NO VIRTUE LIKE NECESSITY

NO VIRTUE LIKE NECESSITY

Realist Thought in International Relations since Machiavelli

Jonathan Haslam

Yale University Press
New Haven & London

Designed by Adam Freudenheim

Set by SNP Best-set Typesetter Ltd., Hong Kong

Printed in Great Britain

Library of Congress Cataloging-in-Publication Data

Haslam, Jonathan.
    No virtue like necessity : realist thought in international relations
since Machiavelli / Jonathan Haslam.
       p.   cm.
    Includes bibliographical references and index.
    ISBN 0-300-09150-8 (hardcover : alk. paper)
    1. International relations – Philosophy – History.   2. International relations – Political
aspects – History.   3. International relations – Psychological aspects – History.   I. Title.
JZ1253 .H37   2002
327.1′01 – dc21   2001006066

A catalogue record for this book is available from the British Library
10 9 8 7 6 5 4 3 2 1

"We are hardly going to mount our Rozinante, to redress all the wrongs, and engage all the windmills in the world."

– William Fox, *The Interest of Great Britain, respecting the French War*

"Though some speak openly against my books, Yet they will read me."

– Marlowe, *Jew of Malta*

Contents

Acknowledgements

A work as broad as this inevitably builds upon foundations laid over the years by others who passed this way before. But rather than trail fashion and create an unwieldy and unoriginal commentary upon the syntheses of others, the intention has been instead to mine primary sources wherever possible.

It is therefore a singular pleasure to highlight my debt to those who generously shared views on the subject and those who took the time to read and criticise various elements of the work in manuscript: Robert W. Tucker (Edward B. Burling Professor Emeritus of International Law and Institutions at the Johns Hopkins University); Quentin Skinner (Regius Professor of Modern History, Christ's College, Cambridge); Adam Roberts (Montague Burton Professor of International Relations, Balliol College, Oxford); Ernst Haas (Robson Research Professor Emeritus of Government at the University of California, Berkeley); Kenneth Waltz (Ford Professor Emeritus of Political Science at the University of California, Berkeley); Robert Jervis (Adlai E. Stevenson Professor of International Relations at Columbia University); Derek Beales (Professor Emeritus of Modern European History, Sidney Sussex College, Cambridge); Stephen Walt (Evron and Jeane Kirkpatrick Professor of International Affairs at the John F. Kennedy School of Government, Harvard University); Giuliano Procacci (Professor Emeritus at the University of Rome, La Sapienza); Nigel Simmonds (Reader in Jurisprudence, Corpus Christi College, Cambridge); Michael Sonenscher (Fellow in History, King's College, Cambridge) and Andrew Hurrell (Lecturer and Fellow, Nuffield College, Oxford).

This is also the place to thank those who arranged visiting professorships during a sequence of productive sabbaticals where the larger part of the research was done and the manuscript was finally completed: David Holloway, Raymond A. Spruance Professor in International History (at Stanford 1994), Paul Kennedy, J. Richardson Dilworth Professor of History (at Yale 1996) and Professor Andrew Moravcsik (at Harvard, 2001), plus membership of the Institute for Advanced Study at Princeton in 1998 (courtesy of Professor Jack Matlock).

Jonathan Haslam   Corpus Christi College, Cambridge

Introduction

"Actually, in matters of business and affairs of state there is never any need to avail oneself of the work of academics [dottori] since with their excessive subtleties they are more likely to ruin them than bring them to a good conclusion."

– Advice from Pope Clement VIII, 26 August 1595[1]

The suggestion that the writings of academics on international relations are irrelevant to the needs of statesmen should come as no surprise. The reasons are twofold. The first is a matter of substance; the second, a matter of form.

In respect of substance, it is the refusal to accept the state as a continuing and critical unit of international relations that renders much analysis redundant. In addition, insistence that the behaviour of states towards one another should be governed by a moral code that rules the behaviour of individuals effectively undermines credibility. In sum, it is for want of greater realism that international relations as an academic subject is discarded by decision-makers.

In respect of form, it is the very effort to turn the subject into a science on the model of the natural sciences which makes for, at worst, arcane inaccessibility and, at best, abstract and dogmatic generalisation that wilfully disregards the provenance of ideas, their historical and cultural specificity. Concepts have to be re-introduced in the circumstances of their birth and evolution in order to discount those elements and associations of no relevance to our own time and situation.

The aim is thus twofold: to reassert the value of the realist approach, but to do so in a way that sensitises our awareness of the context in which realist concepts emerged. Only by these means will international relations as a subject have something to say and find someone to listen at the summit of the state. To the anti-realist this is of no consequence, since, if the state is not the key actor, the statesman is not the most important person to address.

The thrust of Quentin Skinner's history of modern political thought might aptly be described as the study of liberty.[2] What follows, in contrast, may equally well be

---

1   *La Legazione di Roma di Paolo Paruta (1592–1595)*, ed. G. de Leva (Venice 1887) Vol. 1, p. 268. Clement VIII was no mean statesman. As Pope from 1592 to 1605, he brought about peace between Spain and France, simultaneously enlarging the territories of the Holy See.
2   Q. Skinner, *The Foundations of Modern Political Thought*, Vol. 1 (Cambridge 1978).

called the study of power. The text is aimed at three distinct audiences: policy-makers; devotees of political thought; and students of international relations.

The relationship between those who merely write about international relations and those responsible for the conduct of foreign policy has always been problematic, not least because it is one of the few areas where those with no practical experience comment with presumed authority. The Italian Ludovico Zùccolo long ago complained: "He who has not ploughed the sea does not presume to know the art of navigation; he who has made no effort at music makes no claim to understand notes and tones. But there are few men who, though never having governed, do not claim to know how to judge the administration of states [*republiche*] and empires."[3] This is, indeed, the standard complaint of Secretaries of State for Foreign Affairs after prolonged and often ill-informed Cabinet discussion, even if it is arguably also a necessary price to pay for democracy.

In answer to the apparent need to educate all policy-makers in such important matters, early modern Europe witnessed the culling of political maxims from the works of great classical historians such as Tacitus.[4] Girolamo Frachetta (1558–1620) was a figure of considerable political experience in the Italy of the Counter-Reformation. He served cardinals Luigi d'Este and Scipione Gonzaga before working for the Spanish ambassador to the Holy See, later fleeing the capital (for reasons unknown) and settling in Naples, subsequently acting as agent for the Duke of Urbino.[5] In the preamble to one collection of maxims, he remarked that there was no matter of greater importance for the Prince than to know how to govern the subjects of his kingdom in order that they may live in peace. "This discipline or skill [*peritia*] in matters pertaining to the government of the State in peace or to that in war," he noted, "is acquired by the Prince by three means: that is, conveyed orally by those qualified in such matters; through the reading of history and of writers of State and military affairs; and through experience."[6]

Though a successful purveyor of maxims on a grand scale, Frachetta openly acknowledged the limitations of education in statecraft by such means. First, he thought that this was no science in the meaning we now give to the term. As Aristotle had pointed out, the social sciences could not be nailed down with as much precision as mathematics.[7] By the term "political science" (*scienza politica*) Frachetta meant no more than knowledge of, or study of, politics. Second, the fallibility of the human mind led to mistakes, whatever the training given. Third, emotions often got the better of

3   L. Zuccolo, *Della Ragione di Stato* (1621) p. 1: reprinted in ed. B. Croce and S. Caramella, *Scrittori d'Italia: Politici e Moralisti del Seicento* (Bari 1930), p. 25.
4   For an easy introduction to this issue, see R. Mellor, *Tacitus* (New York 1993), Chapter 6. For more detail, see below, pp. 37–8.
5   T. Bozza, *Scrittori Politici Italiani dal 1550 al 1650: Saggio di bibliografia* (Rome 1949) p. 80.
6   G. Frachetta, *Il Seminario de' Governi di Stato et di Guerra* (Venice 1613), "Proemio".
7   Aristotle, "Nicomachean Ethics", Book 1: *Complete Works of Aristotle*, ed. J. Barnes, Vol. 2 (Princeton 1984) p. 1728.

good judgement; and, lastly, God had a tendency to cause events to turn out otherwise than intended:

> One must not esteem them [these maxims] as certainties, as equations in mathematics or the movement of the heavens, which are unchanging: but open to error because of the imbecility of the human mind, which in affairs of state or war frequently forms the wrong opinion; because of the emotions, which often cloud judgement; and because of the will of God, who, either in order to punish some for their failings or for some other end, causes things to turn out the opposite from that which human judgement would have happen.[8]

In weighing up the advantages offered rulers by education in maxims of state, Frachetta concluded that "the Maxims and Rules that make up political science and the art of warfare are necessary for ruling the state and conducting war. And if others without these have on occasion ruled well," he continued, "one would say this occurred by chance, or started by having been given them with which to rule by one who was instructed in such sciences and arts, or by having himself through long experience formed a habit similar to science."[9]

Having made the case for political science, Frachetta was sceptical, however, of the value of merely a training in political science for the creation of effective statesmen:

> In truth it is much better that Princes and Generals [*Capitani generali*] do not learn the sciences, but are instructed in the arts of ruling and military command through experience, or that they rule with the advice of others . . . rather than being taught arts or sciences that have nothing to do with government, or the arts of governing and making war, but furnished through intermediaries. Because taking up disciplines that have nothing to do with government is a waste of time. And information transmitted to Princes or Generals through intermediaries gives rise to doubts rather than solutions. And in affairs of state and of war there is nothing worse than lack of resolution. Apart from which, Princes who have learned a few bits and pieces of affairs of state persuade themselves that they are fully instructed in such matters . . .[10]

It is not our purpose to resolve that dilemma; nor is it to assert that the writings of academics have necessarily had a momentous impact on the course of events, however much they would like to have done so; and any attempt to gauge the degree, if any, of influence they have exerted would be complex in the extreme and would most certainly merit a work of its own. A connexion there is, however, which points to the power of

8   Frachetta, *Il Seminario*, p. 993.
9   Ibid., p. 794.
10   Ibid.

ideas. The liberal critic of US foreign expansion William Sumner wrote, at the turn of the last century, of "the danger of having a doctrine lying loose about the house, and one which carries with it big consequences . . . You accede to it now, within the vague limits of what you suppose it to be; therefore you will have to accede to it tomorrow when the same name is made to cover something which you never have heard or thought of. If you allow a political catchword to go on and grow, you will awaken some day to find it standing over you, the arbiter of your destiny, against which you are powerless, as men are powerless against delusions."[11] Sumner referred to a degree of consciousness. In a much quoted but much truncated passage from his *General Theory of Employment, Interest, and Money* John Maynard Keynes argued the power of the unconscious: "the ideas of economists and political philosophers, both when they are right and when they are wrong, are more powerful than is commonly understood. Indeed the world is ruled by little else. Practical men, who believe themselves to be quite exempt from any intellectual influences, are usually the slaves of some defunct economist. Madmen in authority, who hear voices in the air, are distilling their frenzy from some academic scribbler of a few years back. I am sure that the power of vested interests is vastly exaggerated compared with the gradual encroachment of ideas. Not, indeed, immediately, but after a certain interval; for in the field of economic and political philosophy there are not many who are influenced by new theories after they are twenty-five or thirty years of age, so that the ideas which civil servants and politicians and even agitators apply to current events are not likely to be the newest. But, soon or late, it is ideas, not vested interests, which are dangerous for good or evil."[12]

This classical liberal viewpoint – the pre-eminence of ideas over material circumstance – does not have to carry full conviction to be taken seriously. Moreover, influence comes in different forms; not just at different times. A direct influence is easier to detect but at the same time more rare; indirect influences are at first sight more likely but perhaps too subtle to measure. And whereas scholars like to see themselves as independent, if not in knowledge then in judgement, a close reading of their work in combination with the fullest understanding of their times raises serious doubts about the degree to which intellectual autonomy can be taken for granted. In other words, it may well be the case that policy-makers reflect the learning of academics. One American professor of international relations has insisted that "The shape of the world will depend on which theory we think is true, and what we do to try to make it come true."[13] True or not, it is certainly the case that academics more often than they care to admit mirror the attitudes and assumptions of those in power. It is in the belief that both propositions have at times been true that this book has been written.

---

11   W. Sumner, "War", 1903: *War and Other Essays* (New Haven 1919) p. 38.
12   J. M. Keynes, *The General Theory of Employment, Interest, and Money* (London 1964 edition), pp. 383–4.
13   Bruce Russett of Yale to the editors of *International Security*, Vol. 15, No 3, Winter 1990/91, p. 217.

Policy-makers ought to be aware of the provenance of unwritten assumptions so that they can take care not to be projected by them into positions that may damage interests pursued. Consciousness is of course the first step towards control. The same follows for the rest of us. Only an awareness of the possible interdependence of the ideas and the interests of those in power and international conditions prevailing enables one to discount likely bias before absorbing these ideas in their purest form. And to what extent are the ideas that lie buried in the rare books rooms of leading university libraries likely to be of relevance to those conducting foreign policy in our times? Our predecessors seemed fairly certain that they were. In ancient Greece former general Thucydides wrote of his *History of the Peloponnesian War* that "if these words of mine are judged useful by those who want to understand clearly the events which happened in the past and which (human nature being what it is) will, at some time or other and in much the same ways, be repeated in the future", he must have assumed that the past had something to teach the present and that the fundamental reason for this lay in the eternal character of man.[14] Some are sceptical that events will be repeated in anything like that degree of uniformity. In our own time Albert Hirschman has warned against "trotting out the identical ideas that had been put forward at an earlier period, without any references to the encounter they had already had with reality, an encounter that is seldom satisfactory . . . *vaguely similar* circumstances at two different and perhaps distant points of time may very well give rise to *identical and identically flawed* thought-responses if the earlier intellectual episode has been forgotten."[15]

Frachetta raised the issue as to whether ancient authorities were more deserving of respect than modern. Many argued that modern authorities held greater weight since they were "closer to us and therefore carry more conviction" and the state of affairs in classical times, whether in government or war, was "not as a whole similar to those in our time."[16] Moreover, modern authorities were more likely to persuade the population as a whole, since the people "have no knowledge of antiquity"; indeed the nobility were little better informed. On the other hand, he argued, "It is of no matter that the state of affairs is perhaps today in certain ways different from antiquity, whether in form of government or whether in the manner of making war, because the difference amounts to little or nothing . . ."[17] This is something we need to consider as we continue through this text. Can we assume relevance? Can we assume only partial relevance? Has the conduct of foreign policy changed more substantially for us from the time of Frachetta than it had from the time of Tacitus to the time of Frachetta?

Why should we assume that the rediscovery of the roots of thinking about international relations is of value only to policy-makers and students of world affairs? The subject actually bridges at least two fields, most notably both the theory of

14   I, 22.4: Thucydides, *History of the Peloponnesian War*, ed. M. Finley (London 1972) p. 48.
15   A. Hirschman, *The Passions and the Interests: Political Arguments for Capitalism before Its Triumph* (Princeton 1981) p. 133.
16   Frachetta, *Il Seminario*, p. 993.
17   Ibid.

international relations and the history of political thought. A gulf long lay between them, and to some extent it still does. Giuseppe Ferrari in his *Corso sugli Scrittori Politici Italiani* of 1862 complained that: "The fault of the Italian school, the fault of all schools, from the most distant past through to Locke, Montesquieu and to contemporary political figures, has been to confine the subject to the idea of a state in isolation as though it must be alone on the earth. Plato conceived of his Republic as solitary, as did Machiavelli his State a world unto itself, as did Campanella his universal City, as did Montesquieu his secular Monarchy."[18]

Indeed, the same could be said of those who teach and write the history of political thought today, not least in the last two decades.[19] A division of labour of some kind between those who study domestic politics and those who focus on international relations is essential because it facilitates ever greater degrees of specialisation. This makes possible the excavation of knowledge at ever greater depths. However, the danger thereby arises of distortion. The one half of the subject is cut off from the other because each is conceptually distinct, even though both are organically connected. It is time those who teach the history of political thought interested themselves in international relations and vice versa.

The old authorities that dominate the history of political thought did refer to international relations, though never comprehensively. What they left behind were scattered fragments, partly formed ideas, nascent concepts. Our purpose is to seek a pattern from these fragments, to go deeper and trace the roots of thinking about international relations through the work of the "realist tradition" across the centuries in order, ultimately, to contextualise recent and current dogmas and debates. What we find is interesting. Instead of a seamless progression in comprehension from one generation, one century to another, we find the intermittent emergence and occlusion of certain realist conceptions and a fluctuation in the degree to which realist ideas predominate or give way to their universalist counterpart. It then becomes difficult to determine the degree to which successive generations have re-invented or rediscovered time-honoured notions.

Victorian political economist McCulloch saw this happening at the earliest stages in the development of economics as a science:

Those who have got together a considerable number of works in any department of science or literature, or who have bestowed any pains in tracing its history, can

---

18   G. Ferrari, *Corso sugli Scrittori Politici Italiani* (Milan 1862) p. 793. A rather different view was later given from Harvard by Carl Friedrich: "internal and external security get hopelessly mixed up with each other. This was . . . the inclination of all the older writers, usually without any explicit recognition of the fact." *Constitutional Reason of State: The Survival of the Constitutional Order* (Providence 1957) p. 2.

19   An honourable exception is, of course, Richard Tuck. See, in particular, *The Rights of War and Peace: Political Thought and the International Order from Grotius to Kant* (Oxford 1999).

hardly fail to be struck, on the one hand, with the indications and explanations of sound principles and doctrines to be found among its earlier cultivators, and on the other, with the continued revival of exploded errors and fallacies.

. . . Whether a writer or a speaker undertakes to unfold principles, to set them in a novel or more striking light, or to recommend their application, he should know what has been already undertaken, what has been accomplished, and what remains for discovery and elucidation. The following work gives sundry examples of the inconveniences resulting from the want of this information, by exhibiting able men engaged in the investigation of principles and the development of laws which had been previously established and traced, and putting forward speculations as original which had been long before the public.[20]

That said, the case should not be overstated: to call the writers with whom we are directly concerned "theorists" is almost certainly inaccurate, since it implies a greater degree of coherence and completeness in their work than exists.[21] Their concepts, as noted elsewhere, largely "grow out of original intuitions of actors in interstate politics and are developed into doctrine by former or would-be actors, temporarily or permanently severed from active affairs."[22] They were therefore in some sense tainted goods. "Their proponents are motivated by the desire to reconstruct the essentials of political action intellectually, and thereby to facilitate the action of others and perhaps provide the theorist himself with a substitute for action and authority."[23] It is their utility that interests us, but it is their very utility that presents dangers. "It requires no elaborate penetration, for instance, to realize that the balance-of-power concept has been used in different ways and given distinct meanings. And the critic of this fact should suspect that this variability was appreciated by participants in the system and that from their viewpoint the ambiguity that has been depicted constitutes the concept's chief virtue in many situations, except in the critical ones that tend to dissolve the ambiguity and replace it with a clear imperative whose application may be fraught with practical but not with theoretical difficulties."[24] And the temptation to impose a false coherence from the perspective of the present that did not exist in the works of the past must be

20   J. McCulloch, *The Literature of Political Economy: A Classified Catalogue of select publications in the different departments of that science, with historical, critical, and biographical notices* (London 1845) pp. v–vii.
21   The unfortunate misuse of this term in respect of thinkers we are going to consider is noticeable in T. Knutson, *A History of International Relations Theory* (Manchester/New York 1992). The merit of the work is, none the less, to provide an eclectic introductory text to some elements in the history of political thought deemed relevant to students of international relations.
22   G. Liska, "Continuity and Change in International Systems", *World Politics*, XVI, No 1, October 1963, p. 134. It should be remembered that Liska was, as a very young man, secretary to Jan Masaryk (1886–1948) before the latter's suicide or assassination as Foreign Minister of Czechoslovakia.
23   Ibid.
24   Ibid., p. 135.

resisted. But one cannot afford to discard key principles of statecraft because of the problems in abstracting them for what value they may still contain.

Some thirty years ago the field of political philosophy in the English-speaking world was overturned by the realisation that historical context was vital to an understanding of the great texts, and that these texts themselves should be seen not as self-standing entities but as part of a larger stream of thought. Skinner, the leading progenitor of this approach, wrote: "I have tried not to concentrate so exclusively on the leading theorists, and have focused instead on the more general social and intellectual matrix out of which their works arose . . . I take it that political life itself sets the main problems for the political theorist, causing a certain range of issues to appear problematic, and a cor-responding range of questions to become the leading subjects of debate." What he thus intended was "a history of political theory with a genuinely historical character."[25] That approach, though original for Britain and the United States, was commonplace in Italian historiography; so the revolution in our thinking represented not merely the dawn of perception but perhaps also a timely escape from accustomed insularity. As far back as 1929 Carlo Morandi asserted similar principles in a fierce attack on foreign contemporaries who studied a Bodin or a Hobbes, "transporting them out of their con-crete historical context". Morandi was anxious not to be taken to believe that a politi-cal thinker could be studied purely as a product of his time. Moreover he cautioned against reducing speculative principles to practical motives. "The history of a political doctrine," he wrote, "as of every current of ideas, must be studied in its own terms and then dialectically understood for its universal value. But it is at that delicate moment in which the ideology joins history proper, that one must have an eye to the complexity of motives that cannot be reduced to intellectual criteria . . ."[26] Later, Federico Chabod wrote a preface to an edition of Rudolf von Albertini's classic, *Das florentinische Staatsbewusstsein im Übergang von der Republik zum Prinzipat*, originally published in 1955. Albertini presented his treatise "in the only way that allows one to capture political thought comprehensively and concretely, and that is to say connecting it closely and continually with the political and socio-economic conditions of the age from which this thought emerges, keeping the tightest correlation between the politi-cal problems that occur from time to time and the theoretical discussions."[27] That this was not entirely a new method is also evidenced by the writings of not only Benedetto Croce but also that leading historian of ideas in respect of statecraft, Rodolfo de Mattei, whose key findings will be alluded to below. This is most certainly our point of departure.

The study of thought in international relations stands somewhere close to that of political thought in the English-speaking world in the late 1960s. Many texts, even the

---

25   Skinner, *The Foundations*, pp. x–xi.
26   "Lo studio delle dottrine politiche e la storia", *Rivista internazionale di filosofia del diritto*, 1929: reprinted in C. Morandi, *Scritti Storici*, ed. A. Saitta, Vol. 1 (Rome 1980) pp. 5–14.
27   *Firenze dalla repubblica al principato: Storia e coscienza politica* (Turin 1970) p. xi.

most recent and best informed, display a casual ignorance of and indifference to the provenance of ideas. Moreover, the practice of discussing the realist tradition in inter-national relations as though it began with Carr's *Twenty Years' Crisis* in 1939 or Morgenthau's *Politics among Nations* in 1948 produces a curious distortion in the debate as to what is normally to be expected of realism and what is not.

One instance of this is "A Tale of Two Realisms: Expanding the Institutions Debate", which appeared in 1997. Here the authors, Schweller and Priess, make out a tenden-tious case for "traditional realism's concern for the origins and influence of interna-tional institutions."[28] The sense of traditional realism conveyed is also seriously deficient. Certain assertions are made. One such is that "Traditional realism is rooted in sociology and history (with some attention to psychology, theology, and econom-ics)."[29] This is a puzzling assertion since political science predates sociology and arguably also even history (in the Rankean sense) as the progenitor and portrayal of ideas in international relations. It is no less puzzling in that "traditional realism" was originally founded on assumptions about the nature of man, which are clearly – though not then recognised as such – assumptions about psychology. Furthermore the asser-tion that "traditional realists view power as an end in itself" was most certainly not always true before Morgenthau. Indeed, most traditional realists believed states were inherently expansionist rather than specifically in search of power. Indeed they, like today's neorealists, believed that security was the most vital concern. In this sense, although it may be correct to say that Kenneth Waltz in his *Theory of International Pol-itics* borrowed "most heavily from microeconomics" for the metaphorical framework of the neorealist thesis, his core ideas originate from far into the distant past: not least his assertion that the states system determines behaviour. This certainly does not fit with the not uncommon but misplaced claim that "Traditional realists posit that power and the interests of states drive behavior" while "neorealists examine only anarchy and the distribution of capabilities."[30] And statements such as that traditional realists focus on "the relative distribution (balances and imbalances) of capabilities between specific states or coalitions of states, not on the systemwide distribution of capabilities or the polarity of the system"[31] are clearly incorrect; a quick reading of Lord Bolingbroke will relieve one of that unhappy assumption, if one believes the distinction is anything other than hair-splitting. Another assumption misattributed to realists is that "humans do not face one another primarily as individuals but as members of groups that command their loyalty".[32] This seems plausible, in that it is states which act in international rela-tions (according to realists). But the authors go on to compare this with the liberal

---

28   R. Schweller and D. Priess, "A Tale of Two Realisms: Expanding the Institutions Debate", *Mershon International Studies Review* (1997) 41, p. 1.
29   Ibid., p. 7.
30   Ibid.
31   Ibid.
32   Ibid., p. 6.

assumption that "autonomous individuals and private groups"[33] are the real actors. This distinction is baffling because all of the realists (and more) that Waltz in *Man, the State and War* collects under his category of the first image in international relations talk in terms of the individual, not the collective. Machiavelli is the most obvious instance. Only those falling within his second image can be categorised as reasoning on the basis of collective actors. And even these allow for the effects of "private groups". We also encounter, from the hand of Pulitzer Prize winning journalist Thomas Friedman, the strange assertion: "I am not a realist, who thinks that everything in foreign affairs can be explained by the quest for power and geopolitical advantage – and markets don't really matter."[34] This ignores the stream of thought outlined at length below, in Chapter 3.

Lest readers believe this collective amnesia to be a peculiarly American phenomenon, consider two British writers who talk of realists "thinking of nation states as constituents of an international system which determined their behaviour" as a specifically twentieth-century phenomenon, apparently blissfully unaware of, though more likely casually indifferent to, nearly four hundred years of such usage.[35] Almost ubiquitous on both sides of the Atlantic is the assumption of rationality, in the sense of policy driven and deliberately contrived to achieve goals that maximise whatever target is set (power, security, wealth, etc.). This assumption crosses the battlefield between liberals and realists and inhabits most of no man's land as well. It is, however, only an assumption, and it is worth reminding readers that the key goal of the earliest realists in formulating Reasons of State was to introduce and enforce the dictates of rationality in decision-making. It was thus an aim in and of itself, which was not infrequently breached, and not something one could confidently assume. Particularly in an era where public opinion (including sectional interest) calls the shots in foreign policy, most notably in the United States – ironically also the mother church of assumed rationality – any such assumptions have to be questioned.

Others have become more aware of the need to search out the pedigree of ideas; several texts on theory have emerged with reference back to the more distant past. Yet these backward glances have represented little more; as, for instance, is the case with recent debates about the Peace of Westphalia.[36] History is treated as given, a static, if not decaying, resource from which the occasional illuminating trinket can be drawn merely for illustrative purposes to add colour rather than define the debate in question. Where past thinkers are named – usually the same litany and almost always from secondary sources and then invariably from sources in the English language – their works have rarely been reread afresh and *in toto*. Moreover, the works of less well known contemporaries to the great figures have fallen into neglected obscurity. Even where a

---

33   Ibid.
34   T. Friedman, *The Lexus and the Olive Tree* (New York 2000) p. 23.
35   M. Hollis and S. Smith, *Explaining and Understanding International Relations* (Oxford 1991) p. 92.
36   See, for instance, S. Krasner, *Sovereignty: Organized Hypocrisy* (Princeton 1999).

more thorough-going approach is adopted, as in the case of Waltz and Michael Doyle, forty years apart, the attitude taken – and dictated by contemporary political science – is strictly presentist in terms of preoccupation and strictly instrumentalist in purpose. The writers under scrutiny are not valued in and of themselves so much as illustrations for current theoretical preoccupations. This is, of course, a perfectly acceptable enterprise. The price paid, however, is in the process of simplification; for meaning is specific to context and context itself subject to radical change.

The lessons of the school of political thought can contribute to our understanding of international relations. But rather than treat the subject merely in terms of individual thinkers sequenced purely chronologically, it arguably makes more sense to segment specific areas of thought for contextualisation in greater depth. Our focus is realist thought. Realist thought is to be distinguished primarily from moralist thought not, as might be expected, by being value-free, but by its claim that the conduct of international relations itself should be unconstricted by moral values. It is this claim that marked out Machiavelli from his predecessors and, indeed, from all his immediate successors in political science. But the claim that realist thought is not in itself normative – that is to say, it seeks to further no values but merely reflects reality – is surely untenable.

The most striking instance is the much deployed notion of the Balance of Power. In the late twentieth century it found its most trenchant and convincing critic in the young Ernst Haas, whose PhD thesis strikingly and devastatingly underlined not only the disturbing elasticity of the term over time and in different contexts, but also the fact that it served both as a description of structure and a policy aim adopted from choice and therefore subject to values: "the mere use of the term [Balance of Power] in any diplomatic document", Haas wrote, "proves nothing about the precise motivations of its authors. A detailed analysis of the total diplomatic and domestic political situation is imperative before any light can be thrown on these motivations and only after such an analysis is made can a generalization be ventured as to what each plenipotentiary meant – if he meant anything at all – by the use of the term."[37] A critique of this kind serves notice on all who pretend to timeless concepts claimed for universal validity regardless of provenance. We have to answer to the argument that such concepts have shifted in meaning over time and across space, and that they have thereby forfeited the status of the absolute.

The only means of meeting such a formidable accusation, and the only hope of salvaging something from the wreckage, is to employ the very methods used by those in the adjacent field of political thought: through the closer scrutiny of historical context, to recognise these concepts as historical products. At the very least it may tell us more about the real nature of the international system in more distant eras, along whose

---

37   E. Haas, *Belgium and the Balance of Power: A Critical Examination of some Balance of Power Theories in the Light of the Policy Motivations of the Major European States toward Belgium, 1830–1839* (Columbia University PhD 1953) p. 85.

trajectory we stand today. This would enable us to escape from and guard against the crude transposition of apparently familiar ideas of old to the current and possibly inappropriate context. At most it may indeed enable us to refine further such notions and hone them to current and future needs. Either way, the process of winnowing out the chaff is a task necessary for progress.

To forestall any misunderstanding, let us be clear in more detail what is meant by "realist". For present purposes it may be summed up in the Elizabethan term "statist": that is to say, the focus on international relations is on the behaviour of the state, its security and interests being the highest priority of political life. Additional definitions have been offered. Hans Morgenthau conceived of it as the search for power as the ultimate aim of all states. Waltz, on the other hand, has seen it as the search for security. Robert W. Tucker talks of a self-help system. All assume an anarchical international system. As we can see, there is no single theory; more a collection of approaches with differing points of emphasis, but converging upon a central core they all hold in common.[38] A realist can generally be counted on to take a pessimistic or "Augustinian" view of the behaviour of man or society or both in the conduct of international relations. This definition circumvents the bias implied in treating "realists" as necessarily those in closest touch with reality; in many cases true, perhaps; in some cases, self-evidently false. Added to the list of characteristics are questionable assumptions, most notably the belief that states are "rational" and "unitary" agents pursuing fixed and identifiable interests.[39] It was well said by the Scottish philosopher Adam Ferguson (1723–1816) that the atmosphere in which we judge behaviour influences the causes we put to that behaviour: "we assign as the motives of conduct with men, those considerations which occur in the hours of retirement and cold reflection. In this mood frequently we can find nothing important, besides the deliberate prospects of interest . . ."[40] In that atmosphere the thinker is less likely to seize upon the emotions as a motivation for action. Realists in the past have certainly not presupposed rationality; rationality was a goal, the ideal towards which the statesman progressed. And what are we to make of the bold assertion by Waltz that "Realists think of causes running in one direction, from interacting states to the outcomes of their acts"; that they ignore the impact of the state system on the behaviour of the state?[41] In contrast, he claims, "Neorealism contends that international politics can be understood only if the effects of structure are added to traditional realism's unit-level explanations."[42] But, as we shall see in the chapter on the Balance of Power, traditional realist approaches were by

---

38   See B. Frankel, ed., *Roots of Realism* (London 1996), p. ix.

39   J. Grieco, "Realist International Theory and the Study of World Politics", *New Thinking in International Relations Theory*, ed. M. Doyle and G. Ikenberry (Boulder, Colorado 1997) p. 165.

40   A. Ferguson, *An Essay on the History of Civil Society* (Edinburgh 1767) p. 17.

41   K. Waltz, "Realist Theory and Neorealist Theory", C. Kegley, ed., *Controversies in International Relations Theory: Realism and the Neoliberal Challenge* (New York 1995), pp. 74 and 80.

42   Ibid., p. 78.

no means so limited, neither bounded by assumptions of rationality, nor confined to unit-level explanations.

Yet even if we take the broadest definition of "realist", which usually implies a pessimistic view of human nature, few would contest the assertion that relations between states through the greater part of history have largely been conducted along realist as against utopian or legalist lines. The lineage of realist thought is long, indeed. The written record limits our scope to ancient Greece, India and China. Research on Greek diplomacy – or, rather, the lack of diplomacy in our sense of the term – has highlighted the absence of a co-operative spirit and the enormous and overwhelming emphasis placed on the importance of success in the society of the Hellenic world. War was commonplace and Greek diplomats spoke as all Greeks: bluntly; not least because these practices were open.[43] Bellicosity and threats were the currency of the day; moderation of language in inter-state relations a practice all but unknown. Xenophon (435–354 BC) recounts the Theban request for Athenian assistance against Sparta in 395 BC: "We all know you would like to recover your former empire – don't be afraid because Sparta has many subjects, but . . . take courage from this, reflecting that you too, when you had most subjects had most enemies. But as long as they had no one to support their revolts, they concealed their hatred of you; but when the Lacedaemonians came forward as their champions, then they showed their feelings towards you."[44]

This is the kind of context in which should be seen the notorious dialogue between the menacing Athenians and the victim Melians as related by Thucydides. Here one finds "that in fact the strong do what they have the power to do and the weak accept what they have to accept."[45] Here too one finds reference to "a general and necessary law of nature to rule whatever one can"[46] and the accusation of the Spartans that they were "most conspicuous for believing that what they like doing is honourable and what suits their interests is just."[47] Similarly in Plato's *Gorgias* Callicles tells Socrates that "it's the weaklings who constitute the majority of the human race who make the rules", that in creating these rules "they look after themselves and their own interest, and that's also the criterion they use when they dispense praise and criticism" and "Other creatures show, as do human communities and nations, that right has been determined as follows: the superior person shall dominate the inferior person and have more than him." Philosophers were "completely out of touch with human nature."[48] And in Plato's *Laws* appears the bold assertion from Clinias the Candian that "according to nature there is always an undeclared war involving each city-state against all other city-states".[49]

---

43   J. Grant, "A note on the tone of Greek diplomacy", *The Classical Quarterly*, LIX (XV), 1965, pp. 261–6.
44   Ibid., p. 263.
45   Thucydides, *History of the Peloponnesian War*, ed. M. Finley (London 1972) 5, 89.
46   Ibid., 5, 105.
47   Ibid.
48   Plato, *Gorgias*, ed. R. Waterfield (Oxford/New York, 1998) pp. 65–7.
49   Plato, *Laws*, 626A.

Around the time that Plato wrote (fifth to fourth century BC), the *Arthashastra* appeared in India, a synthesis of political and economic principles put together by Kautilya. Whether or not the name derived, as has been claimed, from the Sanskrit for "shrewd", "astute" and "wicked" (*kutila*) is unknown,[50] but the writing certainly reflects such qualities. Kautilya describes an Indian states system that sounds familiar to those acquainted with medieval and early modern Europe, with states ruled by families, whose personal relations affected inter-state relations, for good and ill. Kautilya focuses on the position of the potential conqueror who always aimed to enhance his own power at the expense of the rest and would do so by establishing himself at the hub of a wheel of states. He then elaborates upon the six methods of foreign policy, which need not concern us here. Suffice it to say that these included the advice that the king should "make peace with an equally powerful or stronger king; he shall wage war against a weaker king."[51] The only time the king should refrain from war-making against a weaker king was "if by taking action there will neither be an increase in his own strength nor a decrease in that of the enemy."[52] Much else that can be found here anticipates Machiavelli, which is also the case – though to a lesser degree – with the work of Shang-chün (known as Lord Shang), who held high office in the Ch'in dynasty between 359 and 338 BC. Again, in a remark eerily reminiscent of the Italian sage, Shang writes: "Force produces strength, strength produces prestige, prestige produces virtue, and so virtue has its origin in force, which a sage-prince alone possesses, and therefore he is able to transmit benevolence and righteousness to the empire."[53]

That we do not begin our account with such thinkers is not least because too large a gap in time separated their work from the modern period, and in some cases also, too large a gap in culture and space. Even with respect to the rediscovery of Thucydides, no discernible influence is evident until thought about international relations had already recovered most if not all of the ground lost in the Dark Ages.

That realist practices and ideas predominated in the past, however, is largely accepted even by those who claim that realism is no answer to today's problems. Indeed, for many their search for alternatives is the result of a moral revulsion against the dogged persistence of realism over the centuries. Two leading international relations theorists at root opposed to realism attest to this. Robert Keohane informs us that "For over 2000 years, what Hans J. Morgenthau dubbed 'Political Realism' has constituted the principal tradition for the analysis of international relations in Europe and its offshoots in the New World."[54] Michael Doyle also sees realism as not only "our dominant theory" but also "our oldest theory".[55] On the other hand, thought about international relations has never accepted this as inevitable. A view has long existed that may

---

50   For this assertion: Narasingha Prosad Sil, *Kautilya's Arthashastra* (London 1985).
51   Kautilya, *The Arthashastra*, ed. L. Rangarajan (London 1992) p. 566.
52   Ibid., p. 567.
53   *The Book of Lord Shang*, ed. J. Duyvendak (London 1963) p. 259.
54   R. Keohane, ed., *Neorealism and its Critics* (New York 1986) p. 158.
55   M. Doyle, *Ways of War and Peace: Realism, Liberalism, and Socialism* (New York/London, 1997) p. 41.

be summed up as the belief that the state is merely passing through, an enema that has unaccountably become lodged in the bowels of international relations. Realist behaviour in international relations, resting upon a pessimistic view of man or society or both, may well be as old as Adam. It is nevertheless true that if it were always and in all places the established norm, realist critics of the current conduct of international relations would have had nothing to criticise. Indeed, a plausible case can be made that universalist and idealist thought predates realist thought by a considerable margin, as we will see below. Moreover, the plain fact is that regimes have not infrequently strayed from the realist path. The argument that, like the dislocation of stock market prices from their fundamental value, governments simply cannot afford to stray consistently over time from the norm or they will lose power to rivals does not tell us how long they may continue in this vein before the inevitable correction asserts itself. The fact that they can and do stray is undeniable. This therefore requires that we take seriously the alternative paths chosen and their rationale. Moreover, the fact that realist behaviour long remained instinctive, undefined and unchallenged also meant that it remained open to abuse, allowing its ultimate purpose – the protection and furtherance of state interests – to become obscured from view in violent indulgence under the forceful influence of unrestrained emotion: "passions" in the language of the time.

This work focuses on several key concepts in realist thought as they evolved from their starting point in public debate into the currency of contemporary discussion.

Reasons of State emerged to articulate the primacy of the state over the medieval vestiges of universal empire, to argue that no value, whether moral or secular, should stand above the security of the state. This effectively meant that the moral rules applicable to the individual were not transferable to the state in its behaviour towards citizens or towards other states. It also represented a significant advance over the conduct of affairs of state according to the passions or whim of the ruler. It thus stood for the subordination of state business to criteria of reason – in this case effectiveness in the security of the community – but the elevation of state business above all other concerns.

Similarly, the notion of the Balance of Power asserted the security of the state against the universalist or imperialist pretensions of other states. But it highlighted an important corrective to the idea that unenlightened short-term interest should irrevocably hold sway. For the Balance rested on the notion that a common interest emerged from Reasons of State in that the survival of the individual state was contingent on the maintenance of the entire states system against the hegemony of any one Power or, indeed, from implosion. In this crucial sense Reasons of State dictated the Balance of Power. And both were elements restrictive as well as liberational of state behaviour. Interestingly, however, whereas there emerged a strong backlash against the notion of Reasons of State (notably from the Counter-Reformation Church), the idea of the Balance of Power was more readily accepted as force of circumstance. Yet nowhere was it assumed that the Balance could be enforced without war. It underlined the fact that both Reasons of State and the Balance of Power held within them assumptions about the tendency of man or society to strive for the domination of others.

These concepts came to prevail on the political plane. But they had their counter-part on another plane – that of economics. Here the notion of the Balance of Trade, otherwise known as protectionism or, more colourfully, "Mercantile Machiavellianism", complemented both Reasons of State and the Balance of Power. The reasoning was that commercial capabilities underwrote political power. Moreover, the power of manufac-turing far superseded the exchange value of primary commodities, and therefore this power should be developed by and harnessed to the state. The economy could not be allowed to run its natural course. The notion of the Balance of Trade thus resisted the universalist and individualist assertions of liberal trade theory since that theory effec-tively sought the ultimate extinction of the state, as did Marxism. It is in this manner that the Balance of Trade highlighted the realist opposition to liberal universalism, the secular successor to *corpus christianum* and medieval ideas of universal empire above and beyond the state. And it was not long before liberal universalism came to challenge the notions of the Balance of Power as well.

The irony was that rampant expansion of market capitalism liberated by Ricardian theory from the shackles of the Balance of Trade in the nineteenth century witnessed in Britain the formation of the largest empire in the world since Rome. The attendant process of territorial extension heightened the issue of space in international relations – space and topography both. The Balance of Power appeared dependent upon over-seas expansion, and imperial extension in turn focused anxious eyes upon the vulner-abilities for communication across the open sea and the intimidating span of the continental land masses. The simultaneous rise of biology, in which the notion of strug-gle was itself borrowed from the realm of international relations, coincided with the emergence of German nationalism, now shorn of liberal illusions. Here the idea arose that space was vital to the state's very existence and that living room was a matter of survival for the state as a form of life. These two processes – the biological and the mechanistic – converged and erupted into the concept of Geopolitics in northern Europe at the turn of the twentieth century.

This assembly of interdependent ideas formed the core of realist thought in the twentieth century. The notion of Reasons of State re-emerged under the cover of Realpolitik in the Germany of the nineteenth century and in due course found its way across the Atlantic. The Balance of Power, under attack from Wilsonian liberalism, re-emerged with a vengeance in reaction to Nazi Germany and Imperial Japan in World War II. The Balance of Trade became the focal point for American, German, Japanese and Russian industrialisation, and later for much of the third world as well. Geopolitical conceptions received a momentous boost in securing the emergence of the United States as a global Power against the expansion of Stalin's Russia.

Chapter 1
REASONS OF STATE

"There is scarcely any term more famous in politics than this. Ministers have ranked it a secret of state, and have carefully locked it in their offices, while professors and men of letters have tortured themselves defining and explaining it."

– Baron de Bielfeld[1]

Common to all realists, consciously or not, is the notion of Reasons of State: the belief that, where international relations are concerned, the interests of the state predominate over all other interests and values. The assumption held by some realists, that such interests predominate of their own accord, by "necessity" – hence the alternative rendering, "necessity of state" – does not hold, however. Reasons of State might therefore be more accurately phrased as the belief that, where international relations are concerned, the interests of the state *should* predominate over all other interests and values. For it is plain to see – as is demonstrated below – that an alternative view has periodically prevailed, not least in the minds of our predecessors reflecting on the conduct of foreign policy.

The following propositions arise from viewing the evolution of Reasons of State since Machiavelli:

Reasons of state emerged to legitimise a new social formation, the state, against a universalist alternative: initially the Holy Roman Empire and universal church.

The state's core claim to legitimacy lay in its role in assuring the security of the community within state frontiers.

On the practical plane Reasons of State also represented an attempt to order policy to cope with a universal predisposition to conflict.

Reasons of State thus played a dual role: one of legitimacy and one of ensuring efficiency in achieving goals set by the state.

Most of the discussion of Reasons of State turned on the assumptions about the origins of the drive to war: since Reasons of State was designed to harness those

---

1 Baron de Bielfeld, *Institutions Politiques* (Paris 1762) Vol. 3, pp. 277–8.

powerful destructive forces – usually identified as "passions" – their provenance had to be known, so too their *modus operandi* and their relationship to intentionality.

Those assumptions more recently became identified as Kenneth Waltz's three images – about the nature of man, the nature of society or the nature of the states system, or combinations of any of the three.

The first two, however, were essentially interchangeable since it was generally accepted that the "passions" which propelled man into conflict also accelerated society into war. The third we will consider at length in the subsequent chapter on the Balance of Power, though for present purposes it could be regarded as a historical product of the first two – in that once action and reaction were in place, expectations of action would determine behaviour; behaviour would thus *appear* to be systemically driven.

The imposition of order in policy-making according to the rational criteria of Reasons of State that purposefully excluded personal or sectional interest as well as obedience to higher moral values or authorities reminds us that rationality in foreign policy-making was a goal not a given (as many now suppose). Even if successful as a goal, it was, as with any political principle, effected only in proximate and therefore imperfect form – as a result of what Clausewitz would have called the introduction of friction – which in many eyes undermined what legitimacy it claimed.

But the same can equally be claimed of universalist principles. Their stature as a legitimising force inevitably made their adoption a convenient cloak for the exertion of particularist claims to universal monarchy.

The universalist alternative changed, arguably as early as the time of Vitoria, certainly with Grotius, from an explicitly religious basis or a backward reach to the glory and security of Rome to the purely secular and unpartisan basis of early cosmopolitan liberalism. That issue is furthest explored in Chapter 3 on the Balance of Trade.

Arguably it is liberal cosmopolitanism, even more than resurgent Islamic universalism, that challenges Reasons of State to this day. But its disentangling from the particularist interests of individual states is as problematic as ever. It could plausibly be argued that at least Reasons of State is more honest about the selfishness of the state's goals – but only in practice if the domestic hinterland allows integrity in the conduct of foreign policy.

Much, however, turns on the assumption that the conduct of international relations is dictated by the same, Platonic forces as it was when Reasons of State first came into being. Has the world really altered for the better?

These are the broad lines that emerge from the historical record outlined below.

In Latin the closest approximation to Reasons of State is *ratio rei publicae*; in the Italian of the fifteenth century it is *ragion* (or *ragione*) *di stato*; in early modern England it is *statism*, later *reason* or *reasons of state*; in Germany *Staatsräson*, and in France *raison d'état*. The French terminology came to predominate because French substituted for Latin as the language of diplomacy in late modern Europe. But whatever the language, it represents the subjugation of those moral principles normally applicable to the behaviour of the individual in the interests of the community for the conduct of government: whether that community is a "nation-state", as we now know it, or other authority, such as the medieval city-state, is really immaterial. But its emergence as an explicitly articulated concept in political life is none the less of considerable significance because it marks acceptance of the state as an enduring mechanism for ensuring the safety and prosperity of the community. It is no accident that the concept emerges into the full light of day only with the rise of the modern state during the late medieval and early modern period, roughly from 1300 to 1600.

The term originated in early modern Italy and arose simultaneously with the rediscovery of the classical world, which had largely disappeared from view in the Dark Ages following the fall of Rome. It therefore occasions no surprise to learn that at least one Italian intellectual, Secondo Lancellotto (1583–1643), exclaimed: "Say what you want, but I always deemed Reason of State [*Ragione di Stato*] not modern but very ancient".[2] Indeed, Rodolfo de Mattei, a leading specialist on the subject, centuries later argued that "The ancient world . . . was well acquainted with it and taught it, deploying a variety of different terms".[3]

They are both right and wrong. Quotations can be found that appear to fit the bill. But on closer observation the language suggests that in ancient Greece and Rome the concept was articulated only in very rudimentary form. For example Eteocles, in the *Phoenician Virgins* by Euripides, states: "For if one must do evil, then it is good to do it for the sake of authority; but otherwise one ought to act rightly".[4] In Cicero the closest terms that can be found mean "the interests of the state" or "public affairs".[5] One reliable litmus test, the epitomist Florus, placed little weight on the term *ratio rei publicae*, which suggests the notion may not have been widespread.[6] Some element at the root of the idea is there, that acting for the community absolves one from observing the customary moral code. But the concept does not appear to have been used by Caesar, Sallust, Livy or Tacitus. And no less an authority than Friedrich Meinecke is insistent that for all the apparent similarity, in the ancient world the notion "never seemed to rise (or at least not at all consistently) towards the conception of a supra-individual and independent state personality, which would stand over against the actual rulers of the time".[7]

It is also striking that there is no such term in Chinese, Russian or, indeed, in Arabic. It is almost exclusively of modern West European invention, vintage and usage. This

2   S. Lancellotto, *L'hoggidì overo Il mondo non peggiore, né più calamitoso del passato* (Venice 1627–36), quoted in R. de Mattei, *Il problema della "Ragion di Stato" nell'età della Controriforma* (Milan 1979) p. 48.

3   R. de Mattei, *Il problema*, p. 40.

4   F. Meinecke, *Machiavellism: The Doctrine of Raison d'Etat And its Place in Modern History* (London 1957) p. 25. This is most certainly a classic in the subject, not least because of the extent of the author's erudition and the savagery of his judgements.

5   Cicero, *Ep. ad Fam.* 10.16.2, and *Pro Sestio* 103, *Pro Sulla* 10. I am indebted to Dr. C. Kelly for these and other such references.

6   Lucius Florus, *Epitome of Roman History*, 1.2.8.

7   Meinecke, *Machiavellism*, p. 26.

illustrates an important point. Why should the term have arisen where it did, when it did, and nowhere else on record?

We must distinguish between language and practice. The absence of the term in other languages and cultures does not mean that the practice which it signifies did not or does not exist. On the contrary, its absence in other societies may well indicate that no alternative arose to challenge the practice – it reigned supreme and was taken entirely for granted. This appears to have been the case in respect of China and in the Slavic and Islamic cultures. The term in a sense merely made explicit what was in part always implicit in customary diplomatic practice. "Nobody worried about codifying it: diplomacy was perpetuated as an art, as a tradition, as the secrets of chancelleries . . ."[8] Tsar Alexander I's foreign policy adviser Prince Adam Czartoryski noted: "The maxims upon which relations between states are founded, since there have been states in the world, are a kind of oral tradition as old as history, an opinion, or, rather, an unthinking practice which people have followed without having ever adequately studied it thoroughly and after having let the initial revelations disappear."[9] It is this that suggests the main reason why the term Reasons of State appeared in early modern Europe: it arose in response to the stubbornly held assumption that some value higher than the state governed political behaviour and determined not merely ultimate political goals but also the means chosen to pursue them. As Tucker noted some years ago with respect to Reasons of State, "The problem of justification need not arise. It does not arise where there is no awareness of an order imposing obligations on the individual and independent of, and in potential opposition to, the order of the collective. Where men identify themselves completely with the collective to which they belong, where they believe that the 'health and strength' of the collective is not only the highest but the only moral imperative, the problem of reason of state does not and cannot arise."[10] Unchallenged orthodoxy does not require justification. This was only one precondition. After all did not Islamic precepts challenge such an idea? The second precondition was the freedom of the printed word, so that the contradictions in world view could be joined in open discussion among those beyond the confines of the court or the council.

What exactly were those values and how did they come to predominate?

In medieval Europe there existed an organic sense of unity that transcended territorial boundaries. The *lingua franca* for the educated was Latin. The Roman Empire had also left a legacy of belief in a common culture, a common authority – either the Pope (spiritual) or the Holy Roman Emperor (legal) – and a common destiny under Christianity. The sense of individual territorial autonomy of the various nationalities that made up Western Europe after the fall of Rome (476) was weak. On one level law

---

8   Maude-La-Clavière, *La Diplomatie au temps de Machiavel*, Vol. 1 (Paris 1892), p. 6.

9   Le Prince Czartoryski, *Essai sur La Diplomatie* (Paris 1864) p. 10.

10   R. W. Tucker, "Peace and War" (a review of R. Aron, *Paix et Guerre entre les nations*), *World Politics*, January 1965, XVII, No 2, p. 322.

worked to undermine territorial jurisdiction through the reigning principle that a man should be tried only by his own people and not by the courts of others, even if the offence he committed breached the law of the host society. On another level, the preservation of principles of Roman law (in bowdlerised form) sustained the myth of a universal empire transcending all particular authority. The bishop of Seville St. Isidoro (560–636), for instance, claimed that the barbarian successors to the former territories of ancient Rome remained mere *Regna* (kingdoms) within an *Imperium* (empire).[11] Since that time, Charlemagne (742–814), ruler of the Francs, had himself crowned by Pope Leo III as *imperator augustus romanum gubernans imperium*: the successor of the Roman emperors.[12] The vast empire he built was thus in need of legitimation, and the church was equally needful of military support.

Roman law (*Corpus Iuris Civilis*) had been synthesised in the form of the Code and Digest of the Emperor Justinian (482–565), who ruled Byzantium. It later became the focal point of scholastic study. These scholars, the Glossators and later the Commentators, increasingly played a key role in both justifying central imperial authority and undermining it. It was in reaction to the claims from German emperors and from the Papacy – which claimed spiritual dominion with political consequences – and, indeed, from internal rivals,[13] that the doctrine of sovereignty began to emerge, formalised in the phrase: *Rex in regno suo est Imperator regni sui* (the king in his own kingdom is emperor of his own kingdom). The doctrine appears to have originated in France. The Papal Bull *Per venerabilem*, of 1202, provided: "*Quum rex ipse superiorem in temporalibus minime recognoscat, sine juris alterius lesione in eo se juridictioni nostrae subjiceri potui et subjecit*".[14] The French court took the first phrase, which recognised the king's superiority in temporal matters, but omitted the second half of the sentence, which qualified his authority. As the historian Ullmann noted, the decretal of Innocent III (1160–1216) contained within it the "germ of the idea of sovereignty".[15] By the end of the thirteenth century, therefore, the jurist Gulielmus Durandus (1237–96) noted with some authority that the King of France "does not recognise a superior in temporal matters".[16] The French then built upon this distortion of doctrine through further commentaries – Jean de Blanot (1255) and Guillaume de Plasions (1303).

11   J. Morrall, *Political Thought in Medieval Times* (Toronto 1980) p. 18.

12   For the context in terms of political thought: H.-X. Arquillière, *L'Augustinisme Politique: Essai sur la formation des théories politiques du moyen-age* (Paris 1934) Chapter 4.

13   See Olivier-Martin, *Histoire du droit français* (Paris 1948) p. 235: cited in A. Bossuat, "La Formule 'Le Roi est empereur en son royaume': Son emploi au XVe siècle devant le parlement de Paris", *Revue historique de droit français et étranger*, Vol. 39, 1961, No 3, p. 371.

14   Bossuat, "La Formule . . .", p. 373.

15   W. Ullmann, "The Development of the Medieval Idea of Sovereignty", *The English Historical Review*, Vol. LXIV, No CCL, January 1949, p. 8.

16   Quoted in F. Ercole, *Da Bartolo all' Althusio: Saggi sulla storia del pensiero pubblicistico del rinascimento italiano* (Firenze 1932) p. 181. Such sentiments were most evident in the writings of a jurist, most likely Thomas of Pouilly, composed in 1296–7: ibid., p. 185.

A similar process occurred in Italy, in particular with respect to the kingdom of Naples and Sicily, linked by the Angevin dynasty to Paris. The Italians cite the work of Marino da Caramanico in this respect.[17] He argued that the Romans acquired their empire illicitly merely by force.[18] This was also the case made by Andreas de Isernia. And since the kingdom of Naples and Sicily originally came under the jurisdiction of the Papacy rather than the empire, Pope Clement V of necessity found himself backing sovereignty against Emperor Henry VII.[19] Whereas the French Glossators asserted continuity with the Roman empire by talking of the king as an emperor in his own kingdom and sought recognition of independence *de facto* rather than *de jure*, Marino instead more radically asserted the existence of *ius gentium* that predated the Roman empire and therefore Roman law. According to the *ius gentium* multiple kingdoms existed. Thus the Neapolitans asserted not merely *de facto* independence but also *de jure* sovereignty.[20] Clement V is said to have consulted a leading jurist, Oldradus de Ponte, before issuing his bull. In a separate consilium, Oldradus outlined his views on the dispute between Robert of Naples and Henry VII, and it is here that he launches a searching investigation into imperial power and authority, amalgamating both French and Neapolitan ideas in the process, dispensing once and for all with the idea that the emperor could be *dominus mundi*.[21] It was only a matter of time before the French followed the Neapolitans to the assertion of *de jure* rights. Bartolus of Sassoferrato (1314–57) paved the way by dissolving the real distinction between *de jure* and *de facto*, by arguing, in effect, that *de facto* power was also legitimate authority.[22] What this reflected was the substantial and irreversible decline in real imperial authority, though it did not forestall repeated attempts by the empire to recover what it believed it had lost illegitimately. The concept of *utilitas regis* (expediency of the king) or *utilitas regni* (expediency of the kingdom) was now in circulation and found its way into political pamphlets of the period, justifying Philip the Fair (1268–1314) against the jurisdiction of the Pope.[23] And when in 1418 the University of Paris made independent contact with the new Pope Martin V, it was called upon by parliament to explain its actions. There the King's counsel, Guillaume le Tur, opened his case with the words: "The King

---

17   F. Calasso, "Origini italiane della formula 'Rex in regno suo est imperator' ", *Rivista Storica di diritto italiano*, III, 1930, p. 213; and, in greater detail and with a reply to critics: *I Glossatori e la Teoria della Sovranità: studio di diritto comune pubblico* (third edition, Milan, 1957). Calasso makes the case that the Neapolitans were the first to originate theories of sovereignty in opposition to the Holy Roman Emperor. It is generally believed that the thesis is unproven, but the point is accepted that the French may not have been alone in being the first. See Ullmann, "The Development . . .", p. 20, footnote 1.

18   Ullmann, "The Development . . .", p. 19.

19   Ibid., p. 26.

20   For a good summary: J. Canning, "Ideas of the state in thirteenth and fourteenth-century commentators on the Roman law", *Transactions of the Royal Historical Society*, Fifth Series, Vol. 33 (London 1983) p. 7.

21   Ullmann, "The Development . . .", pp. 28–33.

22   C. Woolf, *Bartolus of Sassoferrato* (Cambridge, 1913) and Q. Skinner, *The Foundations*, pp. 9–11.

23   Presidential Address, F. Powicke, "Reflections on the Medieval State", *Transactions of the Royal Historical Society*, 4th series, Vol. XIX (London 1936) pp. 5–6.

is emperor in his kingdom, which he holds from God alone without recognising any temporal superior [*seigneur terrien*]."[24] If the empire was waning, so too was the power of the Pope. Arguably the efforts of the Papacy to buttress its secular power through conquest during those very centuries enhanced rather than diminished the process of particularisation. The conflict between Pope Boniface VIII and Philip of France began as a confrontation between competing legal systems – secular (French) versus ecclesiastic (Papal) – and culminated in defeat for the Vatican and resulted in the housing of the papal seat in Avignon for the better part of the fourteenth century.

Given the intimacy as well as the deep rivalry between the kings of France and England, it is not surprising that by the sixteenth century the implications of these developments were absorbed across the Channel. By the time the future Henry VIII, at the age of eighteen, came to alter the draft of his coronation oath, he was merely adjusting form to substance. The original draft had the King "swere at ye coronacion that he shall kepe and mayntene the rights and the libertees of holie churche of old tyme graunted by the righteous cristen Kinges of Englond." This he changed in his own hand to ". . . mayntene the lawfull right and libertees of old tyme graunted by the righteous cristen Kinges of Englond to the holy churche of inglond nott preiudyciall to hys jurysdiccion and dignittie ryall". He also changed "He shall graunte to holde lawes and customes of the realme and to his power kepe them" to "He shall graunte to holde lawes and approvyd customes of the realme and lawful and not preiudiciall to his crowne or imperial jurisdicion to his power kepe them."[25] Thus when he finally broke with Rome, Henry was acting consistently with long-held belief and most probably also established conviction.

A debate as to the future political structures of Europe was under way, stimulated not merely by the upsurge in demands for sovereignty from nascent states but also by the rediscovery of the political and social writings of Aristotle (384–322 BC). From this point the argument about the nature of international relations hinged upon assumptions about the nature of man; and, from the beginning of the eighteenth century, the nature of society. The conclusion drawn in the twentieth century by a leading British diplomat of the postwar period, Sir Nicholas (Nicko) Henderson, reflects a long-standing belief: "The proper study of diplomatic practice", he wrote, "is man, the understanding and reconciliation of some of the deepest instincts of human nature; and these being unchanging it follows that the scope of an Ambassador's responsibility may be less subject to the forces of modern science than are the range and methods of many other professions, the armed services, for instance."[26]

The challenge presented by Aristotle's writings to orthodox theology was met by blending the more optimistic outlook on the nature of man and the legitimacy Aristotle lent to the authority of the state with greater emphasis on the humanism of

---

24   Quoted in Bossuat, "La Formule . . .", p. 374.
25   Quoted in W. Ullmann, "This Realm of England is an Empire", *Journal of Ecclesiastical History*, Vol. 30, No 2, April 1979, p. 183.
26   N. Henderson, *Mandarin: The Diaries of an Ambassador, 1969–1982* (London 1994) p. 3.

the New Testament as against the harsh judgementalism of the Old. Aristotle argued that man was naturally sociable: "he who is unable to live in society, or who has no need because he is sufficient unto himself, must be either a beast or a god: he is no part of a state. A social instinct is implanted in all men by nature . . ."[27] Adoption of this idea in medieval Europe meant ditching the resolutely negative view of man and his works, including politics, that found full expression in the writings of St. Augustine of Hippo (354–430). Although Augustine allowed that some were elected by God to be saved from damnation, every facet of life on earth, except the spiritual, engaged in by man was hopelessly contaminated by original sin. *The City of God against the Pagans* took a jaundiced view of man. Driven by his passions, man inevitably created conflict, even if he was inherently sociable: "mankind everywhere is generally divided against itself, and when one part is the stronger, it oppresses another."[28] This applied equally to the community and to the individual: "the earthly city . . . when it seeks mastery, is itself mastered by the lust for mastery . . ."[29] It was, Augustine argued, "all the more full of perils by reason of its greater size."[30] And he undermined the legitimacy of the state by expressing the striking opinion that, without justice, "what are kingdoms but great bands of robbers?"[31] He quoted the answer given by a captured pirate to Alexander the Great, who asked the pirate what he meant by infesting the sea: "The same as you do when you infest the whole world, but because I do it with a little ship I am called a robber, and because you do it with a great fleet, you are an emperor."[32] All were thus embroiled in conflict, whether sought or not: "it is the iniquity of the opposing side that imposes upon the wise man the duty of waging wars."[33] Conflict is therefore structurally determined.

These were arguments pointing to the necessity of authoritarian control but scarcely designed to win over those who sought higher aims from power as expressed by Aristotle and, later, in the tradition of the Stoics, Cicero (106–43 BC), who resolutely refused to countenance "a distinction between what is expedient and what is right".[34] These arguments were to reappear on the horizon under a variety of sails over the centuries that followed, ultimately cut free from their religious moorings. St. Thomas Aquinas (1225–74), in transforming Aristotle's *Politics* into the contemporary language of medieval Christianity, was more concerned with legitimacy than power, with the common good rather than the doubtful means. In his *Summa Theologica*, he argued that "there is in man a natural aptitude to virtuous action".[35] Man was, on this view,

27   *Politics*, I, ii, 28–30: ed. J. Barnes, *The Complete Works of Aristotle*, Vol. 2 (Princeton 1984) p. 1988.
28   *The City of God against the Pagans*, ed. R. Dyson (Cambridge 1998) p. 822.
29   Ibid., p. 3.
30   Ibid., p. 928.
31   Ibid., p. 147.
32   Ibid., p. 148.
33   Ibid., p. 929.
34   Cicero, *De Officiis*: III, 28.101.
35   *Aquinas: Selected Political Writings*, ed. A. D'Entrèves (Oxford 1965) p. 127.

rational in nature rather than driven by lust, and "naturally a social and political animal."[36] But while casting a veil of legitimacy over the political order, Aquinas simultaneously spurned the particularism that was now the order of the day in Western Europe: "government is the more perfect the more universalist it is, and the further it extends and the higher its aims."[37] To him, "Secular power is subject to the spiritual power as the body is subject to the soul".[38] The church thus held the ultimate authority over everything, temporal as well as spiritual. One leading commentator has noted that in Aquinas: "The *ecclesia* includes the *res publica*."[39] This did not mean that the Pope wielded both swords. But it did mean that the conduct of politics had to fit within a moral framework as defined by God's representative on earth. Although Aquinas acknowledged the state, his outlook also implied that those who followed Aristotle in medieval conditions combined greater humanism with an explicit commitment to universalism. This was even more apparent in the writings of the poet Dante Alighieri (1265–1321).

In his prose work *Monarchia*, Dante pressed for a universal empire. As one learned commentator has remarked, "This is the old cosmopolitanism of the Stoics revised to suit Christian needs and fitted into an Aristotelian system."[40] For the Stoics the universe was governed by seminal reason (*spermatikos logos*), which lay not just in the universe at large but also within man. It was this that gave direction to life and the outer cosmos as a whole. Man was duty-bound to pursue "right reason" in conformity with the *logos*, though on an individual level he exercised choice; but "once it has been given an external stimulus it will move itself for the rest by its own force and nature."[41] This inevitably entailed a vision of politics that embraced a world beyond the confines of the polis or empire. Dante, following Aristotle, believed in man's capacity for reason and, following the Stoics, that man naturally belonged to a universal community, the *humana civilitas*; and witness his comment that "the end of humankind is a necessary means for the attainment of the ultimate ends of universal nature".[42]

Dante's model was Rome. "Time will run back, and fetch the age of gold", wrote Milton. Dante's answer was both authoritarian and universalist: an extreme reaction to the internecine strife that troubled Italy. From Poppi in the Casentino, he wrote that God had "entrusted to the Holy Roman Empire the governance of human affairs so that mankind might have peace under the cloudless sky that such a protection affords." Correspondingly, "when the throne of Augustus is vacant, the whole world loses its way, the

---

36   Ibid., p. 3. This was in his essay "On Princely Government to the King of Cyprus".
37   Ibid., p. 163.
38   Quoted in D. Bigongiari, "The Political Ideas of St. Thomas Aquinas", in ibid, *Essays on Dante and Medieval Culture* (Florence 1964) p. 131.
39   Ibid., p. 132.
40   "The Political Doctrine of Dante", ibid., p. 21.
41   Chrysippus, quoted in A. Long, "Freedom and Determinism in the Stoic Theory of Human Action", Long (ed.), *Problems in Stoicism* (London 1971), p. 182.
42   Quoted by D. Bigongiari, in ibid., p. 27.

pilot and oarsmen in the ship of St. Peter fall asleep, and Italy, unhappy and forsaken, abandoned to private caprice and deprived of all public direction, drifts in such a battering from wind and wave as words could not express, and even the Italians themselves in their misery can scarcely measure it by their tears"[43] – not the first, nor last time that civil conflict turned a sensitive mind to the advocacy of an authoritarian, in this case universalist, solution. The essential requirement for widespread acceptance of the principle of Reasons of State was the removal of the idea that the expedient act of a ruler should also be moral; otherwise a higher value would stand above the needs of the state. Thomists elevated moral principle above politics. It was not until the fifteenth century and in Italy that the ground was cut from under the feet of Thomist reasoning concerning the supremacy of principle over expediency in the conduct of politics.

Marsilius of Padua (c. 1275–1342) led the way with the conception of society as a living organism governed by human laws free of higher moral prescription.[44] That is to say, the spiritual realm should not dictate to the temporal. In one sense the authority of Augustine was thus broken. In another sense, however, it experienced a renascence. The early Christian conception of original sin incorporated in Augustinian doctrine served as the essential premiss for the construction of Machiavelli's political thought that smashed through the fragile moral foundations of politics. Man was by nature inclined to evil and the organization of the state should take that into account. Interestingly this view – later termed a Hobbist view of human nature – was also taken by some in the Islamic world in the fourteenth century. It was here, not in Italy, that the "mirror of princes" literature first appeared. And it was here that the overriding demands of religion were first challenged in the name of secular priorities. Whereas the leading authorities had focused on the construction of a state in accordance with religious law (*shari'a*), al-Tortúshí[45] (1059–1126/30) fixed instead on the needs of the state itself (*siyasa*).[46] Born in Tortosa, Tortúshí studied in Zaragoza, Seville and elsewhere, before leaving Spain in 1083 for Baghdad, Basra, Mecca, and Damascus, and later settling in Egypt. The work which Tortúshí completed in 1122 and by which he is best known was called *Sirach Almoluc*.[47] *Sirach* means lamp or torch. The title thus translated means "Lamp of Princes", or, as later became popularised, "Mirror of

43   Letter VI: *Dante, Monarchy and Three Political Letters*, ed. D. Nicholl (London 1954) p. 103.
44   For a discussion of this, see L. Rothkrug, *Opposition to Louis XIV: The Political and Social Origins of the French Enlightenment* (Princeton 1965) pp. 7–8.
45   His full name was Abú Bekr Muhammad B. al-Walid B. Muhammad B. Khalaf B. Sulaimán B. Aiyub al-Fihrí, known also as Ibn Abí Randaka – *Encyclopaedia of Islam*, ed. M. Houtsma et al., Vol. 2 (London 1927) pp. 355–6.
46   For the background, see R. Khalidi, *Arab Historical Thought in the Classical Period* (Cambridge 1994) pp. 193–7.
47   The full title runs: "A book of the lamp of princes and caliphs, the path of governors and emirs; histories of the prophets, upon whom there is peace; news of Arab and foreign kings, and the rule or government of kingdoms and empires." See F. Pons Boigues, *Ensayo Bio-Bibliográfico sobre los Historiadores y Geógrafes Arábigo-Españoles* (Madrid 1898) pp. 181–4.

Princes". The book was dedicated to his protector, the Wazir of Egypt, Almamúm ben Albathaihí.[48]

Tortúshí, a witness to the dissolution of his native Andalucía under the impact of civil strife, argued the overwhelming importance of advice to statesmen because of the transcendental nature of political power. He claimed obedience to higher authority was essential not merely because it was a refuge against doubts about the faith, but also because "for the people the ruler is what the spirit is for the body".[49] In a work replete with quotation from sources as widely garnered as from India and ancient Greece (Aristotle), Tortúshí insisted upon the importance of justice from the ruler, but for pragmatic rather than moral reasons. And where the needs of justice conflicted with the survival of the state, he placed the latter firmly over the former:

> It may therefore be said that an infidel ruler who complies with the requirements of conventional policy lasts longer and is stronger than a believing ruler who in his own person is just and obedient to a prophetic policy of justice . . ."[50]

Tortúshí's most significant successor was Ibn Khaldun (1332–1406), who wrote his reflections in an introduction to history after having served many years in the upper reaches of government. Khaldun divided politics into two parts: the general issues which came under the laws of Islam, and that "concerned with the interest of the ruler and how he can maintain his rule though the forceful use of power." Here he insisted that people "cannot persist in a state of anarchy and without a ruler who keeps them apart. Therefore, they need a person to restrain them. He is their ruler. As is required by human nature, he must be a forceful ruler."[51] Ibn Khaldun believed in giving advice. Other writers in the Islamic world thought this unnecessary. In *A Mirror for Princes: The Qabus Nama*, for example, written around 1082, Kai Ka'us Ibn Iskandar, Prince of Gurgan, wrote that "princes are like water-fowl in that young water-fowl need never be taught to swim".[52]

There also existed the view, prevalent in England, at least, through to the second half of the seventeenth century, that: "The interests of princes are not proper subjects for ordinary pens . . ."[53] Had this view prevailed in early modern Italy, the chief and most

48   Ibid.

49   M. Alarcón (ed.), *Lámpara de los Príncipes por Abubéquer de Tortosa* (Madrid 1930), Vol. 1, p. 240.

50   Quoted in Khalidi, *Arab Historical Thought*, p. 194. For its place in the text: *Lámpara*, p. 204.

51   Ibn Khaldun, *An Introduction to History – The Muqaddimah*, edited by N. Dawood (London 1967), pp. 257 and 152.

52   Kai Ka'us Ibn Iskandar, *Prince of Gurgan, A Mirror for Princes: The Qabus Nama*, translated by R. Levy (London 1951) p. 214.

53   *A Justification of the present War against the United Netherlands. Wherein the Declaration of his Majesty is vindicated, and the War proved to be just, honourable, and necessary; the Dominion of the Sea explained, and his Majesty's Rights thereunto asserted; the Obligations of the Dutch to England, and their continual Ingratitude: In Answer to a Dutch Treatise, intitled, "Considerations upon the present*

radical exponent of Reasons of State, Niccoló Machiavelli (1469–1527), would never have emerged into print. Although he did not use the term *ragion di stato*, he left no doubt that it captures the essence of his thought. Machiavelli had devoted an unusual amount of time focusing on practices hitherto taken much for granted. He dutifully served the city-state of Florence and it was in that capacity that he imbibed the essence of statecraft. When forced out of office he deeply regretted "being far from the secrets and the affairs [of state]".[54] But he spent his time wrapped in thought about such questions, becoming, as Francesco Guicciardini (1483–1540) described him, an "inventor of new and unusual things".[55]

On 4 April 1513 Machiavelli wrote to friend and diplomat Francesco Vettori: "Fate has determined that, not knowing how to think about the art of silk and the art of wool, nor of profits, nor of losses, it has fallen to me to reason about the state . . ."[56] Formerly the practitioner, Machiavelli turned his "knowledge of the conduct of great men, learned through long experience of modern affairs and continual study of ancient history"[57] into theoretical form and in a vain attempt to win high office incidentally enlightened the layman, from whom this arcane world had hitherto studiously been hidden.

Machiavelli was, indeed, motivated by personal ambition in writing *The Prince*. In a further letter to Vettori, he openly acknowledged that he was short of income and that he also hoped the Medici would "employ" him, even if at the outset in humdrum and burdensome work. On his view, the knowledge he had acquired through the experience of those he studied made him eminently employable.[58] But there was also much more to it than that. Machiavelli blamed the destruction of the civilised world he knew at the hands of invaders on the lack of attention to power. In 1494 the invasion of the French under King Charles VIII destroyed the delicate balance of power between the city-states of Italy:

> Our Italian princes believed, before they tasted the blows of the war from beyond the mountains, that it was enough for a prince at his desk to know how to think up a sharp retort, to write a fine letter, to demonstrate wit and quickness [of mind] in words and sayings, to know how to weave a fraud, to adorn oneself with gems and

State of the United Netherlands." By an Englishman. Reprinted in *The Harleian Miscellany: A Collection of Scarce, Curious, and Entertaining Pamphlets and Tracts, as well as in manuscript as in print. Selected from the Library of Edward Harley, Second Earl of Oxford.* Ed. W. Oldys and T. Park, Vol. 8 (London 1811) p. 129.

54   Quoted in J. Macek, *Machiavelli e il Machiavellismo* (Firenze 1980) p. 55.
55   Ibid.
56   *Opere* di Niccolò Machiavelli, Vol. 3, ed. F. Gaeta (Torino 1984) doc. 208.
57   Dedicatory letter prefacing Machiavelli, *The Prince*, ed. Q. Skinner and R. Price (Cambridge 1988) p. 3.
58   Machiavelli to Vettori, 10 December 1513: *Opere*, Vol. 3, ed. F. Gaeta, doc. 224. A partial translation of the letter is available in Machiavelli, *The Prince*, ed. cit., pp. 93–5.

gold, to sleep and eat with greater splendour than others, to behave sufficiently lasciviously all over the place, to govern one's subjects with meanness and arrogance, to rot in idleness, to give rank to the military from favour, to show contempt if someone pointed out some praiseworthy path, wishing that their words were the answers from the oracle; nor did they notice the wretches who prepared themselves as prey for someone who assaulted them. It was this that later in 1494 gave birth to the great fear, the unexpected retreats and the prodigious losses: thus three of the most powerful states that Italy had were sacked and laid waste several times.[59]

Moreover, he concluded *The Prince* with the exhortation to rescue Italy from "the hands of barbarians".[60] He was thus also driven by a passionate sense of unnecessary loss that resulted from the irresponsible conduct of political life in the city-states that so easily succumbed to invasion.

The circumstances of the time do much to explain the peculiar emphases that mark Machiavelli's writing. For instance, the trauma of invasion and subsequent chaos left many entirely fatalistic, believing "that the affairs of the world are in a way governed by chance [*fortuna*] and by God".[61] If these tragic events were foreordained, then nothing could be done to remedy them. "This opinion has become more credited in our time because of the great changes that have been seen and are seen every day, beyond what any human could conceive. And sometimes when thinking, I am myself to a certain extent inclined to their opinion."[62] Moreover, when the Florentines were spurred to act, they were inclined to rely more on mental agility than on force to protect themselves; *ragione* was their preferred weapon. As was said at the time, they could "resist either with force or with intelligence. And it does not appear possible that we can resist the whole of Italy relying on force. We must take the alternative: intelligence."[63]

Fatalism was anathema to Machiavelli. Chance (*fortuna*) "demonstrates its power where virtue [quality of leadership] is not regulated to resist it . . ." For Machiavelli, therefore, despite the actions of fate, all was not foreordained; human agency was central to failure. He thereby typified Renaissance thinking in seeing man at the centre of things, both for good and evil. And evil was for Machiavelli an ever-present reality. This belief underpinned his aversion to total reliance on *ragione* or *ingegno* (ingenuity) and the realisation that force was critical. He had no faith in human nature and, in a world where God did not intervene on a consistent basis to ensure goodness, man had to be so organised as to bring him into better behaviour.

59   N. Machiavelli, *Arte della guerra e scritti politici minori*, ed. S. Bertelli (Milan 1961) p. 518.
60   Machiavelli, *Il Principe* (Milan 1950 edition) p. 190.
61   Ibid., p. 186.
62   Ibid.
63   Quoted in F. Gilbert, *Machiavelli and Guicciardini: Politics and History in Sixteenth Century Florence* (Princeton 1965) p. 34. This is surely a classic, given Gilbert's extensive research in the city's archives.

Machiavelli's comments on the nature of man are scattered but entirely consonant with an Augustinian pessimism. Strong government is necessary because man is fundamentally not to be trusted: ". . . every armed prophet is victorious and the disarmed is ruined. Because, when everything is said, the nature of the people is changeable; and it is easy to persuade them of a thing, but difficult to keep them to such a persuasion. It is therefore necessary that it be so arranged that when they no longer believe, one can make them believe through force."[64] Similarly, men were "ungrateful, fickle, impostors and dissemblers, cowards, greedy for profit . . ."[65] All in all, therefore, in answer to the question whether it is better to be loved than feared, "because it is difficult to mix them together, it is much safer to be feared than loved, when one has to lose one of the two."[66] The reason was simple: "men have less respect offending one who elicits love than one who elicits fear; because love is maintained by a bond of obligation which, given that men are bad, is broken on any occasion when required; but fear is maintained by being frightened of punishment which never leaves you."[67] This concern for utility meant that for Machiavelli, as indeed for all those committed to Reasons of State, calculation and self-control were mechanisms essential to effective rule. Whereas fear was useful, hatred was counter-productive.

Machiavelli was not against constitutional rule; far from it. But power was the first issue to be considered. "The main bases of all states, whether new, old or mixed, are good laws and good arms. And, since there cannot be good laws where there are not good arms, and where there are good arms there are necessarily good laws I will leave aside discussion of laws and talk of arms."[68] In particular, Machiavelli located that failure in lack of military power and want of wisdom. He had criticised his fellow-countrymen for relying too much on intelligence and too little on force, but he was no less conscious that intelligence itself had been less than successfully deployed. "These . . . two things [military power and wisdom] are the nerves of all governments [*signorie*] . . ." The loss of territory, the fall of cities, and the overthrow of governments were, on his view, all due to "lack of weapons and of judgement".[69] The ruler of Siena, Pandolfo Petrucci, replied to Machiavelli's questioning about the "tricks and intrigues" deployed in dealing with Florence in the following terms: "Wishing to make as few mistakes as possible, I conduct my government day by day, and arrange my affairs hour by hour; because the times are more powerful than our brains."[70] There were other lessons, other teachers by example; most notoriously in ruthlessness. Cesare Borgia

64   *Il Principe*, p. 106.
65   Ibid., p. 153.
66   Ibid., p. 152.
67   Ibid., p. 153.
68   Ibid., pp. 132–3.
69   "Parole da dirle sopra la provisione del danaio, fatto un poco di proemio e di scusa", Machiavelli, *Arte della guerra e scritti politici minori*, ed. S. Bertelli, Vol. 2 (Milan 1961) p. 57.
70   Q. Skinner, "Machiavelli", in *Great Political Thinkers* (Oxford 1992) p. 24.

(Valentino), alerted to a plot by subordinate allies, called them to a meeting and murdered them. Machiavelli was "lost in wonder at this development."[71]

One of his favourite adjectives was "useful" (*utile*). This was his measure of all things. Others had written handbooks of advice for princes. Where Machiavelli differed was in totally detaching recommendation from morality – his very definition of virtue was ability and efficiency, which he elevated to the level of moral qualities, rather than in terms of ethics. He wrote of "cruelty badly employed or well employed. One can call cruelties well employed (if it is legitimate to call bad good) when they are carried out all at once in order to make oneself secure . . . badly employed are those which, even if small within the principality, grow somewhat with time . . ."[72] Good or bad was thus reduced to necessity and utility. Even piety was a matter of utility, and it was here that Machiavelli was to create an immovable barrier between himself and the Catholic revival, with momentous consequences for the fate of his work.

As noted, Machiavelli's position rests on a key assumption about the nature of man which he shared with many "realists". Most men, he wrote, "are not good". It therefore followed that if the prince insisted "on making it his business to be good", he would fail to achieve "great things" and "will surely be destroyed." "And it must be understood that a ruler, and especially a new ruler, cannot always act in ways that are considered good because, in order to maintain his power, he is often forced to act treacherously, ruthlessly or inhumanely, and disregard the precepts of religion."[73] One current ruler "is always preaching peace and trust, although he is really very hostile to both; and if he had practised them he would have lost either reputation or power several times over."[74] Only this would assure the necessary tactical flexibility that would enable him always to adjust to circumstance in changing times: ". . . if it were possible to change one's character to suit the times and circumstances, one would always be successful."[75]

We are thus not told explicitly how to run foreign affairs, even though the experience of human nature Machiavelli drew upon was largely diplomatic. Acute observation of behaviour in the practice of foreign policy appears to have been transmuted into reflections on the domestic realm. Although there is little direct sign of this, the circumstantial evidence lies in his career: missions to France, Rome and various city-states over a dozen years in office. There is also the example of foreign treaties in his discussion of broken promises and deception. "One could give countless modern examples of this, and show how many peace treaties and promises have been rendered null and void by the faithlessness of rulers; and those best able to imitate the fox have succeeded best." But "one must be a great feigner and dissembler. And men are so naive,

71   Ibid., p. 26.
72   *Il Principe*, pp. 120–1.
73   *Great Political Thinkers*, p. 62.
74   Ibid., p. 63.
75   Ibid., p. 86.

and so much dominated by their immediate needs, that a skilful deceiver always finds plenty of people who will let themselves be deceived."[76] As early as 1503 Machiavelli wrote that "between ordinary citizens [*uomini privati*] laws, contracts and agreements are enforced by trust, but between rulers weapons are the only means of enforcement."[77] He polemicised against the eternal optimists who continually found reasons for avoiding rearmament: "every city, every state, must deem hostile all those who could hope to be capable of occupying it and from whom you are not able to defend yourselves. There never was either a government or a republic that wanted to maintain its state at the discretion of others or that, maintaining it, thought to have it secure."[78] He advised his employers: "Leave the house and take a look at whom you have around you: you will find yourself in between two or three cities which prefer that you die rather than live. Go further, leave Tuscany and look at the whole of Italy: you will see it tossing and turning under the king of France, the Venetians, the Pope and Valentino."[79]

The Prince took this much as given, and the focus turned instead on how a ruler could reinforce his power within the state, the problem most apparent from the weakness and division of the city-states that made foreign invasion so easy.[80] Machiavelli explained that "rulers should have two main worries: one is internal, and concerns his subjects; the other is external, and concerns foreign powers. Against the latter threat, good troops and reliable allies are an effective defence; and possessing good armies always results in having allies who are reliable. If external relations are solidly based, internal affairs will give no trouble unless they have already been disturbed by conspiracy."[81] We are also told in a very matter-of-fact manner that "Wanting to annex territory is indeed very natural and normal . . ."[82] Yet Machiavelli's entire book is given over to the complications of internal affairs. Clearly his key obsession can be encapsulated in his comment that "when faction-ridden cities are threatened by an enemy force, they always fall very quickly."[83] No amount of foreign policy is of any avail if the domestic realm is not in good order.

Although Machiavelli never used the term Reasons of State, he did talk of reasoning about the state, and the term was certainly in use during his lifetime. It appeared in print within years of his death variously as *Ragion di Stato* (Giovanni Della Casa) and *Ragione dei Governi* (Palazzo).[84] However differently phrased, there can be no

76   Ibid., p. 62.
77   Machiavelli, "Parole . . .": loc. cit.
78   Machiavelli, *Arte*, ed. Bertelli, p. 61.
79   Ibid., p. 62.
80   For a detailed account of the role of internal divisions in the weakening of Florentine foreign policy: S. Bertelli, "Machiavelli e la politica estera fiorentina", *Studies on Machiavelli*, ed. M. Gilmore (Florence 1972) pp. 31–72.
81   Ibid., p. 64.
82   Skinner, "Machiavelli", p. 13.
83   Ibid., p. 73.
84   R. de Mattei, "Il problema della 'Ragion di Stato' nei suoi primi affioramenti", *Rivista Internazionale di Filosofia del Diritto*, XLI, Nov.–Dec. 1964, pp. 712–13.

doubt what it meant. Francesco Guicciardini used the term *Ragione e uso degli Stati* in his *Dialogo del reggimento di Firenze*, written between 1521 and 1526, while Machiavelli was still alive.[85] Guicciardini also served government, as ambassador to Spain. He was perhaps more like the rest of us than Machiavelli, torn as he was between the need to see the facts "as they are" and as "they should be",[86] yet simultaneously reluctant to take such a fundamentally negative stance on human nature.[87] He found Machiavelli's position "that men do not behave well except out of necessity" too extreme. On his own view there were "many who, including those capable of acting badly, behave well, and not all men are bad."[88] Indeed, in his memoirs he wrote: "Men are naturally inclined to the good, in the sense that for everyone, when the bad does not give pleasure or serve a need, the good is preferred to the bad. But because their nature is fragile and the opportunities which tempt them to the bad are infinite, they derive easily from their own interests from natural inclination."[89] However, it was the same Guicciardini who also wrote: "It will perhaps appear malicious or suspect to say so . . . God would wish it were not true: there are more bad men than good; maxims which direct the interests of property [*di roba*] and of the State . . ."[90]

This "realist" view of human nature found voice in Guicciardini's *Dialogo* in the person of Bernardo, who concludes: "the fact is that in the natural course of human affairs . . . force rather than the reason or wisdom of men is often better."[91] Later on in the same discussion, he sees force as not only a value in and of itself,[92] but also as a consequence of the fact that "men have a taste for corruption; they do not see true honour as made up of anything other than power . . ."[93] He goes on to discuss the threat posed to Florence by stubborn Pisa: "one must always kill every Pisan that takes part in the war, to reduce the number of enemies and make the others more fearful . . ."[94] Of course this would give one a reputation for cruelty and lack of conscience. Bernardo's answer to both was "that he who wishes today to keep hold of his land and the state must, where possible, use piety and good will, and where it is not possible to do otherwise, it is necessary to use cruelty and with little conscience." He cites his interlocutor's great-grandfather, Gino Capponi, as having written that "it is impossible to run governments and states wishing to do so in the manner they do today, according

85   F. Guicciardini, *Dialogo del reggimento di Firenze*, reprinted in *Opere di Francesco Guicciardini*, ed. E. Scarono, Vol. 1 (Turin 1970), p. 465.

86   F. Guicciardini, *Ricordi Politici e Civili*, reprinted ibid., No 179, p. 780.

87   One struggles to see how one can judge Guicciardini as cold, calculating and heartless, as he is presented in B. Brunello, *Machiavelli e il pensiero politico del Rinascimento* (Bologna 1964) p. 121. This is none the less a useful work.

88   "Considerazioni sui 'Discorsi' di Machiavelli", *Opere di Guicciardini*, Vol. 1, p. 613.

89   Ibid., No 3, p. 798.

90   Ibid., No 201, p. 787.

91   "Dialogo del reggimento di Firenze", *Opere di Guicciardini*, Vol. 1, p. 382.

92   Ibid., p. 390.

93   Ibid., p. 443.

94   Ibid., p. 463.

to the precepts of Christian law . . . In what way could one in conscience make war from greed to expand one's domain, in which so much killing, so much violation of women, so much burning of houses and of churches and an infinite number of other evils are carried out? None the less, whosoever in a senate would for this reason and no other reject the undertaking of an enterprise that is both feasible and useful would be refuted by everyone. But we are saying more than that: in what way could you according to conscience undertake a war of defence even of the lands that you possess? Moreover even if there were no war and that no one demanded one, how could you maintain your domain, in which, if you think about it properly, there is perhaps nothing that is your own, your having occupied all or at least most of it through force or by purchasing it from those who had no other choice? The same thing happens to all the others because all states, whoever looks closely at their origins, are violent . . ."[95] Republics were no better than other forms of government. "You see what those who wish to govern states according to the strictures of conscience are reduced to. But when I said to kill or hold prisoner the Pisans, I have perhaps not spoken as a Christian, but I have spoken according to the reason and practice of states [*secondo la ragione e uso degli stati*] . . ."[96]

The sense that international relations governed by such amoral practices were no easy matter to change and that more recalcitrant, constant – or, if you like, structural – factors were at work is evident in attempts to portray the ideal state that emerge in the sixteenth century. Sir Thomas More (1477/8–1535), Chancellor of England from 1529 to 1532, later conceived of his utopia operating in an international system that most certainly was not utopian. A man of firm religious principle, his own preference and that of his fictional Utopians was to act through "intelligence and rationality" rather than by force.[97] For the Utopians war, however, was necessary, though "they go to war only for good reasons: to protect their own land, to drive invading armies from the territories of their friends, or to liberate an oppressed people, in the name of compassion and humanity, from tyranny and servitude."[98]

More, Aristotelian in outlook, believed men and therefore communities were connected by society or a bond of nature. The problem was that they did not behave as though they were. One indicator of More's pessimistic appraisal of the existing state of international relations was his assessment of treaties. Whereas some may believe alliances were a sign of amicability, More saw them as exactly the reverse; indeed, as causes of trouble as much as a consequence of it: "While other nations are constantly making, breaking and renewing treaties, the Utopians make none at all with any nation."[99] "A treaty implies that a people divided by some natural obstacle as slight as

95   Ibid., p. 464.
96   Ibid., p. 465.
97   T. More, *Utopia*, ed. G. Logan et al. (Cambridge 1995) p. 205.
98   Ibid., pp. 202–3.
99   Ibid., p. 197.

a hill or a brook are joined by no bond of nature; it assumes they are born rivals and enemies, and are right in trying to destroy one another except when a treaty restrains them."[100] As an experienced diplomat and statesman More had reason to know what he was saying. Those opposed to Machiavelli and his ideas were therefore hard put to convince others that in the conditions of the time statecraft could effectively operate in ways other than those he commended. It was always easier to prescribe a domestic rather than an international utopia. It meant that those so motivated tended either to idealise the imperial past of universal monarchy as utopia or to idealise an existing and aspirant monarchy (usually of their own nationality) as the long-sought universal empire. To borrow from Robert Conquest: unable to realise the ideal, they resorted instead to idealising the real, as many socialists have done in the twentieth century.

Before long the term Reasons of State was spreading with bewildering rapidity as a fashionable cliché for want of serious opposition. Venetian ambassador Andrea Gussoni wrote in 1576 of "reason of state [*ragion di stato*] and one's own utility which is the only argument that avails in the minds of princes . . ." And three years later Tasso (1493–1569), writing to Scipione Gonzaga, referred to "those who for reason, as they say, of State [*per ragion, com'essi dicevano, di Stato*], vacillate in their faith."[101] Guicciardini, however, had less impact on opinion than Machiavelli.

At first Machiavelli was welcomed. Lord Acton pointed out: "Machiavelli enjoyed a season of popularity even at Rome. The Medicean popes refused all official employment to one who had been the brain of a hostile government; but they encouraged him to write, and were not offended by the things he wrote for them. Leo's own dealings with the tyrant of Perugia were cited by jurists as a suggestive model for men who have an enemy to get rid of. Clement confessed to Contarini that honesty would be preferable, but that honest men get the worst of it . . . Two years after this speech the astute Florentine authorised *The Prince* to be published in Rome."[102] In 1550, however, Machiavelli was denounced to the Inquisition. The Index of proscribed books was instituted seven years later, and Machiavelli was among the first to be named. But what was shocking and to be condemned was less that the behaviour of states was such as described than that such descriptions should be widely circulated as the norm.

It has been said that the strength of *The Prince* derived less from its theoretical contribution to knowledge than its realistic portrayal of affairs.[103] What attracted attention, however, was its startling amorality. Machiavelli was later characterised by the historian Thomas Macaulay (1800–59) as "an enigma" whose "moral sensibility"

---

100   Ibid., p. 201.
101   Both quoted in de Mattei, *Il Problema*, p. 28.
102   Acton's "Introduction to Burd's Edition of *Il Principe* by Machiavelli", *Selected Writings of Lord Acton, Vol. II: Essays in the Study and Writing of History*, ed. J. Fears (Indianapolis 1985) pp. 480–1.
103   A. Sorel, *L'Europe et la Révolution Française*, part 1 (Paris 1908) p. 17. Apart from Meinecke, this is surely one of the best surveys of the subject of Reasons of State.

seemed at once "to be morbidly obtuse and morbidly acute".[104] This was an assessment of a more detached age. At the time of writing the unadorned and brutal directness of Machiavelli's message inevitably sounded shocking. Before long it triggered the revival of moralism in political prescription. But this revival and the associated condemnation of Machiavelli's ideas were not merely spontaneous moral revulsion. Rather, they represented an orchestrated counterblast from a church fighting for the retrieval of its spiritual supremacy against the Protestant Reformation inaugurated in 1517. And the counter-attack represented not merely the resurgence of moral prescription but also a revival of universalist ideals in opposition to the focus on the state as much as on Reasons of State.

The urge to universalism encompassed a variety of different positive motives. In part it was a false nostalgia for a world at peace within one empire. In part it was the utopian search for a secular saviour of mankind. In part it was a spiritually motivated attempt to take the world back into the temporal control of the universal church. But all saw Reasons of State set for destruction. Giovanni Battista Pigna (1530–75) wrote of a heroic prince becoming "Monarch of all of this world".[105] The most famous advocate of universal empire was, however, Tommaso Campanella (1568–1639). Campanella, a Dominican, suffered badly for his fierce independence of mind. Persecuted by the Holy See, tortured, twice accused of heresy, imprisoned for perpetuity, serving 27 years in total, he eventually died in exile in Paris.[106] Only in his rejection of Machiavelli did he stand four-square with the church. Campanella carefully distinguished between "*Prudence*" and "*Craft*". Whereas the former came from God and was therefore good, the latter – "which is called by some, *Ratio Statuum regendorum*, the Reason, or Rule of State-Government" – was bad.[107] Campanella expressly denied Aristotle's dictum that one man could not rule the world and insisted that it would fall to the King of Spain to fulfil that role, whose ultimate purpose was to bring all back under the Holy Church. His reasoning was simple: "all the troubles of the world are born from war or from disease or from famine or from opinion opposed to native religion."[108] Of course, the irony is that this utopian aspiration to universal monarchy was easily twisted to serve Reasons of State. As E. H. Carr (see pp. 186–90) once said, everything is an instrument of foreign policy.[109] The best means of legitimising a bid for imperial hegemony in Europe was to claim universal monarchy, not state interests, as one's true motivation. Few were exempt from this great temptation. Thus even the apparently unworldly French philosopher Guillaume Postel (1510–81) envisaged France as the universal empire.[110]

---

104   "Machiavelli" (March 1827): Lord Macaulay, *Critical and Historical Essays*, Vol. 1 (London 1903) p. 65.
105   Quoted in Rodolfo de Mattei, *Il Pensiero politico italiano nell'Età della Controriforma* Vol. 1 (Milan 1982) p. 222.
106   T. Bozza, *Scrittori politici italiani dal 1550 al 1650* (Rome 1949) pp. 135–6.
107   T. Campanella, *A Discourse touching The Spanish Monarchy* (London 1654) p. 16.
108   Quoted in de Mattei, loc. cit., p. 225, note 13.
109   To the author, in discussing a chapter entitled "Disarmament as an Instrument of Foreign Policy".
110   Quoted in de Mattei, p. 226.

Indeed, the most striking feature of Machiavelli's foremost critics was the degree of hypocrisy, conscious or not, exposed in the vast gap between their public protestations against the immorality of *The Prince* and their own behaviour. Mons. Giovanni Della Casa (1503–56), who launched an assault on Reasons of State in his *Orazione a Carlo V*, is an exemplar. Della Casa was no mere cleric or scholar. He was also a diplomat, familiar with the affairs of state. Pope Paul III had sent him as Papal Nuncio to Venice and he was a confidant of Cardinal Carlo Carafa, head of Pope Paul IV's secretariat.[111] In the *Orazione*, Della Casa polemicised against masking "fraudulent and violent activity under the name of reason". He denied that there could be two types of reason, the private which was simple and pure, and that of state which was "not only hardly Christian but . . . also hardly human."[112] Yet, as has been pointed out, it was this same Della Casa, in his role as Nuncio, who, willingly or no, in fact operated on two moral levels. In two *Orazioni* written to incite the Venetians into an alliance against Charles V, Della Casa does not use the term *ragion di stato*, but he tacitly yields to its dictates. He writes of "the nature of things by which, as between the wolf and the herd, no more or less than between the Empire and the . . . states, eternal dissension and hostility has been ordained according to infallible and perpetual law." He added: "the prosperity of the Emperor is our adversity; and in so far as His Majesty rises and becomes more powerful, so do we decline and fall."[113] Even more striking is his comment that if rulers held a territory unjustly, they should not expect that "others would intervene in merely a legitimate and just manner; because in such questions there is no competent judge, no briefs or petitions are given; but arms, force and industry are together both judges and executioners . . ."[114]

To those who had no practical experience of statecraft, it was easier to take the moral high ground against Machiavelli, and in the years of the Counter-Reformation such writers carried weight. To avoid public opprobrium, therefore, Machiavelli's followers felt obliged to turn instead to ancient Roman precedent, the writings of Cornelius Tacitus (*c.* 55–120), as the authority. The *Annals* were published in 1515. But it was not until about 1580 that Tacitism became widespread. In particular, the publication of Scipione Ammirato's superficial but popular *Discorsi sopra Cornelio Tacito* in Florence in 1594 led to translations which sent these ideas beyond Italy's borders.[115] Instances there were of words claimed as those of Tacitus which were in fact closer to Machiavelli, though the degree to which this became commonplace is now disputed.[116] Indeed, it was the shift from use in support of absolutism to exposure of the secrets of government (*arcana imperii*) in the interests of greater public participation that provoked

---

111   De Mattei, "Il problema . . .", pp. 720–2.
112   Quoted ibid., p. 723.
113   Quoted ibid., p. 730.
114   Quoted ibid., p. 731.
115   In France a translation by Baudoin appears in 1618: Maspétiol, "Les deux aspects . . .", p. 212.
116   See, for instance, J. Freund in *Staatsräson: Studien zur Geschichte eines politischen Begriffs*, ed. R. Schnur (Berlin 1975) pp. 78–9; for a more sceptical view: P. Burke, "Tacitism", in *Tacitus*, ed. T. Dorey (London 1969) pp. 149–171.

deep disquiet. The inevitable reaction from the authorities was to suppress writings on Tacitus.

In 1627 Traiano Boccalini's posthumous *Comentarii sopra Cornelio Tacito* were thus ruled unsuitable for publication by the Venetian Council of Ten, objecting that good government would be jeopardised by open discussion among members of the public of the secrets of statecraft.[117] Indeed, in a play on words the view from the top in Venice was that "*sarebbe stato meglio che Tacito avesse tacito*" (it were better had Tacitus kept quiet).[118] But this was most definitely a futile gesture of orthodoxy. No sooner did they slam one door, than another opened behind them. Ludovico Zùccolo (1568–c. 1631), who published *Della ragion di stato* in 1621, joked that Reasons of State were discussed "not merely by counsellors at court and by academics [*dottori nelle scuole*], but even by barbers and by the lowest of craftsmen in the workshops . . ."[119] And in 1634 *Il forestiero* by Giulio Capaccio (c. 1560–1651) contained the revealing comment that "the world has rediscovered [Reasons of State] in order to lose its mind because, mixed in with every human activity and every event, whether frivolous or serious, useful or damaging, in earnest or for enjoyment, it has no idea how to leave men's mouths alone; it is reasoned in kitchens, its cry is heard in brothels, nobles have a ceremonial place for it, the common people make use of it to sound big [*ci si fan grandi*], and among astrologers they say that the heavens move by reason of state".[120] Similarly, in the satire *La secretaria d'Apollo* by Antonio Santacroce, which appeared in 1653, Tacitus protests at being belittled by having attributed to him "things of which he had never even dreamed."[121]

Suppression was never fully effective. A more subtle and lasting stratagem was, however, to neutralise the impact of Machiavelli by accepting certain prescriptions in dilution while rejecting the amoral thrust of his argument; that is, preserving its form while effectively destroying its content. Giovanni Botero (1533/4–1617) was a clever scholar but an intemperate spirit. He trained as a Jesuit (including an enlightening spell in Paris) but found the discipline all but intolerable. Attaining no proper outlet for mounting ambition, he soon acquired a reputation for intrigue. Indeed, his superiors castigated him in September 1579 as a "person . . . who is more readily at home with secular than with holy wisdom [*che s'accomoda più presto per prudenza umana che divina*]".[122] It was therefore with some relief on all sides that he left the order after twenty-two years of difficulty in December 1580. In Milan he found brief employment with the powerful Archbishop San Carlo Borromeo, for whom he had previously carried out some duties (before falling out with him over an ill-considered utterance denying

117   D. Wootton, *Paolo Sarpi: Between Renaissance and Enlightenment* (Cambridge 1983) p. 73.
118   Quoted in F. Ramorino, *Cornelio Tacito nella Storia della Coltura* (Milan 1898) p. 101.
119   Quoted in B. Croce, *Storia della Età Barocca in Italia* (Bari 1929) p. 77.
120   Ibid., p. 76.
121   Ibid., p. 84.
122   L. Firpo, "Giovanni Botero", *Dizionario biografico degli italiani* (Rome 1971) p. 354 *passim*.

Christ's temporal authority before the crucifixion). What proved a turning-point was an attack on Machiavelli in his manuscript of *De regia sapientia*. Before long he was installed as the Archbishop's secretary and companion. The Borromeos were the leading family of Milan: at last Botero had attained a position of influence under someone from whom he had a great deal to learn. Disaster struck, however, in November 1584, when the Archbishop died. Botero's political experience was then immeasurably enlarged by serving on a diplomatic mission in Paris for Carlo Emanuele of Savoy in 1585. The crisis in France and the intellectual ferment that accompanied it gave pause for profound reflection. On return to Milan he was appointed tutor to San Carlo's young nephew, Federico (1564–1631), accompanying him in September 1586 to Rome to pilot him through the dangerous waters of the Roman court. Success was achieved with Federico's elevation to the purple, achieved just over a year later. There was yet little in Botero's background to suggest that he would become one of the most influential political thinkers of the Counter-Reformation. But the opportunities opened up by Rome made all the difference. Enlarging upon the sketch given in *De regia sapientia*, Botero set out to defend the values of the church in the Counter-Reformation, to restore transcendental religious values to their former supremacy above the conduct of politics. He added water to Machiavelli and made Reasons of State a much easier and less heady mixture to swallow for those of a more trusting or naive disposition. The title of his *Della Ragion di Stato*, published in 1589, would best be translated "Thinking about Government" rather than Reasons of State.

Despite its undeniable success in Italy and abroad, this artful attempt at bowdlerisation did not go unchallenged. The caustic Monsignor Goffredo Lomellini, agent in Rome for the republic of Genoa, and a man with a literary reputation as well as an expert in the art of negotiation, used to meet with others every week at the house in Rome of one of the most powerful figures in the city, Cardinal Cinzio Aldobrandini, nephew of Pope Clement VIII, at what they called the *Accademia di cose di Stato* (the Academy of Affairs of State). It was there that Lomellini delivered an attack on Botero's work on 20 June 1594 and quipped of his book that it "contained nothing about *Ragion di Stato* other than the title".[123] This stinging rebuke echoed beyond the walls of the *Accademia*. A letter from Girolamo Frachetta in March 1594 was no less disparaging.[124] Thus in July Botero was prompted to write to Aldobrandini and other cardinals to protest that the attack by Lomellini was unjustified.[125] Not that this had any great effect, for some years later, in the writings of Boccalini, Apollo complains that the book treats

---

123   Quoted from the Vatican archives: R. de Mattei, *Il problema della "Ragion di Stato" nell'età della Controriforma* (Milan 1979) p. 66. See also E. Baldini, "Le guerre di religione francesi nella trattatistica della ragion di stato: Botero e Frachetta", *Il Pensiero Politico*, XXII, No 2, 1989, p. 309. The precise date of the paper and the comment are from Baldini.

124   Quoted in Luigi Firpo, "Lettere inedite di Giovanni Botero", *Atti delle Accademia delle Scienze di Torino* Vol. 89 (1954–5) p. 213.

125   Letter of July 1594: ibid., pp. 239–40.

only of "politics in general", without any mention "of that reason of State which the title otherwise promises."[126]

That Botero's publication was largely a self-serving act of political opportunism is borne out not least by the fact that his preface contains a dedication to the Archbishop and Prince of Salzburg, himself a man of no admirable reputation. Botero's ostensible indignation at the fact that "Machiavelli bases his Reason of State on lack of conscience and that Tiberius [the focal point of Tacitus' writings] justified his cruelty and tyranny by an inhuman *lex maiestatis . . .*" thus needs setting in its context, as should his expressed "amazement to find that this barbarous mode of government had won such acceptance that it was brazenly opposed to Divine Law, so that men even spoke of some things being permissible by Reason of State and others by conscience."[127]

Botero was by no means alone in this, however. Frachetta, in *L'Idea del libro de' governi di stato e di guerra*, published in 1592, had already distinguished between "*buona ragione di stato*" (good reason of state) and "*cattiva ragione di stato*" (evil reason of state):

> Reason of State comes in two shapes, the one true, which is that which we have . . . called civil prudence, which is not divorced either from moral virtue, or from religion, and is therefore true reason, and true rule of government. The other a facsimile, which only takes into account the convenience of the one who makes use of it, and pays no consideration either to God or to duty. It is of the second, not of the first, that I now intend to speak, because it is this . . . that has usurped the name of Reason of State.[128]

Frachetta continues:

> One cannot justly call this Reason of State Art because Art (as Aristotle teaches in the sixth book of Ethics) applies to things that can be created [*delle cose fattibili*], whereas Reason of State applies to means to an end [*delle cose agibili*], or preferences [*eligibili*], as one would say . . . We would therefore say that Reason of State is a training [*pedia*], or skill [*peritia*], or discipline, that is to say, originating partly in the instruction of others, partly in the reading of histories, and of political writers, partly of diplomatic correspondence [*Relationi*], partly a matter of intuition [*dal seso*], and partly of experimentation in the affairs of the world . . .[129]

---

126   Published in 1613: quoted in ibid., p. 212.
127   Dedication, 10 May 1589: G. Botero, *The Reason of State* (London 1956) pp. xiii–xiv.
128   G. Frachetta, *L'Idea del libro de'governi di stato et di guerra* (Venice 1592) pp. 37–8.
129   Ibid., p. 39. For the relevant section of Aristotle: "Nicomachean Ethics", book 1, in *The Complete Works of Aristotle*, ed. J. Barnes, Vol. 2 (Princeton 1984), p. 1728.

Frachetta also distinguished between Reasons of State and Reasons of War, rather in the manner that those realists who later objected to Hobbes distinguished between the State of Nature and the State of War (see below, pp. 51–6). While attaching himself to Tacitus, Frachetta vented his contempt and outrage upon Machiavelli and those who followed "such an abominable author whom so many had seized hold of in the fine Kingdom of France . . ."[130]

It was, indeed, in France that there emerged the most important realist to follow Machiavelli. Here the term Reasons of State did not emerge into print until the end of the sixteenth century.[131] But the thrust of the idea was evident earlier, in the work of Jean Bodin (1530–96). The *Six Livres de la République* were published in 1576. Like others of a similar disposition Bodin emphasised his differences with the old master while in practice holding a great deal in common. Only a decade earlier he had praised Machiavelli – though never uncritically – as the "first . . . for about 1,200 years after barbarism had overwhelmed everything" to write at length about politics.[132] The St. Bartholomew's Day Massacre of 1572 put an end to such tolerance. On that day Maria de Medici, mother of the young king, in a bid to rid the crown of Huguenot influence, had the leader Admiral Coligny assassinated in a move which set off a series of massacres of Huguenots across the country. Civil war ensued.

Repudiation of Machiavelli should occasion no surprise. Any explicit association with his ideas risked condemnation and worse. Yet the circumstances which gave rise to Machiavelli's *tour de force* existed elsewhere and inevitably led others to prescribe not dissimilar solutions to comparable problems. For just as the breakdown of order in Italy had imperilled the future of the medieval city-state that Machiavelli sought to protect, the dramatic disintegration of France during the brutal wars of religion created a special awareness in Paris of the need for strong measures to reunify the kingdom. The *Six Livres* were thus imbued with an obsession for "the preservation of Kingdoms and Empires and of all peoples" and were rooted in anxiety at the "impetuous storm" which has "tormented the ship of our Republic".[133] Clear differences emerged between Bodin and Machiavelli. But the degree to which the two shared common ground is due to their similar responses to like circumstances: chaos and disorder within the state and the threat of invasion from abroad.

---

130   Frachetta, *L'Idea*, p. 45.
131   Its first appearance is recorded as having been in a Protestant lampoon of May 1593 entitled: "a warning to the King, in which are deduced the Reasons of State [*raisons d'Etat*] for which it is not seemly for him to change religion" – quoted in R. Maspétiol, "Les deux aspects de la 'raison d'État' et son apologie au debut du XVIIe siècle", *Archives de Philosophie du Droit* No 10, 1965, p. 209.
132   *Methodus ad facilem historiarum cognitum*: quoted in E. Beame, "The Use and Abuse of Machiavelli: The Sixteenth-Century French Adaptation", *Journal of the History of Ideas*, Vol. XLIII, No 1, 1982, p. 39.
133   J. Bodin, *Les Six Livres de la République* (Paris 1576; 1594 edition).

It is therefore no surprise that Bodin found therein the reasons for the creation of the state: not as an act of God, of chance or the product of a mythical social contract. On the contrary, he bluntly asserted the premiss that "force and violence provided the source and origin of Republics."[134] Their development was a fundamental response to the demands placed upon them by a threatening environment. "The Republic," he wrote, "having come into being, if it is well founded, secures itself against external force, and against domestic infirmities: and little by little grows more powerful . . ."[135] The accretion of power to an absolute level in the form of total sovereignty was vital for both domestic and foreign policies. "First and foremost," he asserted, "it is a requirement in affairs of state that one must be the strongest or among the strongest: and this rule allows few exceptions, whether within the Republic itself or between various Princes."[136]

Bodin never leaves us in any doubt that strength was essential to protection in a European states system operating through violence. The structure of the system, resting as it did upon societies that were under severe economic constraints, forced a mode of behaviour onto governments, deprived as they were of a multiplicity of choices. "People in a fertile country and surrounded by hungry enemies must be ready for war", he wrote.[137] To him, therefore, the conduct of international relations – which was never his leading concern – was largely a zero-sum game. "At first sight," he noted, "it seems that there is no means of maintaining one's state in its greatness better than to see one's neighbours ruin one another. For the greatness of a Prince, to put it in a nutshell, is nothing other than the ruin or diminution of his neighbours: and his power is nothing other than the weakness of the rest."[138]

Such cold-blooded cynicism extended to seeing international threats as a convenient means to ensuring the internal cohesion of the state: "the finest means of conserving the state and guaranteeing it from rebellion, sedition, and civil war and to keep its subjects on good terms with one another, is to have an enemy against which one can exert oneself."[139] This was advice worthy of a disciple of Machiavelli. But it would be wrong to see Bodin as entirely given over to the amoral dictates of Reasons of State, though recent events had all but driven him entirely into that camp. He followed St. Augustine in recommending that, however powerful a prince might become, he should resort to war only from "necessity".[140] And although Bodin's sensitivity to the overwhelming importance of the factor of power in international relations caused him to warn against the dangers of alliances between the weak and the strong – "The strongest foreigners

134   Ibid., Vol. 1, p. 112.
135   Ibid., Vol. 4, pp. 7–8.
136   Ibid., Vol. 5, p. 179.
137   Ibid., p. 163.
138   Ibid., p. 179.
139   Ibid., p. 137.
140   Ibid., pp. 149–50.

make themselves masters of those who appeal to them for help"[141] – he was troubled by the need to create and reinforce bonds of obligation, a need unrecognised later by Hobbes but explicit in the work of the Thomists (firmly entrenched in the University of Paris) and their successors: Grotius, Pufendorf, Locke and Rousseau. There is "nothing", Bodin wrote, "in all the affairs of state which gives more trouble to Princes and Rulers than to safeguard treaties that one makes with another: whether it is between friends, whether between enemies, whether with those who are neutral, whether even with one's subjects."[142] Treaty observance was thus not just about power, it was also a matter of faith, and "faith", he wrote, "is the only foundation and support for justice, upon which all Republics, alliances and human societies are based . . ."[143]

Bodin's vision of the European system was that of conflict modified, and to some extent circumscribed, by ethics. It is this element in his thought which was developed by the more utopian theologians who ultimately founded the school of international law. Whereas the reaction to Machiavelli in France emerged only after the high intensity of the wars of religion, the reaction in Spain was extreme from the outset.[144] Spain of the Counter-Reformation produced both the most cynical "reasoning" of state and the most forceful and committed reassertion of universalism, both Christian and secular. Among those cited and condemned in 1595 by the Jesuit theologian Pedro de Rivadeneira, in his *Tratado de la Religion*, as the most dangerous proponents of amoral statism were Machiavelli, the French Calvinist La Noué, Duplessis-Mornay, Bodin, and, last but not least, fellow Spaniard Antonio Pérez (*c.* 1540–1611).

Pérez, whose astuteness had initially served him well as secretary of state to King Philip II, ultimately landed in trouble with his direct complicity in the assassination of rival Escobedo, resulting in an escape into exile, first to France, then England. In Paris he published his *Relaciones*, which, he warned, "have nothing to do with Religion." They were an "anatomical body for the teaching of what Princes keep concealed [*privados de Principes*]." The work was imbued with personal experience: "The most dangerous thing here, as elsewhere in centuries past, is to know the most secret secrets of Princes. More dangerous than to have a Prince under a great obligation."[145] This was followed

---

141   Ibid., p. 160.

142   Ibid., p. 165.

143   Ibid., p. 189.

144   Gonzalo Fernandez de la Mora, "Maquiavelo visto por los tratadistas españoles de la contrarreforma", *Arbor*, XIII, 1949, pp. 417–49. Subsequent attempts to modify this picture have found only very marginal evidence that matters were otherwise: D. Bleznick, "Spanish Reaction to Machiavelli in the Sixteenth and Seventeenth Centuries", *Journal of the History of Ideas*, Vol. XIX, June 1958, No 3, pp. 542–50.

145   *Relaciones de Antonio Pérez, Secretario de Estado, que fue, del Rey de España Don Phelippe II. deste nombre* (Paris 1598), pp. 11–12. Arguments as to Pérez's authorship of various works that appeared under his name can be found in the introduction by Modesto Santos to a work originally known as being the product of Pérez, *Discurso Politico al Rey Felipe III al Comienzo de su Reinado* (Madrid

by the publication of his letters, from which a series of aphorisms were drawn and, as with Tacitus earlier in the sixteenth century, separately published. The aphorisms contained little of direct relevance to the conduct of international relations; they were largely concerned with the kind of knowing advice to princes current in the Italy of Machiavelli. It was the fact of Pérez's notoriety which gave the aphorisms a certain piquancy.[146]

A more effective alternative appeared, again in Spain, from the hands of the Dominicans, who, wisely from a tactical viewpoint, accepted the fact of the state but not the implication that the state was therefore the end of the matter. Two theologians reasserted the essential unity of mankind more in the manner of the Stoics against the statist particularism so emphatically asserted by Machiavelli and Bodin. But it was a mark of the growing secularism of this debate that instead of pressing the traditional claim for a universal monarchy based on the *corpus christianum*, they chose instead to frame their case on a premiss independent of religious belief, though entirely consonant with such beliefs. And they did not seek to banish the state so much as contain its excesses in the conduct of international relations.

First, the celebrated academic from the University of Salamanca Francisco de Vitoria (1480–1546) insisted upon a *societas naturalis* of nations and freedom of trade.[147] Vitoria had been trained in Paris under the influence of a Thomist revival and, on returning to his native land, soon acquired a fame that surpassed any of his generation in applying Thomist principles to the issues of the day. These ideas were adumbrated in a series of *relecciones* – two-hour lectures which he was obliged to deliver as part of his duties as professor in Salamanca. There is in Vitoria's writing an obvious tension between the emerging consensus on Reasons of State and what might be called Reasons of War and Thomist universalism. First, he held the state not only legitimate but natural: "States and commonwealths had not their fount and origin in the invention of man, nor in any artificial manner, but sprang, as it were, from Nature, who produced this method of protecting and preserving mortals."[148] Second, he argued that "if States and societies are established in accordance with divine or natural law, the same is true of power, without which States could not exist."[149] Third, he commented that "a prince ought to subordinate both peace and war to the common weal of his State and not spend public revenues in quest of his own glory or gain, much less to expose his subjects to danger on that account."[150] And, last, he claimed that "In war everything is

1990); the author given is Baltasar Alamos de Barrientos. These arguments, here and elsewhere, by others, do not appear entirely convincing, however.

146   *Aphorismos de las Cartas Españolas, y Latinas de Antonio Pérez* (Paris 1605).

147   See J. Barthelemy, "de Vitoria", in *Les Fondateurs du Droit International*, ed. A. Pillet (Paris 1904) pp. 8–9.

148   "De Potestate Civili", in J. Scott, *The Spanish Origin of International Law: Francisco de Vitoria and His Law of Nations* (London 1934), pp. lxxv–lxxvi.

149   Ibid., p. lxxvi.

150   "De Jure Belli", ibid., p. liv.

lawful which the defence of the common weal requires", since the aim of war was "the defence and preservation of the State".[151] This, of course, applied only to a just war, not an unjust war.

Vitoria thus accepted that the state was here to stay and war along with it. His purpose was to create a framework that took one step back from Reasons of State – which were overtly amoral – and once again circumscribe the state in a larger philosophy with ethical ends. In a *relección, De potestate civili*, he postulated that "the entire globe . . . in a certain sense forms a state [*república*]".[152] This underwrote his belief in the general applicability of a *jus gentium* or law of nations. Yet he was not interested in re-establishing the old empire. In his *relecciones* on the position of the indians of the New World, despite living within the jurisdiction of Charles V he openly rejected universal monarchy: "The emperor is not master of the entire globe".[153] He also asserted the right of the indians to be treated as equals. Dismissing the idea that they could be compared with animals, he insisted that even though they were not Christians, they had property rights; "before the arrival of the Spanish, the indians were true masters".[154] By insisting that the world formed a whole but not under one master, and that this whole was shared by equals who were not necessarily Christians, Vitoria effectively provided the basis for the more systematic regulation of relations between these parts according to certain moral precepts. Following Augustine, who had cryptically once referred to unnamed "laws and customs of war",[155] presumably those noted by Cicero,[156] he allowed for the right of states to fight a just war on their own behalf, since, in the absence of higher authority, "princes are judges in their own causes because they have no superior above them."[157] But he also sought to limit their conduct by law.

Jesuit Francisco Suárez (1548–1614), a fellow Thomist and formerly also of Salamanca, further amplified Vitoria's conception of a *societas naturalis* of nations into the requirement for a law of nations (*jus gentium*):

The *raison d'être* of this law consists in the fact that the human race, although it is actually divided into peoples and kings, none the less sustains at any rate a certain unity, not merely that of the species, but almost political and moral as indicated by

---

151   Ibid., p. lv.
152   Quoted in F. Castilla Urbano, *El pensiamento de Francisco de Vitoria: Filosofía política e indio americano* (Barcelona 1992) p. 170. For more on Vitoria: R. Naszalyi, *El estado según Francisco de Vitoria* (Madrid 1948). Also, in English, a significant study is J. Fernández Santamaría, *The state, war and peace. Spanish Political Thought in the Renaissance, 1516–1559* (Cambridge 1977). Also, Scott, *The Spanish Origin*, pp. lxxxii and xc.
153   The second part of his *Relecciones sobre los indios y el derecho de guerra* (Buenos Aires 1946) p. 68.
154   First part of *Relecciones*, p. 63.
155   It is not at all clear what these "laws and customs" were: *The City of God*, p. 52.
156   See Cicero, *De Officiis*, I, 11.36.
157   Quoted in Naszalyi, *El estado*, p. 149.

the natural precept of solidarity and assistance which is extended to all, including foreigners and of any nation whatever.

As a result, although a state – monarchy or republic – is by nature an autarchic community and is possessed of its own constitutive elements, any of these states is, however, also in some sense and in relation to the human race a member of this universal community. Because these states, considered in isolation, never enjoy an autonomy so absolute that they do not require any help, association and mutual exchange, at times for their well-being, progress and development, at others also from real moral necessity and lack of means, as experience itself demonstrates.

And this is the reason for the fact that nations have need of a system of laws: so that these kinds of exchange and mutual association can be directed and organised purposefully. And if we accept that it is in large part allowed for in natural reason, it is not, however, directly or completely so in relation to all matters and circumstances. Hence some special laws could be established by means of the customs of these same nations. Because in the same way that custom is the source of law in a state or country, so too would it be possible to establish international laws by means of custom in the community of the human race.[158]

Although Suárez, like Vitoria, was clearly committed to the moral unity of mankind, it would be a mistake to see him as some kind of early liberal. He was, moreover, not a pacifist. Nor did he conceive of any kind of world government. He accepted war as the only means by which a state could secure justice.[159] Moreover Suárez, Vitoria and compatriot theologians Domingo de Soto (1495–1560) and Luis de Molina (1535–1600)[160] all accepted the key realist assumption that one had to distinguish between what was morally permitted to the individual and what was acceptable for the state. In addition the state was the only judge of its right to wage war since no higher authority stood above it – as Suárez accepted: "no better method, humanly speaking, could be found in the natural order . . ."[161]

What we witness here is a critical adjustment to the state as the highest authority in matters secular; at the same time, however, the reassertion of the existence of a larger community within which the state acts and which in some profound ways contained its freedom of manoeuvre by the exertion of higher values. This represented a bold Thomist renaissance, albeit through the back door. The concept of utility, and therefore interests, buttressed the Thomist case for sociability. And one of those who made

158   F. Suárez, *De Legibus: De Iure Gentium*, ed. L. Pereña et al., Vol. 4 (Madrid 1973), pp. 135–6.

159   L. Rolland, "F. Suárez", in *Les Fondateurs*, pp. 107–10 and 122.

160   Molina is wrongly described as Portuguese by R. Tuck, *The Rights of War and Peace*, p. 9. Molina was born in Cuenca but moved to Coimbra after he began his novitiate: *Enciclopedia Universal Illustrada*, Vol. XXXV, pp. 1464–5.

161   For a summary account: B. Hamilton, *Political Thought in Sixteenth-Century Spain: A Study of the political ideas of Vitoria, De Soto, Suárez, and Molina* (Oxford 1963), chapter vii.

that crucial adjustment was the Spanish priest Juan de Mariana (1536–1624), like Rivadeneira a Jesuit. But he was a much more independent and formidable intellect, best known perhaps for his bold defence of the right to overthrow tyranny. This he asserted in his work *De Rege et Regis Institutione* of 1599. His first chapter begins with the sub-title straight from Aristotle: "Man is by nature a social animal".[162] But Mariana presents that sociability not as something instinctive and native to man, as Aristotle and his followers would have it, but as a direct product of dire need. Man is born into the world comparatively defenceless. "We begin this miserable life with a breath on our lips and tears in our eyes, a certain portent of the unhappiness that will oppress us and of the misfortunes that will threaten us . . ."[163] For everything, including safety, men had to rely upon one another. Mariana followed Augustine in his belief in the just war, coining the eloquent epigram: "one must seek not war in peace but peace in war".[164] That is to say, the purpose of war was to obtain the appropriate peace. But his outlook was consistently tough-minded. Should the king be "weak and hate weapons, he will begin to be held in contempt, firstly by the army, later the entire citizenry, and as you know after disdain comes harm, since the majesty of kings depends less on power and force than on opinion and the respect of men."[165] Also, he wrote, "At time of peace prepare for war", and this included the formation of alliances.[166] Moreover, although he insisted princes must not lie, they could dissimulate.[167] Mariana presented not merely a tough-minded philosophy but also an unhesitatingly utilitarian yardstick. He emphasised: "nothing motivates as much as real utility whether for kings or for individuals, and never believe secure alliances or friendships from which no advantage can be expected."[168]

The power of interests was equally self-evident to the Dutch jurist Hugo Grotius (1583–1645), whose Aristotelianism was only conditional. Evidently as a result of his own private ties to commerce, as well as his commitment to the emerging commercial colossus of the Netherlands, Grotius sought to ground universalist limitations on state sovereignty in self-interest, and this sense of self-interest arose from a strong sense of private property.[169] He rationalised this position as being perfectly in accord with Aristotelean principles, principles which produced "that brotherhood of man, that world state, commended to us so frequently and so enthusiastically by the ancient

---

162   J. de Mariana, *Del Rey y De la Institucion Real: Obras de Padre Juan de Mariana* (Madrid 1854) p. 467.
163   Ibid.
164   Ibid., p. 543.
165   Ibid., p. 545.
166   Ibid., p. 569.
167   Ibid., p. 568.
168   Ibid., p. 567.
169   The overturning of pre-existing suppositions about the purely Aristotelean trajectory of Grotius's thought is the achievement of Richard Tuck, whose most accessible account is to be found in *The Rights of War and Peace*, Chapter 3.

philosophers and particularly by the Stoics".[170] He explained what appeared a para-doxical harmony between individual self-interest and the interests of the larger com-munity of mankind in his first treatise, written to justify the seizure of booty by the Dutch from their hispanic rivals. The Prolegomena to the case, presented in *De Iure Praedae Commentarius*, first establishes the universal society asserted by Vitoria and Suárez – with no reference to them – only in order to open up a justification of state unilateralism:

> When it came to pass . . . that many persons (such is the evil growing out of the corrupt nature of some men!) either failed to meet their obligations or even assailed the fortunes and the very lives of others, for the most part without suffering pun-ishment – since the unforeseeing were attacked by those who were prepared, or single individuals by large groups – there arose the need for a new remedy, lest the laws of human society be cast aside as invalid. This need was especially urgent in view of the increasing number of human beings, swollen to such a multitude that men were scattered about with vast distances separating them and were being deprived of opportunities for mutual benefaction. Therefore, the lesser social units began to gather individuals together into one locality, not with the intention of abol-ishing the society which links all men as a whole, but rather in order to fortify that universal society by a more dependable means of protection, and at the same time, with the purpose of bringing together under a more convenient arrangement the numerous different products of many persons' labour which are required for the uses of human life.[171]

In this crucial form Grotius' sense of universal values was not only secular but also proto-capitalist. It is therefore no mistake to see a kind of loose natural affinity between Grotius and latter-day liberalism.

Like his Spanish precursors, Grotius was determined to reduce the ferocity and barbarity in the conduct of war in the sixteenth century. His thesis was published in 1625 as *De Iure Belli ac Pacis*. But it was only in the second edition of 1631 that he emphasised unequivocally his link with the Aristotelian tradition. The reasons why he did so at this late stage have been a matter of debate. Squarely within the legacy of Aris-totle, he argued that "among the Faculties peculiar to Man, is his Desire of Society, that is, of a Community, not of any kind, but such as is peaceable . . ."[172] Like Suárez, Grotius argued that natural law provided the basis for a law of nations, which law "few have

170   Quoted in ibid., p. 87.
171   H. Grotius, *De Iure Praedae Commentarius: Commentary on the Law of Prize and Booty*, Vol. 1 (Oxford 1950) p. 19.
172   H. Grotius, *Of the Rights of War and Peace, in Three Volumes; In which are explain'd The Laws and Claims of Nature & Nations, and the Principal Points that relate either to Publick Government, or the Conduct of Private Life* (London, 1715) p. 10.

touched upon, and none hitherto treated of universally and methodically; though it is in the Interest of Mankind that it should be done."[173] To Grotius "the Mother of Natural Law is human nature it self, which, though even the Necessity of our Circumstances should not require it, would of it self create in us a mutual desire of Society . . ."[174]

Given only conditional adherence to Aristotelean values, it is not surprising to find Grotius insistent on the unavoidability of interdependence and the need from entirely practical reasons for that interdependence to be properly regulated. Others could counter that whereas citizens were obviously interdependent, whole cities or states by virtue of self-sufficiency as communities had no need for such regulation according to principles of justice; that morality could not properly apply to the conduct of international relations. Grotius therefore asserted the impossibility of sustainable autarchy:

> But whereas many that require Justice in private Citizens, make no account of it in a whole Nation or its Ruler; the Cause of this Error is, first, that they regard nothing in Law but the Profit arising from it, a thing which is visible with Respect to private Citizens, who, taken singly, are unable to defend themselves. But great Cities, that seem to have within themselves all things necessary for their Defence and well-being, do not seem to them to stand in need of that Virtue which respects the Benefit of others, and is called Justice.
>
> But, not to repeat what has already been said, namely, that Law was not instituted for the sake of Profit only; there is no City so strong or well provided, but what may sometimes stand in need of Foreign Assistance, either in the Business of Commerce, or to repel the joint Forces of several Foreign Nations Confederate against it. For which Reason we see Alliances desired by the most powerful Nations and Princes, the whole Force of which is destroy'd by those that confine Law within the Limits of one City only. Most true is it, that by receding from Law all things are reduced into an uncertain fluctuating State.[175]

Law would thus provide for a more orderly and therefore predictable international environment in which states could reach agreements with one another. The argument was based upon will buttressed by necessity; morality could be counted on as a convenient fixative:

> If there is no Community which can be preserved without Law . . . certainly that likewise which joins Mankind in general, or several Nations together in one Society, must stand in need of Law; which was observed by him who said, That a base thing ought not to be done, even for the sake of ones Country.[176]

173   Ibid., p. 7.
174   Ibid., p. 17.
175   Ibid., pp. 19–20.
176   Ibid.

To Grotius, who came from a newly established, wealthy and settled state, there was such a thing as international society, following from the nature and needs of man; moreover justice could and should rule interest in international relations. But whereas Grotius, motivated not least by various imperatives, had reacted to the barbarity of war (at least among white races) from a discreet distance by seeking to regulate its conduct, others who followed him, most notably Thomas Hobbes (1588–1679), whose career spanned the Thirty Years' War that devastated northern Europe as well as the civil war that ruptured the old order in England, were struck less by the need for justice than – like Bodin during and after the wars of religion – by the need for order at home and the inevitability of conflict abroad, prompting a very different reading of the true nature of man. Power and Interest were thus more determinant than Morality and Justice. This was realism in its starkest form. It cannot be accidental that Machiavelli, Bodin and Hobbes reacted similarly in comparable conditions.

It had by now become commonplace for realist thinkers to nod in the direction of morality while pressing home their insistence on the primacy of Reasons of State. But by raising "reason" as the determining principle, realists considered that they were drawing a more practical and disciplined line between purely animal behaviour and policy dictated by overriding moral considerations, even though it was obvious to all that this line lay closer to the former than the latter. The end of *corpus christianum* and the emergence of the secular state were thus paralleled by the decline of orthodox spiritually inspired morality and its gradual substitution by the humanist alternative: the legitimating force of reason. The notorious Cardinal de Richelieu (1585–1642), who had shown few signs of religious scruple in ruling France with ruthless efficiency, wrote in his *Testament Politique* that "reason" should dominate over passion in the conduct of government, because allowing passion free rein would make man indistinguishable from the animal kingdom. On the other hand, Richelieu was insistent that "of all the principles capable of moving a State, fear . . . has the greatest impact" and that "If this principle is of great efficacy within States, it has no less outside, subjects and foreigners seeing with the same eyes a redoubtable power, and the former and the latter avoid offending a prince whom they recognise as capable of harming them, should he wish to do so."[177] He went further. "He who has might often has right in affairs of State and he who is weak will have difficulty escaping culpability in the judgement of most people."[178] This concern for the dominance of disinterested reason is equally apparent in the writing of Jean Silhon, one of Richelieu's secretaries.[179] It is not at all apparent who borrowed from whom.

Like Machiavelli and Bodin but distinct from Grotius, Hobbes was primarily concerned with establishing order at home, within the walls of the state; he believed man

---

177   Cardinal de Richelieu, *Testament Politique*, ed. L. André (Paris 1947) p. 326.
178   Ibid., p. 380.
179   *Le Ministre d'Estat, avec le véritable usage de la politique moderne par le Sieur de Silhon* (Amsterdam 1644) p. 18.

was moved not least by fear.[180] Thomas Hobbes was born on 5 April 1588, at the time of the Spanish Armada, in Westport near Malmesbury in Wiltshire.[181] Deserted by his father but supported by a rich uncle, he went up to Oxford at fourteen years of age. On graduation he became secretary and companion to the son of William Cavendish, then Baron of Hardwicke (later Earl of Devonshire). This gave Hobbes the opportunities of travel and access to the best of libraries. In 1614 he visited France and Italy with the young Cavendish at a time when the advances in science (Galileo and Kepler) were startling educated Europe. Thereafter the contacts with Paris, professional and personal, were as close or closer than anything found in England. A second trip as travelling tutor from 1629 to 1631, after the untimely death of his young companion, included a stay of some eighteen months in France. On this occasion Hobbes witnessed the spectacle of Richelieu's centralisation of monarchical power on behalf of Louis XIII and gained a fortuitous introduction to the deductive certainties of Euclidian geometry; the former doubtless firmed up his belief in royal power, the latter gave him a pronounced taste for axiomatic reasoning. He returned to England at the request of the Dowager Countess of Devonshire to take charge of the son of the previous Earl. But after only three years he could again be found on the continent, accompanying his charge through France and Italy.

The return to England coincided with the growing crisis between King and country over the rights of the monarchy. The Devonshires were firm royalists, as one might reasonably have expected. In 1628, at the time of the first major clash between Charles I and parliament, the Earl of Devonshire was Attorney General. It was in this role that he made the most forceful defence of "reason of state" that Whitehall had yet witnessed.[182] His case was that "if the subject prevail for liberty, he loses the benefits of that state government, without which a monarchy may soon become an anarchy . . ."[183] This he justified as a matter of "the necessities of state".[184] Following the close of parliament, it fell to Cavendish to prosecute in the Court of Star Chamber those members of the House of Commons who had spoken against the King. That Cavendish's case was later formulated into doctrine by the household's tutor should therefore occasion little surprise. And on Hobbes' return to England, he composed a small tract defending Charles I against a renewed and more forceful challenge by parliament – "the said power and rights were inseparably annexed to sovereignty . . ." Although the treatise

---

180   The best treatment of this aspect can be found in H. Trevor-Roper, "Thomas Hobbes", published in 1945 and reprinted in J. Gross, *The Oxford Book of Essays* (Oxford 1992) pp. 566–71.

181   A summary of Hobbes' life and works is to be found in G. Sortais, *La Philosophie Moderne depuis Bacon jusqu'à Leibniz* (Paris 1922), article III, chapter 1. This piece, though not entirely accurate to the last detail, has the inestimable advantage of placing Hobbes in his larger European context. For a different vantage-point and a more speculative account: R. Tuck, *Philosophy and Government 1572–1651* (Cambridge 1993) Chapter 7.

182   The precise date is not known: *The Parliamentary History of England*, Vol. II (London 1807) col. 306.

183   Ibid., col. 318.

184   Ibid., col. 317.

went unpublished, it gained wide circulation and notoriety. He later recalled that "had not his Majesty dissolved the Parliament, it had brought him [Hobbes] in to danger of his life". He added that when the new parliament met in November 1640, it consisted "for the greatest part of such men as the people had elected only for the averseness to the King's interest" and who "proceeded so fiercely in the very beginning, against those that had written or preached in the defence of any part of that power . . . that Mr. Hobbes, doubting how they would use him, went over to France, the first of all that fled . . ."[185]

Entitled *The Elements of Law Natural and Politic*, the treatise drew its image of conflict from the behaviour of man. Later, in the *Leviathan*, Hobbes also took his image from the realm of international relations: a point that appears to have hitherto escaped notice. As indicated above, the treatise was prompted by deep reflection on the ultimate causes of the political bickering, in France as well as England, that eventually broke the back of the social order. Here Hobbes avoided specifics. Elsewhere, and with the Thirty Years' War as much in mind as England's troubles, he argued that "the dispute for [precedence] between the spiritual and the civill power has of late, more than any other thing in the world, been the cause of civill wars in all places of Christendome."[186] Instead he built a picture of society based upon a bleak assessment of the nature of man, with a character not unlike that portrayed by Lucian the satirist (AD 117–180), of insatiable desires that lead to conflict:

> considering the great difference there is in men, from the diversity of their passions, how some are vainly glorious, and hope for precedency and superiority above their fellows, not only when they are equal in power, but also when they are inferior; we must needs acknowledge that it must necessarily follow, that those men who are moderate, and look for no more but equality of nature, shall be obnoxious to the force of others, that will attempt to subdue them. And from hence shall proceed a general diffidence in mankind, and mutual fear one of another.
>
> . . . Farther, since men by natural passion are divers ways offensive one to another, every man thinking well of himself, and hating to see the same in others, they must needs provoke one another by words, and other signs of contempt and hatred, which are incident to all comparison: till at last they must determine the pre-eminence by strength and force of body.
>
> . . . Moreover, considering that many men's appetites carry them to one and the same end; which end sometimes can neither be enjoyed in common, nor divided, it followeth that the stronger must enjoy it alone, and that it be decided by battle who is the stronger. And thus the greatest part of men, upon no assurance of odds,

---

185   T. Hobbes, "Considerations upon the reputation, loyalty, manners and religion of Thomas Hobbes written by himself by way of letter to a learned person", *Works*, Vol. IV, p. 414.

186   Letter to the Earl of Devonshire, 2 August 1641: N. Malcolm (ed.), *Correspondence of Thomas Hobbes*, Vol. I, p. 120.

do nevertheless, through vanity, or comparison, or appetite, provoke the rest, that otherwise be contented with equality.[187]

Hobbes summed up his position thus:

> Seeing then to the offensiveness of man's nature one to another, there is added a right of every man to every thing, whereby one man invadeth with right, and another with right resisteth; and men live thereby in perpetual diffidence, and study how to pre-occupate each other; the estate of men in this natural liberty is the estate of war. For WAR is nothing else but that time wherein the will and intention of contending by force is either by words or actions sufficiently declared; and the time which is not war is PEACE.[188]

In the *Leviathan*, which was completed in 1651, well after the English civil war came to an end and from his place of exile, Hobbes hardened his position considerably, despite attempting to return to his homeland, which he achieved during the following year. The need to leave France was prompted, he has told us, "because he would not trust his safety with the French clergy."[189] His aim, as told in his own hand, was to make "clear to all that it was impossible to establish peace in the Christian world unless that doctrine [the right of kings in both spiritual and temporal terms] was accepted, and unless a military force of considerable magnitude could compel cities and states to maintain that concord."[190] He insisted that there existed "a general inclination of all mankind, a perpetual and restless desire of power after power, that ceaseth only in death . . . he cannot assure the power and means to live well which he hath present, without the acquisition of more", and that "Competition of riches, honour, command, or other power, inclineth to contention, enmity, and war . . ."[191] In his most quoted passage, he stated:

> during the time men live without a common power to keep them all in awe, they are in that condition which is called war, and such a war as is of every man against every man. For WAR consisteth not in battle only, or the act of fighting, but in a tract of time wherein the will to contend by battle is sufficiently known.
>
> Whatsoever therefore is consequent to a time of war, where every man is enemy to every man, the same is consequent to the time wherein men live without other security than what their own strength and their own invention shall furnish them

187   T. Hobbes, *Human Nature and De Corpore Politico* (Oxford 1994) p. 78.
188   Ibid., p. 81.
189   "Considerations . . .": *Works*, p. 415.
190   Memoir in *Human Nature*, p. 248.
191   T. Hobbes, *Leviathan with selected variants from the Latin edition of 1668*, ed. E. Curley (Indianapolis/Cambridge 1994) p. 58.

withal. In such condition there is no place for industry, because the fruit thereof is uncertain, and consequently, no culture of the earth, no navigation, nor use of the commodities that may be imported by sea, no commodious building, no instruments of moving and removing such things as require much force, no knowledge of the face of the earth, no account of time, no arts, no letters, no society, and which is worst of all, continual fear and danger of violent death, and the life of man, solitary, poor, nasty, brutish, and short.[192]

Critics could and evidently did point out that "there was never such a time nor condition of war as this". Hobbes willingly acknowledged that "it was never generally so, over all the world."[193] But, he continued, and here he turned to international relations to support his case, "though there had never been any time wherein particular men were in a condition of war one against another, yet in all times kings and persons of sovereign authority, because of their independency, are in continual jealousies and in the state and posture of gladiators, having their weapons pointing and their eyes fixed on one another, that is, their forts, garrisons, and guns upon the frontiers of their kingdoms, and continual spies upon their neighbours, which is a posture of war."[194]

This picture of man in isolation at war with all, or potentially so, was not significantly altered by Hobbes' acknowledgement that men – with the help of reason – could agree with one another to achieve certain ends in the absence of a sovereign authority. Once again, the example is taken from the international arena. Such agreements were possible but not sustainable. Take alliances: "though they [states] obtain a victory by their unanimous endeavour against a foreign enemy, yet afterwards, when either they have no common enemy, or he that by one part is held for an enemy is by another part held for a friend, they must needs by the difference of their interests dissolve, and fall again into a war amongst themselves."[195] To Hobbes this state of nature by definition precluded justice and – although not addressed explicitly – most certainly any idea of a law of nations: "Where there is no common power, there is no law; where no law, no injustice . . ."[196] And it is striking that instead of "society", Hobbes prefers the colder, more mechanistic term "systems" to refer to "any numbers of men joined in one interest, or in one business".[197]

Until the appearance of Hobbes' *Leviathan* in seventeenth-century England no publicists were willing publicly to appear so firm in their disparagement of human nature and therefore so brutal in their advocacy of the supreme priority of the interests of the

192   Ibid., p. 76.
193   Ibid., p. 77.
194   Ibid., p. 78.
195   Ibid., pp. 107–8.
196   Ibid., p. 78.
197   Ibid., p. 146.

state. And can it be mere coincidence that the breakdown in the security of life in fifteenth- and sixteenth-century Italy and France, which drove home to Machiavelli and Bodin respectively the importance of seeing the world as it was and governing it as it was rather than as it might be, was also a feature of that period of seventeenth-century England in which Hobbes composed his frightening text? The collapse of civic order after the challenge thrown up to monarchical authority by a restless parliament had led to a bloody civil war and then a republican dictatorship. As noted, Hobbes tells us that upon the outbreak of civil war, "fearing for his safety, he returned to France."[198] For such a royalist, the world had, as Christopher Hill notes, been "turned upside down". Hobbes wanted order restored – "a military force of considerable magnitude" to "compel cities and states to maintain" concord[199] – just as had Machiavelli and Bodin, and in almost identical circumstances.

Hobbes does not appear always to have held to such an extreme view. Biographer John Aubrey (1626–97) tells us that Hobbes once worked as secretary to Francis Bacon (1561–1626), Lord Verulam, who clearly respected him, and from whom he must have imbibed some sense of the realities of political life, domestic and international.[200] After a none too principled path to power, Bacon had briefly served as Chancellor before dismissal for corruption. He never accepted in full the view expressed in Plato that war was natural between states, but he was not averse to preventive war if just fears existed. He was particularly dismissive of "some schoolmen (otherwise reverend men, yet fitter to guide penknives than swords)" who insisted that one had to wait to be attacked.[201] Where Plato was right, Bacon argued, was not only "that every state ought to stand upon his guard, and rather prevent than be prevented", but "it bears thus much of the truth, that if that general malignity and predisposition to war (which he [Plato] untruly figureth to be in all nations) be produced and extended to a just fear of being oppressed, then it is no more a true peace, but a name of a peace."[202] Indeed, the latter is the very point Hobbes sought to emphasise.

Evidence exists that Hobbes became more disillusioned under the impact of events rather than through reading. In 1628–9 he prefaced his translation of Thucydides' history of the Peloponnesian war with comments that indicate a disenchantment settling in and a strongly moralist tone. Arguing the value of studying the past, and Thucydides' contribution in particular, Hobbes noted that "in *History*, actions of *honour* and *dishonour* doe appear plainely and distinctly, which are which; but in the present Age they are so well disguised, that few there bee, and those very carefull, that bee not

---

198   Hobbes' own memoir, Hobbes, *Human Nature*, p. 247.
199   Ibid., p. 248.
200   J. Aubrey, "The Brief Life", in Hobbes, *Human Nature*, p. 234. Much is made of this – perhaps too much – by R. Tuck, *The Rights of War and Peace* (pp. 126–7), whose work is otherwise helpful on Hobbes.
201   "Considerations touching a War with Spain. To the Prince" (1624): *The Works of Francis Bacon*, ed. J. Spedding et al., Vol. XIV (London 1874) p. 476.
202   Ibid.

grossely mistaken in them."[203] But it does not appear that the close study of Thucydides itself brought about that transformation – there is certainly no indication in Hobbes' preface to the *Eight Bookes* that this was so. His memoir says only that "Thucydides was his source of particular delight" and that in the history "the weaknesses and eventual failures of the Athenian democrats, together with those of their city state, were made clear."[204] And in his life in verse, Hobbes amplified that point:

> There's none that pleas'd me like *Thucydides*.
> He says Democracy's a Foolish Thing,
> Than a Republick Wiser in one King.[205]

His work on Thucydides thus appears to have done nothing for his understanding of international relations; rather it reinforced him in his monarchism. We are therefore left to conclude that events themselves accomplished the decisive change in his reading of the world and human nature both.

The use of the term "systems" by Hobbes was no accident. He conceived of the world in materialist and individualist terms. This, in the conditions of seventeenth-century England, made him radical. But his solution was a form of absolute sovereignty over the people – the Leviathan – which ultimately made him a conservative. Because his analysis stripped man of the obligations and characteristics then assumed by the Christian religion, he had to found the bases for social order upon man's natural (worst) characteristics. His ruthless assumptions about the nature of man were taken one step further on the continent of Europe by the Dutch Jew Benedict Spinoza (1632–77). Compared with England, a visitor noted, in Holland "there seemed to be among them [the Dutch] too much coldness and indifference in matters of religion."[206] And Sir William Temple (1628–99), the English ambassador during the Restoration, commented that "No Man can here complain of Pressure in his Conscience", adding that "Religion may possibly do more Good in other places, but it does less Hurt here . . ."[207] Unencumbered by the need to tone down the severity of his assumptions by society's sensitivities,

---

203   *Eight Bookes Of the Peloponnesian Warre* (2nd edition, London 1634).

204   "The Prose Life", in Hobbes, *Human Nature*, p. 246.

205   "The Verse Life", ibid., p. 256. Also, see more than one reference in his account of the civil war – *Behemoth* – to the malign effect of the classics on young men: "there were an exceeding great number of men of the better sort, that had been so educated, as that in their youth having read the books written by famous men of the ancient Grecian and Roman commonwealths concerning their polity and great actions; in which books the popular government was extolled by that glorious name of liberty, and monarchy disgraced by the name of tyranny . . ." – *Behemoth: The English Works of Thomas Hobbes*, Vol. VI, ed. W. Molesworth (London 1840) p. 168; also, see p. 218.

206   This was 1664: *Bishop Burnet's History of His Own Time* (Oxford 1823 edition) Vol. 1, p. 357.

207   *Observations upon the United Provinces of the Netherlands* (1672): *The Works of Sir William Temple*, Vol. 1 (London 1740) p. 59.

Spinoza – though a believer – laid bare the selfsame elements but free of the outer religious framework into which Hobbes' work had of necessity to be cast.

Not unlike Hobbes, Spinoza "deduced all these doctrines from the essential nature of man . . . from the universal urge of all men to preserve themselves."[208] His most complete discussion of these matters appears in the *Tractatus Politicus*, which opens with a fierce attack on utopian thinkers who "conceive men, not as they are, but as they would like them to be." Theorists and philosophers were in Spinoza's view much less cogent commentators on political matters than practitioners:

> Statesmen . . . are believed to plan men's undoing rather than their welfare, and have a greater reputation for cunning than for wisdom. No doubt experience has taught them that there will be vices so long as there are men. They therefore try to forestall human wickedness; but since they do so by means of tricks which have been learnt from long practical experience, and which men usually employ out of fear rather than from rational motives, they are regarded as opponents of religion, especially by theologians, who believe that sovereigns ought to handle public affairs in accordance with the same moral rules as are binding on private individuals. Yet there is no doubt that statesmen have written much more successfully about politics than philosophers; for since experience has been their guide, they have taught nothing which could not be put into practice.[209]

The reason why the sovereign could not be judged in his actions by the same moral standard as the private individual was because the sovereign in embodying the state was acting in the same amoral environment as man in nature: "two states are in the same relation to one another as two men in the condition of nature".[210] Here the core idea of Machiavelli – "that shrewd observer", "that wise statesman"[211] – met and joined with the essence of Hobbes. In nature the only limitation on freedom of action was power and will. This applied as much to man as to nature: "man's natural right is not determined by sound reason, but by his desire and his power."[212] In nature "all are equally bent on supremacy . . ."[213] Spinoza continued:

> the right of the state or of the sovereign is nothing but the right of nature itself, and as such determined by power; not however by the power of a single individual, but

208 B. De Spinoza, *The Political Works: The Tractatus Theologico-Politicus in part and the Tractatus Politicus in full*, ed. A. Wernham (Oxford 1958) p. 299. For the most recent and up-to-date account of Spinoza's philosophy: S. Smith, *Spinoza, Liberalism and Jewish Identity* (New Haven 1996).

209 Ibid., p. 261.

210 Ibid., p. 295.

211 Ibid., p. 313.

212 From the *Tractatus Theologico-Politicus*: ibid., p. 127.

213 From the *Tractatus Politicus*: ibid., p. 265.

by that of a people which is guided as if by one mind. In other words, it is clear that what is true of each man in the state of nature is true likewise of the body and mind of the whole state – it has as much right as it has power and strength.[214]

Spinoza believed, as did Hobbes, that "two commonwealths are enemies by nature", and since this was the case then might was right:

> If . . . one commonwealth wishes to attack another and to use extreme measures in order to make it subject, it has the right to attempt this, since all it needs to wage war by right is the will to wage war.

Like Hobbes he also allowed for the formation of alliances, but like Hobbes he also asserted that a "treaty of alliance remains in force as long as the motive for making it, i.e. fear of loss or hope of gain, continues to hold good; but as soon as either commonwealth loses its fear or hope, it is left in possession of its own right . . . and the tie which bound the commonwealths together breaks of its own accord."[215] Statesmen had no right to protest at this, because contracts were reached under specific conditions "and once these change, the reason for the whole arrangement changes as well." This meant statesmen had no grounds for trusting temporary allies: "if a commonwealth complains that it has been duped, it certainly cannot blame the bad faith of its ally, but only its own folly in entrusting its safety to a foreign ruler who is possessed of his own right, and has no higher law than the safety of his own realm." This bleak prospect is only partly relieved by the reflection that the larger the alliance the greater the deterrent to others from making war: "The greater the number of commonwealths that make a treaty of peace together, the less is each to be feared by the rest, or, if you like, the less power each has of making war on the rest; each is more strictly bound to observe the conditions of peace . . . it is less in possession of its own right, and more obliged to comply with the common will of the allies."[216] Lest anyone interpret Spinoza as envisaging the possibility of future world government or a United Nations, it must be understood that this merely allowed for a hegemonic alliance dominating neighbouring states. There is nothing to indicate that the aims of such a system would necessarily be of benefit to those not party to it. The constraint on their ability to make war but not upon the alliance as a whole merely limits their freedom of action without necessarily also providing for their own protection.

The key element in Spinoza's thinking on these questions is his belief, like Hobbes', that "men . . . are led more by passion than by reason."[217] Whatever political decisions are based on calculation are therefore only contingent upon the consequences of

214   Ibid., p. 285.
215   Ibid., p. 295.
216   Ibid., p. 297.
217   Ibid., p. 315.

"passion". This view did not have to be accepted in its entirety to upset the assumption of complete rationality. Moreover awareness of the force of the emotions was not peculiar to England or Holland. Indeed, Jean Paul de Gondi, Cardinal de Retz (1614–79), of France, himself no mean political operator, shared this perspective, albeit from his own, more nuanced angle of vision. He wrote:

> The most correct maxim for accurately appraising the intentions of men is to examine their interests which are the most common motive for their actions. But a truly subtle politician does not wholly reject the conjectures which one can derive from man's passions, for passions enter sometimes rather openly into, and almost always manage to affect unconsciously, the motives that propel the most important affairs of state.[218]

De Retz saw the emotions as a source of interference in politics, but one that could be exploited. Spinoza, on the other hand, resolutely refused to condemn passion since he saw it as entirely natural. The transposition of this approach to the international system produces a vision of behaviour which is no less anarchic than that witnessed and described by Hobbes. Hobbes' insistence on absolutism rested on his particularly bleak reading of human nature: man as a naturally asocial and predatory being. One means of attacking the *Leviathan* was to undermine that premiss. Richard Cumberland (1631–1718), a Fellow of Magdalene College, Cambridge, and later Lord Bishop of Peterborough, argued that man was naturally good, social and relatively pacific. His objective was "to pluck up, by the very Roots, the fundamental Points of Doctrine contained in his Book *De Cive*, and in his *Leviathan*"; these were, in Cumberland's opinion, "wicked, destructive Opinions".[219] To this end he published *A Philosophical Enquiry into the Laws of Nature*. The thrust of the attack was moral, but that should not of itself disqualify it from serious appraisal in an appreciation of realism, since Cumberland did tease practical inconsistencies out of Hobbes' work. And it is his attack which underlines just how radical Hobbes' ideas appeared. Moreover his critique was consciously or unconsciously absorbed by Locke and Pufendorf, and, still later, influenced Bolingbroke and Rousseau, despite the fact that none of them lay far beyond the realist circle.

In contrast to Hobbes, Cumberland suggested: "it is not impossible but that the first Impressions (of true Piety and sound Morality) may be both born within us, and

---

218   Quoted from the Cardinal's memoirs: A. Hirschman, *The Passions and the Interests: Political Arguments for Capitalism before Its Triumph* (Princeton 1977) p. 45.

219   R. Cumberland, *A Philosophical Enquiry into the Laws of Nature Wherein The Essence, the Principal Heads, the Order, the Publication, and the Obligation of these LAWS are deduced from the NATURE of THINGS. Wherein also, The Principles of Mr. HOBBES' Philosophy, both in a State of Nature, and of Civil Society, are examined into, and confuted* (Dublin 1701) p. lxxv.

become deeper engraved upon our Hearts and Minds from outward Causes."[220] His view was "That certain Practical Propositions of unchangeable Truth (diligently exercised, employed in promoting, protecting and preserving the Happiness or Good of all rational Beings collectively taken) are necessarily impressed upon our Minds from the nature of Things . . ."[221] He did not merely maintain that man is naturally good but also argued that man's need for co-operation is a primary urge and requirement, and that in fact Hobbes' Leviathan would be impossible to construct without it:

> all could and must have foreseen (and which is a Point Mr. *Hobbes* himself might freely give up) that a mutual, social Assistance must prove useful, convenient and beneficial; and that the natural Propensity of the human Mind towards such a social State, was capable of full Discovery by proper Signs, Marks & Tokens: For even Mr. *Hobbes* himself lays the Foundation of all society, as established for this very End & Purpose, i.e. as a State of mutual Assistance.[222]

Even were one to allow that the urge to co-operation is not primary, Cumberland also deployed the argument that man learns from behaviour, that not only is the art of co-operation capable of being learnt but so is the principle of deterrence:

> *The Power to commit an Injury, is sufficiently ballanced by an equal Power in others of committing the like: And this, either upon a Principle of Defence or Retaliation.* For which Reason, such a Power cannot, to the Man who prudently consults his own Preservation & Safety, prove any sort of Argument, why he should choose rather to hurt than not to hurt others.[223]

Added to this were three further points: (1) there was always the possibility of assisting others and of being assisted by them; (2) any individual can be overwhelmed by a mass of individuals; and (3) mass assistance is always more valuable than individual assistance. Thus:

> It cannot, indeed, upon any Shew or Appearance of Reason, enter into the Mind of Man to imagine, that, in this general State of War devised by Mr. *Hobbes*, the human Forces & Powers always are so distinctly & clearly separated, that only one single Person only engages & combats with another single person only . . .[224]

Few would go so far as to accept Cumberland's conclusion that in place of Hobbes' image of reality as a "State of War" one should instead insert its antithesis a "State of

220   Ibid., p. xvi.
221   Ibid., pp. xvi–xvii.
222   Ibid., p. 56.
223   Ibid., p. 244.
224   Ibid., p. 247.

Peace".[225] But Cumberland, followed by Locke, did remind one and all of the ambivalent nature of man and that he was fundamentally social, as Aristotle, Aquinas, Vitoria and Grotius had all insisted. Although almost never directly addressed, it is apparent that Cumberland considered these precepts applied also to the conduct of states, as he referred at one point to the evidence of reciprocal benevolence in the creation of agreements between bordering kingdoms.

In 1690 John Locke (1632–1704) described the state of nature as "a *state of liberty*" but "*not a state of licence.*"[226] Born at Wrington, near Bristol, in Somerset on 29 August 1632, Locke, like Hobbes, found the stilted education at Oxford not to his taste. He was none the less "lookt on as the most ingenious young Man in the Colledge"[227] and remained attached to Christ Church indefinitely until put out by the King in 1684. A physician, he drew close to the first Earl of Shaftesbury after operating upon him, and began to share his friend's interest in philosophy. It was this that transformed his life and ultimately turned him into the father of liberalism. In what seems to indicate Cumberland's influence, he argued that the state of nature has "a law of nature to govern it, which obliges every one . . . Every one, as he is *bound to preserve himself*, and not to quit his station wilfully, so by the like reason, when his own preservation comes not in competition, ought he, as much as he can, *to preserve the rest of mankind*, and may not, unless it be to do justice on an offender, take away, or impair the life, or what tends to the preservation of the life, the liberty, health, limb, or goods of another."[228] Thus to him there was a "plain *difference between the state of nature and the state of war*" which "some men [i.e. Hobbes] have confounded". These were, he wrote after Cumberland, "as far distant, as a state of peace, good will, mutual assistance and preservation, and a state of enmity, malice, violence and mutual destruction, are one from another."[229] To Locke as to Cumberland, the state of nature did not mean man stood alone in perpetual war with other men. "Mutual assistance" was possible in the suppression of war. The state of nature was none the less "unsafe and uneasy".[230] Men were thus impelled to create a "civil society" by agreement that would arbitrate between men in the enforcement of agreed laws.

It was this "civil society" that was absent from the international arena; hence "the noise of War, which makes so great a part of the History of Mankind."[231] But this was not continual war of all against all: "all princes and rulers of *independent* governments

---

225   Ibid., p. 397.
226   J. Locke, *Second Treatise of Government*, ed. C. Macpherson (Indianapolis/Cambridge 1980) p. 9.
227   J. Le Clerc, *The Life and Character of Mr. John Locke, Author of the Essay concerning Humane Understanding* (English edition, London 1706) p. 2. Le Clerc (see p. 67) was "one of Mr. Locke's intimate Friends" – preface to *The Life*. They had met when Locke went to Holland in 1683, following Shaftesbury.
228   Locke, *Second Treatise*, p. 9.
229   Ibid., p. 15.
230   Ibid., p. 68.
231   Ibid., p. 91.

all through the world . . . are in a state of nature"[232] and by Locke's definition this meant that governments could make agreements from time to time: "it is not every compact that puts an end to the state of nature . . . other promises, and compacts, men may make with one another, and yet still be in the state of nature . . . for truth and keeping of faith belongs to men, as men, and not as members of society."[233] Locke thus reserved the term "society" for the circumstances in which a "civil society" is established and brings man out of the state of nature. He nevertheless saw man as fundamentally social. Others went on to argue that this meant society in some form pre-existed civil society instituted by man, thereby blurring the original distinction between the state of nature and life under civil society.

Cumberland reluctantly acknowledged the force of passion; but his work is steeped in a very firm belief in the dominance of reason over passion, whereas Hobbes clearly averred the contrary. The danger with Cumberland's view, ironically, is that if transposed to the conduct of state business it assumes predictable rationality and precludes the triggering of conflict as an unintended consequence of faulty human action or, indeed, the Hobbist or Spinozan exertion of plainly primitive and passionate responses that do not yield to the dictates of reason. For the true realists rationality was a goal, not a precondition to behaviour. In this respect Samuel Pufendorf (1632–94) was – no doubt from experience as a practitioner – closer to reality than Cumberland. From the perspective of a former diplomat and from his reading of history, Pufendorf emphasised the importance not just of man and the state but also of the men who run the state.

Pufendorf was born on 8 January 1632 at Dorfchemnitz-bei-Thalheim in Saxony. After university in Leipzig and Jena (where he was introduced to the work of Hobbes), through the good offices of his brother, a diplomat, he went to work for Count Pierre Julius Coyet, the Swedish envoy in Copenhagen, where he was imprisoned on suspicion of intrigue for eight months. He moved on to the Netherlands before being appointed a professor in 1661 at Heidelberg by the Elector: an extraordinary decision given Pufendorf's youth (then barely thirty years of age) and the fact that he, a Protestant, was given such a post in a traditionally Catholic institution. It was apparently the fact that the college needed renovation that explains the appointment. Instead of teaching Roman law as did his colleagues, Pufendorf instead began teaching natural law in line with the writings of Grotius. He so impressed the Elector that he was also asked to become his private counsellor. But his taste for free thinking and controversy before long made his continuation in post problematic. After attacking corruption in the Holy Roman Empire in *De Statu Imperii Germanici*, published in 1667, he moved to Lund at the invitation of Charles XI of Sweden in the year following publication. There Charles asked him to work on the history of the royal family. Although his history of Sweden occupied most of his energies for the next nine years, it was here in 1672 that Pufendorf

232   Ibid., p. 13.
233   Ibid.

completed and published his most noted work, which grew directly out of his teaching in Heidelberg: *De jure naturae et gentium*, otherwise known as *Of the Law of Nature and Nations*. The Swedish interlude was, however, punctuated in 1686 by an offer from the Grand Elector of Brandenburg to come and advise him. Two years later, Pufendorf took up this position, which he held to the end of his life. The Elector's son, Frederick, eventually became Frederick I of Prussia, father of Frederick the Great. It was on his way back from receiving the title of free Baron from Charles XI of Sweden that Pufendorf died in 1694.[234] Pufendorf's life thus emphasises the ardent commitment he excited in his powerful admirers but it no less illustrated the acerbity with which his detractors regarded him. The philosopher Gottfried Leibnitz (1646–1716) described him contemptuously as *Parum jurisconsultus et minime philosophus* (an average legal adviser and a minimal philosopher).[235]

Pufendorf straddles both Aristotelean and Hobbist positions. To him there was a "natural bond among men".[236] On the other hand, he also argued that "nearly constant suspicions and mutual distrust thrive among those living together in a natural state, especially if their situation provides them with opportunities for harming one another. And many of them evince a desire to undermine and impede the growth of others' strength, to augment their own strength out of the latter's ruin and, when an occasion is finally given, to beat them to the blow and crush them."[237] Similarly, in his most famous tract, *Of the Law of Nature and Nations*, he acknowledged, for instance, "that most Empires, which have made a Noise and Figure in the World, if not all in general, have owed their Growth & Progress to War." But he also parted company with Hobbes when he wrote that "this is no reason why we should pitch upon War for the Original & Fountain of Government."[238] He considered harmful "the insistence of those who pronounce the natural state to be one of war, indeed a war of all against all or of anyone against anyone living together in that state."[239] His objections were practical rather than moral: not least that "since no one can do without the assistance of others . . . concern for their own self-preservation makes everyone unable and unwilling to treat all other persons as enemies."[240] While agreeing on "an innate wickedness" in humans, Pufendorf none the less believed that "since the causes that can set men at odds with one another are either not universal or tend not to break out into hostile acts on a constant basis, they should certainly not be deemed a sufficient warrant for simplistically declaring

234 S. Goyard-Fabré, *Pufendorf et le droit naturel* (Paris 1994).
235 Letter to Kastner, 21 August 1709: ibid., p. 18. See also J. Schneewind, "Barbeyrac and Leibniz on Pufendorf", *Samuel Pufendorf und die europäische Frühaufklärung: Werk und Einfluss eines deutschen Bürgers der Gelehrtenrepublik nach 300 Jahren* (1694–1994) (Berlin 1996) pp. 181–189.
236 *Samuel Pufendorf's On the Natural State of Men: The 1678 Latin Edition and English Translation*, ed. M. Seidler (New York 1990) p. 130.
237 Ibid., p. 128.
238 S. Pufendorf, *Of the Law of Nature & Nations* (London 1712), Book VII, p. 488.
239 *Samuel Pufendorf's*, p. 128.
240 Ibid., p. 129.

the natural state a state of war."[241] Moreover he took issue with the idea that men should not "be reckon'd Friends [rather] than Enemies", where friendship meant "where there is neither Will nor Power to injure."[242] "Similarly," he wrote, "we should also not tolerate those who so indiscriminately toss out the claim that someone who is able to injure us also wishes to do so, and that if an opportunity for harming him presents itself we ought not fruitlessly to forego it, since he will surely not fail to destroy us if given a chance to do so."[243]

In some respects, Pufendorf thus appeared to be providing modifications to Hobbes' bleak philosophy, but he stood a considerable distance from the more reassuring picture envisaged by Cumberland or even Locke. In another crucial respect, however, he appears to differ fundamentally. Whereas Hobbes and Spinoza saw man dictated to by passions, Pufendorf like Cumberland saw man ruled by reason. For Pufendorf reason was the arbiter. Where Hobbes assumed that equality of strength would cause men to fight one another from instinct, Pufendorf argued that such equality would "restrain [rather] than . . . provoke a Desire for Hurting. For no Man in his Wits is very fond of coming to an Encounter with his Equal, unless he is either driven upon it by Necessity, or by the Fairness of the Opportunity put in Hopes of Success."[244] Elsewhere he added that "surely reason will not allow me an uncertain fear of the future as a pretext for threatening certain and present evil against another."[245] Complete acceptance of Hobbes' position thus conflicted with the belief in an overwhelming dictate of reason.

He thus comes out in favour of "some kind of middle course":

Because of the bond among men resulting from the similarity of their nature, their mutual need, and natural law's dictate urging peace, the natural state cannot properly be considered a state of war. But because of men's wickedness, their desires, and the passions which struggle vehemently against right reason, it is also characterized by a rather instable and undependable peace.[246]

The deductions that followed were thus equally balanced:

we ought to suppose anyone our friend and be ready to perform the duties of peace and humanity toward him if he is willing to receive them. Just the same, we should also be anxiously concerned about securing our own safety at all times, as if the friendship of others were little to be relied on, and never allow ourselves to slide into passive neglect by trusting in others' moral integrity or innocence.[247]

241   Ibid.
242   Pufendorf, *Of the Law*, p. 112.
243   *Samuel Pufendorf's*, pp. 129–30.
244   Ibid.
245   Ibid., p. 130.
246   Ibid.
247   Ibid.

This apparently academic discussion of man in a state of nature underwrote Pufendorf's advice for statesmen in that "an exact knowledge of the natural state can suggest to leaders of states many things concerning a state's external and internal affairs whose observance is extremely necessary."[248] What is so evident here is that, balancing between the two extremes in the discussion of man in nature, when turning to the practice of states in international relations, Pufendorf tilts the balance decisively in favour of prudence, not least because of "the prime obligation of leaders to seek the preservation of their own states".[249] First, "peace in the natural state is quite unreliable and little to be trusted".[250] Second, and following from that proposition, problems arose in translating "the bond of men's shared kinship" into alliances between states. No presumed general interest in the common welfare of all but particular interests would secure a state's safety against an external threat. An "inborn self-love makes everyone most concerned for their own welfare – which most people far prefer to the safety of others".[251] This meant that "we should seek to ally ourselves with those especially who are bound to us by common interest and to whom it matters that we be safe." Appeals to "the claims of humanity, to mercy, to honor, and to glory" would alone elicit "a sterile sympathy or procure assistance that is too ineffectual".[252] A coincidence of "advantage" was the *sine qua non* of assistance. "And nothing strikes a reader of history more often than the automatic expiration of treaties after times and interests have changed."[253] Third, it followed that "those who value their own preservation must try, as far as they can, to prevent anyone else from excessively and unnecessarily increasing his strength to the point of being able to overwhelm them, and to maintain an equilibrium among their neighbors' strength."[254] But Pufendorf, following Augustine, did not approve of pre-emptive war to limit the power of neighbouring states. Only if that state provokes others into war would united action be justified, and if that state itself were subject to attack it would be justified to abstain from assistance.[255] Fourth, "leaders should do their utmost to make their own states as strong as possible", not least because "states that are suddenly attacked by an enemy after having been enervated during a long, idle peace are in the greatest danger". This also required encouraging the private acquisition of wealth, to cover future military costs.[256]

Pufendorf did not, however, naively assume that, because man is ruled by reason rather than passion, Reasons of State could be pursued purely according to the dictates of reason with no interference from non-rational elements. In this he was not so far from Cardinal de Retz. In *An Introduction to the History of the Principal Kingdoms &*

248   Ibid., p. 131.
249   Ibid.
250   Ibid., p. 132.
251   Ibid., p. 133.
252   Ibid., p. 131.
253   Ibid.
254   Ibid., p. 132.
255   Ibid., p. 133.
256   Ibid., p. 134.

States of Europe Pufendorf discussed Reasons of State in the context of Interests. He divided these interests into the "Imaginary" and the "Real". By imaginary he meant hegemonic and imperialist goals like Universal Monarchy, which would obviously disturb other Powers and prompt their opposition: "the Fuel with which the whole World may be put into a Flame . . ." The "Real Interest" could be subdivided into "Perpetual" and "Temporary". The "Perpetual" were determined by "the Situation & Constitution of the Country, & the natural Inclinations of the People". The "Temporary" was determined by the "Condition, Strength & Weakness of the Neighbouring Nations; for as those vary, the Interest must also vary." And in a passage which would even now serve as a salutary reminder to current theorists of international relations, he wrote:

> Whence it often happens, that whereas we are, for our own security, sometimes oblig'd to assist a Neighbouring Nation, which is likely to be oppress'd by a more potent Enemy; we at another time are forc'd to oppose the Designs of those we before assisted; when we find they have recover'd themselves to that degree, as that they may prove Formidable & Troublesome to us. But seeing this Interest is so manifest to those who are vers'd in State-Affairs, that they can't be ignorant of it, one might ask, how it often times happens, that great Errors are committed in this kind against the Interest of the State. To this may be answer'd, That those who have the Supream Administration of Affairs, are oftentimes not sufficiently instructed concerning the Interest both of their own State, as also that of their Neighbours; & yet being fond of their own Sentiments, will not follow the Advice of Understanding & faithful Ministers. Sometimes they are misguided by their Passions, or by Time-serving Ministers & Favourites. But where the Administration of the Government is committed to the Care of Ministers of State, it may happen, that these are not capable of discerning it, or else, being divided into Factions, they are more concern'd to ruin their Rivals, than to follow the dictates of Reason.[257]

Frederick the Great attacked "Princes who look upon a Misunderstanding between their Ministers as necessary for their Interest: They fancy they are less in Danger of being imposed upon by Men whom a mutual Hatred obliges to watch over one's Actions."[258] This was certainly the manner in which many conducted the affairs of state and it inevitably distorted rational decision-making. But just as decisions could be corrupted by individual fallibility or selfish interest groups and therefore weaken the effectiveness of the state in foreign affairs, so too could outstanding judgement

---

257   Preface, Pufendorf, *An Introduction to the History of the Principal Kingdoms & States of Europe* (2nd edition, London, 1697).

258   *Anti-Machiavel: or, an Examination of Machiavel's Prince with Notes Historical and Political* (London 1741) pp. 249–50. The book was originally published under Voltaire's name. Frederick later betrayed in practice most of the principles he had grandly enunciated in this book before taking the throne.

compensate for lack of material power: "it frequently happens," Pufendorf wrote, "That a State, which in it self consider'd, is but weak, is made to become very considerable by the good Conduct & Valour of its Governors; whereas a powerful State, by the ill management of those that sit at the Helm, oftentimes suffers considerably."[259]

In the eighteenth century Reasons of State was still the ruling standard. But expectations of governments attaining that standard had fallen rather than risen, and a degree of cynicism had settled in among Enlightenment minds. As rulers dressed their policies in the language of ideals, the reaction was predictable. Reference to law or religion was seen as self-serving, as the liberal philosopher and theologian Jean Le Clerc (1657–1736) pointed out:

> Those States which are not powerful enough to invade the possessions of others talk only of Peace and maintain with reason that their neighbours should leave them to enjoy what they have. They do not fail to cite Reason or Religion in defence of snatching from someone else what he owns by Right. But States which are, or which believe themselves to be, superior in strength to those that are in the vicinity, hardly fail to invade, when the opportunity strikes, the lands of their Neighbours, and to retain them by the Law of the strongest; they try to mitigate it sometimes by bad excuses whose feebleness strikes the eye. We could well suppose that if the strongest became the weakest and if the latter became the most powerful, one would soon hear them exchanging language and roles. He who spoke only of Justice and Religion when he had need of Peace would begin searching for frivolous pretexts to crush his Neighbour in turn. The other, on the contrary, would gather up, so to say, the arms which his Enemy had thrown down and would with reason polemicise against the violence and ambition of the one he could not resist. It is in this manner that Human Kind makes use, by turns, of virtues and vices, to attain its ends.[260]

Such cynicism was answered with proposals for perpetual peace. But before we plunge into another pool of thought, let us consider the first of several thinkers who found something of a middle path between Hobbes and Cumberland by emphasising that whereas man was indeed social by nature – that is to say in need of the society of other men – the society of which he formed a part behaved just as badly as the individuals described by Hobbes but that this was due less to the badness of man than to the nature of society.

The first to open the path across this barrier appears to have been Sir William Temple, a great influence on Jonathan Swift, who served as his secretary in the last

---

259   Preface, Pufendorf, *An Introduction to the History of the Principal Kingdoms & States of Europe* (2nd edition, London, 1697).

260   *Negociations secretes touchant la paix de Munster et d'Osnabrug; ou Recueil General des Preliminaires, Instructions, Lettres, Memoires &c. concernant ces Negociations, depuis leur commencement en 1642. jusqu'a leur conclusion en 1648. Avec les Depeches de Mr. de Vautorte, & autres Pieces au sujet du meme Traite jusqu'en 1654. inclusivement*, ed. J. Le Clerc (Amsterdam, 1724) Vol. 1, p. i.

decade of Temple's life. Temple was ambassador to the Hague in 1668, negotiating the Triple Alliance, and when this broke down he negotiated an end to the Dutch war in 1674. Out of step with the corrupt regime under Charles II, he returned to politics in 1681. Temple is perhaps best known for his *Observations upon the United Provinces of the Netherlands*, published in 1672, a brilliant assessment of a neighbouring country's rise and fall as a great Power (see pp. 137–8). Of more direct relevance here is his *Essay Upon the Original and Nature of Government*, also of 1672. Whereas others, notably Hobbes and Cumberland, had seized upon one aspect of the nature of man as his essential characteristic and built a system of politics upon that ground, Temple, much the political practitioner, saw a duality, with behaviour ultimately determined by circumstance. He also had little time for contractualist explanations of the state. Such contracts were entered into for the avoidance either of violence (Hobbes) or of confusion (Cumberland). Temple shared neither assumption: "if Mankind must be ranged to one of these Sorts," he argued, "I know not well to which it will be: And considering the great Differences of Customs and Dispositions in several Men, and even in the same Men at several Times, I very much doubt they must be divided into several Forms. Nor do I know, if Men are like Sheep, why they need any Government: Or, if they are like Wolves, how they can suffer it."[261] It was Macaulay who later suggested that Temple's instinct to split the difference between extremes was, like that of Lord Halifax ("the trimmer"), typical of his time, when memories of the violence of revolution were too fresh to bear repetition. It was therefore only natural that as those memories faded, so too did the inclination to seek compromise.

Hitherto discussion of the causes of conflict in international relations had centred on the nature of man. Those who focused upon man as a social animal (following Aristotle and Aquinas) necessarily assumed he was less given to conflict than those who assumed man was inherently anti-social. The only figure of note who had (privately) suggested that what Hobbes was attributing to the nature of man might indeed, after all, be due to the nature of society was Leibnitz, the German philosopher and mathematician, polymath besides. His interest in matters political is evident from his correspondence with Thomas Burnet, the unorthodox clergyman. In one letter, undated, Leibnitz commented that with regard to the origins of government, he sided more with Aristotle than with Hobbes. On his view what had happened was that "corruption and violence ensured that man was separated from the state of nature at its perfection and obliged to come to terms with nature in disarray."[262] The implication being that society corrupted man. Leibnitz thereby privately anticipated a change in outlook that came about with Rousseau; though the emphasis on society emerges in the work of the Dutch physician Bernard Mandeville (1670–1733), author of *The Grumbling Hive*. Mandeville went so far as to publish (under another name) what at first sight appeared to be an attack on his own work: an *Enquiry into the Original of Moral Virtue*, of 1728. The

261   *Works*, Vol. 1, p. 99.
262   Letters to Thomas Burnet, VIII: Leibnitz, *Opera Omnia*, Vol. 6 (Geneva 1768) p. 268.

author was supposed to be a clergyman deeply disturbed at the immoral presentation of society offered by Mandeville, who had argued that private vice – in the form of expenditure on luxuries – created public benefit, because it produced industry and employment:

> Thus every Part was full of Vice,
> Yet the whole Mass a Paradise;
> Flatter'd in Peace, and fear'd in Wars,
> They were th'Esteem of Foreigners,
> And lavish of their Wealth and Lives,
> The Balance of all other Hives.

Mandeville believed that man was "a compound of various Passions, that all of them, as they are provoked and come uppermost, govern him by turns, whether he will or no."[263] The satirical critique he composed gradually drew the trusting and soon to be betrayed reader through a devious maze of reasoning that resulted in the legitimation of the notion of self-love, interest and pleasure as the true motives of virtuous activity (instead of morality). *Inter alia* the *Enquiry* argued that "The great Aim and Design of *Politicians* and *Princes* generally has been to heap up Riches, to aggrandize their Fortunes, to extend their Conquests, and enlarge their Dominions, to prey upon the Weakness or Necessities of their Neighbours; and, in short, to stick at Nothing that could any wise tend to gratify their Ambitions, Ends and Purposes."[264] How this came about was in part described in terms of man's very sociability: "a Man's wanting or desiring those Things that are now call'd the Necessities and Comforts of Life, and in which People generally make their Interest and Happiness to consist, does plainly arise from his being mixed with others, among whom there has happened an Emulation."[265]

Mandeville managed to unite sociability and self-interest within society. The next step, taken by others that followed, was – as with Leibnitz – to attribute the causes of conflict in international relations not to man but to society itself. This followed logically upon a greater attention to man as a group rather than man as individual and saw the reappearance of analogies between men and ants or men and bees, familiar to the classical world. It is perhaps not accidental that this also followed the assertion of the collective – the class of property-owners in England – against the individual sovereign in the two revolutions (1640–6 and 1688). For the sovereign was no longer an individual called upon to obey Reasons of State and serve the community; the sovereign was

---

263   B. Mandeville, *The Fable of the Bees: or, Private Vices, Public Benefits* (1924 edition, Oxford) p. 39.

264   Alexander Innes, *An Enquiry into the Original of Moral Virtue; wherein The False Notions of Machiavel, Hobbes, Spinoza, and Mr. Bayle, as they are Collected and Digested by the Author of The Fable of the Bees, are Examin'd and Confuted; and the Eternal and Unalterable Nature and Obligation of MORAL VIRTUE is Stated and Vindicated* (London 1728) p. xvii.

265   Ibid., p. 6.

now the community itself – or at least the property-owners who identified themselves collectively as the community. The behaviour of the collective was no longer to be explained merely as the total sum of individual desires and wants, but the realisation made was that the very creation and existence of the collective dictated certain modes of behaviour and indeed moulded man. Reasons of State, in other words, had an existence apart from the will of man; it was integral to society as a society. It was a given from some natural law. The first to draw attention to this phenomenon with respect to international relations was Lord Bolingbroke, who, unlike Temple, was most certainly never a man who instinctively chose the golden mean.

In explaining the origin of government, Temple followed classical thought, seeing the answer in the organic extension of paternal authority from the family outwards into communities and ultimately to the state. Henry St. John, Lord Viscount Bolingbroke (1678–1751), was a great admirer of Temple and a friend of Swift. He took Temple's explanation as his own and developed it further, far beyond Temple's reasonable expectation. As Britain's Foreign Secretary – "a most artful negotiator"[266], in the words of Swift – Bolingbroke brilliantly but ruthlessly ended the War of the Spanish Succession with the Treaty of Utrecht in 1713, against formidable domestic resistance. In a series of letters to the poet and satirist Alexander Pope (1688–1744), he presented a philosophy that had much greater impact in its time than it has had since, not least because those who succeeded him were in all respects more accomplished philosophers. Arguably, though, they built upon the bases of Bolingbroke's intuitions in matters of state, which bear the distinctive hall-marks of rich personal experience. It is, to say the least, ironical that radical utopians should find a ready foundation for their beliefs in the writings of a British statesman, a monarchist, and a convinced Tory. But then this is what enables us to classify them, in matters of international relations, as realist.

Where Bolingbroke began, in setting up the imagined origins of the state, was, like Temple and classical thought, not with the individual but with the primary social unit: the family which, once expanded through the generations, removed itself from single patriarchal control, and in interaction with other families required a greater authority for the maintenance of order. Society thus always existed in some form; men were never "unassociated independent creatures" or "strolling savages".[267] The difference between these basic communities and the state was that the former were "natural societies"; the latter "political societies". Bolingbroke's view of man was not much different from that presented by Hobbes. Men were naturally sociable but only to the point that society answered their basic needs; that is to say, there was no question of their being naturally good and therefore sociable, but in need and therefore sociable – to a point. Moreover, communities – which fulfilled those basic needs – were not naturally sociable

---

266   "Characters", *Annual Register For the Year 1765*, pp. 12–13.
267   "Fragments or Minutes of Essays", *The Works of the late Right Honorable Henry St. John, Lord Viscount Bolingbroke*, Vol. V (London 1754) p. 131.

in their relations with others, but warlike. The state of war was not, he emphasised, the *cause* of the formation of society but its *effect*. It is here, at his most original, that Bolingbroke anticipates Jean-Jacques Rousseau (1712–78) and indeed, later, Immanuel Kant (1724–1804):

> Individuality belongs to communities, not persons. Families might be conceived as individuals, tho not men, in the state of nature; and civil societies much more so in the political state. The reason is plain. We have a natural sociability, that is, we are determined by self-love to seek our pleasure and our utility in society, as it has been said; but when these ends are once sufficiently answered, natural sociability declines, and natural insociability commences. The influence of self-love reaches no further. Societies become in all respects individuals, that is, they have no regard for others except relatively to themselves; and self-love, that promoted union among men, promotes discord among them. Like the philosopher of MALMES-BURY's [Hobbes'] wild men, they act as if they had a right to all they can acquire by fraud or force: and a state of war, so far from being the cause, has been the effect of forming distinct societies, tho by the general plan of nature the propagation of mankind makes it necessary to form them. Such is our inconsistency, such are the contradictions that unite in the human character.[268]

That character, Bolingbroke claimed, was formed by an interaction between passion and reason, both equally essential to survival and success. He thus found something of a half-way house between Hobbes and Cumberland, not dissimilar to Pufendorf in some respects. Unlike ants and bees, men could not be perfectly obedient citizens, because "the rational creatures neglect their reason, or degrade her, in the intellectual oeconomy, and make her the vile instrument of their appetites and passions. This is so much the case," Bolingbroke continued, "that men would have been what HOBBES assumes that they were, if the divine wisdom had not constituted them so that they are, as soon as they come into the world, members of societies which are formed by instinct and improved by reason. What reason cannot do by herself, she does in some degree by the adventitious helps which experience enables her to acquire, by orders and rules of government which every man concurs to maintain; because every man is willing to controul the passions and restrain the excesses of others, whatever indulgence he has for his own. I said, in some degree; for, even with these adventitious helps, reason preserves human societies unequally, and by a perpetual conflict: whereas instinct preserves those of bees in one uniform tenor, and without any conflict at all."[269]

Once these political societies were in being, the behaviour of some set the pattern for the behaviour of all:

268   Ibid., p. 115.
269   Ibid., p. 116.

However unlike nations may be to nations in their dispositions and manners, all of them, even the weakest, seek their own advantage real or imaginary, at the expence of others. Thus have the civil societies of men acted towards one another from their primitive institution; for if some set the example, the others soon followed it, and whilst every particular state has gone thro various forms of government and revolutions of fortune, the universal state of mankind has been little less than a state of perpetual anarchy. Families kept men out of that state of individuality which HOBBES, and even LOCKE, supposes. But political societies have been always individuals.[270]

Where Bolingbroke's conservative instincts had the final word – and where he was to differ in spirit from what Rousseau and Kant were to argue – was in his belief that this situation could not be bettered; man had no alternative, a position summed up in one sentence: "We look up much higher than we are able to rise."[271] What could be expected? Not much: Bolingbroke's dismal view of the behaviour of states was encased in a larger view of "the system wherein this planet rolls".[272] "The several parts of the material world, like the machines of a theatre, were contrived not for the actors, but for the action: and the whole order and system of the drama would be disordered and spoiled, if any alteration was made in either."[273] "The course of things rolls on through a vast variety of contingent events, for such they are to our apprehensions, according to the first impression of motion given to it, and under the direction of an universal providence."[274] The conduct of international relations fitted within this larger frame:

Tho the establishment of civil societies originally, and the maintenance of them since, have caused, in the order of providence, perpetual wars, and much of that misery which injustice and violence bring on the world . . . yet the necessity of establishing and maintaining them arises from the constitution of human nature, and is therefore indispensable. The great commonwealth of mankind, cannot be reduced under one government, nor subsist without any.[275]

Though a firm believer in God and Providence, Bolingbroke nevertheless prided himself on brutally cutting through appearance to reality, which marked him out as a realist par excellence in the more general meaning of the term. His characterisation of

---

270   Ibid., p. 137.
271   Ibid., p. 150.
272   Ibid., p. 326.
273   Ibid., p. 377.
274   Ibid., p. 379.
275   Ibid., p. 149.

moral and legal hypocrisy in respect of the treatment of colonised populations has, as a result, almost a contemporary and radical ring to it. "When the Spaniards sailed to the conquest of America, silver and gold were their objects, but the propagation of the gospel was their pretence", he wrote.[276] He went further, in a vein worthy of E. H. Carr in a subsequent but not more knowing century:

> Our legal violations of natural law have a solemn varnish of policy, and even of reli-
> gion, which the casuists of the law and those of the gospel throw over them, and
> which always disguise, altho they cannot always hide them. Illiterate savage nations
> have no such varnish to employ, and their laws and customs appear to every eye but
> their own, as unnatural and abominable as they really are. To this it may be added,
> that they who can write have a great advantage over those who cannot, in all such
> cases. They can extenuate and exaggerate matters of fact, and they seldom fail to do
> it, with no more regard to truth than is necessary to make the falsehood pass. If we
> had the history of Canaan writ by a canaanite, that of Carthage by a carthaginian,
> or that of Mexico and Peru by a mexican or peruvian, figure to yourself how the
> hospitality, the fidelity, the innocence, and simplicity of manners, of all these
> people, would be exemplified in various instances, and what further proofs would
> be brought of the ferocity, the treachery, the injustice and cruelty of the Israelites,
> the Romans, and the Spaniards, of the first and the last especially.[277]

Bolingbroke's vision in a substantial sense anticipated the kernel of Rousseau. Although not published posthumously until 1756, after the appearance of Rousseau's two discourses in 1750 and 1752, it predated Rousseau's fragmentary comments on international relations. The ideas may well have been in circulation beforehand, courtesy of their recipient, Pope, who raised Bolingbroke's wrath by arranging to publish other such writing without even requesting permission.[278] Their influence was extensive because of Bolingbroke's immense reputation, not yet eclipsed by nineteenth-century moralistic disdain for such a libertine, Jacobite and unscrupulous tactician.

In 1756 a determined assault was launched on Bolingbroke's ideas by the ambitious, young, and instinctively unorthodox Irish Whig, Edmund Burke (1729–97), an assault that made his reputation. He published *A Vindication of Natural Society: or, a view of The Miseries and Evils Arising to Mankind from every species of Artificial Society* in the form of an imitation of Bolingbroke's style and a logical extension of his ideas. "The Design was, to shew that, without the Exertion of any considerable Forces, the same

276   Ibid., p. 266.
277   Ibid., p. 152.
278   Pope none the less held Bolingbroke "the greatest Man in the World, either in his own Time, or with
      Posterity" – Pope to Jonathan Swift, 25 March 1736: Swift, *Works*, Vol. VII (Dublin 1770) Letter
      LXXVI, p. 322.

Engines which were employed for the Destruction of Religion, might be employed with equal Success for the Subversion of Government . . ."[279] As a satire, it made Burke's name, though, as one anonymous reviewer pointed out, "we apprehend, in regard to the little piece before us, that the ingenious writer had more inclination to shew his parts and capacity as an author, than his judgement and principles as a philosopher. We cannot without justice, however, deny him the merit of a good *actor*, who has played his part well, and is not unlike the character he represents . . ."[280]

The reviewer evidently meant that the author was no better at philosophy than Bolingbroke. But there may be more truth to the statement than intended. Are we to assume there was no trace of Burke's ideas behind the satire? A staunch defender of Burke has insisted that when his hero writes of wrongs to the poor in the *Vindication*, he is not mocking but is "in dead earnest".[281] What else might stand under that category? The *Vindication* also extended Bolingbroke's view of international relations, with which it deals at some length, and in a manner entirely consonant with Burke's view of history as presented in his *Annual Register of World Events*,[282] where Burke appears to equate historical events with the occurrence of war.

Whatever the truth of the matter, the *Vindication* is worth considering in its own right. In a state of nature, Burke argued, men faced "Want of union, want of mutual assistance, want of a common arbitrator to resort to in their differences." He continued: "Man found a considerable advantage by this union of many persons to form one family; he therefore judged that he would find his account proportionably in an union of many families into one body politick. And as nature has formed no bond of union to hold them together, he supplied this defect by laws." This was "*political society*. And hence the sources of what are usually called states, civil societies, or governments; into some form of which, more extended or restrained, all mankind have gradually fallen."[283]

But whereas Rousseau was to attribute all evil to the effect of society upon man, the *Vindication* attributed the greater part only to society; a sure sign of a much more moderate spirit of radicalism: "political society is justly chargeable with much the greater

---

279   Preface from the second edition, *A Vindication of Natural Society: or, a view of The Miseries and Evils Arising to Mankind from every species of Artificial Society* (London 1757) p. vii.

280   *Critical Review*, June 1756, Article III, p. 426.

281   J. Cressman, *Burke's Satire on Bolingbroke in a Vindication of Natural Society* (Michigan PhD, 1957) p. 281. This is the most detailed investigation of the subject. Its weakness is that the author imputes motives to Burke for which we have little evidence. The argument that, despite his protestations, Burke in fact drew extensively on Bolingbroke for style and ideas is made forcefully in W. Sichel, *Bolingbroke and His Times*, Vol. 2 (London 1902) Chapter XI.

282   For more on Burke's authorship: T. Macknight, *History of The Life and Times of Edmund Burke*, Vol. 1 (London 1858) pp. 90–95 and 115.

283   "A Vindication of Natural Society: or, a view of The Miseries and Evils Arising to Mankind from every species of Artificial Society" (1756): *The Works of The Right Honourable Edmund Burke*, Vol. 1 (1803) p. 11.

part of this destruction of the species. To give the fairest play to every side of the question," he acknowledged, "I will own that there is a haughtiness, and fierceness in human nature, which will cause innumerable broils, place men in what situation you please; but owning this, I still insist in charging it to political regulations, that these broils are so frequent, so cruel, and attended with consequences so deplorable. In a state of nature, it had been impossible to find a number of men, sufficient for such slaughters, agreed in the same bloody purpose; or allowing that they might have come to such an agreement, (an impossible supposition) yet the means that simple nature has supplied them with, are by no means adequate to such an end . . . Society, and politicks, which have given us these destructive views, have given us also the means of satisfying them. From the earliest dawnings of policy to this day, the invention of men has been sharpening and improving the mystery of murder, from the first rude essays of clubs and stones, to the present perfection of gunnery, cannoneering, bombarding, mining, and all these species of artificial, learned, and refined cruelty, in which we are now so expert, and which make a principal part of what politicians have taught us to believe is our principal glory."[284]

Writing at the outbreak of the Seven Years' War, fought not least between Britain and France for possession of North America, Burke anticipated Rousseau's assessment of international relations. "It is no less worth observing," he wrote, following Bolingbroke, "that this artificial division of mankind, into separate societies, is a perpetual source in itself of hatred and dissension among them."[285]

The first part of the external view of all states, their relation as friends, makes it so trifling a figure in history, that I am very sorry to say, it affords me but little matter on which to expatiate. The good offices done by one nation to its neighbour; the support given in publick distress; the relief afforded in general calamity; the protection granted in emergent danger; the mutual return of kindness and civility, would afford a very ample and very pleasing subject for history. But, alas! all the history of all times, concerning all nations, does not afford matter enough to fill ten pages, though it should be spun out by the wire-drawing amplification of a Guicciardini himself. The glaring side is that of enmity. War is the matter that fills all history, and consequently the only or almost the only view in which we can see the external of political society, is in a hostile shape; and the only actions, to which we have always seen, and still see all of them intent, are such as tend to the destruction of one another. War, as Machiavel, ought to be the only study of a prince; and by a prince, he means every sort of state, however constituted. He ought, says this great political Doctor, to consider peace only as a breathing-time, which gives him leisure to continue, and furnishing ability to execute military plans. A meditation on the conduct of political societies made old Hobbes imagine, that war was the state of

284   Ibid., pp. 30–1.
285   Ibid., p. 32.

nature; and truly, if a man judged of the individuals of our race by their conduct when united and packed into nations and kingdoms, he might imagine that every sort of virtue was unnatural and foreign to the mind of man.

The first accounts we have of mankind are but so many accounts of their butcheries. All empires have been cemented in blood; and in those early periods when the race of mankind began first to form themselves into parties and combinations, the first effect of the combination, and indeed the end for which it seems purposely formed, and best calculated, is their mutual destruction.[286]

And, as to Reasons of State: "All writers on the science of policy are agreed," Burke wrote, "and they agree with experience, that all governments must frequently infringe the rules of justice to support themselves; that truth must give way to dissimulation; honesty to convenience; and humanity itself to the reigning interest. The whole of this mystery of iniquity is called the reason of state."[287] "There was a time," he continued, "when I looked with a reverential awe on these mysteries of policy; but age, experience, and philosophy have rent the veil; and I view this *sanctum sanctorum*, at least, without any enthusiastic admiration. I acknowledge indeed, the necessity of such a proceeding in such institutions; but I must have a very mean opinion of institutions where such proceedings are necessary."[288]

The role of society in making for conflict in international relations was bound up with the presumed importance of collective emotions as much as of the collective interest, and not merely of the ruling class. A key thinker in this sphere was Adam Ferguson (1723–1816), who, at the time of writing his *Essay on the History of Civil Society*, was Professor of Moral Philosophy at Edinburgh. Where Ferguson was at his most interesting was in accepting Aristotle's dictum that man was fundamentally social but, like Juan de Mariana before him, refusing to draw from that premiss the customary conclusions as to what that meant for the conduct of politics. In a delightful and memorable phrase, Ferguson wrote: "To be in society is the physical state of the species, not the moral distinction of any particular man."[289] As he emphasised, "That man is found in society cannot be questioned; that he is by any amicable disposition attached to his kind, has become matter of doubt and of controversy."[290] Society was "the state of those who quarrel, as well as of those who agree. Estrangement is not always a vice, nor association a virtue. Persons may assemble for contest, as well as for concord."[291] Man was "ever disposed to select his company, and to shun,

286   Ibid., pp. 15–16.
287   Ibid., p. 34.
288   Ibid., p. 35.
289   A. Ferguson, *Principles of Moral and Political Sciences*, Vol. 1 (Edinburgh 1792) p. 24.
290   Ibid., p. 22.
291   Ibid., p. 24.

as well as to embrace, an acquaintance."[292] Thus sociability was not only conditional, it could also buttress anti-social behaviour because it could be selective in scope. As he summed it up, "The human species, though disposed to associate, is disposed to separation also."[293]

Ferguson took his cue from Socrates in viewing man as equally given to conflict as to co-operation.[294] Yet Ferguson consistently angled his invective against the Aristotelean tradition. Echoing Hobbes, he wrote:

> Why, in the most peaceful societies, is the magistrate armed; and the very badge of authority a sword of state, or an instrument of violence and an object of terror? Whence is it that nations need so much arrangement, to preserve the peace at home, or to repel invasions from abroad? . . . Whence, on every frontier, are strong holds erected, and military stations selected with so much care? Are these preparations made for the reception of friends from abroad? Or do they not rather betray a conviction, that, beyond the circle, in which men have procured some artificial means of tranquillity, they have nothing to expect but hostility and war.
>
> In answer to these queries, we must admit, that the peace of society is, in many instances, evidently forced and made to continue by a variety of artificial means.[295]

Similarly, he argued that: "It is . . . wise to consider the longest Peace but as a long Truce and a time of preparation for War. Such are human Affairs And no single Party can mend them, without, what never can be obtained, A consent of the whole."[296] That is to say, the behaviour of all states dictated behaviour: the states system itself forestalled a more enlightened conduct of relations. Ferguson was not one to exaggerate the hatred of one nation for another, and he was somewhat complacent about the common level of civilisation and shared public justice. His was, after all, an age of limited wars fought by limited means for limited purposes – "War is made with little national animosity, and battles are fought without any personal exasperation of those who are engaged".[297] But Ferguson was not thereby inclined to overestimate the degree to which reason predominated. His was not quite a Hobbist struggle but was none the less a competition riddled with suspicion:

> Nations are . . . almost in every instance, mutual objects of jealousy and distrust; and must think themselves safe so far only, as they are severally in condition to

292   Ibid., p. 32.
293   Ferguson, *Principles*, Vol. 2, p. 293.
294   A. Ferguson, *An Essay on the History of Civil Society* (Edinburgh 1767) p. 29.
295   Ferguson, *Principles*, Vol. 1, p. 23.
296   Letter to Henry Dundas, 18 January 1802: *The Correspondence of Adam Ferguson*, Vol. 2, ed. V. Merolle (London 1995), No 365, p. 472.
297   Ferguson, *Principles*, Vol. 2, p. 295.

maintain their respective rights. They must keep a watchful eye on the powers by which they may be annoyed from abroad, no less than attend to the means of defence with which they are furnished at home. Their independence must cease to exist, the moment it is held at the discretion of any foreign power: what a neighbour, therefore, is about to gain, may be to them no less a subject of alarm, than what they themselves are about to lose; and a war may be justly undertaken, by one state, to check the dangerous progress of another; as well as to make any other provision necessary to its own preservation.[298]

Although the rules were in a general sense dictated by the states system, non-rational elements made impossible pure calculation and therefore predictability. Thus the practice of Reasons of State hinged on very approximate estimates of intentions, let alone capabilities: "in questions of mere caution or distrust," he wrote, "it is difficult to determine how far one nation may justly oppose the progress of another, and in doing so be supposed to act on principles of mere defence . . ."[299] This had to be factored into decision-making. Ferguson was by no means someone who always sought pre-emptive attack. He cautiously concluded that "In the quarrels of nations . . . much allowance is to be made for the mistake or misapprehension of parties . . ."[300]

However, Ferguson also saw virtue in conflict and emotions at its origins. "Mankind", he wrote, "not only find in their condition the sources of variance and dissension; they appear to have in their minds the seeds of animosity, and to embrace the occasions of mutual opposition, with alacrity and pleasure."[301] No one hitherto had ever mentioned the role of the mass of society in the genesis of conflict in international relations. But, just as did Bolingbroke, Ferguson saw the community as given to conflict, following from one side of man's nature. Within society and between societies, Ferguson believed, the sources of conflict arose naturally from the masses, and not merely self-interest was involved; so were the emotions; and this created a major problem for the pursuit of foreign policy according to reasons of state:

If societies, as well as individuals, be charged with the care of their own preservation, and if in both we apprehend a separation of interest, which may give rise to jealousies and competition, we cannot be surprised to find hostilities arise from this source.

Hear the peasants on different sides of the Alps, and the Pyrenees, the Rhine, or the British Channel, give vent to their prejudices and national passions; it is among

298   Ibid., pp. 300–1.
299   Ibid., p. 301.
300   Ibid., p. 302. This is a notion developed later and extensively by Robert Jervis: *The Logic of Images in International Relations* (Princeton 1970) and *Perception and Misperception in International Relations* (Princeton 1976).
301   Ferguson, *Essay*, p. 30.

them that we find the materials of war and dissension laid without the direction of government, and sparks ready to kindle into a flame, which the statesman is frequently disposed to extinguish. The fire will not always catch where his reasons of state would direct, nor stop where the concurrence of interest has produced an alliance. "My Father," said a Spanish peasant, "would rise from his grave, if he could foresee a war with France." What interest had he, or the bones of his father, in the quarrels of princes?[302]

Ferguson clearly favoured the predominance of Reasons of State, but he also saw the conflict as in itself productive. "Peace and unanimity are commonly considered as the principal foundations of public felicity; yet the rivalship of separate communities, and the agitations of a free people, are the principles of political life, and the school of men."[303] One is here reminded that Britain had done well out of war, having just gained the eastern coastline of North America – excepting Florida, of course – for its exclusive settlement. Ferguson's outlook very much mirrored his times and the interests of the state that sheltered him. Not only were manly virtues created by war, but the very existence of society as a coherent entity owed itself to the ever-present danger of external conflict: "Without the rivalship of nations, and the practice of war, civil society itself could scarcely have found an object, or form."[304] This was unexceptional, in that Hobbes and Pufendorf both accepted this premiss. It was what they built upon its foundation that mattered. Ferguson goes further: "Could we at once, in the case of any nation, extinguish the emulation which is excited from abroad, we should probably break or weaken the bonds of society at home, and close the busiest scenes of national occupations and virtues."[305] He had no thought that this was likely to end:

> It is vain to affirm, that the genius of any nation is adverse to conquest. Its real interests indeed most commonly are so, but every state which is prepared to defend itself, and to obtain victories, is likewise in hazard of being tempted to conquer.
> In Europe, where mercenary and disciplined armies are every where formed, and ready to traverse the earth, where, like a flood pent up by slender banks, they are only restrained by political forms, or a temporary balance of power; if the sluices should break, what inundations may we not expect to behold?[306]

Moreover, he had no desire that it should end:

> The strength of nations consists in the wealth, the numbers, and the characters, of their people. The history of their progress from a state of rudeness, is, for the most

302   Ibid., pp. 34–5.
303   Ibid., p. 93.
304   Ibid., p. 36.
305   Ibid., p. 37.
306   Ibid., p. 235.

part, a detail of the struggles they have maintained, and of the arts they have practised, to strengthen, or to secure themselves. Their conquests, their population, and their commerce, their civil and military arrangements, their skill in the construction of weapons, and in the methods of attack and defence; the very distribution of talks, whether in private business or in public affairs, either tend to bestow, or promise to employ with advantage, the constituents of a national force, and the resources of war.[307]

The role of war in human progress was later taken up by Kant. Rousseau took a rather different view.

Burke may well have read early Rousseau before he wrote the *Vindication*. Indeed, he referred in his preface to "several others" aside from Bolingbroke who dignified these reasonings "with the Name of Philosophy."[308] In direct contrast to Bolingbroke and Ferguson, Rousseau saw man as fundamentally pacific. But the consequences of making this assumption did not lead him to conclude that international relations could be based upon trust, even on the margin, because he took the same view of the behaviour of states as Hobbes had done. Where he and Hobbes differed was that to Rousseau, as to Bolingbroke, Hobbes was wrong to attribute to man in nature characteristics peculiar to man in society. Moreover Rousseau sought also to remove the blame from man entirely: "It is the relationship between things and not men which constitutes war . . ."[309] The fault lay in society, not in man: in his famous phrase, "the state of war is born of the state of society." Once new states spread across the earth it became apparent that there existed between them "relations which tend towards their mutual destruction . . ." "Man", he wrote, "is naturally pacific and fearful . . . he only goes to war under the compulsion of habit or experience. Honour, interests, prejudices, vengeance, all the passions which could make him risk danger and death are far from him in the state of nature. It is only after having come together [*fait société*] with a man that he decides to attack another; and he becomes a soldier only after having become a citizen."[310]

It was not that killings could not occur between individuals in the state of nature but that man isolated in nature had by definition limited capabilities. "The State on the contrary being an artificial body is in no way predetermined in its dimensions; the size which is peculiar to it is undefined; it can always increase it; it feels weak because there are others stronger than itself. Its security, its preservation, require that it makes itself more powerful than all its neighbours. It cannot grow, feed itself, exert its strength except at their expense and if it has no need to look outside itself for its subsistence, it looks incessantly there for new parts which give it a more unshakeable solidity. For the

307   Ibid., p. 357.
308   Preface to the second edition: p. vi.
309   "Du Contrat Social", I, iv: *Oeuvres Complètes*, Vol. 2 (Paris 1971) p. 520.
310   "Fragment sur la guerre", J.-J. Rousseau, *Oeuvres*, pp. 379 and 382.

inequality of men has limits set by the hands of nature, but that of societies can grow incessantly, to the point where one alone absorbs all the rest."[311] Rousseau thus found justification for Reasons of State in society, which was, in essence, not that much different from a customary view current before his own time. "The Iniquity of the Times is often allow'd to be a *Reason of State*, and perhaps one of the best *Reasons of State* that can be given. Circumstances justify Things which are not to be justify'd in themselves, but 'tis a fatal Necessity, which obliges Men either to do Things otherwise hurtful, or omit Things necessary", wrote the novelist and pamphleteer Daniel Defoe several decades before.[312]

The dilemma for all those of a liberal disposition in the late eighteenth century whose head ruled their heart was that progress in all forms of life was self-evident, but that progress in the more civilised conduct of international relations was severely circumscribed. The more enlightened of the realist principles of international relations enunciated in the Renaissance – such as Reasons of State and the Balance of Power – were an advance, but not entirely realised, and, where effected, ultimately proved only a solution *ad interim*: making for greater stability, forestalling hegemony, but obtaining neither an overarching justice nor a permanent peace. Rousseau was not one to be taken in by appearances. Where Reasons of State were concerned, he took the view – as had Le Clerc – that there was not as much reason as there should have been. Rousseau and Hobbes converged in the belief that passion prevailed over reason. "Thousands of writers have dared to say that the body politic [and the State] is without passion and that there are no other reasons of state than reason itself. It is as if one did not see on the contrary that the essence of society consists in the activity of its members and that a State without movement would be nothing less than a corpse."[313] What this highlights is the value of Reasons of State recognised by Machiavelli and Richelieu as an appeal to reason over passion and corruption in the conduct of state affairs. Reasons of State, which in retrospect are seen as entirely conservative if not reactionary in intent, were, in the context of early modern Europe, liberational, because they aimed at securing the primacy of reason common to all men rather than the primacy of the state as the personal property of the monarch.[314]

Rousseau saw the European states system in all its complexity. It is probable that he would have wished to be convinced by the Abbé de Saint-Pierre, whose project on perpetual peace consumed a great deal of his time and attention. But, as Kant was to find for himself before the century was out, the subject of international relations was too complex to be dealt with in its totality in the time available. Indeed, in his masterwork, *The Social Contract*, Rousseau acknowledged that he had laid to one side everything

311   Ibid., p. 383.
312   Writing in *The Manufacturer: or, The British Trade truly Stated*, 5 January 1720.
313   "Fragment . . .", p. 384.
314   J. Freund, "Raison d'état", *Encyclopédie philosophique universelle*, II – *Les Notions Philosophiques, Dictionnaire*, ed. S. Auroux (Paris 1990) pp. 2152–3.

concerning "international law, trade, negotiation, treaties, etc.", which formed "a new subject too vast for my short survey . . ."[315] His outlook has therefore to be garnered from various brief commentaries, inevitably somewhat disjointed and contradictory taken as a whole.

Like Grotius, Locke and Pufendorf, Rousseau allowed for functional international integration "through a union of interests, through . . . conformity of custom, or by other circumstances which permit mutual relations to exist between diverse communities. Thus it is that all the Powers of Europe form between themselves a kind of system which unites them by the same religion, by the same law, by custom, by learning, by commerce, and by a kind of balance which is the necessary effect of all that, and which, without anyone actually dreaming of sustaining it, would not however be as easy to break as many people believe."[316] However, turning to present realities:

> To see, on the other hand, the endless squabbles, robbery, unlawful seizure, revolts, wars . . . a policy so wise in books and so harsh in practice, rulers so well-meaning and a populace so wretched, governments so moderate and wars so cruel: one scarcely knows how to reconcile these strange contradictions; and this vaunted camaraderie of the people of Europe appears to be nothing but a term of derision to express ironically their mutual animosity.

Why should this be so? Here Rousseau's answer echoes Hobbes' pessimism:

> Any society without law or without a ruler, any union formed or maintained by chance, must of necessity degenerate into squabbling and dissension at the first change in circumstance. The ancient union of the people of Europe has complicated their interests and their rights in thousands of ways; they come in contact with one another at so many points that the slightest movement of some cannot fail to collide with others; what divides them is so much more deadly than the intimacy that brings them together, and their frequent quarrels have almost the cruelty of civil wars.
>
> Let us therefore agree that the state particular to the Powers of Europe is simply a state of war, and that all the partial treaties between some of these Powers are more passing truces than a veritable peace: whether because these treaties have jointly no other guarantees than the contracting parties; or whether because the rights of the one and the other are never completely decided that way, and these rights wrongly attained, or the claims which arise out of them between Powers which do not recognise any superior, will infallibly become sources of new wars, as soon as different circumstances have given new strength to the claimants.[317]

---

315   "Du Contrat Social", IV, ix.
316   "Extrait du projet de paix perpétuelle de M. l'Abbé de Saint-Pierre", *Oeuvres*, p. 161.
317   Ibid., p. 164.

The bitter realism was equally evident where Rousseau discussed Reasons of State. In his essay "On the government of Poland" he told Polish rebels that the Christian Powers "knew no other ties than those of their interests". On the other hand, like Pufendorf, he was not entirely convinced that such interests were pursued in a rational and objective manner:

> But it is almost never Reason of State that guides them: it is the momentary interest of a minister, of a girl, of a favourite; it is a motive which no human wisdom could foresee that moves them at times for, at times against, their true interests. Of what can one be assured with people who have no fixed system at all and who conduct themselves merely by fortuitous impulses? Nothing is more frivolous than the political science of the courts: as it has no assured principle, one can draw no certain consequences; and the whole of this fine doctrine of interests of princes is a children's game which makes sensible men laugh.[318]

Clearly Reasons of State were in these terms a distant goal rather than a dominant standard. Rousseau allowed for the possibility of conducting international relations according to more elevated principles through the creation of a federative league of states, but believed it could be accomplished only by means of revolution, "and, on this principle, who of us would dare say whether such a European league is to be desired or feared? It could perhaps do more damage in one blow than could have been anticipated in centuries."[319] For the educated man of the eighteenth century, fear of anarchy – fear of the mob – was as strong as fear of despotism; and, faced with the alternatives, many – even aspirant liberals – chose the latter, a known evil, in preference to the former, a flight into dangerous oblivion.

To the Scots philosopher David Hume (1711–76), international relations, as for Hobbes, was primary. The origin of states lay in international relations: ". . . I assert the first rudiments of government to arise from quarrels, not among men of the same society, but among those of different societies."[320] But like Pufendorf and Rousseau, though a believer in the force of interest and the power of reason, Hume also saw serious limitations in an explanation of politics and Reasons of State which built its foundations solely upon those premises. And he clarified his position by outlining a dialectic at work between states: between reason and passion, between short-term interest and long-term interest. "Nothing is more certain", he wrote, "than that men are in a great measure governed by interest . . ." Yet he also allowed that "men are mightily governed by the imagination, and proportion their affections more to the light under

---

318 "Sur le gouvernement de Pologne": ibid., pp. 505–6.
319 Ibid.
320 Hume, "Of the Origin of Government": from *A Treatise of Human Nature* and reprinted in D. Hume, *Political Writings*, ed. S. Warner and D. Livingston (Indianapolis 1994), p. 51.

which any object appears to them, than to its real and intrinsic value."[321] "This" was "the reason why men so often act in contradiction to their known interest . . ."[322] Hume saw men taking decisions for short-term gain in neglect of long-term advantage. Like Hobbes and Spinoza, he was struck by the fact that men were "perpetually carried, by their unruly passions . . ."[323] These presuppositions had obvious implications for the conduct of international relations. States could not be expected always to behave "rationally" since statesmen were subject to short-term – otherwise described as short-sighted – advantage and driven by emotion. The "selfishness and ambition" of states were, he wrote, "perpetual sources of war and discord."[324] There was no hope of altering this aspect of human nature, which Hume regarded as perpetual, but there were possibilities of altering behaviour through a change "of their situation . . ."[325] Moreover, interests could be counted upon to a degree. "Where possession has no stability, there must be perpetual war. Where property is not transferred by consent, there can be no commerce. Where promises are not observed, there can be no leagues nor alliances." The logic of this reasoning suggested that states, like men in a state of nature, would seek to create an over-arching authority to ensure "peace, commerce and mutual succour".[326]

Thus the conduct of international relations could not be purely Hobbist, and here Hume follows Cumberland. Yet no sooner can one detect a clear departure from Hobbes than we witness also a clear distancing from Cumberland. "There is a maxim very current in the world," Hume added, "which few politicians are willing to avow, but which has been authorized by the practice of all ages, *that there is a system of morals calculated for princes, much more free than that which ought to govern private persons.*" This maxim proved convincing enough to Hume, but, concerned to convince those unhappy at the marginalisation of morality in affairs of state, he distinguished between a governing morality and capacity for enforcement. For whereas in domestic society the morality that ensured co-operative and peaceful intercourse could be enforced from above, in the European states system, such an authority did not exist: "though the morality of princes has the same *extent*, yet it has not the same *force* as that of private persons, and may lawfully be transgressed from a more trivial motive."[327] In other words: "though the intercourse of different states be advantageous, and even sometimes necessary, yet it is not so necessary nor advantageous as that among individuals, without which it is utterly impossible for human nature ever to subsist. Since, therefore, the *natural* obligation to justice, among different states, is not so strong as among individuals, the *moral* obligation which arises from it must partake of its weakness;

321   Ibid., p. 47.
322   Ibid., p. 48.
323   Ibid., p. 61.
324   Ibid., p. 74.
325   Ibid.
326   Ibid.
327   Ibid., p. 75.

and we must necessarily give a greater indulgence to a prince or minister who deceives another, than to a private gentleman who breaks his word of honour."[328]

Thus while dissociating himself from purely Hobbist assumptions and building upon Locke and Pufendorf, Hume gave a moderate and reasoned, but no less effective, justification for Reasons of State as a maxim effectively free from the normal constraints of ethics. It is nevertheless strange that those who, like Hume, would by any other measure fit the label Liberal in the contemporary age were to a large extent realists in their view of international relations. They differed from the hardline realists like Hobbes in their belief that a better and more humane European order was ultimately possible. They differed from those one would label utopians in that for them "ultimately" was, indeed, a very distant goal. In part we can explain the acceptance of Reasons of State as a logical consequence of concern to guard against both passions and arbitrary rule. However, tension none the less existed between their more utopian aspirations and the acceptance of immediate laws of the jungle. That this was not an easy adjustment is evident in Rousseau; it is no less apparent in the writings of Immanuel Kant (1724–1804), an admirer of both Hume and Rousseau.

Whereas Hobbes saw the problem of international conflict in the nature of man, and Bolingbroke and Rousseau saw the problem in the nature of society, Kant instead focused on man's interaction with society as a dynamic making for war and as ultimately an opportunity for peace. Kant's philosophy has always been something of a puzzle because of his ambiguous, indeed ambivalent, attitude to war. In this Kant follows Ferguson. As a result commentators have usually found their own Kant and ignored the other. But Kant, like Rousseau, was both a realist and a utopian, though not to the same degree: a utopian in matters domestic and the ultimate potentiality of international relations, but a realist in the foreign affairs of the short to medium term. By the time we reach the end of the eighteenth century man's understanding of society had much advanced, to the point where a distinction could be drawn between intentionality and result and where the paradoxical nature of man could be openly admitted, celebrated even. The way had been paved, first by Mandeville, then by Adam Smith (see pp. 42–4); both in the sphere of the economy, but with implications for society in general. Kant thought man by nature bad. His image of man was not dissimilar to that of Hobbes and Lucian the satirist: an irresistible drive towards total freedom, inevitably at the expense of others. But he was, unlike Hobbes, also a believer in the betterment of man, as his polemic with Moses Mendelssohn – *Über die Gemeinspruch* (1793) – demonstrated. Echoing the Stoics, Kant conceived of a teleology. It worked by tension: a struggle between opposites. As outlined in the *Idee zur einer allgemeinen Geschichte in weltbürgerlicher Absicht* (1784), the end point, the *telos*, was the full development of man's capacities, most notably his use of reason. Man did not originate with reason but only with the capacity for reason. Nature provided the means for its evolution through a dialectic between man's natural inclinations and civilising culture. It is here that

328   Ibid.

Rousseau's influence is most marked. For Kant the contradiction apparent in Rousseau between his attack on civilisation in the *Discours* and *Héloïse* and his belief in the value of the state and education in the *Contrat social* and *Émile* is resolved as culture develops man's capacities as a moral species such as to eliminate the conflict between the moral and the natural.[329] But whereas Rousseau in fact saw civilisation as key to man's decay, Kant saw it in reverse. Just as many have found the Kant in their own image, so too did Kant find his own Rousseau.

On Kant's view, that which at first sight appeared entirely negative was turned by nature to the forces of progress: natural laws determined man's behaviour, however foolish that behaviour might at any one time appear to be. Kant shared with Machiavelli, Hobbes and Bolingbroke – but certainly not with Rousseau – the belief in man's "animal inclinations",[330] but they were not critical to conflict. Kant had no coherent understanding of how society came into being. One perceptive commentator has listed several of his separate explanations: that families come together naturally; that "civil societies" come together from need; that states come into being because of war.[331] It was social progress, however, that was responsible for accelerating conflict between societies. Kant therefore looked forward to social change as the distant mechanism for ultimately bringing a lasting peace. Kant's judgement on the nature of man and society thus lay in a "teleological theory of nature",[332] whereby he came to share more with Hegel and Marx than those we commonly associate with liberalism. "Individual men and even entire nations little imagine that, while they are pursuing their own ends, each in his own way and often in opposition to others, they are unwittingly guided in their advance along a course intended by nature. They are unconsciously promoting an end which, even if they knew what it was, would scarcely arouse their interest."[333] Hence Kant's celebrated reference to man's "*unsocial sociability*".[334] The influence of Mandeville is here apparent. For Mandeville the lesson drawn was clear – private vice led to public benefit. For Kant, however, the result was by no means so certain, but the means to the ultimate end was equally paradoxical. "The means which nature employs to bring about the development of innate capacities is that of antagonism within society, in so far as this antagonism becomes in the long run the cause of a law-governed social order."[335] That goal had in some respects been achieved but it could not be fully attained until the outer environment of international relations was also brought to order. Thus

---

329   M. Mori, "Il problema della guerra nella filosofia della storia di Kant", *Filosofia*, Anno XXX, Fasc. II: Aprile 1979, p. 214.
330   "Idea for a Universal History with a Cosmopolitan Purpose": I. Kant, *Political Writings*, ed. H. Reiss (Cambridge 1977 edition) p. 41.
331   G. Vlachos, *La Pensée Politique de Kant: Métaphysique de l'ordre et dialectique du progrès* (Paris 1962) p. 216.
332   "Idea . . .", p. 41.
333   Ibid.
334   Ibid., p. 44.
335   Ibid.

for Kant international relations was primary. For "Nowhere does human nature appear less admirable than in the relationships which exist between peoples."[336] The same seemed true in respect of the attainment of a global order.

Kant was, like many contemporaries, disturbed and preoccupied with the need to create peace between states; but not peace at any price. Although war was accepted as an evil, universal monarchy and the extinction of the rights of states were no lesser evil. Moreover, war was also a force for cohesion within society (Bodin's view) and, indeed, a veritable engine of progress (Ferguson's vision):

> if the constant fear of war did not compel even the heads of state to show this *respect for humanity*, would we still encounter the same culture, or that close association of social classes within the commonwealth which promotes the wellbeing of all?[337]

Kant looked harsh realities in the face, as did Rousseau, and it is this that gives him a reputation for realism as well as idealism. There is no trace of moralising in his work. In the tension between head and heart, the head usually won out. The rising level of civilisation of states, "along with their growing tendency to aggrandise themselves by cunning or violence at the expense of the others, must make wars more frequent", he argued.[338] This dialectic between the advancement of civilisation and the recurrence of war through a growing appetite for aggrandisement was most certainly a feature of his time. But instead of enquiring into what in particular acted as the locomotive for war in the development of society, Kant instead placed his weight on the argument that a greater degree of democratisation would ultimately solve the problem, if at all. The nature of the complex interaction between radical domestic change (or perfection of the constitution) and external conflict is thus described:

> All wars are accordingly so many attempts (not indeed by the intention of men, but by the intention of nature) to bring about new relations between states, and, by the destruction or at least the dismemberment of old entities, to create new ones. But these new bodies, either in themselves or alongside one another, will in turn be unable to survive, and will thus necessarily undergo further revolutions of a similar sort, till finally, partly by an optimal internal arrangement of the civil constitution, and partly by common external agreement and legislation, a state of affairs is created which, like a civil commonwealth, can maintain itself *automatically*.[339]

---

336 "On the Common Saying: 'This May be True in Theory, but it does not Apply in Practice'", ibid., p. 91.
337 "Conjectures on the Beginning of Human History", ibid., p. 232.
338 "On the Common Saying: 'This May be True in Theory, but it does not Apply in Practice", ibid., p. 90.
339 "Idea . . .", p. 48.

It is here that Kant the realist finally gives way to the idealist and thereby passes beyond our immediate attention.[340] In the distant future Kant looked forward to man reacting against the mounting costs of war by turning instead to international co-operation. In the meantime, however, "the barbarous freedom of established states" and its "resultant evils" compelled the discovery of "a law of equilibrium" to regulate hostility.[341] This was that other innovation of the Renaissance: the Balance of Power.

340   For a thorough account of this aspect of Kant's thought: A. Hurrell, "Kant and the Kantian paradigm in international relations", *Review of International Studies* (1990), 16, pp. 183–205. My only misgiving is that the author does not acknowledge the ambiguity in Kant's assessment of war.
341   "Idea . . .", p. 49.

Chapter 2
THE BALANCE OF POWER

". . . it is a thing of pure opinion, which each interprets according to his views and his particular interests . . ."

– Instruction du marquis d'Hautefort, 1750.
Recueil des Instructions, Autriche[1]

Critics have attacked the Balance of Power on many counts – some convincingly, some less so. Yet its utility has persisted for the best part of five hundred years. And public criticism of it began only two hundred and fifty years ago. This suggests either that for the previous two hundred and fifty years the consensus was under a sustained misapprehension, or that circumstances so changed by the time criticism arose that the notion had become suddenly redundant, or that conditions unknown and unconnected with the merits of the concept prompted criticism with other purposes in mind.

What emerges with some clarity from a close study of the idea in context is: that the notion was extended from the Italian city-states system to the emerging European states system; that, in stark contrast to the notion of Reasons of State, it went substantially unchallenged for several centuries; that, as the events of the nineteenth century well demonstrate, not merely was its adoption occasionally cover for nefarious aims but its very rejection could prove equally self-serving, and that rejection in at least two major instances was dramatically reversed when the consequences of rejection were shown to be disastrous.

Reasons of State were, some have argued, as old as Adam; on the other hand, the idea publicly expressed was new to the Europe of Machiavelli. The same could be said of the Balance of Power. "It is a question whether the *idea* of the balance of power be owing entirely to modern policy, or whether the *phrase* only has been invented in these later ages?", asked David Hume.[2] But this was merely a rhetorical flourish; he had an answer in mind. Among the Greek city-states, Hume wrote, "every prevailing power

---

1   Quoted by C. Dupuis, *Le Principe d'Équilibre et le Concert Européen de La Paix de Westphalie à L'Algésiras* (Paris 1909) p. 36.
2   "Of the Balance of Power", in D. Hume, *Essays: Moral, Political and Literary* (Indianapolis 1985 edition) p. 332.

was sure to meet with a confederacy against it, and that often composed of its former friends and allies."[3] Hiero King of Syracuse understood the principle when, although an ally of Rome, he sent assistance to Carthage, "Esteeming it requisite . . . both in order to retain his dominions in SICILY, and to preserve the ROMAN friendship, that CARTHAGE should be safe; lest by its fall the remaining power should be able, without contrast or opposition, to execute every purpose and undertaking. And here he acted with great wisdom and prudence. For that is never, on any account, to be overlooked; nor ought such a force ever to be thrown into one hand, as to incapacitate the neighbouring states from defending their rights against it." As Hume pointed out, with a quotation from Polybius, "Here is the aim of modern politics pointed out in express terms."[4] The Balance of Power was thus almost certainly practised in the ancient world.

Ignorance of the notion in early medieval Europe most probably derived from its discontinuation in Roman history, since Rome eventually created a universal empire that blotted out the collective memory of former times. Small states were no longer free to balance one another and collide at will. Rome thus became a rock of stability. As Justus Lipsius (1547–1606) noted of the Roman empire, quoting Plutarch, "it was like an anchor to the floating world."[5] After the sack of Rome, the splintering of empire did not immediately give rise to a Balance of Power system because the shattering of the over-arching infrastructure was not yet fully made up by the expansion of commerce. As Hume's contemporary, William Robertson, noted, "We find . . . that the first effect of the settlement of the barbarians in the Empire was to divide those nations which the Roman power had united. Europe was broken into many separate communities. The intercourse between these divided states ceased almost entirely during several centuries . . . Even between distant parts of the same kingdom, the communication was rare and difficult."[6] These distances amplified a sense of separation, which in turn led to a short-termism in the conduct of foreign politics; and this in turn made impracticable the operation of the Balance of Power. "The expectation of remote advantages, or the prospect of distant and contingent evils," Robertson reminds us, "were not sufficient to excite nations to take arms. Such only as were within the sphere of immediate danger, and unavoidably exposed to injury or insult, thought themselves interested in any contest, or bound to take precautions for their own safety."[7]

The Balance of Power thus became an openly acknowledged, popular concept only in early modern Europe. Like so many notions in international relations, it was an analogy drawn from the world of the natural sciences and, indeed, from everyday life.

---

3   Ibid., p. 334.
4   Ibid., p. 337.
5   Quoted in R. Tuck, *Philosophy and Government 1572–1651* (Cambridge 1993) p. 62.
6   *The History of the Reign of the Emperor Charles V with A View of the Progress of Society in Europe from the subversion of the Roman Empire to the Beginning of the Sixteenth Century* (London 1769) – *The Works of William Robertson*, Vol. IV (London 1818) p. 92. The work, a model of its kind, took ten years to complete.
7   Ibid., p. 105.

Anyone who shopped in the market was familiar with the scales upon which goods were weighed. Statics is the study of the conditions of equilibrium resulting from the distribution of weights. In statics the calculation of much larger weights presented intractable mathematical problems. The ancient Greeks were pioneers in this field. The Romans, however, had built little upon their findings. The breakthrough in statics did not await Galileo and Newton. It was in late medieval Europe, at a time not noted for original scientific thought, that the study of statics – then known as *scientia de ponderibus* – came into its own, and not merely as the reiteration of classic teaching. The need to create precise standards for the measurement of weight had by then become a commercial priority. The key work was that produced by Jordanus in the thirteenth century: *Liber de ratione ponderis.*[8] According to the French historian of science Pierre Duhem, the ideas of Jordanus excited enormous intellectual interest at the time.[9] With educated minds so focused on the problems of equilibrium, it was an easy step for scholars to interpret the behaviour of non-physical objects in analogical terms.

The conceptualisation of Reasons of State followed and mirrored established practice in Renaissance Italy. The logical next step was the conceptualisation of the Balance of Power. The situation which prompted the emergence of the Balance as a ruling principle of international relations was the period in Italy, commonly thought of as stable and peaceful, from the peace of Lodi (1454) to the invasion of the French under Charles VIII (1494), during which five Powers maintained a balance on the peninsula: Venice, Milan, Florence, Rome and Naples. In fact it was not quite so peaceful a period as later represented.[10] Moreover, the bounded nature of inter-Italian relations was by no means as complete as subsequently claimed. The aggressively rich and powerful republic of Venice was an extra-Italian as well as an Italian Power. Florence had close trading relations with France. And a key element to the maintenance of the balance was the stability of each regime, of each kingdom or city-state. When that broke down intervention was all but inevitable, as Machiavelli rightly warned. The Italian system also operated only because the Venetians were afraid of Ottoman expansion, which caused them to pull together rather than continue to exert pressure on their neighbours on the peninsula.

The operation of the Balance of Power as a system may have originated in early modern Europe with the Italian city-states, but it is to that brilliant writer, French statesman Philippe de Commynes, that we owe the first published description of the system of balance, written between 1488 and 1501[11] and printed in 1524. "To the

8   E. Moody and M. Clagett (eds.), *The Medieval Science of Weights* (Madison 1952) pp. 3–20, 57–63, and 169–73.
9   P. Duhem, *Les Origines de la Statique* (Paris 1905).
10 For the best informed and most elegant treatment of the subject: G. Pillinini, *Il sistema degli stati italiani 1454-1494* (Venice 1970).
11 The estimate given in the English-language edition of his works: *The Memoirs of Philip de Commines, Lord of Argentin*, ed. A. Scoble, Vol. 1 (London 1855). The translation is very readable but rather too

princes of Italy", he wrote, ". . . God has given as counters the communes as they are called in Italy, such as Venice, Florence, Genoa, Bologna, Sienna, Lucca and others which, in certain respects, are counters to the principalities and the principalities to them: and each keeps an eye lest his neighbour grow powerful."[12] De Commynes was the first to publicise the balance, but too much should not be made of this: these notions and the associated terminology were almost certainly in general circulation at the time among those in government throughout the Italian states; de Commynes' service as ambassador in Venice will have given him direct access to and complete familiarity with the language and concepts prevalent at the time.

The myth of a perfectly balanced system to which de Commynes himself appears to have subscribed arose soon after France invaded in 1494. It gave Italians a sense of an ideal world to which they might one day return. Every myth has a central figure, and in this case the Florentines threw up the image of Lorenzo de Medici. Not surprisingly, perhaps, the first writer to immortalise him was his brother-in-law, Bernardo Rucellai, in *De bello italico*.[13] Rucellai wrote that both Ferdinand of Aragon, who held Naples, and Lorenzo de Medici, in Florence, "by far the most prudent of all the princes of Italy", strove "for those things by which the affairs of Italy might stand and (to use the words of those men) might hang in equal balance [*examine aequo penderent*]."[14] The manuscript fell into the hands of Guicciardini during the composition of his *History of Italy*, and appears to have prompted him to begin the account at the turn of the century and to present a similar picture in some detail.[15] Indeed his *History* wrote of Lorenzo de Medici that he "took every care that the affairs of Italy were sustained in balance so that the weights were not heavier on the one side than the other."[16]

What then appears to have happened is that an idea current within the semi-enclosed Italian city-states system was transported to the body of Western Europe. At that earlier period, as Robertson points out, "In each kingdom of Europe great events and revolutions happened, which the other powers beheld with almost the same indifference as if they had been uninterested spectators to whom the effect of these

free for direct and accurate quotation. It has therefore been put aside for the original. The claims that the Venetian Francesco Barbaro (1395–1454) was the first to put forward the notion of the Balance of Power are not accurate, at least given the quotations adduced in evidence by Sabbadini, Carotti and Morandi. For a conclusive refutation: G. Pillinini, "L'Humanista Veneziano Francesco Barbaro e l'Origine della Politica di Equilibrio", *Archivio Veneto* (Venice 1963) Anno XCIV, V Serie N. 107, pp. 23–8.

12 *Mémoires de Philippe de Commynes*, ed. R. Chantelauze (Paris 1881) p. 391. For Scoble's rendering, see *The Memoirs*, p. 379. De Commynes was not a realist in international relations: he took a moralistic position as to how governments should behave and condemned the kind of behaviour by rulers that Machiavelli advocated.

13 *Bernardi Oricellarii de Bello Italico Commentarius, Iterum in lucem editus* (London 1733) pp. 4–5, in particular.

14 Ibid., p. 4.

15 This was revealed by Roberto Ridolfi in his *Genesi della storia d'Italia guicciardina* (Florence 1939).

16 *Opere di Guicciardini*, Vol. 2, p. 89.

transactions could never extend."[17] The rise of Spain thus occurred almost unre-marked. What changed was, of course, the growing centralisation of power within certain kingdoms and the emergence of more conscious Reasons of State. As Robertson states, "during the course of the fifteenth century, various events happened which, by giving princes more entire command of the force in their respective domin-ions, rendered their operations more vigorous and extensive. In consequence of this, the affairs of different kingdoms becoming more frequently as well as more intimately connected, they were gradually accustomed to act in concert and confederacy, and were insensibly prepared for forming a system of policy, in order to establish or to preserve such a balance of power as was most consistent with the general security. It was during the reign of Charles the Fifth, that the ideas on which this system is founded first came to be fully understood. It was then that the maxims which it has been uniformly main-tained since that era were universally adopted."[18] Indeed, Robertson argued, the very election of Charles V as Holy Roman Emperor, which united the greater part of Western Europe under one throne in 1519, testified to the slowness with which notions of the Balance of Power took hold:

> The other European princes could not remain indifferent spectators of a contest the decision of which so nearly affected every one of them. Their common interest ought naturally to have formed a general combination in order to disappoint both competitors, and to prevent either of them from obtaining such a pre-eminence in power and dignity as might prove dangers to the liberties of Europe. But the ideas with respect to a proper distribution and balance of power were so lately introduced into the system of European policy, that they were not hitherto objects of sufficient attention. The passions of some princes, the want of foresight in others, and the fear of giving offence to the candidates, hindered such a salutary union of the powers of Europe, and rendered them either totally negligent of the public safety, or kept them from exerting themselves with vigour in its behalf.[19]

Charles V firmly installed, it was above all neighbouring France that was most sensitive to the shift in the Balance of Power. Florentine publicist Donato Giannotti (1492–1573), like Machiavelli, with whom he was closely acquainted, was anguished at the degradation of the Italian city-states, the continued target of Great Power rivalry. The system thrown up in the sixteenth century consequent upon Charles V's election, uniting Austria, Spain, the Low Countries and Germany, was essentially bipolar and it was this that lay at the root of Italian misery, producing a tit-for-tat action and reaction in jostling for primacy of influence. Giannotti saw matters thus: "it is evident enough", he wrote in 1535, "to those considering the characteristics of the state not only

17   Robertson, op. cit.
18   Ibid., pp. 107–8.
19   Ibid., Vol. 2: *Works*, Vol. V (London 1818) p. 68.

in Italy but in Christianity as a whole, that the king of France and the emperor are as two monarchs and primary leaders of the latter [Christendom], such that any incident which arises within it cannot but be due to them . . .".[20]

It was from France, and at a time of growing debilitation induced by the wars of religion in the second half of the sixteenth century, that Jean Bodin wrote of the security of princes and states to be found in "an equal balance between the Powers".[21] That was the Balance as policy, to which we will return later. Giovanni Botero, on the other hand, saw the Balance of Power dictated by circumstance: the structure of what soon became known as the system of states dictated behaviour. In his *Relatione della Republica Venetiana*, published in 1605, Botero was the first to explain how and where a balance would come into being in terms that illustrate well the novelty of the emerging states system:

> where there is no plurality of princes . . . the balance of power [*contrapeso*] which we are discussing can have no place. This can be clearly seen in Spain, England, France, Poland and in other kingdoms that were initially divided into more principalities, and later united under one crown. Furthermore, if the entire world were one republic or one principality, the art of counter-balancing would be superfluous and completely unnecessary: but given the plurality of princes it follows that a balance of power is useful and good not as a result of volition [*non per natura sua*], but circumstances [*per accidente*]. And it is of two kinds, because at times its goal is the peace of a republic, composed of other different states, such as Italy, Germany, and Christianity in its entirety: at other times the security and prosperity of a particular state. In the first case the balance of power consists in a certain equipoise according to which the body of the republic has no parts which are not in proportion and balanced in a kind of equality; excess weight exerts its force now from this side and now from that . . .[22]

The main example cited was the familiar one of the Italian city-states system led by Lorenzo de Medici.

Botero saw the search for balance and the finding of that balance as a predictable process resulting from the multiplicity of states in contention. He concluded that "the balance of power has as its basis the order of nature and the light of reason, as a result of which . . . each must seek to offset power not only suspect and hostile but also

---

20   D. Giannotti, "Discorso delle cose d'Italia" (Al Santissimo Padre e Nostro Signore Papa Paolo Terzo): *Opere Politiche*, ed. F. Diaz, Vol. 1 (Milan 1974) p. 372. For more on Giannotti: *Dizionario Biografico degli Italiani* (Rome 2000) pp. 527–33.

21   Quoted in G. Zeller, "Le principe d'équilbre dans la politique internationale avant 1789", *Revue historique*, Vol. 215, 1956, p. 27.

22   Botero, *Relatione della Republica Venetiana* (Venice 1605), p. 9.

trusted and allied to itself . . . [*a ogni uno convenga cercar oppositione alla potenza non solo sospetta, e nimica, ma anche confidente e congiunta seco . . .*]."[23] It is striking that whereas Botero, unhesitating in his commitment to the Counter-Reformation against heretical thought, spearheaded the onslaught against the writings of Machiavelli and thereby emptied Reasons of State of its true significance, he none the less felt at perfect liberty to enunciate the principle of the Balance of Power with no qualms at all. Whereas his reading of Reasons of State, and that of all the Catholic writers of the sixteenth and seventeenth centuries, implied choice for the ruler between moral and immoral action, the Balance of Power was presented as a given, about which there could be no discussion of equating the morality of means with the morality of ends. If it were a law of nature, then nothing could be done about it. This is the first but by no means the last indication of the degree to which the idea of the Balance of Power found ready consensus in early modern Europe as an obvious and natural solution to a perennial problem. Not only was the idea unchallenged, it attained even a moral quality, which later made it vulnerable to attack, since its very incantation could be used to hide a multitude of misbehaviours. Only in the eighteenth to nineteenth centuries did the very idea come under serious challenge on moral grounds, and then from those new secular universalists, the liberals.

By the end of the sixteenth century – with the Holy Roman Empire now disentangled from Spain – the notion of the Balance was firmly entrenched in Elizabethan England, which, of course, was a minor Power in comparison with its weightier continental counterparts: a clear reminder that, at least in its original formulation as policy, the Balance was primarily an instrument of the weaker against the stronger. "God has put into your hands the balance of power and justice, to poise and counterpoise at your will the actions and counsels of all Christian kings of your time", wrote Geoffray Fenton.[24] It might be said that this was to make a virtue of dire necessity. Francis Bacon, former Chancellor of England, pointed to it as "the main piece of wisdom in strong and prudent councils":

> to be in perpetual watch that the states about them should neither by approach nor by increase of dominion, nor by ruining confederates, nor by blocking of trade, nor by any the like means, have it in their power to hurt or annoy the states they serve: and whensoever any such cause did but appear, straightways to buy it out with a war, and never to take up peace at credit and upon interest. It is so memorable, as it is yet as fresh as if it were done yesterday, how that triumvirate of kings, Henry the eighth of England, Francis the first of France, and Charles the fifth, Emperor and king of Spain, were in their times so provident, as scarce a palm of ground could be

---

23 Ibid.
24 Fenton translated Guicciardini's history into English: quoted in A. Vagts, "The Balance of Power: Growth of an Idea", *World Politics*, Vol. 1, No 1, October 1948, p. 97.

gotten by either of the three, but that the other two would be sure to do their best to set the balance of Europe upright again.[25]

What this paean also suggests is that the currency of power was essentially land. The balance was to be sustained between the three Powers on the basis of territorial distribution. And war was the means by which the balance would be sustained or, failing that, restored. Elsewhere, however, Bacon was more circumspect. In his essay for James I on the "true greatness of the Kingdom of Britaine", one of the earliest assessments of the components of national power in modern Europe, Bacon argued that "in the measuring or balancing of greatness, there is commonly too much ascribed to largeness of territorie." Other factors were of equal significance. Apart from a degree of wealth, true greatness "doth require a fit situation of the place or region" (geography). It "consisteth essentially in population and breed of men" (demography). It "consisteth alsoe in the valour and militarie disposition of the people it breedeth" (morale). It also required that every subject "be fit to make a soldier" (national health). It depended upon "the temper of the government" (identification with the state). And, lastly, true greatness "consisteth in the commandement of the sea."[26] Territorial extension could become "matters of burden than of strength", he insisted.[27] None the less this continued to be the main basis for calculation.

Generally speaking the relative weights of France and Spain were separately more impressive than that of England. The Italian city-states eclipsed as fully independent entities, first France and then Spain raised the Balance of Power as a principle of foreign policy to guard against hegemony of the other. Charles V incorporated all his inherited possessions (Spain, Naples, the Low Countries, Germany and Austria) into one empire. Faced with Spain under the Habsburgs increasingly dominant in Europe, but with Austria and Spain now under separate administration, in 1584 Duplessis-Mornay, a friend of Henri of Navarre, commented:

All states are considered strong and weak only in comparison with the strength or weakness of their neighbours . . . For some time the house of Austria has greatly increased in power and grown in both esteem and territory: such that the balance is without doubt over-weight on one side; and it is time to add weight to the other, if one does not want our France to be stamped out in the end.[28]

25 "Considerations touching a War with Spain. To the Prince", 1624, in *The Works of Francis Bacon*, ed. J. Spedding et al., Vol. XIV (London 1874) p. 477.

26 "Of the true greatness of the Kingdom of Britaine, to King James", *Letters, Memoirs: Parliamentary Affairs, State Papers, & c. With some Curious Pieces in Law and Philosophy Publish'd from the Originals of the Lord Chancellor Bacon*, ed. R. Stephens (London 1736) p. 194.

27 Ibid., p. 196.

28 *Discours au roi sur les moyens de diminuer l'Espagnol*, 23 April 1584: G. Zeller, "Le principe d'équilibre . . ." p. 28.

Likewise Venice – a shadow of its former pre-eminence as a trading colossus and as the leading Power in Italy – became preoccupied with the enormous preponderance of power established by the Habsburgs. While the Pope was agitating to form a general alliance of the whole of christendom against the hated Turk, in Rome Paolo Paruta (1540–98) was putting the Venetian case for a more limited union against Spain. Paruta began as a teacher but moved into politics, a career culminating in the post of ambassador to Rome (1592–5).[29] "For the security of Italy", he wrote in November 1592, "it is sufficient as well as more beneficial that the forces of the Kingdom of France were able, not by themselves, but properly allied to the Italian Powers, to counterbalance the King of Spain: so that, when he thought of touching the state of any Italian, the forces of all the Italian princes would come together, as could easily happen, for the common defence, and those of France which would always be ready for such an opportunity, if it arose, when the need occurred, to act vigorously against such attempts."[30]

The theme continued. In 1635 the *Mercure d'Estat* published a "Discours des Princes e Estats de la Chrestiente plus considerables a la France, selon leurs divers qualites & conditions", written by Henri Duc de Rohan, which argued:

> All Christian Princes and States not subjects or supporters of Spain have an interest in forming a necessary counter-weight against it, and in sustaining those who are bearing arms against so formidable a House . . .[31]

This instrument, the Balance of Power, may have been a constant of English foreign policy because of persistent weakness relative to the continental Powers in Europe; but for the continental Powers themselves it was more a means of exchange, to be traded in when times were good, to be resorted to when rivals emerged. Following the wars of religion France was rebuilt into a powerful and encroaching Power under Louis XIV and then threatened to establish the very universal monarchy once so feared of Spain. In 1667 François Paul, Baron de Lisola, published the *Bouclier d'Estat et de Justice*. De Lisola approved the Duc de Rohan's maxim that the peace of Europe rested upon the maintenance of a balance between the two great monarchies of France and Spain. But he accused the French of abusing this principle by deploying it to draw the other Powers behind France on the false presumption that "the power and the designs of Spain are more formidable than those of France, and that according to these same reasons of state they are obliged to place their counter-weight on its side."[32] Louis XIV of course disingenuously denied it: "Far from dreaming of the famous idea of universal monarchy,

---

29   Bozza, *Scrittori*, p. 54.
30   *La Legazione di Roma di Paolo Paruta* (1592–1595) p. 25.
31   *Le Mercure d'Estat ou Recueil de Divers Discours d'Estat* (1635) p. 399.
32   *Bouclier d'Estat et de Justice, contre Le dessein manifestement decouvert de la Monarchie Universelle, Sous le vain pretexte des pretentions de la REYNE DE FRANCE* (1667) p. 227.

with which Austria's supporters have often alarmed the whole of Europe, I merely claim to uphold this equal balance which the neighbouring Powers have always envisaged as their security."[33] But how striking it is that the concept was so legitimised that such an obvious expansionist as Louis should seek to cloak his plans for aggression under the banner of the Balance of Power.

Indeed the Balance was now so universally accepted – if to be applied only to others and not oneself – that the movement was under way to elevate it to the exalted status of moral principle. Pragmatism was somehow not seen as sufficient justification, at least in continental Europe. Archbishop of Cambrai, François Fénélon (1651–1715), in his "Directions pour la Conscience d'un Roi", written for Louis XIV's grandson, argued that the Balance of Power was essential for safety's sake. Usually those who expressed themselves in such terms turned their backs on the more idealistic appeals to the universalist ideals of mankind. But Fénélon, reaching back to Vitoria and Suárez, also argued that states must act in the common interest by creating "a kind of society and general republic".[34]

Being too light to act as one of the basic weights in the balance, the English sought to act as the pivot between both France and Spain or their successors as leading Powers on the continent. To work successfully such a system required an entirely pragmatic, unbiased and ideologically neutral policy, otherwise it would lack credibility. In 1648 acceptance of the principle of *cuius regio, eius religio* [to each kingdom its own religion] in the treaties of Osnabrück and Münster (the Peace of Westphalia)[35] after the disastrous Thirty Years' War, prepared the way for such a system, though it took more time for Reasons of State to be freed entirely from religious preference. Declarations of principle take one only so far; observance was quite another matter. Lord Halifax (1633–95), once First Lord of the Treasury, reflected in 1689 that when England played the role that nature had given it as the fulcrum of the balance in a neutral manner between France and Spain, the country had benefited: "To be a perpetual umpire of two great contending powers . . . was a piece of greatness which was peculiar to us, as we did it for a considerable time, it being our safety as well as our glory to maintain it." However, "by a fatality upon our councils, or by the refined policy of this latter age, we have thought fit to use industry to destroy this mighty power which we have so long enjoyed; and that equality between the two monarchs, which we might for ever have preserved, hath been chiefly broken by us, whose interest it was above all others to maintain it . . . instead of weighing in a wise balance of power of either crown, it looketh as if we had learnt only to weigh the pensions [bribes], and take the heaviest."[36]

33   20 May 1700: Zeller, "Le principe . . .", p. 33.
34   *Oeuvres Complètes de François de Salignac de la Mothe Fénélon, Archeveque-Duc de Cambrai, Prince du Saint-Empire*, Vol. VI (Paris 1810) p. 334.
35   *The Consolidated Treaty Series*, ed. C. Parry, Vol. 1 (New York 1969).
36   "The Character of a Trimmer", *HALIFAX: Complete Works*, ed. J. Kenyon (London 1969) pp. 86–7.

England had thrown its weight in one direction only – against France. It was that which caused Halifax so much concern. An effective Balance of Power policy could be sustained in the long term only if it operated through a neutral and objective assessment of the relative weights of each power in the system; otherwise its entire purpose would be nullified. This was no easy matter. The very measurement of power was problematic. Bacon, as long ago as the 1620s, had reflected that "the just measure and estimate of the forces and power of an Estate, is a matter than the which, there is nothing among civil affaires more subject to error, nor that error more subject to perilous consequences."[37] Towards the end of the century the perils of correct computation were exacerbated by prevalent corruption. England had abandoned its key interest because, Halifax asserted, statesmen or the court itself had been bribed to do so. Thus it was not merely religion that prevented a clear understanding of national interests. And this raised a larger question: how could there be any objective interpretation of Reasons of State, and therefore how could there be a truly objective assessment of the Balance of Power? Indeed, how rational were men of state?

Ever aware of the intricacies of foreign policy, Pufendorf was, as we have already noted, one of the first to outline the dilemma:

> seeing this Interest is so manifest to those who are vers'd in State-Affairs, that they can't be ignorant of it; one might ask, How it oftentimes happens, that great Errors are committed in this kind against the Interest of the State. To this may be answer'd, That those who have the Supreme Administration of Affairs, are oftentimes not sufficiently acquainted with the Interest both of their own State, & of their Neighbours; . . . Sometimes they are misguided by their Passions . . . or else, being divided into Factions, they are more concern'd to ruin their Rivals, than to follow the dictates of Reason. And for this Reason, some of the most exquisite parts of Modern History consists in knowing the just Character of the Person who is the Sovereign, or of the Ministers, which rule a State; their Capacity, Inclinations, Caprices, Private Interests, Manner of proceeding, & the like; since upon this depends, in a great measure, the good & ill Management of a State. For it frequently happens, That a State which in it self consider'd is but weak, is made to become very considerable by the good Conduct & Vigilance of its Directors; Whereas a powerful State, by the ill Management of those that sit at the Helm, oftentimes declines apace.[38]

The danger of course stemmed not merely from Hobbist passions that might blind statesmen to the true Reasons of State, from the personalities of rulers, the political in-fighting that characterises every government or, indeed, from the venal appetites of those in power, but also from the limitations of purposive rational thought,

37 "Of the true greatness . . .", *Letters, Memoirs*, p. 193.
38 S. Pufendorf, *An Introduction to the History of the Principal Kingdoms and States of Europe* (London 1719).

particularly in an era when "public opinion" began to play a significant role in the making of foreign policy. This became a particular preoccupation in early eighteenth-century Britain.

Daniel Defoe was a cynical figure who took money from all comers and worked both sides of the fence as a spy in Queen Anne's reign. Indeed, one writer later claimed that Defoe polemicised against his own previous publications merely for money.[39] His commentaries, ingeniously composed, were none the less not without influence. He presented himself as a hard-headed and cool realist who decisively rejected "Projects of Peace form'd without Doors, and built on private Opinion only . . ."[40] He had no illusions about the way international relations were conducted: "The Faith and Honour of the best Princes in the World being too weak a Basis to build a Thing of that Consequence upon [a peace treaty], especially while, according to the present Practices, the Faith and Honour of Treaties are always Interpreted by Princes their own way, when they have any Pretensions to make, or find it for their conveniency to break in upon their Word given."[41] In 1701 Defoe expressed his concern at the difficulty of carrying on a policy that worked purely through reason and skirted irrational opinion. For public opinion – even if only that of the ruling class – was now a factor in the formulation of foreign policy, at least in Britain. "Of all the Nations of the World there is none that I know of, so Entirely Govern'd by their humour as the *English*. There's no more to do to make way for any General undertaking, than by some Wonderful Surprize to Rouse the Fancy of the People, and *away they go with it*, like Hounds on a full Cry, till they over-run it, and then they are at a Halt, and will run back against as fast as they came on." He added: "Natural antipathies are no just ground of a War between Nations. Nor Popular Opinions."[42]

In early modern Europe, when influence upon policy-making was confined to the few, when individual passions therefore threatened reasoned decision, the notion of Reasons of State was seen as a crucial safeguard of the needs of the community. The expansion of participation in the most important decisions of foreign policy – namely war or peace – was evident in England as early as 1620. It was prompted by the need for funds. Bacon had then to draft a proclamation for parliament on behalf of the King. "For although the making of War or Peace, be a secret of Empire," he wrote, "and a thing properly belonging to our high Prerogative royal, and imperial Power; yet nevertheless,

---

39   He "sometimes found his account in answering his own productions . . .": *The Critical Review*, October 1756, p. 279.

40   *A Review of the Affairs of France: Purg'd from the Errors and Partiality of News-Writers and Petty-Statesmen, of all Sides*, Vol. V, No 155, 24 March 1709, p. 617.

41   *A View of the real Dangers of the Succession, from The Peace with France: Being A sober Enquiry into the Securities proposed in the Articles of Peace and Whether they are such as the Nation ought to be satisfy'd with or no* (London 1713), pp. 40–1.

42   Defoe, but published anonymously, *Reasons against a War with France, or an Argument shewing That the French King's Owning the Prince of Wales as King of England, Scotland and Ireland; is No Sufficient Ground of a War* (London 1701) pp. 1 and 3.

in causes of that nature, which we shall think fit not to reserve, but to communicate: we shall ever think our selves much assisted and strengthened, by the faithful advice, and general assent of our loving Subjects."[43] Before long those "loving Subjects" overthrew the monarchy and put in their own men. Greater democracy then compounded the problem of subordinating the conduct of foreign policy to principles of reason, including the Balance of Power. Now as the influence on policy-making spread to an entire class of society, collective passions threatened to inflame debate and distort decisions that resulted. In these terms calculations based solely upon the Balance of Power – "that little understood, but very popular and extensive Word"[44] – were seen as an advance upon emotion; indeed, before long it came to be seen as the final triumph of reason. As Defoe explained it, "To prevent . . . the Eternal Confusions, which Ambition and Pride would keep the World continually agitated by, they [our predecessors] drew this Consequence from the whole, and which pass'd for an uncontroverted Maxim ever since, among all the Politicks of *Europe*, *viz*. That to preserve the publick Peace of this Part of the World, A BALLANCE OF POWER should be maintain'd among all the several Monarchies, Commonwealths, and Governments of Christendom – And thus *Exorbitant Power*, the horrid Monster we have been talking of, has been shut out, and banish'd by Human Society in these Parts for several Ages."[45]

The tendency, however, was – just as Halifax complained – for British statesmen and news writers to interpret the Balance purely against France, an old enemy and a Catholic nation, and to give a Protestant but troublesome rival like Holland the benefit of the doubt. Even so astute and self-controlled a Secretary of State for Foreign Affairs as Lord Bolingbroke, who was more aware than others of the adverse impact of the emotions, could speak of Holland as "the frontier of Britain" and as "the two nations together as the bulwark of the Protestant interests."[46] The War of the Spanish Succession was fought and led by Britain to forestall France's attempt to absorb Spain through royal inheritance, which, if it succeeded, would break the Balance of Power for decades if not longer. In generating the Francophobe fears necessary to the successful conduct of the military campaign, emotions were unleashed which could so easily cloud the minds of policy-makers. The collective passions of society thus swelled the individual emotions of statesmen. And as society became more democratised and as other societies followed suit, these problems came to multiply and further complicate events.

---

43   "Draught of a Proclamation for a Parliament, referred to in the preceding letter", 18 October 1620: *Letters, Memoirs*, p. 125.

44   *A Review of the Affairs of France*, Vol. VI, No 7, 19 April 1709, p. 26.

45   Ibid., Vol. VI, No 3, 9 April 1709, p. 11.

46   Letter to Drummond, 3 December 1710: *Letters and Correspondence, Public and Private, of the Right Honourable Henry St. John, Lord Viscount Bolingbroke, during the time he was Secretary of State to Queen Anne; with state papers, explanatory notes, and a translation of the foreign letters, & c.*, ed. G. Parke (London 1798) Vol. 1, p. 22.

The other danger was that Britain would abandon the self-imposed constraints of the Balance of Power as policy and take France's place in a bid for hegemony "and so set up our selves as publick Enemies to *Europe*, in the room of that publick Enemy we pull down."[47] In his *Review of the Affairs of France: Purg'd from the Errors and Partiality of News-Writers and Petty-Statesmen, of all Sides*, Defoe reminded readers what the War of the Spanish Succession was all about:

> The End of this War is to reduce exorbitant Power to a due Pitch, to run it quite down . . . Every Power, which over ballances the rest, *makes its self a Nuisance* to its Neighbours. *Europe* being divided into a great Variety of separate Governments and Constitutions; the Safety of the whole consists in a due Distribution of Power, so shar'd to every Part or Branch of Government, that no one may be able to oppress and destroy the rest.
>
> . . . When that Power is reduc'd, it ceases to be any more the Object either of Jealousie or Resentment of the rest; but if any of the united Powers erect themselves upon the Ruin of that; or by any other method set themselves up too high; the Nusance is transpos'd to that Power, which before it was thought convenient to assist, and it becomes necessary to the rest to reduce that Power or Prince, as it was before to reduce the other. [48]

With victory over the French came a peace brokered by London. "*Britain*", Defoe proclaimed in 1712, "now holds the Ballance, and will turn the Scale, and that which Side soever pushes to Extremity, must split upon this Rock, must have the *British* full in their Way; it is not that I desire it, but the Nature of the Thing is such, it cannot be otherwise."[49] Once again the notion of the Balance of Power was presented as an ineluctable law of nature rather than mere choice. Perhaps not too much should be made of this, coming as it did from such an unscrupulous pen; there is, after all, no better way of advocating policy than presenting it as necessity. And Defoe's motives soon came into question. No sooner did the Dutch seek more than their due – they wished to continue a war that the British Government now sought to end on conditions France had originally proposed – than Defoe published a pamphlet on *The Justice and Necessity of a War with Holland, in Case the Dutch Do not come into Her Majesty's Measures, Stated and Examined*.[50]

In 1713 Secretary Bolingbroke ruthlessly and deviously secured the Treaty of Utrecht, which at last ended the War of the Spanish Succession in victory for the opponents of Franco-Spanish union. Treaty-makers could therefore afford to take the larger view and provide for the general stability of Europe, particularly once Britain had satisfied itself with territorial and other gains. The treaty aimed, among other things,

47   *A Review of the Affairs of France*, Vol. III, No 65, 1 June 1706, p. 262.
48   Ibid.
49   Ibid., Vol. VIII, No 204, 12 July 1712, pp. 817–18.
50   Published in London in 1712.

"to settle and establish the peace and tranquillity of Christendom, by an equal balance of power (which is the best and most solid foundation of a mutual friendship, and of a concord which will be lasting on all sides) . . .".[51] This was the first international agreement which was explicitly based on that principle. As already noted, Bolingbroke, being a man who confessed openly "how much indulgence" he had for "his passions", his "fancies, his "weaknesses",[52] was all too conscious of the dangers of too great a subjectivity in judgement and thus made it a point of principle that reason dominate the conduct of public affairs. His remarks on the Balance of Power show both sensitivity to the distorting impact of the emotions, no doubt born of bitter experience, and a strong belief in the need to conceptualise the conduct of foreign policy to assure the primacy of reason:

> The precise point at which the scales of power turn, like that of the solstice in either tropic, is imperceptible to common observation . . . they who are in the sinking scale do not easily come off from the habitual prejudices of superior wealth, or power, or skill, or courage, nor the confidence that those prejudices inspire. They who are in the rising scale do not immediately feel their strength nor assume that confidence in it which successful experience gives them afterwards. They who are the most concerned to watch the variations of this balance, mis-judge often in the same manner & from the same prejudices. They continue to dread a power no longer able to hurt them, or they continue to have no apprehension of a power that grows daily more formidable.[53]

Assessment of likely threats to security were thus all too fallible. The danger was always that of preparing to fight the last war and failing to anticipate the source of the next.

As the states of Europe grew in population, in industry, agriculture, and in foreign trade, there had been no comparable improvement in the means of communication with the world beyond the sub-continent. Europe seemed claustrophobic. And after decades of peace the Seven Years' War broke out in 1756. The prevailing attitude of mind not unnaturally became entirely zero-sum. "Europe today", wrote Réal de Curban (1682–1752), "forms only one Body, because of the way the different States which compose it relate to one another. But in this body each part has its own interests, and is busy only with is own aggrandisement; it would like to achieve it at the expense of all the others . . ."[54] Thus a Europe that for several centuries had worried "at the

---

51 Treaty of Utrecht between Britain and Spain, 13 July 1713: *The Consolidated Treaty Series*, ed. C. Parry, Vol. 28 (New York 1969) pp. 325–6.

52 Quoted in H. Dickinson, *Bolingbroke* (London 1970) p. 166.

53 "A plan for a General History of Europe", Letter VII: *The Miscellaneous Works of the Rt. Honourable Henry St. John, Lord Viscount Bolingbroke* (Edinburgh MDCCLXVIII) p. 143.

54 Réal de Curban, *La Science du Gouvernement, Contenant le Traite de Politique par rapport au dehors & au dedans de l'État, & aux moyens de concilier les interets respectifs des Puissances qui partagent la domination de l'Europe*, Vol. 6 (Aix-La-Chapelle 1762) p. 437.

slightest movement in ambition that it perceives in a Power" saw its security in the Balance of Power, though this was never easy.[55] "This balance, which must make each his own master, is so dangerous to seek, and even more so to find; and if one has found it, it is impossible to preserve. Do not the passions of Princes, the inclinations of the People, the maxims of States, the changes of regime, and domestic revolutions render the point of balance difficult to find?"[56]

It was in British hands that the Balance of Power in Europe was the most effective. Entirely taken up in expansion overseas, Britain posed no threat to purely continental European Powers. And the one continental Power which posed a threat to that overseas expansion – namely France, in North America – always faced rivals in Europe. By positing the issue of the Balance of Power purely in terms of the European states system, London effectively limited France's ability to expand overseas. "In this we must always have a great advantage over France," noted one MP in 1754, on the eve of Britain's war with France over possession of North America, "because none of them can ever be jealous of this nation, and most of them must always be jealous of France; consequently, it will at all times be easy for us to form such a confederacy upon the continent, as will be able to set bounds to the ambitious views of France when she attempts to extend them too far, either against us, or against any of our allies."[57]

Yet scepticism persisted, even in Britain. Relations between Powers in the European system seemed so fickle, the atmosphere so fouled by mistrust, for the very reason that they were held in balance, so that although alliances were frequently contracted and wars no less frequently fought, outstanding quarrels were never fully resolved, but festered to near putrefaction. The young Irish publicist and politician Edmund Burke, in his account of the progress – or, rather, the lack of it – of the Seven Years' War, echoed the earlier misgivings of Sir Thomas More:

> The balance of power, the pride of modern policy, and originally invented to preserve the general peace as well as freedom of Europe, has only preserved its liberty. That political torture by which powers are to be enlarged or abridged according to a standard, perhaps not very accurately imagined, ever has been, and it is to be feared will always continue a cause of infinite contention and bloodshed. The foreign ambassadors constantly residing in all courts, the negociations incessantly carrying on, spread both confederacies and quarrels so wide, that whenever hostilities commence, the theatre of war is always of a prodigious extent. All parties in those diffusive operations have of necessity their strong and weak sides. What they gain in one part is lost in another; and in conclusion, their affairs become so balanced, that all the powers concerned are certain to lose a great deal; the most fortunate acquire

---

55   Ibid., p. 442.
56   Ibid., p. 447.
57   Colonel Henry Conway, 14 November 1754: *Parliamentary History of England*, Vol. XV (London 1813), col. 340.

little; and what they do acquire is never in any reasonable proportion to charge and loss.

Frequent experience of this might prove one of the strongest grounds for a lasting peace in Europe. But that spirit of intrigue, which is the political distemper of the time, that anxious foresight which forms the character of all the present courts, prevents the salutary effects which might result from this experience. These modern treaties of peace, the fruits not of moderation but necessity; those engagements contracted when all the parties are wearied and none satisfied, where none can properly be called conquerers or conquered, where, after having fought in vain to compel, they are content to over-reach them in the very moment they are formed, and from the very act of forming them, with the seeds of new dissensions, more implacable animosities, and more cruel wars. For if to forward the work of peace any member in these alliances should acquire a cession of any importance in its favour, this afterwards becomes a ground for another alliance, and for new intrigues to deprive them of their acquisition.[58]

This was the first moralistic attack on the Balance of Power, where Burke impetuously identifies the Balance with the overall conduct of international relations. Yet this was not a sustained or considered judgement. For once the system was threatened with destruction, barely a decade later, Burke saw it in a much more positive aspect.

The challenge that finally undermined the fragile claim of the Balance as a moral or legal precept came in the form of the most questionable application of the principle: the division of Poland between Austria, Prussia and Russia in 1772, 1793 and 1795. To sustain a balance between Powers that sought to expand, they agreed to split the difference: which just happened to be Poland. What this underlined was that only the Great Powers were full participants in the system; others were disposable. The British Government, invariably all too sensitive to shifts in the Balance in Western Europe, looked on with calculated indifference. To the British, Poland was not fully a part of Europe and therefore had no place in the scales. Its status was thus akin to overseas plantations; nothing more. Burke took up his cudgels to continue the critique he began during the Seven Years' War. If he had objected to the Balance of Power as a motivating force in 1760, so much more did he object to the manner of its operation in 1772, which he described as a "Revolution in the political system of Europe."[59]

In Burke's words, this was "a revolution as unexpected as important, in that general system of policy, and arrangement of power and dominion, which had been for some ages an object of unremitting attention, with most of the states of Europe."[60] The "violent dismemberment and partition of Poland" was not "sapping by degrees the

---

58   *The Annual Register, or a View of the History, Politics, and Literature, For the Year 1760* (7th edition, London, 1789) pp. 2–3.

59   Ibid., *For the Year 1772* (London 1773) p. 1.

60   Ibid.

continuation of our great western republic"; it was "laying the axe at once to the root, in such a manner as threatens the total overthrow of the whole." Burke continued to the body of the argument:

> The surprize of a town, the invasion of an insignificant province, or the election of a prince, who had neither abilities to be feared, nor virtues to be loved, would some years ago, have armed one half of of Europe, and called forth all the attention of the other. We now behold the destruction of a great kingdom, with the consequent dis-arrangement of power, dominion, and commerce, with as total an indifference and unconcern, as we could read an account of the exterminating one hord of Tartars by another, in the days of Genghizcan or Tamerlane.
>
> The idea of considering Europe as a vast commonwealth, of the several parts being distinct and separate, though politically and commercially united, of keeping them independant, though unequal in power, and of preventing any one, by any means, from becoming too powerful for the rest, was great and liberal, and though the result of barbarism, was founded upon the most enlarged principles of the wisest policy. It is owing to this system, that this small part of the western world has acquired so astonishing (and otherwise unaccountable) a superiority over the rest of the globe. The fortune and glory of Greece proceeded from a similar system of policy, though formed upon a smaller scale. Both her fortune and glory expired along with the system.[61]

Burke argued that Asian provinces had suffered in the past for want of such a system. "Each state", he wrote with respect to the rise of Rome, "looked on with indifference or enjoyed a malignant pleasure at the ruin of its neighbour, without reflecting that the weapons and power of which he was deprived, would be quickly employed to its own destruction."[62] Only too conscious of the misgivings so eloquently expressed a decade before, he granted:

> It will not be denied, that the idea of supporting a ballance of power has in some cases been carried to an extreme; that by artfully employing it to operate upon the passions and jealousies of mankind, it has been made an engine subversive to the designs of interested and ambitious persons, and has perhaps thereby, been productive of some unnecessary wars.

But the same could be said of civil liberty. "Even that, the noblest quality of the human mind, has been productive of wars, and of other evils."[63] The Balance of Power was thus essential:

61 Ibid., p. 2.
62 Ibid.
63 Ibid., p. 3.

The same principles that make it incumbent upon the patriotic member of a republic, to watch with the strictest attention the motions and designs of his powerful fellow-citizens, should equally operate upon the different states in such a community in Europe, who are also the great members of a larger commonwealth. Wars, however it may be lamented, are inevitable in every state of human nature; they may be deferred, but they cannot be wholly avoided; and to purchase present quiet at the price of future security, is undoubtedly a cowardice of the most degrading and basest nature.[64]

Burke also argued that independence from the system was at odds with national security. Isolationionism was therefore no option:

It may not . . . be altogether an hazardous opinion, that a single man, cast out from the laws, the protection, and the commerce of his whole species, might in that solitary situation, with as rational and well-grounded a probability, propose to himself convenience and security, as any single state, in the present political and physical state of Europe, could expect independence and safety, unconnected with all the others.[65]

As Burke now sought to emphasise, the operation of the Balance of Power rested upon a sense of community, even if only between the Great Powers. Religion had all but disappeared as a threat to these calculations. No one anticipated an equivalent force which, built on utopian yet secular foundations, could dislodge Reasons of State, and along with it the Balance of Power, and overturn the controlled use of limited force within shared values integral to the European states system; though, as Burke attested, the system was already in serious decomposition. He argued that "France must behold with the greatest uneasiness a new arrangement of power, which threatens totally to unhinge the ancient system of Germany and the North." Moreover, its total exclusion from the process was bound to have serious consequences:

By the lead which she had for so many years assumed in the affairs of Europe, she [France] had acquired a habit of being looked up to, and by the address and dexterity of her ministers, all negociation and intrigue seemed to originate from them. It must therefore be very galling, exclusive of all other considerations, to see a measure of so extraordinary a nature adopted and nearly executed, without her participation or consent; at the same time that it calls up an unwelcome recollection of that weakness, which has hitherto tied her down to be a mere spectator.[66]

64   Ibid.
65   Ibid.
66   Ibid., p. 5.

That trouble should eventually emerge from Paris was thus not entirely unexpected; but the form in which it arose did come as a complete surprise. It was the revolution of 1789 – more particularly its lurch to the left in the summer of 1792 as conflict arose with neighbouring Powers still seeking partition as a means to expansion – that gave rise to a secular universalism which threatened the integrity of the entire system: universal monarchy by a different name. All forms of monarchical government came under attack, even constitutionalism in Britain. Members of radical British corresponding societies were treated in Paris as allies. London no less than the other capitals of Europe waited in anxious anticipation while the Austrians and others attacked. The decree of the National Convention of 19 November 1792 put a match to the tinder. The British Government described the decree as "the formal declaration of a design to extend universally the new principles of government adopted in France, and to encourage disorder and revolt in all countries, even in those which are neutral."[67] Within a year the two countries were at war; it was France that moved first but only after the Foreign Secretary had already concluded: "I do not see how we can remain any longer *les bras croisés*."[68]

As to reasons for going to war, an element of ambiguity was inescapable. Some emphasised that by seeking to control the Scheldt in the Low Countries, the French had broken the Balance of Power; others emphasised the ideological menace posed by the French, a very different kind of danger – the very nature of the Republican regime. In respect of the former, a *modus vivendi* could in principle be established with French Republicanism; in respect of the latter, only the destruction of that regime could bring order to the system. And if other such regimes emerged, co-existence was equally impossible. While the ideologues remained the minority in London – Edmund Burke and followers – they were in command of other countries, notably Russia and Austria. "Our distance protects us for a certain time: we will be the last, but we too will be victims of this epidemic", wrote the Russian ambassador to London.[69] Yet the distance between Burke, the Russians and Austrians, and the British Government was not quite as great as some would have us believe. As Prime Minister William Pitt himself eloquently put the matter in introducing to parliament the Alien Bill, which was Britain's direct repressive response to the National Convention, "Was it possible to separate between the progress of their opinions and the success of their arms?"[70]

---

67   Grenville to Chauvelin, 31 December 1792: *Foundations of British Foreign Policy from Pitt (1792) to Salisbury (1902): Old and New Documents.* Edited by H. Temperley and L. Penson (London 1938) doc. 1.

68   Grenville to Lord Auckland, 24 January 1793: M. Hutt, *Chouannerie and Counter-Revolution: Puisaye, the Princes and the British Government in the 1790s* (Cambridge 1983) Vol. 1, p. 98.

69   Prince Vorontsov to his brother, at the end of 1792: K. Dzhezhula, *Rossiya i velikaya frantsuzskaya burzhuaznaya revolyutsiya kontsa XVIII veka* (Kiev 1972) p. 152.

70   4 January 1793: *The Parliamentary History of England from the Earliest Period to the Year 1803,* Vol. XXX (London 1817) col. 235. For a rather different view trenchantly presented: T. Blanning, *The French Revolutionary Wars* (London 1986) and P. Schroeder, *The Transformation of European Politics* (Oxford 1994). Curiously, though, neither refers to the parliamentary debates on the subject.

The French justified themselves not least with the argument that the old system of public law, including the Balance of Power, had already irretrievably broken down. This was the foundation of the case laid before the world by Napoleon Bonaparte, who, at the turn of the century, enlisted the eloquence, learning and experience of the head of the first division of political correspondence in the French Foreign Ministry, Alexandre-Maurice Blanc de Lanautte, Comte d'Hauterive (1754–1830), to put into organised and published form his ideas on international relations. The resultant book, *De L'État de La France à La Fin de L'An VIII*, was essentially a sustained polemic against the British, who were ultimately held to blame for most calamities that befell the European states system. "In the judgement of all publicists," the book claimed, "the treaty [sic] of Westphalia founded, in the middle of the seventeenth century, the public law of modern times."[71] Three events, on this view, disrupted the bases of the settlement: first, the emergence of Russia as a Power; second, the elevation of Prussia from a position of subordination within the German Empire; and, last but not least, the enormous growth in the colonial and maritime system "in the four quarters of the Universe."[72]

With respect to Russia, the attack deftly echoed Whig concerns expressed at the time of the partition of Poland:

A theory unknown in preceding centuries was from that time introduced into Europe. Combined plans for invasion, agreement on partition and a guarantee for new demarcations by the co-partitioners were prepared with so much mystery that their violent execution necessarily caused a scandal. The appearance of these views and above all their realisation awakened the greed of all the Great Powers, sounded the alarm among the Powers of the second rank and announced to the small states that there existed for them no safeguard and that their fate depended henceforth more or less upon the ease with which their incorporation in a neighbouring state could offer a powerful neighbour . . .[73]

The emergence of Prussia had no such resonance in Britain, particularly the assertion that it broke the balance within the Holy Roman Empire and cut France out of the game. All of this, though, was more or less merely prelude to attacking on the British.

The opening of the New World was a phenomenon to be welcomed. "The first era is one of the most brilliant additions to the history of Europe in the 15th and 16th centuries . . ." It was an age of heroic adventure and remarkable scenes of "courage, barbarism and greed." "But these events had little influence on the general organisation of Europe; they were almost unconnected with its politics; and it was only by the partial role that they played in the decadence of Spain and the destiny of Holland that they are connected to the events of the second era, on which I must dwell in

---

71   *De L'État de La France à La Fin de L'An VIII* (Paris 1800), p. 3.
72   Ibid., p. 6.
73   Ibid., pp. 11–12.

particular."[74] This era dated from the middle of the eighteenth century and was characterised by a mad rush overseas for wealth. Here the British, initially by stealth
(notably the Navigation Acts established under Cromwell), secured domination of the
seas, enabling them to play a key role in Europe by using Britain's accumulated profit
to divide and rule on the continent.[75] Hauterive concluded by dismissing the possibility of creating the kind of Balance of Power in Europe envisaged by Great Britain,
arguing in part that since France was central to Europe, it could and should be called
in to maintain local balances in various parts of the continent!

The analysis and polemic are interesting, although blatantly self-serving, not merely
because they raised an alternative view of international relations but also because of
what was prompted in response, from both Berlin and London. The first came from the
talented and increasingly celebrated pen of Friedrich Gentz (1764–1832), a former
pupil of Kant, who worked in the Prussian War Office from 1793, took money from the
British (at the time his reply to Hauterive was published) and later worked as a close
adviser to Metternich in Austria. Gentz published his response to Hauterive in London
in 1802. He criticised the elevation of the Peace of Westphalia as the legal basis of the
European states system as ridiculous since it "did not even fulfil the first condition of
a compact designed to be the basis of a federative system; it did not include all the
nations even then important; and still less did it embrace all the relations of the states
which it did include."[76] Moreover,

> The fate of empires is no less subject to vicissitudes than that of individuals: owing
> to the inequality of their respective progress, to the unexpected growth of new
> branches of industry and power, to the personal and family connexions, and, still
> more, to the opinions, the characters, and the passions of their rulers, there must
> necessarily happen many changes which no human wisdom can foresee, much less
> provide against. Each of these changes occasions new wants, new plans, and new
> pretensions; endangers or destroys the former equilibrium; presents fresh difficul-
> ties to the statesman, and renders it necessary to revive the system, and define the
> respective rights anew. Impossible as it is for the code of laws of any nation to provide
> for every possible future variation in the character and manners, civil and moral,
> and domestic condition of its inhabitants; even so impossible is it to establish an
> eternal system of public law, by means of any general treaty, however numerous
> the objects which it may embrace, with whatever care and ability it may have been
> combined.[77]

74   Ibid., p. 23.
75   Ibid., pp. 25–9.
76   F. Gentz, *On the State of Europe before and after the French Revolution being An Answer to L'État de la France à La Fin de L'An VIII* (London 1802) p. 10.
77   Ibid., pp. 8–9.

Gentz did not much disagree with Hauterive with regard to Russia: "it cannot be denied", he wrote, "that the formation of this new empire has served to render the political relations of states more intricate, and their combinations more difficult; to multiply plans and counter plans, pretensions and oppositions; wars offensive and defensive; and to give a new impulse to that restless activity which so particularly distinguishes the present times."[78] As to the partition of Poland, Gentz was less disturbed by the fact of partition – he was, after all, a Prussian, and his country gained by it – than by the fact that it was legitimised in traditional terms which were now seriously devalued as a result:

> The plans of conquest and partition, of which a great part must be laid to the account of this empire [Russia], were less hurtful in their immediate than in their remote consequences. They attacked the foundations of all political, and social security; they loosened and invalidated all principles; they made it doubtful whether the law of nations was not an empty name, invented as a cloak for power, and secretly despised by the powerful: they were the model, the pretence, and the excuse for all future usurpations; and so much did they corrupt the public opinion, that the terms, *sound policy, system of equilibrium, maintenance or restoration of the balance of power*, were too often applied, to what, in fact, was only an abuse of power, or the exercise of arbitrary will.[79]

This was the issue highlighted by the young, ambitious and enterprising, radical Scots Whig, Henry Brougham (1778–1868), a founding editor of the new *Edinburgh Review*. Brougham identified neither with Fox, who had originally vigorously supported the French Revolution, nor Burke, who vehemently supported the cause of war against France. Brougham sought to preserve the original aims of the Balance of Power system and described "the partitioning system" as:

> a natural, though a very alarming corruption of that very balancing system upon which we have relied so implicitly for protection from all such disasters. The balancing system arms all against the usurpation of one, and secures us completely in ordinary times from the danger of universal dominion; but it affords no protection to the smaller states against the combination of two or three ambitious sovereigns, and even seems to facilitate the concentration of all power and authority into the usurping hands of a few great potentates. Such combinations are evidently the devices upon which the ambition of those who would formerly have conquered alone, have recently been driven by the prevalence of the system of

78   Ibid., pp. 15–16.
79   Ibid., p. 17.

balance; and they seem only to give that ambition a greater steadiness of direction, and greater assurance of success.[80]

Brougham – no doubt reflecting the vantage-point of one of the leading Powers – did not wish to argue, as had Gentz, that the Balance of Power system should seek an equality between states. He took the more conservative view, that its aim was "to protect and secure the irregularities to which fortune has given existence: to make wealth and poverty alike safe and independent; to defend the weak and the humble against the rapacity of their superiors; and to maintain legitimate power and authority against the combinations of discontented inferiors."[81] He and Gentz did not disagree that "All the substantial benefits of the modern system are lost, as soon as the smaller states are annihilated", but Brougham none the less held that "the prosperity and independence of all Europe is just as effectually ruined by dividing it into two or three great and equal empires, as by giving it up to the dominion of one universal monarch."[82]

Brougham acknowledged that the "partitioning system is the undoubted offspring of the system of balance; it proceeds on the very same principles, and merely applies, for the purposes of destruction and partial aggrandisement, those artificial powers that had been created to preserve independence, and repress ambition." It was a corrupting deformation of the original system because it appeared to legitimise and facilitate expansionism by the Great Powers at the expense of the weak in the name of preserving the balance:

> The ambition of great and powerful states seldom aims at the subjugation of a great and powerful antagonist; it is satisfied, in the beginning, with the easier acquisition of some petty dominion; and their weaker neighbours are only protected by the jealousy which such an act of depredation would excite among the peers and equals of the spoiler. By the system of partition, however, all this jealousy is disarmed; the great powers are united; they are bribed with a share of the plunder, they proceed in concert, and deliberately trim the ponderous balance of their empires, by a skilful division of the booty upon which they have seized.

Brougham saw this as ominous. "Unless nations can be effectively taught that there are limits to the salutary extension of territory and power, it does not appear to us by any means chimerical to suppose, that, in the course of another century, the partitioning system may have entirely subverted the old constitution of Europe."[83]

It was very much Brougham's aim to rescue the Balance of Power from its recent deformation. Hauterive claimed that the system had already been overthrown and that something new was needed in its place. Brougham believed it too fundamental to the

---

80   "Gentz, *État de l'Europe*", *Edinburgh Review*, No III, April 1803, p. 16.
81   Ibid.
82   Ibid., pp. 16–17.
83   Ibid., p. 18.

conduct of international relations to be so easily erased. He argued that "it seems to be rather a figure of rhetoric, than a sober statement of the fact, to allege that the whole system of the balance is fundamentally overthrown. That system did not consist in treaties or alliances, so as to perish by their violation; but it consisted in a principle, that from its very nature was immortal; the knowledge and the influence of which can never perish, while men continue rational and civilized, and which will easily find a way to manifest and apply itself in every new combination of circumstances to which the destiny of nations may give rise."[84]

The appearance of Gentz's *Fragments Upon the Balance of Power in Europe* in 1806 gave Brougham a further opportunity to enlarge upon these views. By then Gentz was at Metternich's side and had hurried to release what was a preliminary section of a larger work forthcoming.[85] Here Gentz revised the opinion originally attacked by Brougham that the Balance of Power system required an equality of weight between the participating Powers. Instead his "theory of a balance of power" called for "a system of *counterpoise*. For perhaps the highest of its results is not so much a perfect *equipoise* as a constant alternate vacillation in the scales of the balance, which, from the application of *counterweights*, is prevented from ever passing certain limits."[86] But the work was marred by Gentz's partisan attention to current policy and the needs of both the Prussian and Austrian Governments in the war with France. It was this bias which Brougham challenged in the *Edinburgh Review* in the following year, as also Gentz's "turn for apologizing, wherever France is not concerned."[87]

Indeed, Gentz appeared to have framed his argument for the maintenance of the Balance around the history of the conflict with France and the needs of the struggle to come. He claimed that the intervention against the revolutionary regime by Austria and others in 1792 was justified by the fact that France was dissolving as a Power and was therefore throwing the balance into jeopardy. Brougham objected. "In our apprehension," he wrote, "the attempt to partition France in 1792 resembled the scheme which had begun the calamities of Europe twenty years before, in every thing but the event."[88] "This is the precise language of 1772 [the year of the first partition of Poland]", he argued. "Neither the Poles nor the French were left to themselves, lest their anarchy should continue, and lead to a kind of national suicide. Their neighbours must attack them, to save their existence, not to defend themselves; and, in consequence of this interference, had the Poles been as strong as the French, we should in all probability have seen Europe overrun from the Vistula westward, soon after 1772, instead of finding it conquered from the Rhine eastward, a few years later."[89] Brougham was always

---

84   Ibid., p. 22.
85   The work was reportedly written in September and October 1805 and was published in April 1806.
86   F. Gentz, *Fragments Upon the Balance of Power in Europe* (London 1806) p. 63.
87   "Gentz *on the State of Europe*", *Edinburgh Review*, No XVIII, January 1807, p. 259.
88   Ibid., p. 264.
89   Ibid., p. 265.

anxious to cut the ideological underpinnings from beneath foreign policy in order to preserve the basic principles he saw as essential to the stability of the European system in the long term. And he saw a clear danger in assuming anything too optimistic about man's nature. "For our present purpose," he continued, "it is sufficient to observe, that the changes which Mr Gentz admits to have subsequently deformed and degraded the original project are essential to the very nature of all such combinations; that there is no real difference between uniting to partition a neighbouring nation because it has become too feeble, and uniting to attack it because its internal destruction may eventually prove dangerous; that, so long as the nature of man continues the same, all combinations of the latter description will speedily degenerate into the nature of the former; and that the certainty of this constitutes precisely the evil of interfering or attacking upon Mr Gentz's principle, and abandoning the safe and wholesome doctrine so often maintained in this Journal, of strictly confining offensive leagues to those cases wherein evident danger is threatened by the overgrown power of any one state."[90] Brougham argued, equally, that a mere accretion of the domestic basis of power was no just reason for intervention. Others – notably Burke, here unnamed – had argued that France had to be attacked before she spread her ideas across the continent. Burke and Gentz alike represented the arguments of the war party. "Its doctrines," Brougham wrote, "after making the round of Europe, with the exception of two or three very feeble powers, have at last realized the very fears of universal sovereignty, upon which they were originally founded; and the Continent of Europe has been piecemeal subdued by France, in twelve years, by dint of attacking France to prevent her from conquering the Continent of Europe at some distant period. Such being at any rate the fact, it is not altogether unfair to suspect the soundness of the principles upon which the war party have proceeded; and to conjecture, that if ever the zealots of this faction are to assist in repairing the evil which their counsels have occasioned, it must be by revising their fundamental doctrines, or by correcting the application of them."[91]

Brougham's reflections were not entirely without influence. He rapidly became a celebrated figure in London society. The Balance of Power continued to hold sway over British policy. Indeed, it was now seen as giving rise to a more elaborate and organised system for the maintenance of European security. Later on into the war against France, which was typically expected to be brief,[92] Prime Minister Pitt redefined his aim as the establishment of "the closest Union of Councils and Concert of Measures", which would in turn create "a general and comprehensive system of Public Law in Europe, and provide, as far as possible, for repressing future attempts to disturb the general Tranquillity, and above all, for restraining any projects of Aggrandizement and

---

90   Ibid.
91   Ibid., pp. 270–1.
92   For the recollections of Canning, who worked under Pitt: *The Speeches of the Right Honourable George Canning with a Memoir of His Life*, ed. R. Therry (London 1828) p. 123.

Ambition similar to those which have produced all the Calamities inflicted on Europe since the disastrous era of the French Revolution."[93]

Victory over France was finally achieved in 1815. The settlement at Vienna largely reflected the British order of priorities. However, true to their original aims, the Russians and Austrians also formed an alliance with every intention of going further and intervening in the internal affairs of other states to sustain the social and political status quo. Precedent there was. The states of early modern Europe intervened in the domestic affairs of their neighbours to sustain religious principles. After the defeat of the French Revolution intervention was justified by the need to forestall the re-emergence of revolutionary principles.[94] Granted, Metternich repeatedly expressed concern for the Balance of Power, but he also consistently subordinated these concerns to the priority of forestalling revolution."All governments have to fight the same enemy; these enemies are the men who would govern in their place", Metternich wrote.[95] Similarly in 1830, during the crisis over the issue of independence for Belgium, Metternich wrote to the Tsar's representative:"In no epoch of modern history has society been presented with more dangers than in the present, because of the upheaval in France. The true . . . and last anchor left for the welfare of Europe lies in the understanding between the great powers, based on the conservative foundation of their happy and grand alliance."[96] The other half of that alliance was Russia. Nicholas I's foreign minister, Nesselrode, wrote to his son in the aftermath of the 1830 revolutions: "We are more preoccupied than even you with the terrible madness which has taken hold of men and pressed them to overthrow kingdoms . . ."[97] It was an overriding anxiety about the threat of revolution that prompted a sense of urgency to sort out troublesome questions of international relations: "as long as we live there will never be another moment of tranquillity in the world", Nesselrode added. "Consequently, let us make haste to settle in Belgium, Greece and Poland. In two months, perhaps, there won't be any more time for it."[98]

In contrast, Britain's interests consistently pointed towards the more neutral mechanism of the Balance of Power applied without ideological or religious distinction at a time when all the Powers sought to use the same principle to cloak less disinterested actions. When in 1823 a revolution broke out in Spain and the French, now back under a Bourbon monarch, intervened to suppress it, the British Government, under the direction of George Canning, defended the system established at the Congress of

93   Memorandum on the Deliverance and Security of Europe, 19 January 1805: *Foundations*, doc. 2.
94   This is a point emphasised in Chabod's review of W. Kienast, *Die Anfänge des europaischen Staaten-systems im späteren Mittelalter: Rivista storica italiana*, Series V, Vol. 1, Fasc. IV, 31 December 1936, pp. 86–9.
95   Quoted in Haas, *Belgium and the Balance of Power*, p. 157.
96   Ibid., pp. 166–7.
97   Ibid., p. 171.
98   Ibid.

Vienna as "an alliance never intended as a union for the government of the world, or for the superintendance of the internal affairs of other states."[99] Canning subsequently reinforced this with the remark that in the past he had said "that the position of this country in the present state of the world was one of neutrality, not only between contending nations, but between contending principles; and that it was by neutrality alone that we could maintain that balance, the preservation of which I believed to be essential to peace and safety of the world." He had come under attack from Whigs like William Wilberforce – whom he maliciously, though perceptively, described as "mixed in the business of the world without being stained by its contaminations"[100] – for not siding directly with Spain against France. But he was most disinclined to give way, only too conscious of the fear that "the next war which should be kindled in Europe, would be a war not so much of armies, as of opinions . . ."[101]

Britain thus remained the only Power truly committed to the neutral detachment critical to the conception of the Balance of Power – of course by virtue of its interests, not as the result of an overpowering commitment to good above evil. Moreover, only certain Powers qualified as legitimate parts of the European states system. Over a century earlier Defoe had acknowledged that "Sweden or Muscovy, Hungary or the Turks" were "in Europe", yet they were not "the governing Part of Europe . . ."[102] Since then Russia had joined the system with a vengeance and Prussia was now a Power to be reckoned with.

The system was still confined to Europe. But the prospect of further enlargement loomed on the distant western horizon. The British had increasingly held open the option of a revolution in South America against the Spanish as a means of redressing the balance with Spain. As early as March 1790 Francisco de Miranda, Simon Bolívar's disappointed precursor, offered as much to Pitt. In return for British support, he promised "very extensive Trade to offer with preference to England" and that "these two nations [England and South America as a whole] may form the most respectable and preponderant Political union in the World."[103] But Miranda was to be sorely disappointed. He later vented to the Russian ambassador his hatred of Pitt as "a monster who seems to have no other guide than the counsels of Machiavelli's Prince."[104] However, with the emergence in Latin America of a more active movement for independence from the Spanish, in 1815 rebel leader Bolívar wrote a letter appealing for aid from the British and in so doing laid down a momentous marker for change. This part of the New World – Venezuela – offered immense riches for British industry:

99   Speech to the House of Commons on "Negociations Relative to Spain", 28 April 1823: *Speeches*, ed. Therry, p. 63.
100   Ibid., p. 64. For Wilberforce's attack: Hansard, *The Parliamentary Debates*, Vol. VIII (London 1823) cols. 1361–4.
101   Speech, 12 December 1826: *Foundations*, doc. 7.
102   Quoted in W. Roosen, *Daniel Defoe and Diplomacy* (London 1986) p. 35.
103   W. Robertson, *The Life of Miranda* (Chapel Hill 1929) Vol. 1, p. 101.
104   P. Bartenev, ed., *Arkhiv khnyaza Vorontsova* (Moscow 1870–83) Vol. xxx, p. 293.

I will not speak of the other regions which are hoping for freedom only to take to their bosom the continental Europeans and in a matter of years form of America another Europe with which England, by increasing its weight in the political balance, will fast diminish that of its enemies who indirectly and inevitably would come here to recreate against England commercial predominance and an increase in military power capable of sustaining a giant which held every part of the world in its arms.[105]

And in a further letter, to Sir Richard Wellesley, Duke of Wellington and the liberator of Spain from Napoleon, Bolívar grandly referred to "The balance of the universe and the interests of Great Britain" which "perfectly accord with the salvation of America!"[106]

It was Canning, a conservative but desperate Foreign Secretary, who had little choice but to take on board these views a decade later when France jeopardised the new balance of power by invading Spain. He urgently required a neat rationalisation for avoiding the costly option of war and a means of containing the expansion of French power none the less:

I have already said, that when the French army entered Spain, we might, if we chose, have resisted or resented that measure by war. But were there no other means than war for restoring the balance of Power? – Is the balance of power a fixed and unalterable standard? Or is it not a standard perpetually varying, as civilization advances and as new nations spring up, and take their place among established political communities? The balance of power a century and a half ago was to be adjusted between France and Spain, the Netherlands, Austria, and England. Some years afterwards, Russia assumed her high station in European politics. Some years after that again, Prussia became not only a substantive, but a preponderating monarchy. Thus, while the balance of power continued in principle the same, the means of adjusting it became more varied and enlarged. They became enlarged, in proportion to the increased number of weights which might be shifted into the one or the other scale.

. . . What, if the possession of Spain might be rendered harmless in rival hands – harmless as regarded us – and valueless to the possessors? Might not compensation for disparagement be obtained, and the policy of our ancestors vindicated, by means better adapted to the present time? If France occupied Spain, was it necessary, in order to avoid the consequences of that occupation – that we should blockade Cadiz? No. I looked the other way – I sought materials of compensation in another hemisphere. Contemplating Spain, such as our ancestors had known her, I

---

105   Simon Bolívar to Maxwell Hyslop, 19 May 1815: S. Bolívar, *Obras Completas*, Vol. 1, ed. V. Lecuña (La Habana, 1947) doc. 114.

106   Bolívar to Wellesley, 27 May 1815: ibid., doc. 117.

resolved that if France had Spain, it should not be Spain "with the Indies." I called the New World into existence, to redress the balance of the Old . . .[107]

What Canning was careful not to say in public was of no less significance for the future:

The other and perhaps still more powerful motive is my apprehension of the ambition and ascendancy of the United States of America. It is obviously the policy of that Government to connect itself with all the Powers of America in a general Trans-Atlantic league, of which it would have the sole direction. I need not say how inconvenient such an ascendancy may be in time of peace, and how formidable in case of war.[108]

Canning thus talked of enlarging the political system in which the Balance operated, but only because he saw France drawing the Americans in on a lasting basis. In so doing, he was acting a century in advance of events. And nothing came of it in practice, not least because it was not in British interests to act.

The Americans – at least, those who so called themselves – were not interested in direct participation in an extension of the European states system. Nothing affronted the United States more than suggestions from Europe that the rules of that system be extended to the North American sub-continent, not least because the US Government was embarking upon an ever more rapid process of territorial expansion; as President James Polk (1795–1849) claimed, "it is due alike to our safety and our interests that the efficient protection of our laws should be extended over our whole territorial limits."[109] When Texas broke from Mexico, it was recognised as independent by Britain and France. They granted recognition in 1837 only on condition Texas remain independent. But in 1845 the US Government annexed Texas. This led to demands from Europe that the Americans be subjected to the same rules of behaviour as prevailed in Europe. President Polk decisively rebutted those demands:

The rapid extension of our settlements over our territories heretofore unoccupied, the addition of new States to our Confederacy, the expansion of free principles, and our rising greatness as a nation are attracting the attention of the powers of Europe, and lately the doctrine has been broached in some of them of a "balance of power" on this [North American] continent to check our advancement. The United States, sincerely desirous of preserving relations of good understanding with all nations, can not in silence permit any European interference on the North American

---

107   Speech on Portugal, House of Commons, 12 December 1826: K. Bourne (ed.), *The Foreign Policy of Victorian England, 1830–1902* (Oxford 1970) doc. 3.

108   Quoted in H. Temperley, *The Foreign Policy of Canning, 1822–1827* (London 1925) p. 553.

109   First annual message to Congress, 2 December 1845: *A Compilation of the Messages and Papers of the Presidents 1789–1907*, ed. J. Richardson (1908) p. 399.

continent, and should any such interference be attempted will be ready to resist it at any and all hazards . . .

. . . Jealousy among the different sovereigns of Europe, lest any one of them might become too powerful for the rest, has caused them anxiously to desire the establishment of what they term the "balance of power". It can not be permitted to have any application on the North American continent, and especially to the United States. We must ever maintain the principle that the people of this continent alone have the right to decide their own destiny. Should any portion of them, constituting an independent state, propose to unite themselves with our Confederacy, this will be a question for them and us to determine without any foreign interposition. We can never consent that European powers shall interfere to prevent such a union because it might disturb the "balance of power" which they may desire to maintain upon this continent.[110]

Not that all in Europe were so pleased with the Balance of Power. Up to the nineteenth century it had, with the momentary exception of Burke, come under attack in practice only from those states and statesmen who sought universal empire. In Britain it so successfully rationalised the national interest that it aroused little opposition. But with the emergence of idealistic concepts of international relations on the back of Smithian free market economics (see pp. 142–8), instead of war being seen as the natural complement to trade, the idea gained ground that trade not only required peace, it created peace and that, on the contrary, the Balance of Power was associated with war.

John Bright, MP for Birmingham, summed up this position:

I think I am not much mistaken in pronouncing the theory of the balance of power to be pretty nearly dead and buried. You cannot comprehend at a thought what is meant by that balance of power. If the record could be brought before you – but it is not possible to the eye of humanity to scan the scroll upon which are recorded the sufferings which the theory of the balance of power has entailed upon this country. It rises up before me when I think of it as a ghastly phantom which during one hundred and seventy years, whilst it has been worshipped in this country, has loaded the nation with debt and with taxes, has sacrificed the lives of hundreds of thousands of Englishmen, has desolated the homes of millions of families, and has left us, as the great result of profligate expenditure which it has caused, a double peerage at one end of the social scale, and far more than a doubled pauperism at the other.[111]

Similarly MP Richard Cobden said: "The balance of power is a chimaera! It is not a fallacy, a mistake, an imposture – it is an undescribed, indescribable,

---

110   Ibid., p. 398.
111   18 January 1865: *The Foreign Policy*, doc. 82.

incomprehensible nothing . . ."[112] In all this there was much posturing, a good deal of emotion, and even more rhetoric, but little thought. What lay behind the more aggressive side of policy against which these high-flown attacks were directed were the very trading interests which these Radicals falsely assumed made for peace. How else did the British empire come into being? For all their high-mindedness about sustaining a balance on the European continent, the British were never interested in creating a balance overseas, where their interests were protected and extended through an incessant series of naval and military advances.

France, since the decline of the Spanish empire, was most often the unwilling object of the Balance of Power in action. It was therefore no great admirer of the principle and with the emergence of an alternative, that of national self-determination – *nationalités* – in post-Napoleonic Europe, the French sought to identify themselves with resurgent nationalism across the continent, which generally left even Britain, but most certainly Austria and Russia, uneasily defensive. As one French commentator wrote, "the ideal political system must not be to balance power to immobilise a state contrary to law, but rather to organise humanity according to the principle of nationality and to establish peace as a condition for the development of mankind."[113]

In so doing the French Government unwittingly aided forces that ultimately proved its own undoing. The type of national self-determination the French backed was essentially the creation of confederations, not new unitary states on the French model. It was on this basis that in 1858–9 Napoleon III supported Count Cavour's unification of northern Italy. But his motivations were more complicated. It allowed him to take Nice and Savoy, much to British fury. France was so focused on reducing the power of Austria, which was actually in decline, that it overlooked the power of Prussia under Bismarck, which was on the rise. After Austria joined Prussia against Denmark in 1864, Prussia then turned against Austria. But the French were so keen to eject the Austrians from Venetia and turn it over to the Italians that Prussia continued to be seen as ally rather than potential adversary. The sense of complacency was well expressed in a Quai d'Orsay memorandum. France's indifference to Prussian behaviour was thus to be "effective proof of our goodwill" towards Germany, as though this would make any difference to Bismarck. "Released from troubling memories of a past that weighed on France, the policies of European cabinets are taking a new direction. Germany, which no longer doubts that we will let its divisions go by without seeking to profit from them [*qui sait à n'en plus douter que nous laissions passer ses divisions sans chercher à en tirer profit*], can no longer sustain any jealousy in our regard. Prejudices are dissipating, nations are coming closer together, and every day one better appreciates that the system of economic solidarity inaugurated since 1860 was not mere verbiage."[114]

112   Quoted in M. Anderson, *The Rise of Modern Diplomacy 1450–1919* (London 1993) p. 190.
113   F. Laurent, *Études sur L'Histoire de L'Humanité: Les Nationalités* (Paris 1865) p. 48.
114   "Note pour l'exposé de la situation. – Nord. – Affaires d'Allemagne", 27 December 1866: *Les Origines Diplomatiques de la Guerre de 1870–1871*, Vol. XIII (Paris 1922) doc. 3977.

Not all Frenchmen or French statesmen were so sanguine, however. One acute French commentator, Louis Reybaud, attributed British desertion of its cherished commitment to the Balance of Power to the dominant influence of free trade. On this view the critics of the Balance of Power in London had finally won out, albeit posthumously. Reybaud was describing London's reluctance to act with force when France aided the dismemberment of Austrian power in Italy:

> England has recently presented a spectacle to which Europe has not been at all accustomed. It has been seen to assist, gun in hand, in a war which two Powers of the first order had engaged on the continent, exchanging notes while they exchanged gunfire. She has let them bring about the dismemberment of states, some pleasing, others repugnant, without intervening other than with official consent or vain remonstrations. From both sides of the Channel, this behaviour has excited some surprise, it has even provoked blame. The neglect, the abandonment of traditions were flagrant; some have gone so far as to talk of decline. This was no longer, they said, the policy of the Pitts and Castlereaghs, that which had aroused and raised spirits in long and painful struggles. This policy of another era in no way matched those compromises which accommodate difficulties instead of confronting them; it would in no way have given way to the kind of inertia that aims at cleverness but results in weakness [*vise à l'habilité et côtoie la faiblesse*]; it would have been better to act with firmer resolve, more determined to prevail. This is what the most severe critics have said.

Where did all this come from? The Manchester school, said the critics. "The accounts of a great state are not ordered like the inventory of a factory, where each object is valued only in respect of what it costs and what it returns", Reybaud continued, only on the surface playing the role of disinterested observer. When the men of the Manchester school had joined together twenty years before to fight the Corn Laws, "they well knew that the success of their reform would profoundly affect the politics of their country. This crisis occurred, and they persist in believing it to be healthy." They claimed that the interests upon which they relied were "merely the instrument of Christian and moral thought. In the development of commerce, they see above all the closest union of nations. More frequent interchange must lead to better behaviour; the more they know one another, the less will they be inclined to fall out and break off relations. In this work of conciliation neither the dominant classes nor governments have the right spirit: they jeopardise the peace and interests of the community; it was thus the community that they were addressing in calling for resistance to the taste for adventure familiar to the dominant classes and governments."[115]

115   L. Reybaud, "Économistes Contemporains: Richard Cobden et L'École de Manchester", *Revue des Deux-Mondes*, Vol. 27, 15 May 1860, pp. 257–9.

Warnings at a higher level came from former Foreign Minister and Prime Minister Adolphe Thiers, following the Austro-Prussian war to seize Schleswig-Holstein from Denmark in 1864. All of a sudden France – at least, one of its most vocal and articulate statesmen – discovered the virtues of the Balance of Power. Thiers also rediscovered what had hitherto been all but forgotten since 1648, namely "the old European principle that Germany should be composed of independent states", a principle which, he claimed, was "one of the great principles of European public law."[116] To bolster his case, Thiers also raised the spectre of Germany not merely reunified under Prussian arms but also linked to unified Italy. The process he described was initially that of interconnected but separate aims. "Italian unity (this is what I have always reproached him [Napoleon III] for), Italian unity had inevitably to lead to German unity, just as I indicated at the time, by the stages I pointed out to him [*avec les degrés que je lui assignais*], beginning this time with the direct reunification of a certain number of Germans, and indirectly of all the rest, under the hand of Prussia. Italian unity and Germany unity were bound to give each other a helping hand over the Alps, and today you see the realisation of the very phenomenon that I pronounced as unstoppable less than two years ago."[117] Thiers raised the alarm. This was, in his words, "a revolution" which France had the right to stop since it was directly threatened: "we will see the recreation of a new German empire, the empire of Charles V which previously stood in Vienna would now stand in Berlin, would be very close to our borders, would press upon them, would seal them; and, to complete the analogy, this empire of Charles V, instead of, as in the XV and XVI centuries, leaning on Spain for support, would lean upon Italy!"[118] Putting a suitably one-sided and patriotic colouring on two hundred years of history, Thiers went on to claim that France "fought for two centuries, from the time of that great day at Marignan in 1515 to those at Villaviciosa and Alamanza in 1707 and 1710, to divide the crown of Charles V, throwing half in the direction of Madrid, another in the direction of Vienna . . ." Had France accomplished so much "to destroy this colossus" just to see it rebuilt under its very eyes?[119]

Britain, under Gladstone, was inclined to knowing disdain. The prevailing sentiment was that the British had nothing to fear from the continent, which would, sooner or later, follow the islands into free trade, prosperity and peace. Liberal utopianism had triumphed. Nothing could dislodge the Prime Minister from aloof and complacent neutrality. Moreover London still considered Paris, if not a threat, then certainly no particular friend to British interests. Was not Napoleon III now paying for his own opportunism? Was it altogether wrong that some, at least, in France now recognised the virtues of the Balance of Power? As if to confirm British fears of the French, when Prussia finally decided to take the final step to reunification of Germany, Napoleon

---

116   Speech, 3 May 1866: *Discours Parlementaires de M. Thiers*, ed. M. Calmon, Vol. X (Paris 1881) p. 646.
117   Ibid., p. 618.
118   Ibid.
119   Ibid. p. 620.

threw caution to the winds and declared war. Britain remained neutral. Former Prime Minister Benjamin Disraeli, however, spoke from the opposition benches urgently calling for action, as had the French Cassandra Thiers. (It is remarkable how removal from the seat of power can clarify the mind.) With the approach of war, Disraeli, sensing "vast ambitions stirring in Europe", suggested a deal should be sought with Russia to deter France from attacking Prussia to forestall unification.[120]

Over-confident of winning, the French rapidly lost to the Prussian onslaught. Gladstone was remorseless in his bitter contempt. He readily acknowledged that "These events have upset . . . every joint of the compacted fabric of Continental Europe. There is not one considerable State, whose position and prospects were not funda-mentally modified between the 5th of August and the 5th of September. Of some States, indeed, they were more than modified. France had lost, at the latter date, the military primacy which she had borne at the former, and which she had loftily carried for two hundred and fifty years." He went on: "The dominant force of the European system has travelled from one point to another; the centre of gravity has shifted." But the appalling lack of judgement that Gladstone freely condemned in Napoleon III was as nothing compared with his own. The true impact on the Balance of Power in Europe he entirely missed. In its stead he focused on the positive. The final downfall of "the evil star of Napoleonism" was "a cause of congratulation to Europe". Defeat would, he concluded, sober France into becoming "the head of a pacific policy on the continent of Europe."

Gladstone's Panglossian perspective did not stop there. "On the whole, it seems rea-sonable to hope that the practical character of our Teutonic cousins, together with their huge actual mass of domestic sorrows, will assist them to settle down into a mood of peace and goodwill. But whether they do or not, it is idle to believe that they have before them a career of universal conquest or absolute predominance, and that the European family is not strong enough to correct the eccentricities of its peccant and obstreperous members." Gladstone characteristically placed all too great a weight upon "that lofty influence belonging to that general and fixed opinion entertained by civilised man, which happily in our times no state or nation, however powerful, can afford to disre-gard." Echoing Florus the epitomist and his liberal universalist successors (see below, p. 133), Gladstone opined that with all the countries of Europe "and with the vast multitudes of persons in each of them, we have constant relations both of personal and of commercial intercourse, which grow from year to year; and as, happily, we have no conflict of interests, real or supposed, nor scope for evil passions afforded by our peaceful rivalry, there is nothing to hinder the self-acting growth of concord." Indeed, Gladstone sought "to found a moral empire upon the confidence of the nations, not upon their fears, their passions, or their antipathies."[121]

120   Speech to the House, 1 August 1870: *Hansard's Parliamentary Debates*, 3rd series, Vol. CCIII (London 1870) cols. 1288 and 1292.
121   "Germany, France, and England", *Edinburgh Review*, Vol. CXXXII, October 1870, pp. 554–93.

This extraordinary misreading of the situation created by French defeat was by no means universally shared. Disraeli saw matters with great clarity and deep foreboding:

It is no common war, like the war between Prussia and Austria, or like the Italian war in which France engaged some years ago; nor is it like the Crimean War. This war represents the German revolution, a greater political event than the French revolution of last century. I don't say a greater or as great a social event. What its social consequences may be are in the future. Not a single principle in the management of foreign affairs, accepted by all states for guidance up to six months ago, any longer exists. There is not a diplomatic tradition which has not been swept away. You have a new world, new influences at work, new and unknown objects and dangers with which to cope, at present involved in that obscurity incident to novelty in such affairs. We used to have discussions in this House about the balance of power. Lord Palmerston, eminently a practical man, trimmed the ship of State and shaped its policy with a view to preserve an equilibrium in Europe . . . But what has really come to pass? The balance of power has been entirely destroyed . . .[122]

Later Disraeli identified this "German revolution" as "a great revolution in all our diplomatic relations" in which "the principles and traditions with respect to external affairs" were made "obsolete".[123]

At least in part, British indifference to French defeat at the hands of Prussia reflected London's imperial priorities. And as the European Powers embarked upon a further extension of their expansion across the burning line, the British, having called the bluff of the French at Sadowa, proceeded to mop up most of the continent of Africa largely unopposed. As in the previous century, with the expansion through North America, the Balance of Power, if applied as a containing principle of international relations, was not to rule out a universal empire overseas. The only obstacle to the onward march of British power and capital in southern Africa came from the descendants of Dutch settlers, the Boers. As the century turned, British forces attacked Transvaal, opening a war that did nothing for London's image abroad. Comment from Paris raised the core issue:

Another France than that of today would not have impassively facilitated what is going on in southern Africa, and, if it had concluded that it was unwilling or even unable to stand in the way, it should at least have taken precautions and it should have been given pledges against the disturbance that will result in the African balance; because there is not only henceforth a European balance, there is also an African balance and an Asiatic balance.[124]

122   Ibid.
123   Speech to the House, 24 February 1871: ibid., col. 840.
124   Francis Charmes, "Chronique de la Quinzaine", 31 October 1899: *Revue des Deux-Mondes*, LXIXe Année, Vol. 156, 1899, p. 240.

But was any Balance of Power being sustained? Memories of 1871 still fresh, the same commentator bitterly reflected: "Why should Europe intervene for the benefit of the African balance, when it has not intervened to maintain the European balance itself?"[125] The point was, though, that Britain would find it difficult to convince anyone that a Balance of Power should be maintained in Europe but not overseas, given the enormous reach of its imperial possessions and its insatiable appetite for still more.

After the defeat of the French at Sedan, the emergence of Germany in Europe over-shadowed all discussion of foreign policy in Paris. For so long the French had seen the Balance of Power as an instrument targeted directly at their interests and security; now they reinterpreted and adopted it as a sacrosanct principle that dovetailed with the eternal interests of the fatherland. There is nothing like the loss of power to sensitise a state to the value of power. For this reason if for no other, French officialdom viewed with deep scepticism the signature of the Hague convention in 1899. International arbi-tration had its positive aspect, wrote one anonymous senior French official in 1905, since it might make wars less frequent and less destructive; but it did not really deal with the fundamental problem. Wars were not, or at least no longer, the result of rulers' ambitions. "The time for wars of conquest for Europe has passed. But continuous contact of those great human societies called nations creates between them opposing interests, rivalries, differences, struggles that easily degenerate into wars."[126] What was international law anyway? The official then describes what later became known as the "pure theory of law" (see below, p. 191). The distribution of states within the European states system "above all has originated in wars, following which the situation respective to each State changes. The principles flowing from these actions, or serving as their basis, constitute the 'law' that is invoked later as the rule regulating differences that emerge between States in times of peace. But this law itself is not some abstract principle, fixed, preceding or leading the arrangements concluded between States. It flows from them, it is the consequence of them and constitutes merely the formula of the balance of power, led by war, the forces that find themselves in conflict. One must therefore admit, if not that force determines law, at least that it precedes it and that the latter emanates from it." Law was relative to the times: "As long as the treaties and arrangements in force correspond to the realities of power and the respective value of States, they are respected and there is peace."

In Britain Disraeli had interpreted the Balance of Power as a synonym for the struc-ture of the European states system. To him the "whole machinery of States" had been "dislocated".[127] The Foreign Office in London now raised the Balance as a banner beneath which to rally forces to deter a German advance. In a secret memorandum of 1907 the Senior Clerk, Eyre Crowe, elaborated the case for an alliance with France against Germany:

125   Ibid., 14 November 1899: ibid., p. 479.
126   Anonymous, "L'Équilibre Politique et La Diplomatie", *Revue des Deux-Mondes*, LXXVe Année, Vol. 30, 1 December 1905.
127   Speech to the House, 9 February 1871: *Hansard's*, Vol. CCIV, col. 93.

History shows that the danger threatening the independence of this or that nation has generally arisen, at least in part, out of the momentary predominance of a neighbouring State at once militarily powerful, economically efficient, and ambitious to extend its frontiers or spread its influence, the danger being directly proportionate to the degree of its power and efficiency, and to the spontaneity or "inevitableness" of its ambitions. The only check on the abuse of political predominance derived from such a position has always consisted in the opposition of an equally formidable rival, or of a combination of several countries forming leagues of defence. The equilibrium established by such a grouping of forces is technically known as the balance of power, and it has become almost an historical truism to identify England's secular policy with the maintenance of this balance by throwing her weight now in this scale and now in that, but ever on the side opposed to the political dictatorship of the strongest single State or group at a given time.

If this view of British policy is correct, the opposition into which England must inevitably be driven to any country aspiring to such a dictatorship assumes almost the form of a law of nature . . .[128]

The implementation of that policy cost the country a devastating loss of human life and capital resources. Gone was the awe-inspiring self-confidence of the eighteenth and nineteenth centuries. The sense in the postwar world was that any balance was difficult to sustain, resting as it did on such vulnerable foundations. Former diplomat Harold Nicolson caught the mood precisely in an uncharacteristically florid metaphor:

Ponderous and uncertain is that relation between pressure and resistance which constitutes the balance of power. The arch of peace is morticed by no iron tenons: the monoliths of which it is composed are joined by no cement. Impressive in their apparent solidity, these granite masses lean against each other, thrust resisting hidden thrust. Yet a swarm of summer bees upon the architrave, will cause a millimetre of displacement, will set these monoliths stirring against each other, unheard, unseen. One night a handful of dust will patter from the vaulting: the bats will squeak and wheel in sudden panic: nor can the fragile fingers of man then stay the rush and rumble of destruction.[129]

Yet the failure to sustain the Balance of Power from 1933 to 1939 almost cost Britain its independence. Either way, the Balance of Power as a prescription for policy clearly met the needs imposed upon Britain in the international system. As a form of explanation of state behaviour, however, it obviously captured only one side of the spectrum. The drive for universal empire lay elsewhere.

128   1 January 1907: *The Foreign Policy*, doc. 144.
129   H. Nicolson, *Public Faces: A Novel* (London and New York 1932) p. 99.

It would also be wrong to see the Balance of Power as the only determinant of policy, even in Britain. Commercial imperatives, which from the beginning of the twentieth century were sufficiently satiated to make the country the status quo Power par excellence, earlier drove Britain to seek a universal empire overseas. These imperatives also found form in the public debate of the time. Reasons of State surfaced in the literature of early modern Europe to accompany the emergence of the nascent nation-state. Writings on the Balance of Power in Europe appeared in order to avert the absorption of the sovereign state within a universal empire. The much-touted and traduced notion of the Balance of Trade similarly emerged to safeguard the interests of the state by economic means, but, like other philosophies of security, in its turn it became the justification for aggrandisement, and on a global scale. By 1763 the Italian writer Francesco Algarotti judged that "Trade is now giving rise to wars and the bases for treaties of peace, and is perhaps the most valid means of acquiring dominion or the most powerful counterweight with which to sustain the balance of Europe . . ."[130] Trade increasingly became a determinant of the weight in the balance. The Balance of Power thus came to hinge on the Balance of Trade.

130   F. Algarotti, "Saggio sopra il commercio", *Saggi* (Pisa 1763), ed. G. Da Pozzo (Bari 1963) pp. 442–3.

Chapter 3
THE BALANCE OF TRADE

"The Balance of Trade, I cannot too often repeat it, is in Fact the Balance of Power."

– Malachy Postlethwayt[1]

It may be argued that statesmen have always recognised wealth as the precondition for power. It may also be true that one does not have to be a practitioner and that mere common sense tells us that this is so. When US President Clinton visited Uganda in March 1998 he met pupils from Kisowera primary school. An eleven-year-old, Annie Nakayemba, commented that this was the president of the world. "He is more important than my president, because he has a bigger army and more money."[2] Yet not everyone always recognised the validity of Annie's intuition.

It was also said that in the days of ancient Rome the Emperor Vespasian's lieutenant Mucianus gathered "countless sums" into public coffers and "was for ever declaring that money was the sinews of sovereignty . . ."[3] But, as has been said of Reasons of State, commerce did not have anything like the same significance, in political terms, for the classical world as it came to acquire in modern Europe. Where, for example, are the great texts on economics from the libraries of Athens or Rome? Plato dismissed commerce from his *Republic* on moral grounds. Xenophon at one point insists that private enterprise be encouraged, but elsewhere doubts whether it is a good thing. Clearly there was no consensus on this point.[4]

By the fifteenth century the Venetians – known as the *signori delle coste* (Masters of the Coast) – founded their power on the growth of trade. Whereas wars between ancient Rome and Carthage were for the domination of Europe, those between Venice and Genoa were aimed at control over trade with Asia.[5] Mucianus' dictum thus became a commonplace in medieval Italy, though by no means a unanimous opinion.

---

1   M. Postlethwayt, *Great-Britain's True System* (London 1757) p. 234.
2   *Financial Times*, 25 March 1998.
3   *Dio's Roman History*, Vol. 8 (London 1961) p. 261.
4   F. Algarotti, "Saggi sopra il commercio", *Saggi* (Pisa 1763), ed. G. DaPozzo (Bari 1963) pp. 437–8.
5   Ibid., p. 439.

Machiavelli, for one, was singularly unimpressed: ". . . it is not gold, as public opinion cries, that is the nerves of war, but good soldiers: because there is insufficient gold to find good soldiers, but good soldiers are more than sufficient to find gold."[6]

Guicciardini, an experienced diplomat as well as a noted historian, most vehemently dissented from perverse interpretation of such sage advice. "Whoever was author of the sentence that money is the nerves of war . . . did not mean that money alone is sufficient to wage war, nor that it was more necessary than soldiers, because that would be not only a false opinion but also totally ridiculous; but it means that whoever wages war would have massive need of money and that, without it, it would be impossible to sustain a war, because not only is it necessary to pay the soldiers but provide arms, supplies, spies, munitions and all the means used in war . . . it is much easier to find soldiers with money than find money with soldiers."[7] But even Guicciardini's admirers were not always so ready to swallow his advice on these matters. They seized on his assertion that possession of wealth created another risk, that of dangerous complacency. Bacon reminded his sovereign, King James I, of Guicciardini's remark that the prosperity of "the wisest State of *Europe*, the Senate of *Venice*" had "made them secure, and underweighers of perils."[8] Moreover, Bacon generally considered "That there is too much ascribed to treasure or riches in the ballancing of greatness."[9] Indeed, he considered Machiavelli's scepticism justified. Were not the invading French armies "needie, and ill provided"?[10] Moreover "that verie text or saying of *Mutianus* which was the original of this opinion [that money was the sinews of war], is misvouched, for his Speech was *Pecuniae sunt nervi belli civilis*, which is true, for that civil Warres cannot be between people of differing valour; and againe, because in them men are as oft bought as vanquished. But", Bacon concludes, "in case of forrein Warres, you shall scarcelie find any of the great Monnarchies of the world, but have had their foundations in povertie and contemptible beginnings . . ."[11]; "most of the great Kingdomes of the World have sprung out of the hardness and scarceness of means, as the strongest herbs out of the barrenest soyles."[12]

Most, however, reflected on the advantages rather than disadvantages of greater wealth. Even Bacon was forced to acknowledge that, courage in place, it is better to have money for war rather than do without, but that "it be in those hands, where there is likest to be greatest sparing, and encrease, and not in those hands, wherein there useth to be greatest expence and consumption."[13] The Dutch were the most successful example. "Nothing is of greater importance for increasing the power of a

---

6   Book 2 of the Discourses: N. Machiavelli, *Il Principe e Discorsi*, ed. S. Bertelli (Milan 1960) p. 304.
7   "Considerazioni sui 'Discorsi' del Machiavelli", *Opere di Guicciardini*, Vol. 1, p. 661.
8   Letter of 31 July 1617: *Letters, Memoirs*, p. 56.
9   "Of the true greatness . . .", Ibid., p. 204.
10   Ibid., p. 205.
11   Ibid., pp. 205–6.
12   Ibid., p. 210.
13   Ibid., p. 211.

state and gaining for it more inhabitants and wealth of every kind than the industry of its people and the number of crafts they exercise"; "the power of a state is today judged as much by its wealth in money as by its size." So wrote the Venetian Giovanni Botero, author of *Della Ragion di Stato*.[14] The early economic counterpart to Reasons of State was the notion of the Balance of Trade, otherwise labelled mercantilism; later, protectionism.[15]

Before proceeding further it should be borne in mind that in the early modern age – certainly till Adam Smith and David Ricardo – no coherent science of economics existed. As Sir Francis Brewster noted in 1695,

I know no Subject that hath been more writ on, and worse handled, than that of Trade; nor is it to be wondred at, since it is the misfortune of that Mystery not to be in the hands of the Philosophers, or men bred to the Liberal Sciences; but such whose Education hath been more in the *Cantore*, than Schools: And when men of finer Heads and Studies engage in it, they commonly make Flights as far above the genuine Meaning and Nature of Trade, as others that are better versed in it do cover and deface it with Incoherence and Lumber.[16]

The ideas that did arise emerged directly from practice, and such practices as commercial protection were no stranger to government. In 1603 Gerrard de Malynes (*c.* 1586–1641) recalled that King Edward III of England "had a great care, that the forraine Commodities, should not over-ballance his home Commodities: knowing that if hee payed more for them, then he made of his Commodities, the difference must be made up and ballanced with the treasure or money of the realme."[17] The term Balance

---

14   G. Botero, *The Reason of State* (London 1956) pp. 134 and 150–1.
15   The standard basic text has long been E. Hecksher, *Mercantilism* (1934; reissued New York 1983), but for all its undoubted authority it is an unsympathetic and narrow treatment of the subject. For two effective attacks on Hecksher: D. Coleman, "Eli Hecksher and the Idea of Mercantilism", *Scandinavian Economic History Review*, Vol. V, No 1, 1957, pp. 3–25; and L. Herlitz, "The Concept of Mercantilism", ibid., Vol. XII, No 2, 1964, pp. 101–20. For accounts published much earlier than Hecksher which link the economics to the politics, see E. von Heyking, *Zur Geschichte der Handelsbilanz-theorie* (Berlin 1880), G. Schmoller, *The Mercantile System and its Historical Significance* (London 1896), and W. Cunningham, *The Growth of English Industry and Commerce* (Cambridge 1907, 1910). For an excellent survey of the early, English literature: Br. Suviranta, *The Theory of the Balance of Trade in England: A Study in Mercantilism*, Suomalaisen Tideackatemian Toimituksia, Annales (Helsinki 1923). Also, W. Minchinton, ed., *Mercantilism: System or Expediency?* (Lexington, Mass. 1969); D. Coleman, *Revisions in Mercantilism* (New York 1969); and, more recently, a view from economists: R. Ekelund and R. Tollison, *Politicized Economies: Monarchy, Monopoly, and Mercanatilism* (College Station, Texas, 1997). For current relevance: R. Gilpin, *The Political Economy of International Relations* (Princeton 1987).
16   *Essays on Trade and Navigation* (London 1695) p. i.
17   G. de Malynes, *Englands View, in the Unmasking of Two Paradoxes: With a replication unto the answer of Maister Iohn Bodine* (London 1603) p. 70.

of Trade was first expressed in print by the English merchant Edward Misselden (*c*. 1608–1654) in 1623:

> For as a paire of Scales or Ballance, is an Invention to shew us the waight of things, whereby we may discerne the heavy from the light, and how one thing differeth from another in the Scale of waight: So also this *Ballance of Trade*, an excellent and politique Invention, to shew us the difference of waight in the *Commerce* of one Kingdome with another: that is, whether the Native Commodities exported, and all the forraine Commodities Imported, doe ballance or overballance one another in the *Scale of Commerce*.
>
> If the Native Commodities exported doe waigh downe and exceed in value the forraine Commodities imported; it is a rule that never faile's, that then the Kingdome growe's rich, and prosper's in estate and stocke: because the overplus thereof must needs come in, in treasure.[18]

Whereas the doctrine of *laissez-faire* meant freeing the economy from governmental interference, sustaining the Balance of Trade required direct intervention to secure the national economy against competition from foreign rivals. A great deal of ink has been spilt in the attempt to differentiate mercantilism from protectionism, the most prominent argument being that the mercantilists believed in hoarding gold bullion for its own sake as against the industrial protectionists of the late modern era who were mainly concerned to protect the development of domestic manufacturing. This description accurately portrays a good deal of mercantilist thought, but by no means all of it. In fact the most prominent theorists of mercantilism of the seventeenth century had precisely the same objectives as had the protectionists of the nineteenth century.

Mercantilism came naturally to the nascent nation-state, though, as with all political reasoning, the process of articulating the ideas that lay behind it followed well behind practice. It was France that first gave birth to the elaboration of the case for economic protection. Ironically it was France that had first given birth to the enunciation of the principle of free trade, and it was the latter that came first. In his *Response à M. de Malestroit*, Jean Bodin put the argument for free trade in the context of a discussion of the impact of the importation of gold bullion from the New World upon the level of prices in the old, which was clearly inflationary. He wrote: ". . . the flow of trade . . . must be unimpeded and free to secure the wealth and greatness of a

---

18   E. M. Merchant, *The Circle of Commerce. OR The Ballance of Trade, in defence of free Trade: To Malynes Little Fish & his Great Whale, & poized against them in the Scale. Wherein also, Exchanges in generall are considered: & therein the whole Trade of this Kingdome with forraine Countries, is digested into a Ballance of Trade, for the benefite of the Publique. Necessary for the present and future times* (London 1623), p. 116.

kingdom [*le cours de la trafique . . . doibt estre franche et libre, pour la richesse et grandeur d'un royaume*]."[19] He also believed, and this was an opinion ultimately derived from the Roman epitomist Lucius Florus (see overleaf), that trade secured the friendship of other states; and his is the first written record of this idea in modern history.[20]

Bodin was far in advance of his time, initially much more liberal in his reaction to events than his contemporaries in France. Those events were the devastating wars of religion that tore the country apart and threatened the very existence of the state. When he wrote the *Response*, the wars of religion had yet to reach their appalling apogee; three waves (1569–70, 1572–3 and 1574–6) succeeded one another with brutal ferocity. This had its effect. By the time Bodin published the *Six livres* in 1576 no trace of this liberalism remained. Far from seeing trade as the healer of relations between states, he recommended war as a means of uniting the now badly divided nation. Thus the warlike and centralising tendency became most pronounced in French political and economic thought in the backwash to the wars of religion, in particular because France's weakness relative to that of its neighbours tolled against it in the brutal struggle for survival and competition that constituted the international relations of the day. And out of the window went any inclination to follow Bodin's initial precepts on trade.

These were the circumstances in which the first recorded coherent doctrine on mercantilism emerged in France from the pen of Barthélemy de Laffemas (1545–1611), who became the *contrôleur général du commerce* under Henry IV. Laffemas argued "It is very necessary to shut out these [foreign] manufactures so that the good and loyal merchants may be busy henceforth in causing to be made goods and products for the profit of France."[21] This was a natural economic complement to Bodin's call for strongly centralised government in the aftermath of the internecine wars of religion, which nearly destroyed France as a unitary kingdom. It also reflected the

---

19   *Les Paradoxes du Sergneur de Malestroict, conseiller du roy, & Maistre ordinaire de ses comptes, sur le faict des Monnoyes, presentez a Sa Maieste, au mois de Mars, M. D. LXIV, Avec la response de M. Iean Bodin in ausdicts paradoxes* (Paris 1568), reprinted in Paris 1932 in an edition by Hauser from the Sorbonne Under the title *La Response de Jean Bodin à M. de Malestroit 1568* p. 35.

20   ". . . *deverions nous tousjours trafiquer, vendre, achepter, echanger, prester, voire plustost donner une partie de nos biens aux etrangers, et mesmes a noz voisins, quand ce ne seroit pour communiquer et entretenir une bonne amitie entre eux et nous.*" – ibid., p. 33. He also applied this notion to domestic society: "*ce que Dieu semble avoir fait, pour entre-tenir tous les sujets de sa republique en amitie, ou pour lemoins empechere qu'ils ne se facent longtemps la guerre, ayans tousjours afaire les uns des autres.*" – ibid., p. 34.

21   Quoted in C. Cole, *Colbert and a Century of French Mercantilism*, Vol. 1 (New York 1939) p. 31. The assertion commonly made is that the true originator of mercantilism in economic thought is Antonio Serra of Cosenza, author of the *Breve trattato delle cause che possono far abbondare li regni d'oro et d'argento dove non sono miniere* (Napoli 1613). But this volume passed unnoticed by contemporaries and did not reach public attention until it was reprinted in 1780 by Galiani: *Enciclopedia italiana di scienze, lettere ed arti* (Roma 1936–44) p. 454.

extraordinary growth in European trade, which hastened the development of primitive manufacturing and thereby accentuated existing commercial rivalry between the major Powers. Bodin was immediately succeeded by Antoine de Montchrétien (1575/6–1621) whose xenophobic *Traicte de l'oeconomie politique*, published in 1615, built upon his predecessor's legacy: "Let Your Majesties make the experiment and forbid the importation of many articles which are made by the skill of men, and let no raw materials and products be exported from this realm, and you will have the satisfaction of seeing that your State has as many resources, natural and acquired, as it needs to get on well and live well."[22] Not so many years later, Montchrétien was killed as a Huguenot and his work all but disappeared from the libraries of Paris[23]; but the legacy lingered in the corridors of power.

These ideas did not go unchallenged. But it was no accident that the strongest and most consistent case for industrial protection originated within a state that was faltering economically after civil war and in the face of strong foreign competition; nor should it come as a surprise to learn that the argument for freeing trade from customs duties designed to protect the domestic economy should at this point come from within those states that were doing the damage. Sir Thomas Overbury noted at the beginning of the seventeenth century with respect to the Dutch that that "whereupon the most part of their revenue and strength depends, is their traffick; in which mystery of state they are at this day the wisest."[24] Although by no means a political economist, Grotius started where Bodin had left off and took up with approval the argument of Lucius Florus advocating free trade for its supposed contribution to international peace: "So Florus," Grotius wrote, "*Take away Commerce, & you break the Bond that ties Mankind together.*"[25]

English writers did not link trade to politics in this idealistic manner. Not until the latter half of the eighteenth century did an explicit connection of this kind re-emerge, and not until after the Napoleonic Wars did it become integrated in Britain with an entire political philosophy. But there were those who complained, as early as 1645, that: "Those immunities which were granted in the infancy of trade, to incite people to the increase or improvement of it, are not so proper for these times, when the trade is come

---

22 Ibid., p. 95.
23 We are told that his book was put on reserve at the Bibliothèque Nationale and that the only other library in Paris which held a copy was the Mazarine in later years: Th. Funck-Brentano, "La Diplomatie et L'Économie Politique", *Revue D'Histoire Diplomatique*, No 1, 1887, p. 237.
24 *Sir Thomas Overbury's Observations in his Travels, upon the State of the Seventeen Provinces, as they stood, Anno Domini 1609; the Treaty of Peace being then on Foot* (Published in 1626). Reprinted in the *Harleian Miscellany*, Vol. 8, p. 363.
25 H. Grotius, *The Rights of War & Peace in Three Books. Wherein are explained, The Law of nature & Nations, and the Principal Points relating to Government* (English translation edited by Barbeyrac, London 1737). Florus' text read: ". . . *sublatisque commerciis, rupto foedere generis humani . . .*" – Lucius Annaeus Florus, *Epitome of Roman History*, edited and translated by E. Forster (Cambridge, Mass., 1984) p. 190.

to that height of perfection . . ."[26] By this time England was beneficiary of the Thirty Years' War.[27] The situation was well described by Sir Thomas Culpepper:

> the Dutch had then their hands full of their war with Spayne which (although Prosperous enough) was some curb to their growth in Commerce; Germany was so harassed and embroy'd, that it could neither Trade nor Till; Sweden was a mere limb of the French interest; we alone (sitting under the shadow of our own Vines) might afford to give them all great Odds, for all the Markets of the World were full of our Growth, and thin of theirs . . .[28]

When the treaties were signed in Westphalia, however, and peace returned to the European sub-continent, the resurgence in the trade of England's traditional rivals led to a sharpened awareness of the importance of economic factors in world power and a vigorous debate about the degree to which the state should intervene.

The resurgence in France was due not least to Louis XIV's new Minister, Jean-Baptiste Colbert (1619–83), who took full power in 1661. No original thinker, Colbert none the less applied mercantilist principles with a rigour and energy previously unseen. The emphasis was on manufactures as a means to wealth as a path to power. "The trading companies are armies of the King and the manufactures of France his reserves", Colbert is quoted as saying.[29] He summed up the new economic philosophy in a notorious aphorism which captures the spirit of international relations in the seventeenth and eighteenth centuries and so clearly distinguishes the protectionist from the free trader in terms of politics: "I must add that commerce causes a perpetual conflict in peace and war between the nations of Europe, which the best party will win."[30]

Only two years after attaining power, Colbert drew up a damning indictment of France's failure hitherto to sustain a positive balance of trade. Up to 1620, he argued, England and Holland did not manufacture their own cloth; they sent raw fabric to

---

26   Quoted in J. Viner, "English theories of foreign trade before Adam Smith", *Journal of Political Economy*, Vol. 38, August 1930, No 4, p. 417.

27   The collapse of export earnings in the early 1620s does not appear to have continued into the 1640s. For the best account: J. Gould, "The Trade Depression of the Early 1620's", *The Economic History Review*, Vol. VII, No 1, Second Series, 1954, pp. 81–90.

28   *A Discourse Showing the Many Advantages by the Abatement of Usuary*: quoted in R. Conquest, "The State and Commercial Expansion: England in the Years 1642–1688", *Journal of European Economic History*, Vol. 14, No 1, January–April 1985, p. 157.

29   Quoted in P. Boissonnade, *Colbert: Le Triomphe de l'Étatisme. La Fondation de la Suprématie industrielle de la France. La Dictature du Travail (1661–1683)* (Paris 1932) p. 6.

30   "Dissertation sur la question: quelle des deux alliances de France ou de Hollande peut estre plus avantageuse a L'Angleterre." March 1669: *Lettres, Instructions et Mémoires de Colbert. Publies d'après les ordres de l'empereur sur la proposition de son excellence M. Magne, Ministre Secrétaire d'état des Finances*, Vol. 6, ed. P. Clement (Paris 1869) doc. 33, p. 266.

France for processing. Thereafter, due to the war, want of effort and many other factors, France had fallen behind. "In such a manner that before the people made a lot from manufactures (no money left the kingdom as a result of this trade and, on the contrary, a lot came in) at the present time the people make nothing (a lot of money leaves the kingdom and nothing at all comes in)."[31] Not only did Colbert launch a series of companies and regulations designed to further manufactures and trade, he also pressed forcefully for the creation of a powerful merchant marine to capture overseas trade. The opposition argued that a Great Power like France should not soil its hands in such business: "Powerful States have never applied themselves to trade . . . so that this kind of effort is characteristic of weak States . . ."[32] Colbert's answer lay in the example of the Venetians, who had dominated trade with the East until 1480, when alternative routes were opened by the voyages of discovery. Then there were the Dutch who had then taken the commanding role, while France was caught up in civil war and wars of religion and Spain was obsessed with universal monarchy, its eyes focused on Europe. What France had to do was to follow the Dutch.

The obsession with matching the other leading Powers and, indeed, surpassing them drove Colbert in search of every conceivable means of advantage whatever its provenance. An illustration of this is a letter to his brother, ambassador in London, on 20 March 1669:

as . . . it is a subject of the first importance which always touches every issue in England, always bend your efforts towards focusing on and penetrating everything that can throw light on what is good and of advantage in trade, together with the reasons for its growth and of its decline. It is absolutely certain that the extreme greed and the tyrannical manner with which the Dutch conduct trade gives great cause for complaint against them from the English and from every nation in Europe.

Colbert went on to instruct his brother to check on the level of demand for various goods and added, for good measure, the cautionary advice that it was "very important to handle this kind of matter in great secrecy, more especially because, by our efforts, we are learning from foreigners that which it would be very convenient that they were unaware of. I believe you know well enough that these kinds of matters are important to kingdoms."[33]

As to the Dutch, Colbert was by no means the first to introduce the notion of power to the world of commerce. "It is a received aphorism amongst the Hollanders, that the flourishing condition of England is a diminution of their glory; also, that trade, and the

---

31   "Discours sur les manufactures du royaume", 1663: *Lettres et Mémoires*, Vol. 2, Part 1 (Paris 1863) pp. cclvii–cclviii.
32   "Mémoire sur le commerce", 3 August 1664: ibid., p. cclxvi.
33   To Colbert de Croissy, Ambassadeur en Angleterre, 20 March 1669: *Lettres et Mémoires*, Vol. 2, Part 2, doc. 37.

repute of strength, are inseparably linked together . . ."[34] Colbert took the lesson further, to the notion of the Balance of Power. Of the Dutch, he wrote:

they use . . . every means, all their power and all their industry to place in their hands alone the trade of the whole world and to deprive every other nation of it. On which they establish the principal maxim of their government, knowing full well that in so far as they are masters of trade, their land forces and their naval forces will grow continuously and render them so powerful, that they could make themselves the arbiters of peace and of war in Europe and set the limits, such as they please, to the justice and to all the plans of kings.[35]

Trade, in other words, was power and the means to the political domination of Europe. Colbert then advocated a balance:

The political maxims of the greatest princes have always been that it could never be advantageous for a weak prince to ally voluntarily with a prince much more powerful than himself, for fear that his power overwhelm and destroy him, as has happened so many times; but that the same sense of caution requires that the weak princes work always to maintain an equal balance by allying with the nearest Power to hinder too great an expansion [*accroisement*] of the other.

   In applying the same maxims to the matter in question: the Dutch are the most powerful in trade that there are and ever have been in the world, the English are weaker, and the French infinitely so; therefore prudence dictates that neither of these two States should ally with the Dutch, for fear that instead of benefiting their trade, it would be overwhelmed and entirely destroyed; and the same prudence dictates that the two States should join together out of interest to use all their industry to fight a secret war on the trade of the Dutch . . .[36]

One could scarcely conceive of more convincing evidence of the degree to which economic supremacy had become consciously vital to world power and the degree to which its acquisition was seen as a purely zero-sum game. Colbert, indeed, proved so successful that it was not long before the English were turning to France as a model for advancement. This was, indeed, in the words of the Marquis de Condorcet, "a time when mercantile Machiavellianism was, for the politicians of Europe, almost a new form of knowledge [*science*] in which they honoured themselves in self-instruction and in making discoveries."[37]

---

34   *A Justification* . . . : *Harleian Miscellany*, p. 129.
35   "Dissertation . . .": *Lettres et Mémoires*, Vol. 6, p. 264.
36   Ibid., p. 266.
37   *Oeuvres complètes de Condorcet*, Vol. IV (Paris 1804) p. 210.

First came the recognition that England was falling behind. Sir William Temple, as envoy to the Hague, gained invaluable first-hand knowledge of the conditions that favoured the rise of the Netherlands as the leading trading Power. Temple noted the emergence of Venice, Lombardy, then Antwerp and Lisbon as the successive centres of commerce within Europe and between Europe and the East. "But in all this Time," he pointed out, "the other and greater Nations of *Europe* concerned themselves little in it; their Trade was War . . ."[38] "In short," he continued, "the Kingdoms and Principalities were in the World like the Noblemen and Gentlemen in a Country; the Free-States and Cities, like the Merchants and Traders: These at first despised by the others; the other served and revered by them; 'till, by the various Course of Events in the World, some of these came to grow Rich and Powerful by Industry and Parsimony; and some of the others, poor by War and by Luxury: Which made the Traders begin to take upon them, and carry it like Gentlemen; and the Gentlemen begin to take a Fancy of falling to Trade."[39]

All this changed with the Peace of Westphalia. "For since the Peace of *Munster*, which restored the Quiet of Christendom in 1648, not only *Sweden* and *Denmark*, but *France* and *England*, have more particularly, than ever before, busied the Thoughts and Counsels of their several Governments, as well as the Humours of their People, about the Matters of Trade."[40] The explanation was obvious. In recognition of the need to assess the Balance of Power, states had become more than ever conscious – not least with the spectacular rise and decline of Spain, and now the equally meteoric rise and decline of Holland, of the role of the economic component. As Temple noted, "The Decay and Dissolution of Civil, as well as Natural Bodies, proceeding usually from outwards Blows and Accidents, as well as inward Distempers or Infirmities, it seems equally necessary for any Government to know and reflect upon the Constitutions, Forces, and Conjunctures among their Neighbouring States, as well as the Factions, Humours, and Interests of their own Subjects: For all Power is but comparative; nor can any Kingdom take a just Measure of its Safety by its own Riches or Strength at Home, without casting up at the same Time, what Invasions may be feared, and what Defences expected from Enemies or Allies Abroad." Thus, as he wrote, "Trade is grown the Design of all Nations in *Europe*."[41]

This was not least the reason why Temple published an assessment of the causes of Dutch supremacy and decline in his *Observations upon the United Provinces of the Netherlands* in 1672. There he highlighted the fact that the Dutch had few natural advantages for a thriving economy, and that indeed their very disadvantages, most

38   Temple, *Observations . . .* , *Works*, Vol. 1, p. 68.
39   Ibid.
40   Ibid., p. 67.
41   *A Survey of the Constitutions and Interests of the Empire, Sweden, Denmark, Spain, Holland, France, and Flanders; with their Relation to England, in the Year 1671* – Temple, *Works*, Vol. 1 (Miscellanea, Part I) p. 83.

notably a large population packed into a small space, vulnerable to inundation from the sea, had impelled them into ingenuity and trade with the outside world as the only means to prosperity. With the rest of Europe embroiled in the Thirty Years' War, and with England distracted by civil war, the Dutch had seized their chance to dominate trade. But with peace, and the return of rivals to the market, the Netherlands had fallen as rapidly as it had risen.

Temple's concerns were taken up by others, equally involved in the affairs of state. The author of *Some Considerations About the Commission for Trade*, since identified as government adviser Benjamin Worsley, argued forcefully:

> Trade . . . Being well understood by our neighbours, and made so much the Concerne of them as they now place the very vigilant part of their Interest and Government in it this seems to take away all choice from us, and to lay a necessity now Inevitable upon us; That eyther we must leade this great and general affayre of State by making ourselves the Masters of Commerce or Keeping up an Equality a least in it; Or we must be content to be lead by it and humbled under the power of them that have the ability to Rule and Governe it.[42]

Similarly strong opinions were expressed by Charles D'Avenant two decades later, with exports still in relative decline. He argued in terms of Reasons of State. Commerce was the key to political power:

> For war is quite changed from what it was in the time of our forefathers; when in a hasty expedition, and a pitched field, the matter was decided by courage; but now the whole art of war is in a manner reduced to money; and now-a-days, that prince, who can best find money to feed, cloath, and pay his army, not he that has the most valiant troops, is surest of success and conquest.
>
> . . . For the profit from trade is not the advantage the merchant makes at home, but whatt the whole nation gets clear and nett, upon the balance in exchange with other countries of its commodities and manufactures.
>
> So that if we can protect our trade to that degree as to be the gainers by the general balance, the expence and length of the war will not so much affect us . . .[43]

D'Avenant made plain that France was a model to follow:

> A nation that by its whole dealing gets in the general balance, visibly encreases in strength and power, as the northern kingdoms have done since the war, and as

---

42   Quoted in Conquest, "The State . . .", p. 155.
43   "An Essay upon Ways and Means", 1695: *The Political and Commercial Works of that celebrated Writer Charles D'Avenant, Ll.D. Relating to the Trade and Revenue of England, The Plantation Trade, The East-India Trade, And African Trade. Collected and revised by Sir Charles Whitworth, Members of Parliament*, Vol. 1 (London 1771) pp. 16–17.

England and Holland did before it; and a country that by its dealings loses at the foot of the account, does visibly grow weak and decline, as Spain has done for these last 60 years; and of this matter, such as have not been bred merchants are as competent judges as any trading person Whatsoever; for it was to the deep judgements of the ministers of state, Richelieu and Colbert, and not to the merchants, that France owes the prosperity their trade was lately in, and it was their wisdom, more than the industry of their merchants, that laid the foundation of it.[44]

D'Avenant may be described as an advocate of very limited protection. He was against the "bullionists", who were also severely castigated by free traders like Sir Dudley North (1641–91) and Nicholas Barbon (1640–98).

In 1691 North wrote an eloquent pamphlet, *Discourses upon Trade*, which resounds with phrases that foreshadow the writings of the Physiocrats (see p. 142) and Adam Smith. He attacked the notion of the Balance of Trade head on, arguing, inter alia, that "whenever Men consult for the Publick Good, as for the advancement of Trade, wherein all are concerned, they usually esteem the immediate Interest of their own to be the common Measure of Good and Evil." And North's commitment to free trade as stated must have sounded curiously out of place in Colbert's world of commercial war: "Now it may appear strange to hear it said," he wrote, anticipating the sharp intake of breath in surprise, "That the whole World as to Trade, is but as one Nation or People, and therein Nations are as Persons." He added: "That the loss of a Trade with one Nation, is not that only, separately considered, but so much of the Trade of the World rescinded and lost, for all is combined together."[45]

Five years later Barbon published a forceful and lucid attack on bullionism in particular, and protection in general. His argument against the notion of the Balance of Trade rested almost entirely on grounds of practicability. On his view it was next to impossible to make an accurate calculation of the trade balance, even from customs receipts, not least because what we now call "invisibles" (banking, insurance and shipping) were not centrally recorded. Two of Barbon's maxims struck his French successors and undoubtedly Adam Smith as essential truths: "For a Nation, as a Nation, never Trades; t'is only the Inhabitants & Subjects of each Nation that Trade . . ."[46]; "For all Merchants get by their Trade; & if they grow rich, the Nation thrives."[47]

Barbon was followed by the merchant John Cary in *An Essay on the State of England, In Relation to its Trade, Its Poor, and its Taxes, For carrying on the present war against*

---

44   "Discourses on the Public Revenues, and on the Trade of England. Which more immediately treat of the Foreign Traffic of this Kingdom. Pt. 2" (no date): ibid., pp. 386–7.

45   *Discourses upon Trade; Principally Directed to the Cases of the Interest, Coynage, Clipping, Increase of Money* (London 1691), Preface.

46   N. Barbon, *A Discourse Concerning Coining the New Money lighter. IN Answer to Mr. Lock's Considerations about raising the Value of Money* (London, 1696) p. 36.

47   Ibid., p. 4.

FRANCE, published in 1695. Here Cary set his argument for free trade in the context of a discussion of tariffs levied on tobacco from America. "I do not think", he wrote, "new Imposts upon the Importer will so much advance Your Majesty's Revenue as they will discourage the Merchant, 'twould be better to take away those already laid, & instead thereof to raise a far greater Summ on the Consumer . . ."[48] He found it "strange that a Nation whose Wealth depends on Manufactures, & whose Interest is to outdo all others . . . should load either [imports or exports] with Taxes."[49] Cary was in turn followed by Defoe, who, through his journal *Mercator*, in 1713 protested at those blocking a commercial treaty with France now that the War of the Spanish Succession had been won. "How Trade came to be embarass'd with the Strifes and Contentions of Nations, is not easy to learn; and that it is so with us, is the great Misfortune and Disaster of this Nation", *Mercator* protested. Defoe, raising the principle of "the Reason of Trade", even went so far as to object to economic blockade in time of war. "To bar up Trade with a Nation because we differ in State-Matters and Politick Interests, is the greatest Absurdity that a Nation can be guilty of."[50] This was the doctrine said to have first been coined by a merchant in conversation with Colbert: *laissez-nous faire*.[51] Neither Barbon nor Cary came out explicitly for free trade. But the attack on bullionism – "Gold & Silver are but Commodities; & one sort of Commodity is as good as another, so it be of the same value"[52] – and on mercantilist practices in general – "there is nothing so prejudicial to the Trade of *England*, as the many Laws for prohibiting Commodities, or laying too high a Duty, which amounts to Prohibition"[53] – leave little doubt where Barbon stood in the debate.

Nothing could have been further from the mind of Colbert or closer to the spirit of Adam Smith, a century later. But this was still the minority view. One perspicacious foreign observer in 1763 pointed to the Navigation Acts, which required all British goods to be transported in British bottoms, and the Corn Laws, which protected British grain production, as the basis for "that immense power by means of which they [the British] now wage offensive war in all four parts of the world, and in all four have triumphed and are triumphant still."[54] The greater part of the eighteenth century was in fact given over to a series of wars fought against the French largely, if not entirely, for commercial reasons: notably the Seven Years' War (1756–62). Colbert was the model, the French the threat, in the British justification. Quoting Colbert, in his enquiry into

48   John Cary, *An Essay on the State of England, In Relation to its Trade, Its Poor, and its Taxes, For carrying on the present War against FRANCE* (Bristol 1695), preface addressed to the King.
49   Ibid., pp. 23–4.
50   *Mercator: or Commerce Retrieved: being Considerations on the State of the British Trade, &c.*, 23–25 July 1713.
51   D. Stewart, *Biographical Memoirs, of Adam Smith, LL.D of William Robertson, D. D. and of Thomas Reid, D. D.* (Edinburgh) p. 142.
52   Barbon, *A Discourse*, p. 40.
53   Ibid., p. 42.
54   Algarotti, "Saggio . . .", p. 441.

"the *secret Causes* of the *present Misfortunes* of the Nation", Postlethwayt commented: "Thus commerce is to bring in riches, the treasures of the Indies; and these are to be employed in raising armies and navies, and making the world their own . . . Conquest is the design of the French; trade is only attended to as the instrument."[55] The British victory in the Seven Years' War assured control over North America. In the debate on the peace treaty in the House of Commons at the end of 1762 it was generally agreed that "the original object of the war was the security of our colonies upon the continent . . ."[56] The government's supporters "shewed the great increase of population in those colonies within a few years. They shewed that their trade with the mother country had uniformly increased with this population. That being now freed from the molestation of enemies and the emulation of rivals, unlimited in their possessions, and safe in their persons, our American planters would, by the very course of their natural propagation in a very short time, furnish out a demand of our manufactures as large as all the working hands of Great Britain could possibly supply. That there was therefore no reason to dread that want of trade which their adversaries insinuated, since North America alone would supply the deficiencies of our trade in every other part of the world. They expatiated on the great variety of climates which the country contained, and the vast reasons which would thence arise to commerce. That the value of our conquests thereby ought not to be estimated by the present produce, but by their probable increase. Neither ought the value of any country to be solely tried on its commercial advantages . . ." MPs spoke then in pride of Britain as "a great, powerful, and warlike nation."[57] Victory enabled the full implementation of protectionist measures to Britain's commercial advantage (and to the disadvantage of the colonists). As Edmund Burke described it, "These colonies were evidently founded in subservience to the commerce of Great Britain. From this principle, the whole system of our laws concerning them became a system of restriction. A double monopoly was established on the part of the parent country: 1. a monopoly of their whole import, which is to be altogether from Great Britain; 2. a monopoly of all their export, which is to be no where but to Great Britain, as far as it can serve any purpose here. On the same idea it was contrived that they should send all their products to us raw, and in their first state; and that they should take every thing from us in the last stage of manufacture."[58]

The irony is that the France that produced Colbert, the ultimate expression of protectionist ideas, went on to produce its precise antithesis in the century that followed. A further irony, in an age of perpetual wars over trade between London and

---

55   M. Postlethwayt, *Britain's Commercial Interest Explained and Improved; In a Series of Dissertations on Several Important Branches of her Trade and Police: containing A Candid Enquiry into the secret Causes of the present Misfortunes of the Nation. With Proposals for their Remedy. Also The Great Advantages which would accrue to this Kingdom from a Union with Ireland*, Vol. 2 (London 1757) pp. 360–1.

56   9 December 1762: *Parliamentary History of England*, Vol. XV (London 1813) col. 1271.

57   Ibid., col. 1272.

58   *The Works of the Right Honourable Edmund Burke*, Vol. 1 p. 371.

Paris, was that the French Physiocrats drew on English writers for the development of their conception of free trade in a debt openly acknowledged.[59] Most notable among the Physiocrats were François Quesnay (1694–1774), Anne-Robert Turgot (1727–81), and Victor de Riqueti, the Marquis de Mirabeau (1715–89). France, following the triumphs of Louis XIV, was economically a much more assertive Power, particularly after the eclipse of Dutch naval predominance. Quesnay in particular took Barbon one step further and denied the application of the principle of nationality to trade and traders altogether. "The businessman is a foreigner without a country", he wrote. He referred off the cuff to "so-called *national* businessmen"[60] and, a decade later, he wrote of "the universal republic of business strewn across different countries . . . little nations purely engaged in business who are merely parts of this immense republic and who can be looked upon as the capital cities or, if you wish, the main counters . . ."[61] Similarly Mirabeau wrote that the businessman must regard "the world as his country."[62]

The increasingly secular and particularist European states system had emerged from the all-embracing and notionally unitary *corpus christianum*. Political thinking moved to the particular rather than the universal, and horizons narrowed rather than broadened. Economic thought in contrast took the opposite direction. Out of the shell of particularism – that of mercantilism – appeared a new political economy that was rightly described as cosmopolitan in outlook and in aim, prefigured by the Physiocrats and taken into Britain by leading figures of the Scottish enlightenment, notably David Hume (1711–76) and Adam Smith (1723–90). As the Italian historian Fanfani noted with regard to the Physiocrats and the leaders of the Scottish enlightenment: "The two groups move on the same level, but in different directions."[63] The Physiocrats, of course, themselves borrowed from the more liberal tradition in Britain. But, as Leslie Stephen pointed out, the writers within that tradition were themselves far from consistent: "For one moment they reach an elevation from which they can contemplate the planet as a whole, and at the next moment their vision is confined to the horizon visible from an English shop-window."[64]

Hume took the notion of the Balance of Trade and, instead of using it to justify protectionist policies, argued that like water the balance would naturally find its own level if allowed to move without hindrance. Like his friend and successor Smith, he unconsciously articulated a British national interest, that of the only real industrial

59   See Turgot's acknowledgement in his elogy to Vincent de Gourney: *Oeuvres de Turgot*, Vol. 3 (Paris 1808), cited in Stewart, *Biographical Memoirs*, p. 139.
60   Quesnay, *Du Commerce* (Paris 1766): quoted in Silberner, *La Guerre*, p. 197.
61   "Analyse du Tableau économique", in F. Quesnay, *Oeuvres économiques et philosophiques* ed. A. Oncken (Paris 1888) pp. 326–7.
62   Mirabeau, *Les Économiques* (Amsterdam 1769): ibid., p. 214.
63   A. Fanfani, *Storia delle dottrine economiche: Il naturalismo* (2nd edition, Milan, 1946) p. 143.
64   L. Stephen, *History of English Thought in the Eighteenth Century*, Vol. 2 (1962 edition) p. 253.

power which could undercut everyone in their own market, as a universal interest in favouring free trade. And as with Smith the connexion between the two becomes most apparent when an exception is found to the golden rule. Hume attacked the prevalence of protectionist and mercantilist practices throughout Europe, Britain included, though he typically reflected British national interests in allowing for particular tariffs – for example on German linen – that would encourage home manufacture "and thereby multiplies our people and industry."[65]

The vantage-point of the new political economy devised by Smith in *An Inquiry into the Nature & Causes of the Wealth of Nations* was both individualistic and universal. The level that it almost entirely obliterated was that of the nation-state, with very few exceptions. The mercantilists focused on the power of the state relative to that of other states. Smith, on the other hand, was interested only in the origins of wealth, not in its utility in international relations. This is the key difference between the mercantilist and the free trader.[66] Smith's angle of vision was essentially that of the individual property-holder and there was a distinctly moralistic undertone to the apparently pragmatic advice offered to the powers that be. "To give the monopoly of the home-market to the produce of domestick industry, in any particular art or manufacture, is in some measure to direct private people in what manner they ought to employ their capitals, and must, in almost all cases, be either a useless or a hurtful regulation."[67]

Smith had a clear political and moral agenda. And unless one absorbs the tremendous impact of the Seven Years' War fought exclusively for commercial gain, it is difficult to appreciate just how radical were his views. His interpretation of the laws of economic behaviour, for good or ill, derived directly from his ideals. His friend and biographer Dugald Stewart noted the "connection between his system of commercial politics, and those speculations of his earlier years, in which he aimed more professedly at the advancement of human improvement and happiness."[68] And Stewart remarked upon the fact that Smith's comments "with respect to the jealousy of commerce are

---

65   D. Hume, "Of the Balance of Trade", in *Essays and Treatises on Several Subjects*, Vol. 4 (London 1754) pp. 73–86.
66   This point is made with the greatest clarity by the Cambridge economic historian and tariff reformer William Cunningham, *The Growth of English Industry and Commerce in Modern Times* (Cambridge 1882) p. 434. Subsequent editions cover more ground than the original, but they in no way alter the interpretation.
67   A. Smith, *An Inquiry into the Nature & Causes of the Wealth of Nations* (London 1776) p. 36.
68   D. Stewart, *Biographical Memoirs*, p. 87. For more on what the German historian Oncken coined "Des Adam Smith Problem" (*Zeitschrift für Socialwissenschaft*, 1878), see the introduction to Smith's book by Edwin Cannan, who originally uncovered notes of Smith's lectures which preceded the trip to France to meet the Physiocrats: E. Cannan (ed.), *An Inquiry into the Nature and Causes of The Wealth of Nations*, Vol. 1 (London 1904; reprinted 1950), and for more of the context: I. Hont and M. Ignatieff (eds.), *Wealth and Virtue: The Shaping of Political Economy in the Scottish Enlightenment* (Cambridge 1983).

expressed in a tone of indignation, which he seldom assumes in his political writings".[69] Observe Smith's attack on the "Mercantile System":

> the sneaking arts of underling tradesmen are erected into political maxims for the conduct of a great empire. By such maxims as these, nations have been taught that their interest consisted in beggaring all their neighbours. Each nation has been made to look with an invidious eye upon the prosperity of all the nations with which it trades, and to consider their gain as its own loss.[70]

Echoing Florus, Grotius and the Physiocrats, Smith wrote: "Commerce, which ought naturally to be, among nations, as among individuals, a bond of union & friendship, has become the most fertile source of discord & animosity."[71] War was, on this view, a direct consequence of protection. Freeing trade would liberate the world from the lethal consequences of inter-state rivalry which so scarred European life in the eighteenth and preceding centuries: "Were all nations to follow the liberal system of free exportation & free importation, the different states into which a great continent was divided would so far resemble the different provinces of a great empire."[72] This was the rebirth of the notion of universal empire, one based not on a unifying religion or under a unifying hegemony of one Power, but under the disinterested unifying power of capital. This vision was then further extended, in continental Europe, by Smith's great populariser, Jean-Baptiste Say, a collaborator of Mirabeau at the *Courrier de Provence* and one of the manufacturers ruined by Napoleon's Continental System.[73] In Britain the cudgels were taken up by David Ricardo, and Whig Radicals such as the young Palmerston and, perhaps better remembered, Cobden and Bright. Of course, this "disinterested" approach just happened to match the current interests of the world's only major manufacturer: Great Britain. That Smith was not entirely uninfluenced by the country's specific needs is apparent in more explicit fashion. At least one of the only two exceptions he would grant to the need for free trade was not unnaturally entirely in the British interest: the demands of defence, requiring a monopoly of the carrying trade at sea (the Navigation Acts). As an admirer of Smith, the French political economist Charles Genilh, rather uncharitably noted, "This manner of viewing the English act [sic] of Navigation betrays in the author a greater attachment to his country than to truth."[74]

Say was, like Misselden but unlike Smith or Hume, a true practitioner, a small manufacturer. His writing has all the hall-marks of the French enlightenment: a talent

69   Ibid., p. 90.
70   Smith, *An Inquiry*, pp. 90–1.
71   Ibid., p. 82.
72   Ibid., p. 125.
73   See Fanfani, *Storia*, pp. 148–9.
74   C. Genilh, *An inquiry into the Various Systems of Political Economy; Their Advantages and Disadvantages, and The Theory Most Favourable to the Increase of National Wealth* (New York 1812) p. 279.

for systematisation and an extraordinary matter-of-fact lucidity, the product at best of a sharp and observant mind but with a tendency to over-simplification where matters of policy were concerned. His claims for the new science of "political economy" were not modest; he boldly asserted "truths which can be useful at all times and in all countries."[75] He had an in-built tendency to interpret the subject-matter of the moral (social) sciences in positivist terms: on his view there were established facts in the moral sciences as in the natural sciences.[76] To effect this he necessarily claimed to be removing the politics from political economy. "Politics proper – the science of organising societies – has long been confounded with Political Economy which teaches how wealth is created, is distributed and is consumed. Wealth, however, is essentially independent of political organisation."[77] The form of government was, on this view, an irrelevance. Yet he weakened his own case by using political economy as an explanation for international relations. Tariff preferences, he asserted, caused wars.[78] It was "not in the interest of nations to fight one another . . .", he argued, and with equal lack of evidence went still further: "All nations are by the nature of things friends; and two governments which make war are not so much enemies of their adversaries so much as enemies of their own subjects."[79] The protectionist economic historian William Cunningham later described Smith as having "severed economic science from politics".[80] This is not really true. What Smith actually did was to reverse the relationship between the two. Whereas for the mercantilist political requirements were always prior to economic need, for Smith economic need was not only prior to but also determinant of political results. Smith's economics was thus not "positive" but as "normative" as that of the political economists who preceded him.

Political prescription went side by side with a determination to judge prior economic matters solely in term of economic values. Say asserted that trade created equal dependence between economies, whether they were raw material exporters or primarily manufacturers. This position conflicted head on with that taken by Montesquieu (1689–1755), who argued that Poland, an agrarian country, had only grain for export. It was not those countries that had need of something that lost by trade, Montesquieu wrote, but those "which have need of everything. It is not people who are self-sufficient but those who have nothing who find an advantage in not trading with anyone."[81] One might almost be hearing Raúl Prebisch at the United Nations Commission on Trade and Development (see below, pp. 216–17).

75   Jean-Baptiste Say, *Traité d'Économie Politique ou Simple Exposition de la manière dont se forment, se distribuent et se consomment les richesses*, Vol. 1 (4th edition, 1819) p. v.
76   Ibid., p. xxv.
77   Ibid., p. ix.
78   Ibid., p. 228.
79   Vol. 2, pp. 299–300.
80   Cunningham, *The Growth*, p. 440.
81   Montesquieu, *De l'Esprit des lois*, Vol. 2 (Book 20, chapter 23), ed. P. Derathé (Paris, 1973 edition) p. 18.

The general assumption of the mercantilist was that trade was a zero-sum game: someone's loss was necessarily someone else's gain and vice versa; all could not win at one and the same time. This acted as an absurd constraint on trade and bore some responsibility for the wars of the latter half of the seventeenth century and most of the eighteenth century. The new assumption of the free traders was that unrestricted commerce would be of benefit (not necessarily equal) to all economically. They argued that in so doing it would thereby bring peace between competing societies, the assumption being that this competition was in some fundamental sense an artificial consequence of protection and a condition that would be brought to an end with free trade. Thus, in so far as the state was considered at all, it was in respect to its eventual demise. This was in effect a new challenge to the supremacy of *raison d'état* and its substitution by the supranational *raison de commerce*, or, as Defoe called it, "Reason of Trade". The net result would be the hegemony of the market.

It was quite naturally in Britain and in British policy that free trade first made its impact. The industrial revolution had created its economic supremacy over the rest of the world. Even swingeing taxation during the Seven Years' War and the Napoleonic Wars had failed to halt the unprecedented rates of growth, tiny though they were by present-day standards. Inevitably economic development was seen as a panacea for all ills, and along with it imperial expansion. The none-too-subtle John Stuart Mill, in his *Principles of Political Economy with Some of Their Applications to Social Philosophy*, claimed for commerce the role of civilising the world. "Commerce is now what war once was," he asserted, "the principal source . . . of contact." He added: "it may be said without exaggeration that the great extent and rapid increase of international trade, in being the principal guarantee of the peace of the world, is the great permanent security for the uninterrupted progress of the ideas, the institutions, and the character of the human race."[82]

These high-flown claims now penetrated the upper reaches of the state. The brilliant financier turned economist David Ricardo published *On the Principle of Political Economy and Taxation* in 1817, two years before entering the House of Commons, where he led a long and sustained battle against agricultural protection. The text, which gave birth to the law of comparative advantage, stated:

> Under a system of perfectly free commerce, each country naturally devotes its capital and labour to such employment as are most beneficial to each. This pursuit of individual advantage is admirably connected with the universal good of the whole. By stimulating independence, by rewarding ingenuity, and by using most efficaciously the peculiar powers bestowed by nature, it distributes labour most effectively and most economically: while, by increasing the general mass of productions, it diffuses

---

82   J. S. Mill, *Principles of Political Economy with Some of Their Applications to Social Philosophy*, ed. J. Robson (Toronto 1965) p. 594.

general benefit, and binds together by one common tie of interest and intercourse, the universal society of nations throughout the civilized world.[83]

The young and liberal Viscount Palmerston had been sent to Edinburgh to study Smith's ideas and in the House of Commons debate on the abolition of the Corn Laws in 1842, long after Ricardo's demise, he delivered a speech worthy of Florus, Grotius and Smith:

there are larger grounds on which this doctrine [of autarchy] ought to be repudiated by this House. Why is the earth on which we live divided into zones and climates? Why, I ask, do different countries yield different productions to people experiencing different wants? Why are they intersected with mighty rivers – the natural highways of nations? Why are lands the most distant from each other, brought almost into contact by the very ocean which seems to divide them? Why, Sir, it is that man may be dependent upon man. It is that the exchange of commodities may be accompanied by the extension and diffusion of knowledge – by the interchange of mutual benefits engendering mutual kind feelings – multiplying and confirming friendly relations. It is, that commerce may freely go forth, leading civilisation with one hand, and peace with the other, to render mankind happier, wiser, better. Sir, this is the dispensation of Providence – this is the decree of that power which created and disposes the universe; but in the face of it, with arrogant, presumptuous folly, the dealers in restrictive duties fly, fettering the in-born energies of man, and setting up their miserable legislation instead of the great standing laws of nature.[84]

But this was a fairly modest claim compared to those made for free trade by the Victorian factory-owner and Member of Parliament Richard Cobden: "Free Trade is God's diplomacy, and there is no other certain way of uniting people in bonds of peace."[85] His enthusiasm knew no bounds for the political benefits flowing from such a policy. As he declared in 1846,

I believe that the physical gain will be the smallest gain to humanity from the success of this principle. I look farther; I see in the Free-trade principle that which shall act on the moral world as the principle of gravitation in the universe, – drawing men together, thrusting aside the antagonism of race, and creed, and language, and uniting us in the bonds of eternal peace. I have looked even further. I have speculated, and probably dreamt, in the dim future – ay, a thousand years hence – I have

83   D. Ricardo, *On the Principles of Political Economy and Taxation* (London 1817) p. 156.
84   16 February 1642: *Hansard's Parliamentary Debates*: 3rd Series, Vol. LX (London 1842) cols. 618–19.
85   Quoted in *The Foreign Policy of Victorian England*, p. 85.

speculated on what the effect of the triumph of this principle may be. I believe that the effect will be to change the face of the world, so as to introduce a system of government entirely distinct from that which prevails. I believe that the desire and the motive for large and mighty empires; for gigantic armies and great navies – for those materials which are used for the destruction of life and the desolation of the rewards of labour – will die away; I believe that such things will cease to be necessary, or to be used when man becomes one family, and freely exchanges the fruits of his labour with his brother man. I believe that, if we could be allowed to reappear on this sublunary scene, we should see, at a far distant period, the governing system of this world revert to something like the municipal system; and I believe that the speculative philosopher of a thousand years hence will date the greatest revolution that ever happened in the world's history from the triumph of the principle which we have met here to advocate . . .[86]

The critique of free trade that followed Smith came from various quarters. Perhaps the most unlikely source was the one-time libertarian utopian socialist Johann Fichte (1762–1814). In *Der geschlossene Handelsstaat* (The Closed Commercial State), published in 1800, he sought to protect the individual and the state from the damaging effects of open competition, which ruined both. Fichte's view of how states behaved in trade matched the very practices so evident in eighteenth-century Europe and so vigorously attacked by Smith: a mercantilist world in which trade was seen in zero-sum terms, where the preponderance of one nation was challenged and weakened by another.[87] On Fichte's view – which anticipates the one Lenin expounded in *Imperialism: The Highest Stage of Capitalism*, over a century later – the "conflict-causing commercial interest is frequently the real cause of war, even if another pretext is given."[88] And Fichte fully expected matters would get worse, with "an endless war of all against all in public trade, as the war between the buyers and sellers; and these wars will become more violent, more unjust and more dangerous in their consequences" as the world became more populated.[89] Believing that trade was naturally uneven rather than given to equilibrium, as Smith and David Ricardo believed, and believing that these inequalities provoked war, it was logical for Fichte to see as the best way of avoiding conflict: "that the state totally close itself off from all commerce with foreign countries . . ."[90] The state he envisaged was thus one which protected its own industry and, indeed, protected others from it too. The thrust of his arguments was surely not lost on his fellow countrymen, certainly as he became more closely identified with

86   15 January 1846: ibid., doc. 38.
87   Fichte, *Der geschlossene Handelsstaat* (Tübingen 1800), in *Johan Gottlieb Fichte's sammtliche Werke* (Berlin 1845) Vol. 3, pp. 467–8.
88   Ibid.
89   Ibid., pp. 457–8.
90   Ibid., p. 476.

German nationalism. The French revolutionary wars sharpened his insights and made more urgent his message. His celebrated *Reden an die Deutsche Nation* were delivered during the winter of 1807–8 at the Academy in Berlin "while a French Marshal was governor of the city, while regiments with bands playing passed by, while spies were scattered in the audience . . ."[91] There Fichte argued: "May we at last recognize that while the airy theories about international trade and manufacturing for the world may do for the foreigner, and belong to the weapons with which he has always invaded us, they have no application to Germans, and that, next to unity among ourselves, internal independence and commercial self-reliance are the second means to our salvation, and through them to the welfare of Europe."[92] Fichte had no illusion that his proposals were an immediate option for any particular state; even for the Germany of his time. Yet it has invariably been the case that once written, such ideas acquire a life of their own and when implemented often bear little direct relation to the original intention of their author.

Those closest to the centre of things were naturally more moderate and, in the short term at least, more influential. Jacques Necker (1732–1804), Minister to Louis XVI and ultimately to the revolutionary convention in France, was thus more typically rooted in present realities. "Undoubtedly", Necker acknowledged, "if all nations, through a common treaty, wished to abrogate all the tariffs and rights over entry, France should not refuse; for it is likely that it will gain by these agreements." However, this was a chimera: "the Powers which would lose by this freedom would not adopt it at all, and those that would gain would desire it in vain; moreover, if one wished to introduce it by setting the example, one would follow the folly of an individual who, in the hope of establishing a commune, let all his neighbours in to share out his heritage." He added: "One can easily draw a beautiful picture of the fraternity of nations; one can label as barbaric the precautionary laws that separate the different states of Europe, by which each manages its natural resources for creating prosperity; but to discover at the same time that the flames of war are lit without hesitation in dispute over some deserted island is to form a bizarre association of the most contradictory ideas."[93]

This was not an untypical reaction by a former senior civil servant to utopian schemes. The first coherent reaction against the new doctrine appeared in the United States, however. This was not accidental. It was the new republic that, having attained political independence from Britain, now sought to industrialise itself not least in opposition to fierce British economic competition. Whereas a Scotsman, as indeed any Englishman, could build into his economic model the easy assumption that

---

91 From a newspaper article of 19 September 1822. Quoted in H. Engelbrecht, *Johann Gottlieb Fichte: A Study of his political writings with special reference to his Nationalism* (New York 1933) p. 125.

92 Quoted in ibid., p. 120.

93 "De L'Administration des Finances de la France" (Paris 1784): *Oeuvres complètes de M. Necker, publiées* par M. le Baron de Sael, son petit-fils. Vol. 4 (Paris 1821) p. 559.

all economies were competing on an even playing field, it was most unlikely any American would choose to do so. Although in principle committed to free trade, the leaders of the movement for independence differed in respect to the degree to which they followed it in practice. James Madison acknowledged that "Interest does not always regulate itself to the best purpose. Hence the propriety and policy of the interference of commercial regulations, of giving bounties and laying restrictions."[94] Moreover, George Washington made a point of dressing in homespun cloth for his inauguration in 1789.[95] Not much later, in 1791, Alexander Hamilton wrote in his celebrated "Report on the Subject of Manufactures": "the United States cannot exchange with Europe on equal terms; and the want of reciprocity would render them the victim of a system, which should induce them to confine their views to Agriculture and refrain from Manufactures. A constant and encreasing necessity, on their part, for the commodities of Europe, and only a partial and occasional demand for their own, in return, could not but expose them to a state of impoverishment, compared with the opulence to which their political & natural advantages authorise them to aspire."[96] Hamilton was not exaggerating. Exiled to the United States in 1793 the former and future Foreign Minister of France Talleyrand engaged in business to pay his way. He commented that imports were supplied "so completely by England that one has reason to doubt whether England enjoyed this privilege more exclusively at the time of the most severe protection vis-à-vis what were then its colonies than that which it currently enjoys vis-à-vis the independent United States." Talleyrand from first-hand knowledge attributed this to the overwhelming power of British manufacturing and capital markets which allowed sales at low prices and with extensive credit on the basis of annual repayment, which provided a seamless web of distribution, debt and circulation.[97]

Events conspired in support of Hamilton's views. The revolutionary wars in Europe cut the continent off from British trade when Napoleon imposed the Berlin decree of 21 November 1806, resulting in British retaliation in 1807 (Orders in Council) and further French measures (the Milan decree) to isolate the British economy. The folly of British retaliation came under sharp attack from Henry Brougham in the House of Commons and inter alia from the pages of the *Edinburgh Review* in the country beyond. Because France was so little dependent upon overseas trade and therefore her threats empty of substance, it was only Britain and neutral shipping which suffered. The highest price was paid in terms of the sales of British manufactures to the United States, however. By 1812 the *Edinburgh Review* noted "how intimately our commercial

---

94   Quoted in F. List, *Werke*, Vol. 2: *Grundlinien einer politischen ökonomie und andere beitrage der Amerikanischen Zeit 1825–1832*, ed. W. Notz (Berlin 1931) p. 183.

95   Ibid., p. 184.

96   "The Report on the Subject of Manufactures", 5 December 1791: *The Papers of Alexander Hamilton*, Vol. X, ed. H. Syrett et al. (New York 1966) p. 263.

97   "Les États-Unis et L'Angleterre en 1795: Lettre de M. De Talleyrand": *Revue D'Histoire Diplomatique*, 1889, Year Three, pp. 71–2. The letter was sent to Lord Lansdowne.

prosperity depends upon our intercourse with that country, and how much their wants must be dependent on our supply . . ."[98]

As a result of British shortsightedness, for the first time the Americans were substantially left to their own devices. It was in these conditions that Hezekiah Niles of Baltimore (one of the three major ports in the country) began publishing *The Weekly Register*. When he was "yet a lad", Niles "was impressed with an opinion that the republic never could arrive at its rightful power to do good or punish wrong, while dependent on any other country for iron manufactures, articles of clothing, &c. hardly less necessary than food . . ."[99] The first edition, imbued with this principle, appeared on 7 September 1811, after Napoleon had rescinded all measures affecting US trade but with the British still commandeering American merchant shipping and empressing US sailors into the Royal Navy. War soon broke out between Britain and the United States. On the eve of war Niles opened his journal, which soon became an authoritative voice on many issues, not least the issue of industrial protection, with the announcement that he would publish Hamilton's report. He added: "The present is a period naturally leading to the establishment of manufactories. Deprived of our accustomed commerce by the arbitrary and illegal proceedings of the belligerent nations of Europe . . . it is imperiously demanded of the American people that they should look to themselves . . . The prejudice which existed against manufactures have been dispelled or are dispelling by the influence of experience, the sure criterion of all things."[100] There was little need to advocate special measures to aid manufacturing until the belligerents made peace, the net effect of which was to release British manufactures that flooded US markets. On 27 January 1816 Niles published an editorial on "The Manufacturing Interest". The United States was, he asserted, arriving at "a most important crisis". The current session of Congress would determine "whether our manufactories shall go on and increase, and be extended to the general wants of the country, or dwindle into nothing, through a sacrifice to a time-serving policy – a policy, that regards the present moment and pays no respect to the future." He went on:

It is been the practice of every enlightened nation, and especially of Great Britain, (in which, though there is much to condemn, there is a great deal to approve) whose resources have confounded the calculations of the wise and astonished the world, to give a decided, active and unequivocal preference to the product of the labor of its own people.

---

98   A review of *The Speech of Henry Brougham Esq. M.P. in the House of Commons, on Tuesday the 16th of June 1812, upon the present State of Commerce and Manufactures* (London 1812): *Edinburgh Review*, p. 241.

99   *Niles' Weekly Register*, Vol. XXVI, No 659, 1 May 1824.

100 *The Weekly Register containing Political, Historical, Geographical, Scientifical, Astronomical, Statistical, and Biographical Documents, Essays, and Facts; together with Notices of the Arts and Manufactures, and a Record of the Events of the Times*, Vol. 1, No 1, 7 September 1811.

It was this "universal practice of nations" that Niles urged on the US Congress:

> A variety of circumstances – the British orders in council and the French decrees – our self-restrictions on trade – and, finally, the late war [with Britain, 1812–15], gave a new direction to wealth and industry in the United States. Manufactories grew up as if by magic . . . These establishments have made wonderful progress towards protection; but they have not yet arrived at a degree of strength competent to meet, on equal grounds, the more wealthy and older institutions of Europe. They must be protected and assisted for a while by the government . . . the manufacturers of the United States stand to the government in the precise relation of an infant to its mother . . .

Niles, moreover, did not merely believe that industrial protection was a politically neutral course to pursue; he, like Colbert, also assumed that commerce was a form of war, albeit a war imposed by others; and it has to be said that he was not entirely mistaken in this assumption:

> England, no doubt, will do all that she can, fairly or clandestinely, in any shape and every shape, to destroy our manufacturing establishments, and ruin all who have embarked their capital in them. It remains to be seen how far a congress of the United States will assist her in bringing about so great a desideratum – an object of more real importance to her than was the downfall of the hated and feared *Napoleon Bonaparte*.[101]

Congress, which answered to the landed interest and shipping interests, was more receptive to the need for manufacturing than it had ever been; yet manufacturing by definition represented a very small proportion of the national income and therefore had proportionally less representation than rival interests whose profits came from trade with Britain. Niles thundered forth to redress the balance, and on 2 March 1816 he produced a further leading article in the spirit of Colbert on "Prospective Policy":

> It is now more than a year since we closed a contest in arms with Great Britain, in glory. A new struggle has already commenced with the same nation in the arts, as connected with agriculture, commerce and manufactures. The high ground so fairly won in the honorable and happy result of the former, can be maintained only by activity, vigilance, and perseverance in the latter. If the object of the one was to reduce us to "unconditional submission" – "to cripple us for fifty years," the effect of the other will not be less calamitous in bringing upon us a state of dependence and

101   *The Weekly Register*, Vol. IX, No 22, 27 January 1816.

penury, if we blindly reject the dictations of reason and common sense, as founded upon the experience of nations.

Here Niles found a new branch deserving of protection: shipbuilding. The shippers had previously suffered most from the loss of British trade and therefore stood in the opposing camp to manufacturing interests. With the recovery of that trade, however, British rather than American bottoms came to predominate. Niles – echoing John Evelyn and anticipating Alfred Mahan (see below, pp. 171–2) – spoke out for naval as well as the commercial interest:

> It is a matter of universal regret that this branch of industry should fail, and fail they must, if peace continues in Europe. It is an object of great importance to *Great Britain* to destroy it, as having afforded and as furnishing the means of humbling her naval pride, and chasing away the shadows that have surrounded her supposed invincibility on the ocean – that broke the charm of superiority and created a new epoch in maritime affairs.

In Niles' view there was "emphatically, 'no friendship in trade.'" Whatever the causes of the Great War, with peace Britain was now free "to govern, as well in the frozen regions of the north, as control the destinies of millions on the burning line." And how had Britain won against France? "The purse, in the hand of her *Castlereagh*, has won more battles than the sword in the hands of her *Wellingtons*." The power of the navy and the power of the purse were in Niles' mind tightly intertwined. And what was a British peer heard to say to an American? "*You spread too much canvas*."[102]

The view Niles took of Britain's achievements, aims and interests, in 1816 was not short of the mark. The Whig MP Henry Brougham addressed the parliamentary Committee on the Distressed State of Agriculture barely a month after *The Weekly Register* had discharged its cannon from the other side of the Atlantic. Brougham ably summarised the new economic supremacy won at war almost in tones that suggest surprise at what had been achieved but in anxiety lest it be lost:

> The commencement of hostilities in 1793 produced the stagnation of trade and manufactures which usually accompanies a transition from peace to war; but these difficulties were of uncommonly short duration, and the brilliant success of our arms at sea, the capture of some of the enemy's colonies, the revolt of others and the crippled state of his mercantile resources at home from internal confusion, speedily diminished his commerce to an extraordinary degree, augmenting our own in nearly the same proportion. As his conquests or influence extended over other nations possessed of trade or colonial establishments, these in their turn

102   Ibid., Vol. X, No 1, 2 March 1816.

became exposed to our maritime hostility, and lost their commerce and their plantations; so that in a very short time this country obtained a mercantile and colonial monopoly altogether unprecedented even in the most successful of her former wars.[103]

The "final result of Buonaparte's continental and military-system" was thus "the completion of our commercial and manufacturing monopoly, by the destruction of almost all other trade and peaceful industry . . ."[104] When in the spring of 1814 the continental market opened up in Europe, "a rage for exporting goods of every kind burst forth" and was accompanied by an unprecedented wave of financial speculation, sucking in the savings of even household servants who could ill afford losses.[105] The same happened with respect to exports to the United States – £18 million in one year alone – and here Brougham and Niles converged in their view of this trade as a zero-sum game: "it was well worth while to incur a loss upon the first exportation," Brougham noted, "in order, by the glut, to stifle in the cradle those rising manufactures in the United States, which the war had forced into existence contrary to the natural course of things."[106]

Mathew Carey was born in Ireland in 1760 and emigrated to the United States as a young man. He thus had direct experience of two societies which were hit by cheap British manufactures to the disadvantage of local industry. Carey was above all an energetic publicist with a strong sense of mission and although on good terms with Niles, his ego and his verbosity gave him the reputation of being something of a bore among those fighting the same cause. On 21 August 1819 and in response to the slump that hit the economy, citizens of Philadelphia "friendly to American manufactures" met to set up a society to promote American industry. Carey managed to obtain only a seat on the corresponding committee.[107] Yet within three months he was chairman of the board of manufactures of the society.[108] There followed the Philadelphia Society for the Promotion of National Industry and a Pennsylvania Society for the Protection of Domestic Industry.[109] In 1820 he published *The New Olive Branch, or an attempt to establish an identity of interest between Agriculture, Manufactures, and Commerce, and to prove, that a large portion of the manufacturing industry of this nation has been sacrificed to commerce; and that commerce has suffered by this policy nearly as much as manufactures*. It attacked the US Government for abolishing duties on imports which had "beggared and

103   9 April 1816: Hansard, *The Parliamentary Debates*, Vol. XXXIII, 1816, cols. 1087–8.
104   Ibid., col. 1091.
105   Ibid., col. 1098.
106   Ibid., col. 1099.
107   *The Weekly Register*, Vol. XVII, No 1, 4 September 1819.
108   Ibid., 20 November 1819.
109   K. Rowe, *Mathew Carey: A Study in American Economic Development* (Baltimore 1933) p. 48.

bankrupted" the country.[110] "*The war protected the domestic industry of the nation*", Carey claimed. "It throve and prospered under that safeguard, which the peace tore down *de fonds en comble*."[111]

There was little or nothing in *The New Olive Branch* that had not been said better (and with greater brevity) by Niles. Its momentary impact was a symptom of the times. And after making an initial splash Carey found that "the spirit died away in Philadelphia and New York, and everywhere else throughout the union."[112] He "made repeated attempts from year to year to arouse the parties interested", forming "at various times three or four societies, but they generally died in the course of a few months."[113]

A more important and original, though more moderate, formulation of some of the ideas first expressed by Niles appeared in *The Elements of Political Economy*, published in Baltimore – Niles' home town – by Daniel Raymond, a practising lawyer, in 1823. The book, in two volumes, is very repetitive but is at least crystal-clear. In Raymond's view, Smith's assumption that the interests of the individual was necessarily identical with the interests of the nation could not be "more unsound . . . in principle, or a more abominable one in its consequences . . ."[114] In Raymond's view, "the question, whether the importation of manufactures should be prohibited, or the tariff raised, does not at all depend upon the fact, that they can be procured by the consumer cheaper in foreign countries, than in his own. Buying goods where they may be had cheapest may be the best policy for some individuals, while buying them where they come dearest, may be the best policy for the nation."[115] "If a nation has not full employment in its ordinary vocations," Raymond continued, "is it not better to employ its unoccupied time in manufacturing cotton and woollen cloths, than in doing nothing? And will this not be a saving of just so much, as it cost to manufacture the cloths in foreign countries?"[116] Raymond anticipated Keynes and Roosevelt of the New Deal. It was the "duty of the legislator to find employment for all the people, and if he cannot find them employment in agriculture and commerce, he must set them to manufacturing. It is his duty to take special care that no other nation interferes with their industry. He is not to permit one half of the nation to remain idle and hungry, in order that the other half may buy goods where they may be had cheapest."[117] "Every man is to be left free to

110   M. Carey, *The New Olive Branch, or an attempt to establish an identity of interest between Agriculture, Manufactures, and Commerce, and to prove, that a large portion of the manufacturing industry of this nation has been sacrificed to commerce; and that commerce has suffered by this policy nearly as much as manufactures* (Philadelphia 1820) p. 45.
111   Ibid., p. 141.
112   M. Carey, *Signs of the Times* (Philadelphia 1832) p. 3.
113   Ibid.
114   D. Raymond, *The Elements of Political Economy*, Vol. 2 (2nd edition, Baltimore 1823) p. 215.
115   Ibid., pp. 228–9.
116   Ibid., p. 229.
117   Ibid., pp. 230–1.

engage in what business he pleases," he wrote, "but he ought not to be allowed to afford patronage and support to the industry of foreigners, when his own fellow-citizens are in want of it."[118] Raymond's philosophy undoubtedly had an effect, but not so decisively as to ensure that when Carey persuaded a university to set up a chair for him, there were those willing to donate sufficient funding to make it possible. This was also the case with respect to Friedrich List.

It was in Carey's Philadelphia, from 1825 to 1832, that Friedrich List first began to formulate his ideas on industrial protection for infant industry. List had come in exile from Germany to find fortune in Pennsylvania, where the greatest number of German migrants were concentrated in North America. Here he bought a farm but met with difficulties. Within a year of his arrival the Society for the Encouragement of Manufactures and the Mechanic Arts was set up, not under Carey's chairmanship but that of the establishment in Philadelphia: William Tilghman, Chief Justice of the Pennsylvanian Supreme Court, with Charles Ingersoll, the Attorney General for the Eastern District of Pennsylvania, as his deputy.[119] Carey was as before made merely corresponding secretary and considered that the movement he considered that he had founded (but had been unable to make a going concern) had been hijacked by "eleventh hour men" who treated him "with an indignity" with which he "would not have treated a decent sweep-chimney or scavenger . . ."[120] Not least was the resentment at the Society's patronage of List who – unsuccessful at farming and seeking rapid advancement – applied academic precision, order and logic to ideas that Carey propagated with rambling verbosity. The attack on free trade from Hamilton, Niles and Carey had never really generalised from the limited American experience to graduate to the status of a universal theory. It was List who took that further, decisive step, ironically largely because, having formulated his approach to meet American conditions, he was then unable to find a permanent academic position from which to preach his doctrine and had to return to Germany, reformulating his ideas for a more general audience in the process.

Both Smith and List were, perhaps less consciously in the case of the former, responding to the economic requirements of their own communities. Having industrialised first, it was in Britain's interest to open up all foreign markets (while if possible keeping some of its own closed); London could easily dominate in the competition for the sale of manufactures. List on the other hand came from Germany, which, like the fledgling United States, was still struggling to compete with British imports, not yet possessing a substantial or sufficiently advanced industrial base. List's argument followed logically from these constrained circumstances and echoed Niles and Colbert to a fault. Until recently he had been a "very faithful disciple of Smith and Say" and "very

---

118   Ibid., p. 231.
119   List, *Werke*, p. 353.
120   Ibid., p. 358.

zealous advocate" of free trade.[121] But he then witnessed the destructive effects on German industry of the raising of the continental blockade after the defeat of Napoleon and its sudden exposure to cheap imports from Britain.[122] He had access to *The Weekly Register* while still in Germany and as early as 1819, just at the time when he needed a coherent explanation for the economic problems that surrounded him.[123] By the time his ideas were formulated – and nothing on protection appeared by his hand until after he arrived in the United States – they were put together with Niles' trenchant attacks on free trade and the dangers from British manufactures already in mind.

It was not necessarily in the interests of all states regardless of their level of industrialisation to open their markets to goods from abroad. It was in the national interest to bolster economic (hence industrial) power vis-à-vis other states. To give time for industrialisation to succeed, infant industry would have to be protected. And even after protection had succeeded in this minimal aim, it might still be required thereafter if reasons of state so dictated.

List argued for the primacy of politics over economics; economics as the continuation of politics by other means. His experience of Philadelphia further highlighted for him the dominance of the British economy: "a supremacy such as that which exists in our days the world has never before witnessed."[124] This supremacy undoubtedly was of enormous benefit to the world as a whole. "But ought we on that account also to wish that she may erect a universal dominion on the ruins of the other nationalities? Nothing but unfathomable cosmopolitanism or shopkeepers' narrow-mindedness can give an assenting answer to that question."[125]

List spoke from Necker's script:

In proportion . . . as the principle of a universal confederation of nations is reasonable, in just the same degree would a given nation act contrary to reason if, in anticipation of the great advantages to be expected from such a union, and from a state of universal and perpetual peace, it were to regulate the principles of its national policy as though this universal confederation of nations existed already. We ask, would not every sane person consider a government to be insane which, in consideration of the benefits and reasonableness of a state of universal and perpetual peace, proposed to disband its armies, destroy its fleet, and demolish its fortresses?

121 At one moment he claimed the conversion came in 1815: Letter, 15 July 1827: "Outlines of American Political Economy in a Series of Letters addressed by Frederick List Esq. to Charles J. Ingersoll" (Philadelphia 1827) in M. Hirst, *Life of Friedrich List and Selections from his Writings* (London 1909) pp. 172–3. At another, in his speech of 3 November, he spoke of doubts concerning Smith not occurring until 1817: List, *Werke*, p. 159. It may well be that he was converted on arriving in Pennsylvania and seeing a good opportunity to jump on a bandwagon.
122 Ibid.
123 Ibid., p. 355.
124 F. List, *The National System of Political Economy* (London 1885) p. 365.
125 Ibid.

> But such a government would be doing nothing different in principle from what the popular school requires from governments when, because of the advantages which would be derivable from general free trade, it urges that they should abandon the advantages derivable from protection.[126]

Freeing trade between unequals meant unequal distribution of rewards. States included "giants and dwarfs, well-formed bodies and cripples, civilised, half-civilised, and barbarous nations . . ."[127] The main difference was between industrialised and agricultural economies. "The popular school [free trade] betrays an utter misconception of the nature of national economical conditions if it believes that such nations can promote and further their civilisation, their prosperity, and especially their social progress, equally well by the exchange of agricultural products for manufactured goods, as by establishing a manufacturing power of their own."[128] Writing of Smith's classic, List argued: "Not taking into consideration the different state of power, constitution, wants and culture of the different nations, his book is a mere treatise on the question: how the economy of the individuals and of mankind would stand if the human race were not separated into nations, but united by a general law and by an equal culture of mind."[129] But "under the existing conditions of the world, the result of general free trade would not be a universal republic, but, on the contrary, a universal subjection of the less advanced nations to the supremacy of the predominant manufacturing, commercial, and naval power."[130]

The free traders focused on the individual rather than the state or society. To List the notion that society was merely a collection of individuals was a fallacy. "Is it in the interests of individuals to take into consideration the wants of future centuries, as those concern the nature of nations and the State?"[131] If no account were taken of pre-existing economic development, the assumption that free exchange between individuals was best would lead one to an extraordinary conclusion: "according to this doctrine savage nations ought to be the most productive and wealthy of the earth, for nowhere is the individual left more to himself than in the savage state, nowhere is the action of the power of the State less perceptible."[132] The fact was that nation-states existed and "so long as other nations subordinate the interests of the human race as a whole to their national interests, it is folly to speak of free competition among the individuals of various nations."[133] List followed Colbert: "War is nothing but a duel between nations,

---

126   Ibid., p. 181.
127   Ibid., p. 175.
128   Ibid., p. 179.
129   Letter, 10 July 1827: Hirst, *Life*, p. 153.
130   List, *The National System*, p. 126.
131   Ibid., p. 165.
132   Ibid., p. 172.
133   Ibid.

and restrictions of free trade are nothing but a war between the powers of industry of different nations. But what would you think, sir, of a Secretary of War, who, embracing the doctrine of the Friends [Quakers], should refuse to build fortresses and men-of-war, and to supply military academies, because mankind would be happier if there were no war on earth?"[134] The first industrialisers had used protection to establish their national supremacy. "History is there to prove that protective regulations originated either in the natural efforts of nations to attain their prosperity, independence, and power, or in consequence of wars and of the hostile commercial regulation of predominantly manufacturing nations."[135]

The first advocates of the universal republic of commerce were, of course, the Physiocrats, who aroused nothing but open contempt from List: "Following the philosophers of their own age and country, who, in view of the total disorganisation of the national condition of France, sought consolation in the wider field of philanthropy and cosmopolitanism (much as the father of a family, in despair at the break-up of his household, goes to seek comfort in the tavern), so the physiocrats caught at the cosmopolitan idea of universal free trade, as a panacea by which all prevailing evils might be cured."[136] By taking humanity in general rather than the national economy as the object of study, the free traders "assumed as being actually in existence a state of things which has yet to come into existence."[137]

Moreover, List argued, the assumption that individual trading interests were consonant with particular national economic interests could not safely be made. "This perversity of surrendering the interests of manufactures and agriculture to the demands of commerce, without reservation, is a natural consequence of that theory which everywhere merely takes into consideration present values, but nowhere the powers that produce them, and regards the whole world as but one *indivisible republic of merchants*. The school does not discern that the merchant may be accomplishing his purpose (viz. gain of values by exchange) at the expense of the agriculturalists and manufacturers, at the expense of the nation's productive powers, and indeed of its independence."[138]

In asserting "national economy" as against "cosmopolitan economy", List also reasserted the interconnexion between economics and politics. Of what value was Smith's open market without national power? List's world was thus Hobbist rather than the Grotian, Physiocratic or Smithian world of growing harmony under the impact of increased trade: "national wealth is increased and secured by national power, as national power is increased and secured by national wealth. Its leading principles are therefore not only economical, but political too. The individuals may be very wealthy;

134   Letter, 10 July 1827: Hirst, *Life*, p. 154.
135   List, *The National System*, pp. 180–1.
136   Ibid., p. 344.
137   Ibid., p. 126.
138   Ibid., p. 259.

but if the nation possesses no power to protect them, they may lose in one day the wealth they gathered during ages, and their rights, freedom, and independence too."[139] "Smith and Say advise us to buy cheaper than we can manufacture ourselves, in contemplating only the gain of matter in exchanging matter for matter. But weigh the grain of matter with the loss of power, and how stands the balance?"[140]

List's attestation to the self-interestedness of the advocates of free trade was echoed by Karl Marx (1818–83). Marx agreed with the free traders that the economic advance brought by capitalism would transform international relations. Both he and they shared an essentially economistic form of explanation. Where he disagreed was how it would transform those relations. "Is the whole internal organisation of nations," he asked Pavel Annenkov, "are their international relations, anything but the expression of a given division of labour? And must they not change as the division of labour changes?"[141] Thus whereas the free traders saw the growth of the free market drawing the world together in peace because of the growing interdependence of producers, Marx saw free trade exacerbating tensions between wage labour and capital on an international scale. Moreover he saw free trade exacerbating relations between the raw material producers, doomed by the law of comparative advantage to exchanging commodities for manufactures, and the industrialised economies.

For Marx the fate of society and international relations was to be determined by class. Speaking on free trade in Brussels in January 1848 he acknowledged the value of protection. It served as an instrument of the rising bourgeoisie against feudalism and the *ancien régime*, a means of concentrating the power of capital and creating freedom of trade within a society. But it had by now become a "conservative" force. The claims for free trade, however, were claims for greater freedom for capital, and no matter how favourable the conditions under which one good was exchanged for another, there would always exist a class of exploiters and a class of exploited while the relationship between capital and wage labour was maintained. Far from diminishing, the antagonism between labour and capital would become more acute. Translate this free trade from within the state to the universal scale, and "Every one of the destructive phenomena to which unlimited competition gives rise within any one nation is reproduced in more gigantic proportions in the market of the world."[142] Marx thus supported free trade because it hastened "the Social Revolution".[143]

Just as Smith expressed the interests of the dominant industrial Power, so too did List express the interests of subordinate but aspirant economies in a way that found an echo just over a century later when the third world broke free from Western political

139   Letter, 12 July 1827: Hirst, *Life*, p. 162.
140   Letter, 27 July 1827: ibid., p. 235.
141   Marx to Annenkov, 28 December 1846: Karl Marx, Friedrich Engels, *Collected Works*, Vol. 38 (London 1982) p. 98.
142   Public meeting, 9 January 1848: ibid., p. 464.
143   Ibid., p. 465.

but not economic dominance. Given that by definition most states resembled Germany rather than Britain, List's ideas inevitably struck home. It is of note that the great motive force in Russian industrialisation from above, Finance Minister Sergei Witte, chose to introduce List's ideas to the Russian public. Witte put together a pamphlet summarising these ideas in the late 1880s, before he took power.[144] List's work was then translated and published in a Russian edition in 1891. Witte was also an open admirer of Bismarck, who had put into practice with a series of tariffs exactly what List had recommended. "When List wrote his work," Witte wrote, "Germany stood in the same economic dependence on England, in which we stand now on Germany . . ."[145] Little more needed to be said.

The irony is that, although it was Witte who introduced these ideas into Russia, it was Lenin who took them to their logical conclusion in a manner no previous advocate of industrial protection – even Colbert – could have envisaged. In the first list of economic measures Lenin drew up, less than a month after seizing power in 1917, the "state monopoly of foreign trade" was by no means last.[146] The appropriate decree was drawn up within weeks.[147] Its purpose was made explicit by Lenin when it came under attack from within the regime. It was, he wrote in March 1922, impossible to retreat further from the state monopoly of foreign trade: "Otherwise the foreigners will buy up and export everything we have of value."[148] The system was subsequently cast into steel by Stalin, who created a bastardised version of Fichte's *geschlossene Handelsstaat*, which ended only with the collapse of the Communist order in 1992.

The Balance of Trade doctrines highlighted a facet of the Balance of Power easily overlooked. A further factor easily taken for granted was that of geography, whether as limitation or as a prompt for expansion.

144   Graf' S. Yu. Vitte, *Po povodu Natsionalizma. Nasional'naya Ekonomiya i Fridrikh' List'* (2nd edition, St. Petersburg 1912) p. 3.
145   Ibid., p. 69.
146   "Nabrisok programmy ekonomicheskikh meropriyatii", c. 10 December 1917: V. Lenin, *Polnoe sobranie sochinenii*, Vol. 35 (5th edition, Moscow 1962) p. 124.
147   "K proektu dekreta o provedenii v zhizn' natsionalizatsii bankov i o neobkhodimykh v svyazi s etim merakh", c. 27 December 1917: ibid., p. 429.
148   Letter to L. Kamenev, 3 March 1922: ibid., Vol. 44 (Moscow 1964) p. 427.

Chapter 4
GEOPOLITICS

"We cannot do anything about geography"

– Stalin[1]

The term Geopolitics has had an elasticity of meaning far greater than the Balance of Power. It is striking, for instance, that former statesman Henry Kissinger refers to the fact that he had "a better knowledge . . . of the conceptual side of geopolitics" than President Nixon.[2] Yet, despite deploying the term over a dozen times in his memoir, nowhere does he define what exactly he means.[3] In this respect he is not untypical. There has been, none the less, as in the case of the Balance of Power, a core upon which all have generally agreed: the influence of geography in determining the conduct of foreign policy. Beyond that point lies disagreement. Two distinct lines of thought emerge from the belief in the importance of geography. One sees the factor of geography as part of the complex of Reasons of State, essentially an extension of the Balance of Power, which takes in the constraints on the exercise of power dictated by the factor of space; the other essentially sees geography itself determining the nature of the state, thereby dictating the trajectory of foreign policy independently of the exercise of Reason. Whereas the first tends to focus on the limitations imposed by space, the

---

1   In negotiation with the Finns, October 1939: President Paasikivis Minnen, *Moskva och Finland 1939–1940* (Stockholm 1958) p. 40.

2   H. Kissinger, *Years of Renewal* (London 1999) p. 47.

3   This appears to be habitual and it is for this reason that Kissinger finds no place in this volume. In a characteristically perceptive portrait reviewing Kissinger's career and works up to the time of writing (1975), the late Philip Windsor points to Kissinger's "weakness as a theorist." Windsor finds Kissinger "a conservative who has not troubled to spell out his philosophy or his history; and whose concepts of power and order have not really taken either the study or the practice of international relations very much further. His memoirs", Windsor concludes prophetically, "will be read with fascination by millions when he retires. One hopes he will also find the time and energy to write the sustained and comprehensive work which would elucidate his philosophy and draw his ideas together." P. Windsor, "Henry Kissinger's scholarly contribution", *British Journal of International Studies*, April 1975, pp. 33 and 37. In this crucial respect Kissinger's interim study of diplomacy, despite its robust defence of anti-Wilsonian values, scarcely meets Windsor's criticism as either history or philosophy.

second rationalises the remorseless process of expansion of the state as a fact of life. It was thus not accidental that the former grew most notably out of reflections by the British at the height of empire, whereas the latter originated in northern central Europe at a moment when the German empire sought violently to escape confinement to Mittel-Europa.

For centuries the known confines of the civilised world, centred on the Mediterranean, circumscribed any sense of the factor of geography in the conduct of international relations. The first signs of change came with the great discoveries from the late fifteenth century, when the notion of the Balance of Trade also first come to the fore. The opening up of the Atlantic to the New World and the dependence upon that New World for bullion vulnerable to predation from other Powers created a sudden awareness of the factor of space in strategic calculation. "Look, Sir, at the Indies; which is the part where the money comes from, and with it also the substance of this Monarchy . . .", wrote Philip II of Spain's perspicacious one-time chief minister, Antonio Pérez. Pérez very quickly saw the momentous significance of these changes for the future conduct of international relations.[4] "Personal experience and the universal lesson teaches us", he noted, "that the Prince who is Lord of the sea will be Monarch and master of the earth, as absolute distributor of the things by which one is sustained and lives, which by means of navigation pass from some regions and from some nations to others, and with which one can build a unique City master of all the world . . ."[5] Spain's chief enemy, England, witnessed a similar observation. Francis Bacon argued that "if wee truely consider the greatnesse of *Spaine*, it consisteth chiefly in their Treasure, and their Treasure in their *Indies*, and their *Indies* (both of them) is but an accession to such as are matters by sea; so as this axell-tree whereupon their greatnesse turnes is soon cut a two by any that shall be stronger than they at sea."[6]

The colonisation of distant lands thus highlighted the importance of communications across the open seas. Only a few years after Pérez penned these words, Grotius' polemic *Mare Liberum* was published, apparently without his express permission. It set down a critical marker in stating the case for freedom of the seas in a manner which every Dutchman, faced with Portuguese and Spanish protectionism, could swiftly understand.[7] An entirely new and much larger realm of calculation thus emerged. Yet this vision did not immediately and materially alter the fundamentally Eurocentric outlook in the conduct of foreign policy that reasserted itself with the Thirty Years' War,

---

4   The original manuscript, in Salamanca, is dated 1602: *Norte de Principes, virreyes, presidentes, consejeros, y governadores, y advertencias politicas sobre lo publico y particular de una Monarquia Importantisimas a los tales: Fundadas en materia y razon de Estado, y Govierno. Escritas por Antonio Perez, Secretario de Estado que fue de Rey Catholico Don Phelipe, segundo de este nombre. Para el uso de duque de Lerma, gran Privado del Senor Rey Don Phelipe tercero* (Madrid 1788) p. 146.

5   Ibid., p. 147.

6   "Notes of a Speech, concerning a War with Spaine", *Letters, Memoirs*, p. 230.

7   C. Roelofsen, "Grotius and the International Politics of the Seventeenth Century", *Hugo Grotius and International Relations*, ed. H. Bull et al. (Oxford 1992 edition) pp. 106–7.

the Seven Years' War (which was only in part an Anglo-French war for the possession of North America), the War of the Spanish Succession and the Napoleonic Wars. It took several centuries to rise to the surface. The explanation and the solution for such conflicts long remained squarely within the idea of the Balance of Power.

As a concept the Balance of Power served to limit the threat that any one state or group of states could pose to the rest of the European states system. That is to say, it recognised an interest above the state, though only for a very clearly defined purpose. Geopolitics as a world view not only widened the compass of calculation in terms of distance, it also effectively extended the realm of the state's needs and further diminished, if not completely supplanted, other competing requirements. Under Kant the state became a legal entity. Under Hegel it was elevated into a logical abstraction. Leading progenitors of anthropomorphic Geopolitics – unconsciously leading back to Marsilius of Padua – now transformed the state into an organism with a life and needs of its own. But this was the least realistic end of a new spectrum of thought about international relations which essentially and usefully sought to contextualise state behaviour in terms of geographical constraints and dynamics.

By the end of the nineteenth century, for all the reflections on the nature and conduct of international relations over the previous five hundred years, there still existed no coherent and comprehensive theory that explained the behaviour of states. The Balance of Power was associated with greater stability and freedom from major war, at least until 1914. It rested still on a sense of mutuality, at least among the Great Powers, expressed in terms like Christian civilisation, and stoutly reinforced by fears generated by the French Revolution and wars that followed. In Europe the Balance was disturbed but not abandoned with the unification from above of Italy and of Germany, the latter accomplished with the bloody reconquest of territory seized by France during the prolonged dismemberment of the Holy Roman Empire. But as a concept which had successfully explained a great part of relations within the European states system for as long as anyone could recall, it no longer seemed adequate for an understanding of why and how in the last decades of the nineteenth century the seizure of obscure islands in the Pacific or tracts of darkest Africa had seemingly taken precedence in international relations over the more vital affairs of the European sub-continent.

Not for the first or the last time in recorded history forces beyond the conscious control of man appeared to be determining events. The notorious German officer turned academic Karl Haushofer (see pp. 177–8) later noted: "Towards the end of the 19th century one had the general impression that the technical and scientific equipment of the era which had developed and grown at break-neck speed had largely overtaken the art of politics, not only in Europe but throughout the world."[8] Geopolitics thus appeared at the very end of the century, when this process reached its peak, as a comprehensive approach to explaining international relations which, in the absence of anything more

8   K. Haushofer, *De la géopolitique*, ed. J. Klein (Paris 1986) p. 98.

convincing and despite its conceptual poverty, came to dominate realist discussions for some years to come. The concept emerged at a time of rapid imperial expansion "as a revolutionary attempt to measure and to harness" those expansionist forces.[9]

The emergence of Geopolitics also reflected the transition from a purely European states system to an international system, a process that began with the liberation of Spanish America and was not finally completed until the Second World War, which then saw the jettisoning of Geopolitics as a mode of explanation and its absorption into the study of international relations in its own right. In this sense Geopolitics was something of a chrysalis which incubated the subject of international relations in its most recent phase of gestation.

In more distant times it is not easy to find evidence for consciousness of the dead weight of natural forces in the writings of statesmen or pamphleteers, perhaps in part because it was so much a part of life that it barely merited any mention. Francis Bacon took up the matter in his reflections on "the true greatness of the Kingdom of Britaine" in terms of "the natural and fit situation of the Region or Place." He defined it thus:

> I mean nothing superstitiouslie touching the fortunes or fatal destinie of anie places, nor philosophicallie touching their configuration with the superiour Globe . . . there doth arise a triple distribution of the fitness of a Region for a great Monarchie. First, that it be of hard accesse. Secondlie, That it be seated in no extreme Angle, but commodiously in the middest of manie Regions. And Thirdly, That it be Maritime, or at the least upon great navigable Rivers; and be not Inland or Mediterrane.[10]

Bacon's outpouring was most obviously little more than a matter of self-congratulation for good Englishmen. Another rare reference comes from one who never held back from stating the obvious in international relations: Antoine Pecquet, admirer of Montesquieu, whose book, *The Spirit of Political Maxims*, claimed to be a sequel to Montesquieu's *Spirit of the Laws*. Here a section can be found which does at least broach the effects of geography on foreign policy. "The conditions given by nature being almost invariable," Pecquet wrote, "the relationship between reciprocal interests that may result from them must be the same; and it is perhaps this of all the relationships upon which one could most clearly base predictable political maxims [*des maximes certaines de politique*], and the best indication of the principles of alliances that seem to accord with this particular relationship."[11] Thus by the time Napoleon Bonaparte wrote to the King of Prussia on 10 November 1804 caustically evaluating Tsar Alexander 1's unrealistic demands in the European system, he was merely reiterating a commonplace, at least in

9   R. Strausz-Hupe, *Geopolitics: The Struggle for Space and Power* (New York 1942) p. viii.

10   *Letters, Mémoirs*, p. 214.

11   Pecquet, *L'Esprit des Maximes Politiques pour servir de suite à L'Esprit des Loix du Président de Montesquieu* (Paris 1758) p. 178.

France: "without doubt", Bonaparte noted, "one day this Power [Russia] will become aware that if she wishes to intervene in the affairs of Europe, she must adopt a reasoned and coherent approach [*un système raisonné et suivi*] and abandon principles springing merely from fantasy and passion, because the policy of all the Powers is a matter of geography."[12]

The constraints of nature were thus seen as intimately bound into the constraints of reason in determining the conduct of foreign policy. But Russian consciousness of geography had always played its role in foreign policy: hence Peter the Great's conquest of the outlet to the Baltic, which led to the momentous foundation of St. Petersburg and the perpetual search thereafter for warmwater ports. In this sense a landlocked Power could not but be ever-conscious of the constraints of geography. Yet once again this was a given rather than an item to be debated, quite apart from the fact that the scope for debate in the Russia of that era was severely circumscribed. Later, leading Slavophile Nikolai Danilevskii, in his popular polemic *Rossiya i Evropa*, referred to the claim that Russia's massive weight overshadowed Europe as "*landkartnoe davlenie*" (literally, "geographical map pressure"), only to dismiss the idea as wrong-headed: to him Russia was victim rather than bully; geography left Russia vulnerable rather than threatening.[13] The term Geopolitics was not yet in broad circulation.

This highlights the main difference between those who saw geography as a limitation on a state's freedom of action and those who saw it as the ultimate determinant of its behaviour. Clearly Napoleon saw geography as a constraint on Alexander's ambitions and an obvious limitation he should have assimilated into his foreign policy-making. Space was not, however, as serious a problem as it became when the world beyond Europe became closed to further expansion. The completion towards the end of the nineteenth century of the conquest of territories that began with the great discoveries of the fifteenth century turned the outer world into a closed system, displacing the gathering tensions of rival overseas empires into the delicately balanced mechanics of the European system. What made matters worse was that the unification of Germany within the confinement of Europe necessarily came about at the expense of France, whose historic role had been to keep the Holy Roman Empire splintered and therefore weak, and that with Britain's domination of the world overseas and the colonial world no longer open to further expansion, the German empire could find accretion of territory – for resources, for markets and for settlement – only through war in Europe. That it sought expansion in those terms, rather than through the peaceful alternatives of industrial and commercial expansion, owed something to the form of

12   *Correspondance de Napoleon 1er*, publiée par ordre de l'Empéreur Napoléon III, Vol. X (Paris 1862) doc. 8170.

13   N. Danilevskii, *Rossiya i Evropa: vzglyad' na kul'turnyya i politicheskiya otnosheniya* (5th edition St. Petersburg 1895) p. 20. The Russian term *landkarta* came straight from the German, *Landkarte*, and was in use from 1744.

government, a great deal to protectionism, but something also to the frame of mind developed by geopolitical thinkers.

The source of those ideas sprang from various and distinct channels: first, organic conceptions of the state rooted in the distant past; and second, a more recent and practical concern to define the boundaries of imperial expansion. The idea of the state as a body that evolved, matured, declined and died was something of a truism since medieval times. Machiavelli wrote: "like all other natural things that are born and grow rapidly, states that grow quickly cannot sufficiently develop their roots, trunks and branches, and will be destroyed by the first chill winds of adversity."[14] It was, after all, an easy and obvious analogy to draw. But political philosophers since Hobbes had seen the state as an artificial construct consciously made by man to provide for a secure civil society. Of this Prussia was perhaps as good an example as any. The Leviathan and its successors were notionally brought into being by contract. There was nothing organic about the state; it was an abstract entity. As Rousseau had pointed out, "One can kill the state without killing even one of its inhabitants."[15] Moreover the Grotian tradition in international relations laid the groundwork for the definition of the state as a legal entity, as we have seen, a feature fixed upon by Kant, and a feature that harmonised well with the contractual explanation for the origins of the state.

Whereas in relatively satisfied nation-states like Britain and France, intellectuals had no need to seek statehood and therefore could afford to view it mechanistically as a functional means to the larger ends of security and prosperity, many Germans, divided and impoverished since the Thirty Years' War, necessarily sought to harness the energies of their countrymen through an appeal to the emotions. In such conditions the image of the contract was hardly a clarion cry to mobilise mass opinion. It was surely for this reason that when in post-Enlightenment Europe German philosophers began to take up the notion, commonplace at court but hitherto ignored in public, of the state as an organism, the idea came as a blinding revelation to the politically conscious, unhappy at the dour image of contract theory.

In the era of Romanticism and under the impact of the Napoleonic invasion and occupation, Adam Müller published *Die Elemente der Staatskunst* in 1809. It emphasised that the organic nature of the state was revealed in war, which was, he asserted, as natural as peace, and in competition with other states: *lebendige Bewegung*.[16] By the end of the century this notion had reached its apogee with the works of Heinrich Ahrens[17] and Friedrich Ratzel's "Der Staat als Organismus" ("The State as an

---

14 Machiavelli, *The Prince*, ed. Skinner and Price (Cambridge 1988) p. 23.
15 "Notes pour le Contrat Social": *Oeuvres*, Vol. 1, p. 422.
16 See F. Coker, *Organismic Theories of the State: Nineteenth Century Interpretations of the State as Organism or as Person* (New York 1910).
17 *Naturrecht oder Philosophie des Rechtes und des Staats auf dem Grunde des ethischen Zusammenhangens von Recht und Cultur* (6th edition, 1870–1).

Organism").[18] It was Ratzel who coined the term political geography, and it was Ratzel who used Malthus' term 'living room' to describe the space required for the development of the nation-state.[19] The main complaint which he sought to remedy, and which shared ground with contract theory, was that "The majority of sociologists study man as if he was formed in the air, without ties to the soil."[20] But other than repeat the analogy of the state as an organism his main work merely underlined the very point made by Napoleon, namely that geography constrained state behaviour. Other Germanic writers of a more liberal persuasion accepted that the state was "in no way a lifeless instrument, a dead machine",[21] much more than a collection of atomised parts, while at the same time arguing that it was a "moral" rather than a "natural" organism.[22]

Either way, the organic theory of the state had caught on in Germany. And it found fertile soil that simultaneously favoured the re-emergence of a forceful Reasons of State doctrine emphasising the centrality of power. It was here, in Germany, after the failure of the 1848 revolutions that the publicist and increasingly conservative Ludwig von Rochau (1810–73) published his *Grundsätze der Realpolitik angewendet aus die staatlichen Zustände Deutschlands* in 1853. It is this work that coins the term *Realpolitik*. The true spirit of the book is summed up in the following terms:

> The political organism of human society, the state, originates and subsists in virtue of a natural law which man, with or without consciousness or will, carries out . . . The imperative of Nature on which the existence of states depends is fulfilled in the historically given state through the antagonism of various forces; its condition, extent and achievements varying infinitely according to space and time. The study of the forces that shape, sustain and transform the state is the starting-point of all political knowledge. The first step towards understanding leads to the conclusion that the law of the strong over political life performs a function similar to the law of gravity over the material world.[23]

But like Machiavelli, von Rochau focused almost entirely upon effective internal reconstruction. This, no doubt, is what gave Machiavelli a second lease of life, in Germany as it did in his own Italy, in the mid-nineteenth century, at a time of resurgent nationalism and the search for statehood. Acton describes the phenomenon thus:

---

18 *Die Grenzboten*, Vol. 55, No 52, 1896.

19 See, for example, F. Rätzel, "Der Lebensraum: eine biogeographische Studie", *Festgaben für Albert Schäffle* (Tübingen 1901) pp. 103–89.

20 F. Ratzel, "Le Sol, La Société et L'État", *L'Année Sociologique 1898–1899*, 1st Part, p. 1.

21 J. Bluntschli, *The Theory of the State* (Oxford 1885) p. 18.

22 Ibid., pp. 72–3.

23 *Grundsätze der Realpolitik angewendet aus die staatlichen Zustände Deutschlands* (Stuttgart 1853) p. 1.

The national movement which united, first Italy and then Germany, opened a new era for Machiavelli. He had come down, laden with the distinctive reproach of abetting despotism; and the men who, in the seventeenth century, levelled the course of absolute monarchy, were commonly known as *novi politici et Machiavellistae . . .* But the immediate purpose with which Italians and Germans effected the great change in the European constitution was unity, not liberty. They constructed, not securities, but forces. Machiavelli's time has come.[24]

Thus on the eve of Italian unification, in 1859, the Tuscan state issued a decree providing for the publication of Machiavelli's entire oeuvre at the expense of the state. And the leading German thinkers were no less grateful.

Within the Machiavellian framework, though, the notion of the state as an organism and the importance of space were a peculiarly German phenomenon. The emphasis Ratzel placed on the importance of geography, however, did find a strong echo in Britain. Here in a more prosaic and "conservative" society, the interest was severely practical rather than semi-mystical and romantic as it had been in Germany. The sense of a shortage of space – or *Lebensraum* – had first been emphasised by Thomas Malthus (1766–1834), whose essay on the subject was published in 1798, perhaps not accidentally, "at a period of extensive warfare . . ."[25] Malthus was born on 17 February 1766 in Dorking, Surrey. A scholar at Cambridge, he was then elected a Fellow of Jesus College. His declared purpose was "to examine the effects of one great cause intimately united with the very nature of man . . . the constant tendency in all animated life to increase beyond the nourishment prepared for it."[26] "Man", he stressed, "is necessarily confined in room."[27] By the time he produced his later editions the message seemed more rather than less urgent: "War, the predominant check to the population of savage nations", had "certainly abated, even including the late unhappy revolutionary contests . . ."[28] The dangers of overpopulation thus appeared more threatening than ever, particularly since the rest of the century was marked by the absence of serious conflict in Europe.

This conception fed into the work of Charles Darwin (1809–82), notably *On the Origins of Species by Means of Natural Selection, or Preservation of Favoured Races in the Struggle for Life*, and into sociologist and journalist Herbert Spencer's obsession with the survival of the fittest. It is notable that Darwin, like Hobbes, and in fact several writers in biology and geology, drew a key metaphor from international

---

24   "Introduction to Burd's Edition of Il Principe by Machiavelli", *Selected Writings of Lord Acton*, pp. 89–90.
25   Preface to the 5th edition of 1817: *An Essay on the Principle of Population; or A View of its Past and Present Efforts on Human Happiness; with an inquiry into our prospects respecting the future removal or mitigation of the evils which it occasions* (6th edition, 1826) p. xi.
26   Ibid., p. 2.
27   Ibid., p. 7.
28   Ibid., p. 534.

relations. Darwin considered using the term "War of nature" to head a section on the struggle for existence in the "big book" of which the *Origin* was a hurried anticipation.[29] He began that section with the words "all nature is at war . . ."[30] And the *Origin* itself is marked by references to "Battle within battle", "war between insect and insect", "one species victorious over another", "the great and complex battle of life" and "war of nature".[31]

Recently some have sought to save Darwin from more militaristic admirers by exclusive emphasis on one aspect alone of his definition of the struggle for existence: the dependence of one species upon another.[32] However, in the very same part of the text Darwin describes this dependence in two forms: the one as assistance from one form of life to another, but the other as the dependence of a bird feeding on an insect. The latter might technically be qualified as dependence, but it is self-evidently not the kind of dependence the insect seeks from its environment! Those seeking to change Darwin's message to support a beneficent and peaceful world have also failed to see that he uses the term struggle in three distinct ways: struggle between individuals within a species which ensures the evolution of the most favourable qualities for survival – the core of this theory; struggle between the species and the environment; and struggle between one species and another.[33] Real dependence was scarcely at the core of his system. Indeed, this almost certainly troubled him. Darwin felt his heart at odds with his head. "Nothing is easier than to admit in words the truth of the universal struggle for life", he wrote in some anguish, "or more difficult – at least I found it so – than constantly to bear this conclusion in mind."[34]

In all events, it was the main thrust of Darwin's message, not the partial qualifications, that had the greatest impact on political thinking. Rätzel himself had trained in zoology and was steeped in the Darwinian heritage. Writings on the natural world, which borrowed from the world of international political conflict, thus fed back into attempts to explain the identity and behaviour of states. They contributed to an intellectual atmosphere in which these organic metaphors acquired a life of their own. If the nation were organically attached to the soil and its numbers were growing exponentially, and the new lands opened by the discoveries were now being closed to

---

29   *Charles Darwin's Natural Selection being the second part of his big specie book written from 1856 to 1858*, ed. R. Stauffer (Cambridge 1975) p. 172.

30   Ibid.

31   Listed in B. Gale's pathbreaking article on "Darwin and the Concept of a Struggle for Existence: A Study of the Extrascientific Origins of Scientific Ideas", *Isis*, September 1972, Vol. 63, No 218, pp. 323–4.

32   Notably G. Beer, *Darwin's Plots: Evolutionary Narrative in Darwin, George Eliot and Nineteen Century Fiction* (London 1983); but also P. Crook, *Darwinism, War and History* (Cambridge 1994).

33   P. Bowler, "Malthus, Darwin, and the Concept of Struggle", *Journal of the History of Ideas*, Vol. 37, No 4, 1976, pp. 632–3.

34   C. Darwin, *On the Origin of Species by Means of Natural Selection, or Preservation of Favoured Races in the Struggle for Life* (London 1859) p. 62.

further entry, so that the gains of one Power could be secured only through losses to the competing Power, was conflict in the form of war not inevitable?

Another strand – much more distinctively realist – originated in the intensification of imperialist rivalry across the "empty" territories across the globe, of what was later to be called the third world. The awareness of the sense of space was compounded by consciousness of the vulnerability of assured communication across that space, which was largely sea. It is startling that, rather like the simultaneous but independent discoveries of evolution through natural selection by both Charles Darwin and Alfred Wallace,[35] both Regius Professor of Modern History at Cambridge Sir John Seeley (1834–95) and retired US Naval Captain Alfred Mahan (1840–1914) drew similar conclusions regarding the relationship between war and the expansion of trade and the empire, at the very same time.

"It so epitomized the general drift of my book on Naval History that I at once forwarded it to the publishers", Mahan wrote of Seeley's published lecture to the Aldershot Military Society of 24 April 1889.[36] But Mahan was surely exaggerating. The central similarity was Seeley's finding that "after the nation had begun to devote itself to commerce, England waged war more frequently and on a greater scale than ever before . . ."[37] This was particularly noticeable of the period after 1689. "The truth is that war and trade went hand in hand throughout this period; it was because we were devoted to trade that we engaged in war; the wars were waged in the interest of the trading classes, and the grounds of war in the main were found just where the trade was, that is, in the New World."[38] War thus arose from empire rather than from conflicts in Europe. Seeley never attempted to cover the growth of British naval power, which formed the focus of Mahan's account, but these assumptions underlay Mahan's thesis. If Britain had built a successful empire by fighting for one at sea, why should not the United States do the same? "When I was first asked to lecture on Naval History at our War College," Mahan told a correspondent, "I proposed to myself at once the question, 'How shall I make the experience of wooden sailing ships, with their pop-guns, useful in the naval present?' The first reply was: 'By showing the tremendous influence Naval Power, under whatever form, has exerted upon the Course of History' . . ."[39]

Mahan was first and foremost an advocate of US naval expansion; all this reasoning was secondary to that primary goal. Thus although *The Influence of Sea Power upon History 1660–1783*, which he published in 1890, was on the surface historical, it

35 *Charles Darwin's*, p. 1.
36 *Alfred Thayer Mahan: The Man and His Letters*, ed. R. Seager (Annapolis 1977) p. 199; J. Seeley, "War and the British Empire", *Journal of the Military Service Institution of the United States*, September 1889, pp. 488–500.
37 Ibid., p. 488.
38 Ibid., p. 492.
39 Mahan to William Henderson, 5 May 1890: *Letters and Papers of Alfred Thayer Mahan*, ed. R. Seager and D. Maguire, Vol. 2 (Annapolis 1975) p. 9.

was most definitely prescriptive in intention and Hobbist in tone. "The history of Sea Power", he wrote in its opening pages, "is largely, though by no means solely, a narrative of contests between nations, of mutual rivalries, of violence frequently culminating in war." Mahan was also consciously responding to "the conditions and signs of these times, and the extra-territorial activities in which foreign states have embarked so restlessly and widely . . ."[40] But the mainsprings for this frantic struggle lay hidden. "It is odd", he wrote, "to watch the unconscious, resistless movements of nations, and at the same time read the crushing characteristics or by accident, happen to be thrust into the position of leaders, when at the most they not only guide to the least harm forces which can no more be resisted permanently than can gravitation."[41]

The expansion of Europe, at its apogee, underlined the fact that control of the seas was the key to power. It is telling, however, that Mahan's conclusion was little more than the reiteration of a maxim coined by John Evelyn in his book *Navigation and Commerce, Their Original and Progress*, published in 1674, with which Mahan was certainly familiar: ". . . whoever Commands the Ocean, Commands the Trade of the World, and whoever Commands the Trade of the World, Commands the Riches of the World, and whoever is Master of That, Commands the World it self . . ."[42] "Let us start from the fundamental truth warranted by history," argued Mahan, "that the control of the seas, and especially along the great lines drawn by national interest or national commerce, is the chief among the merely material elements in the power and prosperity of nations. It is so because the sea is the world's greatest medium of circulation. From this necessarily follows the principle that, as subsidiary to such control, it is imperative to take possession, when it can be done righteously, of such maritime positions as contribute to secure command."[43] Here the natural isolationism of the American people presented an obstacle. Within the economy the overriding focus on tariff protection epitomised this troubling introspection. "Within," he argued, "the home market is secured; but outside, beyond the broad seas, there are the markets of the world, that can be entered and controlled only by a vigorous contest, to which the habit of trusting to protection by statute does not conduce."[44]

Mahan thus emerged from across the Atlantic heralding the United States' emergence as a world Power. He drew from the history of the Royal Navy the lessons that the US Navy should learn to acquire a similar reach. But Britain was now a near-satiated Power of impressive imperial proportions. The dominant preoccupation was how to hang on to all its possessions and how to cope with the claustrophobic friction consequent upon closing the world's frontiers, which threatened the danger of war. The

---

40   "The Future in Relation to American Naval Power", June 1895: Mahan, *The Interests of America in Sea Power, Present and Future* (1897; 1970 edition, New York) p. 139.

41   "A Twentieth-Century Outlook", May 1897: ibid., p. 227.

42   J. Evelyn, *Navigation and Commerce, Their Original and Progress* (London 1674) p. 15.

43   "Hawaii and Our Future Sea Power", March 1893: Mahan, *The Interests*, p. 52.

44   Ibid., p. 4.

situation was ably framed by Halford Mackinder (1861–1947). Born in Gainsborough, Lincolnshire, on 15 February 1861, one of his earliest recollections was of being caned for sketching maps during his Latin class. Geography, although all the rage in Germany, "was then almost completely ignored in the Universities and schools of Britain."[45] A scholar in natural sciences at Christ Church, Oxford, at the early age of only twenty-six, no doubt because of his legendary lectures as a missionary for this comparatively novel subject, he was appointed to the new post of University Reader in Geography. The subject, however, was regarded with deep suspicion in liberal circles. Life in Oxford thus proved uncongenial. One objection raised was "that the study of maps by the young promoted strategical, that is to say militarist and imperialist ways of thinking."[46] Political correctness is not entirely a recent innovation.

Thus it was the Royal Geographical Society in 1904 that hosted Mackinder's lecture entitled "The Geographical Pivot of History".[47] The paper was the result of "many years of observation and thought" and was prompted by the experience of the British war in South Africa against the Boers and Russia's war in Manchuria.[48] His portrayal of the progress of international relations through the centuries was both schematic and to the point. The previous four hundred years had been an age of exploration and expansion. In Christendom threats from outside and the need for resistance by communities had led to the forging of nation-states. "European civilization is", Mackinder opined, "in a very real sense, the outcome of the secular struggle against Asiatic invasion."[49] The defeat and the expulsion of the Moors from Spain, the securing of Europe against Ottoman invasion and the voyages of discovery and subsequent colonisation of the world beyond European shores had given a new stability through the release of pressures that had built up within the closed European states system. "Every explosion of social forces, instead of being dissipated in a surrounding circuit of unknown space and barbaric chaos, will be sharply re-echoed from the far side of the globe, and weak elements in the political and economic organism of the world will be shattered in consequence. There is a vast difference of effect in the fall of a shell into an earthwork and its fall amid the closed spaces and rigid structures of a great building or ship."[50] Elsewhere Mackinder used an equally apt metaphor, strongly reminiscent of Bolingbroke: "we now have a closed circuit – a machine complete and balanced in all its parts. Touch one, and you influence all."[51]

45   E. W. Gilbert, "The Right Honourable Sir Halford J. Mackinder, P.C., 1861–1947", *Geographical Journal*, Vol. CX, No 1–3, July-December 1947, p. 94.
46   Mackinder quoted by Gilbert: loc. cit.
47   H. Mackinder, "Geographical Pivot of History", *Geographical Journal*, Vol. XXIII, No 4, April 1904.
48   Mackinder, "The Round World and the Winning of the Peace", *Foreign Affairs*, Vol. 21, No 4, July 1943, p. 596.
49   Mackinder, "The Geographical . . .", pp. 422–3.
50   Ibid., p. 422.
51   Mackinder, "The Great Trade Routes (Their Connection with the Organization of Industry, Commerce and Finance)", 13 December 1899: *The Institute of Bankers Journal*, Vol. XXI, Part V, May 1900, p. 271.

Although Mackinder followed Napoleon in his assertion that "Man and not nature initiates, but nature in large measure controls",[52] his persuasive characterisation of the evolution of the European states system suggested that the change in the nature of that system by the beginning of the twentieth century brought with it a seriously increased danger of catastrophic war. However, Mackinder did not entirely see the implications of his own discovery. His obsession with the "yellow peril" and Russia's role as the pivotal state in the "Heartland" of the "World-Island", as a barrier against Asia, distracted him from fundamental truths. It remained for the Liberal and anti-imperialist economist John Hobson, and the Marxist Lenin, to draw more far-reaching conclusions than Mackinder was willing to make; and to Haushofer and Hitler, on the Right. Not all that Mackinder said met with general acclamation, however, even from the Right. Fellow of All Souls and journalist Leo Amery, who before long became a noted spokesman for the British empire and the leading intellectual in the Tory Party, found Mackinder's lecture a source of stimulation for further thoughts, one of which all but undermined Mackinder's message entirely. "What I was coming to is this", Amery said at the meeting, "that both the sea and the railway are going in the future – it may be near, or it may be somewhat remote – to be supplemented by the air as a means of loco-motion, and when we come to that (as we are talking in broad Columbian epochs, I think I may be allowed to look forward a bit) – when we come to that, a great deal of this geographical distribution must lose its importance, and the successful powers will be those who have the greatest industrial base. It will not matter whether they are in the centre of a continent or on an island; those people who have the industrial power and the power of invention and of science will be able to defeat all others. I will leave that as a parting suggestion."[53] Thus did Amery anticipate the power of growth in military technology to curb the limitations imposed by geography.

But Mackinder was not without judgement, and certain of his statements in retro-spect sound eerily prophetic. Both before and after World War I, he reacted to Mahan's message of naval supremacy by asserting, to the contrary, the superiority of landpower. From the Heartland key sea routes such as the Suez Canal could be threatened and a lifeline cut above all by countries such as Germany and Russia, "each with a powerful historical momentum." The Heartland was thus critical: "Nature there offers all the prerequisites of ultimate dominance in the world; it must be for man by his foresight and by the taking of solid guarantees to prevent its attainment."[54] The assumption was very much that of an international system prone to continuous conflict of one sort or another, and the underlying explanation was a geographical or economic one. "The great wars of history", he wrote in 1919, "– we have had a world-war about every hundred years for the last four centuries – are the outcome, direct or indirect, of the

52   Mackinder, "The Geographical . . .", p. 422.
53   Intervention: ibid., p. 441.
54   Mackinder, *Democratic Ideals and Reality: A Study in the Politics of Reconstruction* (London 1919) p. 221.

unequal growth of nations, and that unequal growth is not wholly due to the greater genius and energy of some nations as compared with others; in large measure it is the result of the uneven distribution of fertility and strategical opportunity upon the face of the Globe. In other words, there is in nature no such thing as equality of opportunity for the nations."[55] From history and strategy Mackinder moved just as easily to questions of economics, as in his series of lectures delivered to the Institute of Bankers, in which he warned that now geographical discovery was at an end, there would be "the dispersion and equalisation of industrial and commercial activity throughout the world."[56]

Politicians, too, were drawn to the debate in Britain. Mackinder himself stood for parliament. The future Foreign Secretary George Curzon returned at the turn of the century from India, where as Viceroy he had indulged his long-held fascination for the problem of establishing secure frontiers for the British Empire in Asia. At Oxford he spun a fascinating lecture out of his experiences. As Viceroy and later at the India Office Curzon was fully alerted to the growth of the very pressure alluded to by Mackinder. This, he claimed, was as a result "a period of great anxiety when the main sources of diplomatic preoccupation, and sometimes of international danger, had been the determination of the Frontiers of the Empire in Central Asia, in every part of Africa, and in South America."[57] He turned attention to the particular problem of frontiers. Consciously following Mackinder, Curzon referred to "wars arising out of the expansion of states and kingdoms, carried to a point, as the habitable globe shrinks, at which the interests or ambitions of one state come into sharp and irreconcilable collision with those of another."[58] In a passage also very reminiscent of both Malthus and Mackinder, he argued that "with the rapid growth of the population and the economic need for fresh outlets, expansion has, in the case of the Great Powers, become an even more pressing necessity. As the vacant spaces of the earth are filled up, the competition for the residue is temporarily more keen."[59] Yet, like Mackinder, Curzon – though by no means a Liberal – failed to follow through to the most obvious conclusion: a major war. Instead he anticipated an end to the competition and a more settled situation governed by the rule of law – a very Victorian and, indeed, Liberal sense of the inevitability of progress through controlled, peaceful change: convincing testimony to the dominance of Liberal ideology at the turn of the century.

Curzon's lecture is interesting for its portrayal of the solutions adopted to deal with disputed frontier territory where competing empires homed in from opposite directions. Such expedients included protectorates, which extended political or strategic as against direct administrative control and provided for defence against external attack

55   Ibid., p. 2.
56   Mackinder, "The Great Trade . . ." p. 271.
57   Curzon, *Frontiers* (Oxford 1907) p. 2.
58   Ibid., p. 5.
59   Ibid., pp. 7–8.

and attacks on property within the region. Protectorates then shaded "by imperceptible degrees into the diplomatic concept now popularly known as Spheres of Influence." This implied "a stage at which no exterior Power but one may assert itself in the territory so described, but in which the degree of responsibility assumed by the latter may vary greatly with the needs or temptations of the case."[60] One form of expansion naturally blended imperceptibly into another: "Of all the diplomatic forms or fictions which have . . . been described, it may be observed that the uniform tendency is for the weaker to crystallize into the harder shape. Spheres of Interest tend to become Spheres of Influence; temporary Leases become perpetual; Spheres of Influence to develop into Protectorates; Protectorates to be the forerunners of complete incorporation."[61]

Meanwhile the German school of Geopolitics evolved a separate existence from this and other elements blended into a curious and potent concoction: the Romantic revival of the notion of the state as an organism rather than a legal entity; Ratzel's tradition of political geography which emphasised the spatial dimension; Malthus' concerns for overpopulation and the struggle expected to emerge from it; the Darwinian development of evolutionary biology which carried the metaphor to more scientific heights; and the absorption of the writings of Mahan and Mackinder. Some of these ideas were then refracted through the writings of a rather dull but industrious Swedish political scientist, Rudolf Kjellén (1864–1922).

Obliged to cover geography as part of his duties on taking the Chair of Political Science at Göteborg University in 1899, Kjellén read extensively and then began integrating the two subjects.[62] The synthesis resulted in a series of lectures, delivered in 1908, which formed the basis of a book with the simple but delightful title *Staten som Lifsform* – "The State as a Form of Life" – published in 1916.[63] By then he had already coined the term Geopolitics.[64] Yet *Staten som Lifsform* devoted only Chapter Two – *Staten some rike (geopolitik)* – directly to the subject. The book deals also with the state as a people (*etnopolitik*), the state as an economy (*econompolitik*), the state as a society (*sociopolitik*) and the state as government (*regementspolitik*). "Geopolitics", Kjellén wrote, "is the study of the state as a geographical organism . . ."[65] Drawing on the writings of Ratzel, from whom he had all but snatched the title for his book, Kjellén emphasised that the state was rooted in the soil: "Territory is the state's body",[66] he wrote; "The state cannot move"[67] – hence the importance of geography. As an organism, the

60   Ibid., p. 42.
61   Ibid., p. 47.
62   E. Thermaenius, "Geopolitics and Political Geography", *Baltic and Scandinavian Countries*, Vol. IV, No 2 (9), May 1938, p. 166.
63   Preface, R. Kjellén, *Staten som Lifsform* (Stockholm 1916).
64   Kjellén, "Studier ofver Sveriges politiska granser", *Ymer*, Vol. 19, 1899, pp. 283–331; also, Kjellén, *Inledning till Sveriges geografi* (Göteborg 1900).
65   Kjellén, *Staten*, p. 39.
66   Ibid., p. 63.
67   Ibid., p. 44.

state was also perishable like the Roman empire, the Inca kingdom and Moorish Andalucía.[68] He explained:

The state as an empirical fact is not only a legal entity, a constitution and an administrative system . . . It is above all not complete, not stationary . . . It has a life . . . It is, like a private individual, placed in a struggle for existence which absorbs a great part of its power and creates an incessant, stronger or weaker, friction with its surroundings.[69]

Thus the real test of the organism's survival was war. "A country's organic nature never stands out more clearly than in war." And, reflecting no doubt at the time of writing (1915–16) on the shocking devastation of the First World War, Kjellén added: "Modern war has as its object to break the will of the opponent; the most radical means to that end is to seize the entire country, for that is the same as depriving him of the right to dispose of his own body."[70]

Kjellén was hardly the most stimulating writer. He saw his work largely as a form of political morphography – classifying political terminology rather as a botanist identifies plants, but never rising much above this to a more conceptual level. His works never the less had a profound impact on the German Right, not least because they provided a core idea that answered desperate needs. It was Haushofer who pulled Rätzel, Kjellén and Mackinder into a synthesis to bolster German attempts to break out of the Versailles settlement of 1919. Leo Amery, once again watching, wrily, from the sidelines, found it "amusing" that, via Haushofer and Rudolf Hess, Mackinder's *Democratic Ideals and Reality*, which he had neglected to read when it appeared in 1918, "largely influenced Hitler in Mein Kampf!"[71]

Haushofer was born in Munich on 27 August 1869 into the professional classes. He embarked on a military career and it was as a colonel at the front in the summer of 1916 that he read a translation of Kjellén's *Staten som Lifsform*, with which he immediately identified the current "fight for our own life and our existence."[72] By May 1917 he was set on a study of the subject.[73] And, after completing a thesis on the Japanese empire with great rapidity, in the summer of 1919 he was appointed to the Institute of Geography at Munich University. Only a few months before, he had met the young Rudolf Hess. Rudiger Hess has since recalled that "For my father these conversations were the first step leading from an instinctive political thought to a conscious political thought."[74] Haushofer's concern, like that of most Germans after 1919, was

---

68 "Staters och nationers forganglighett": R. Kjellén, *Politiska Essayer. Studier ill Dagskronikan (1907–1913): Internationell Politik och Geopolitik* (Stockholm 1914) p. 3.
69 *Staten*, p. 63.
70 Ibid., p. 51.
71 Diary entry in 1943: *The Empire at Bay – The Leo Amery Diaries 1929–1945* (London 1988) p. 874.
72 Quoted in Hans-Adolf Jacobsen's introduction to K. Haushofer, *De la géopolitique* (Paris 1986) p. 52.
73 Ibid., p. 53.
74 Ibid., p. 63.

dismemberment of the country: the "stones fallen from the wall".[75] The states of Eastern Europe, such as Czechoslovakia, were not true nation-states, which meant they were "incomplete" organisms.[76] Geopolitical ideas were thus put to work to press for a foreign policy that would right these wrongs. Haushofer saw his purpose, inter alia, as that of educating his fellow countrymen into *Raumsinn* or *Raumauffassung*: consciousness of space.[77] In 1924 he founded the journal *Zeitschrift für Geopolitik*. Writing within the limited context of the peaceful revision of Germany's postwar frontiers sought by the leaders of the Weimar Republic, he defined the subject thus: "Geopolitik is one of the most powerful weapons in the struggle for a more just distribution of vital spaces of the east, a distribution based on the capacity to work and the cultural achievements of peoples rather than on settlements imposed by force."[78] Similarly, in another obvious reference to the German problem: "A great nation has to break out from a singularly narrow space, crowded with people, without fresh air, a vital space narrowed and mutilated for the past thousand years . . . unless either the whole east is opened up for the free immigration of the best and most capable people or else the vital spaces still unoccupied are redistributed according to former accomplishments and the ability to create."[79] All that had to be added was dictatorship under a man who soaked up such ideas from Haushofer's academic musings to become the ideology of an entire regime bent on foreign conquest, colonisation and, ultimately, genocide.

The ideas of Seeley, Mahan, Mackinder, Kjellén and Haushofer in turn percolated through into the academic study of international relations in North America just as the United States began to emerge as a world Power. It found expression in the writings of those trying to hasten the process. After the First World War the US Government had essentially withdrawn from the European states system, having made the critical contribution to victory against Germany. It had, however, never withdrawn from Far Eastern affairs, nor indeed from Latin America. The proponents of Geopolitics in the United States wished to project their country back into the centre of the international system. It was at Yale that this process began. Nicholas Spykman (1893–1943), an American of Dutch origin, opened the campaign in two articles published by the *American Political Science Review* early in 1938, as the European crisis was reaching its peak.

Born in Amsterdam on 13 October 1893, Spykman worked as a freelance journalist, first in the Middle East (1913–19) and then the Far East (1919–20) before arriving in California, where he enrolled at the University and graduated within a year. After taking

---

75   Quoted in J. Paterson, "German geopolitics reassessed", *Political Geography Quarterly*, Vol. 6, No 2, April 1987, p. 110.
76   Haushofer to Hans-Otto Roth, 24 June 1935: Haushofer, *De la géopolitique*, p. 240.
77   "German geopolitics . . ." p. 109.
78   Quoted in G. Kiss, "Political Geography into Geopolitics: Recent Trends in Germany", *Geographical Review*, Vol. XXXII, October 1942, No 4, p. 642.
79   Ibid., p. 643.

a PhD just two years later, he taught briefly before translating in 1925 to Yale, where within three years he rose to become full professor. What he brought to the study of international relations from the real world of events covered for the press during the war was an acute sense of the inevitability of conflict based on geographical determinants. This was a message no more popular in the United States of the time than it had been in Mackinder's Oxford. "Politically oriented geography was associated with strategy", a fellow academic noted at Columbia; "Strategy was associated with war-making. Teachers of international subjects were advised to concentrate on peace, not on war."[80]

In 1934 Yale created a separate International Relations department, chaired by Spykman, within the graduate school. He simultaneously applied for and received funding from the Rockefeller Foundation to establish an Institute of International Studies as the research division of the department. It was created in 1935. In his report on the Institute, Spykman outlined the approach he was going to take. He would focus on the foreign policy of the United States rather than international institutions, and when listing the chapters he proposed to write, geography came first.[81] But it did not yet predominate. The proposals for the Institute in general contained the usual litany of the period – the League of Nations, moral sanctions, the prospects of international government etc. So either Spykman was careful to conceal his real intentions or, more likely, the critical nature of geography had not yet occurred to him. Not until 1938 did geography emerge as the dominant element. The first results appeared that year in the *American Political Science Review*. Quoting Napoleon, Spykman sought to establish geography as "the most significant" factor in the conduct of international relations. At the same time, however, he differed from the "organicists" and held more in common with Mackinder and Mahan in seeing geography as a "conditioning" rather than the "determining" element. Location was the key. It made isolationism possible for the United States, in contrast to landlocked countries such as those in Eastern Europe. Their fate was to force their way to the sea (Poland's possession of Danzig, for example, though this was a gift of the Entente rather than unilateral action) or be split by their neighbours.

All geographical factors had their influence on foreign relations – space, topography, climate – and although the advance of technology had reduced their impact in many respects, their role was still critical.[82] All this was anodyne compared to what the German school had said. But a subsequent pair of articles, written jointly with research assistant Abbie Rollins and published in 1939, were more outspoken, at least with respect to Spykman's fundamental assumption about international relations, which

80   H. Sprout, "Geopolitical Hypotheses in Technological Perspective", *World Politics*, No 2, January 1963, p. 190. Sprout had taught at Stanford 1929–30, before moving to Columbia.
81   Yale Institute of International Studies Report for the Year 1935–1936: *Rockefeller Foundation Archives*, RG1.1 series 200 Box 417 Fldr 4952.
82   "Geography and Foreign Policy 2", *American Political Science Review*, No 2, April 1938, pp. 213–36.

reached back to Machiavelli. "Other things being equal," the first article stated, "all states have a tendency to expand."[83] The search for "natural frontiers" formed a focus for such expansion. And there also appears a distinctly Hobbist reference to that "temporary armistice called peace."[84] Moreover, the international system was once more, as in Botero and Bolingbroke, portrayed in the language of natural science, though in this case that of physics rather than mechanics:

> Shifts in frontier, which are the physical manifestations of the dynamics of expansion, are not, however, the only or first indications of a shift in the balance of forces. The realm of international politics is like a field of forces comparable to a magnetic field. At any given moment, there are certain large powers which operate in that field as poles. A shift in the relative strength of the poles or the emergence of new poles will change the field and shift the lines of force. A reorientation and realignment of the small powers in such a field may be the first result of a shift in the balance of forces between the large powers.[85]

These articles formed the groundwork for the book *America's Strategy in World Politics*, which was completed by the end of October 1941 and was in galley proofs the day after the Japanese bombed Pearl Harbor on 8 December.[86] It is impressive indeed that at this stage only twenty pages needed changing. Spykman had planned a parallel study on British security policy from the geographical standpoint and a second study on the United States, but poor health, which had caused him to give up directing Yale's Institute in 1939, supervened, cutting short his life on 26 June 1943.

America's Strategy in World Politics was timely and controversial. It insisted upon the need for the United States to remain engaged in Europe and the Far East. Building upon Mackinder's notion of a World Island, Spykman argued that it would continue to be in the interests of the United States to prevent its domination by any one Power. Mahan had structured his case for global US seapower on the basis of the British experience. Spykman now constructed his case for a US policy of maintaining the world Balance of Power on his interpretation of the history of British foreign policy. He was above all anxious to rid the United States of Wilsonian illusions. "Nations which renounce the power struggle and deliberately choose impotence will cease to influence international relations either for good or evil", he stressed. *Life* magazine subsequently ran a sensationalist long article on the subject of Geopolitics attacking Spykman from a

---

83   N. Spykman and A. Rollins, "Geographical Objectives in Foreign Policy, I", ibid., Vol. 33, No 3, June 1939, p. 394.

84   Ibid., p. 395.

85   Ibid.

86   Frederick Dunn (Yale) to Joseph Willits (Rockefeller Foundation), 16 March 1942: *Rockefeller Foundation Archives*, RG 1.1 Series 200, Box 416, Fldr 4945. Dunn took over from Spykman as director of the Institute.

Wilsonian standpoint: "This policy parallels, on a grander scale, the historic policy of Britain towards the continent of Europe. It is cold-blooded power politics. It assumes that wars are inevitable and seeks to assure that the U.S. will hold the balance of power."[87] Spykman was hurt. "My interest in a balance of power", he responded, "is not merely inspired by a concern for our power position, but also by my conviction that only in a system of approximately balanced powers is collective security workable. Only under such conditions can common action create overwhelming power on behalf of the international community. If there is no possibility of balancing power, there is no possibility of resistance and the less power required to checkmate aggression, the more likely are states to make good on their guarantees."[88] For all the tough talk, Spykman thus stood at the moderate end of the geopolitical spectrum, and, among others, led the way towards a synthesis of the traditional concepts of realism into a late twentieth-century attempt to account for the age-old problem of international conflict. Mackinder and Spykman's warning of the dangers of a preponderance of one Power on the Eurasian landmass inevitably prompted an emotive reaction from some quarters. It is salutary in this connexion to note how blind most were to what lay not so far ahead. A reader, Philip Nordell, wrote in to complain that "some will think that we must beware of Russia. On the basis of this sheer bunk, I have already heard one seemingly normal person portentously announce that because Russia controls the Heartland she is a menace to the whole world."[89]

The general interest in Geopolitics, though confined to a minority under attack in the West, continued to grow in the United States, so much so that Mackinder was invited to relaunch his ideas in *Foreign Affairs*, journal of the influential Council on Foreign Relations, just before he too died in the summer of 1943. Answering critics who recently echoed the reservations originally made by Amery concerning the likely impact of air-power on the conduct of war, Mackinder insisted that his concept of the Heartland – essentially Eurasia and later the USSR – was as valid as ever. The conclusions he drew from this central concept, as applied to current conditions, were no less prophetic than his earlier observations and no less offensive to those readers of *Life* who objected most to Spykman: "All things considered, the conclusion is unavoidable that if the Soviet Union emerges from this war as conqueror of Germany, she must rank as the greatest land Power on the globe. Moreover, she will be the Power in the strategically strongest defensive position. The Heartland is the greatest natural fortress on earth. For the first time in history it is manned by a garrison sufficient both in number and quality."[90] He did not see airpower as critical and in this he was proved right by the survey of the use of airpower made at the end of the war. The atomic bomb had yet to appear, but even

87   J. Thorndike, "Geopolitics: The Lurid Career of a Scientific System which a Briton Invented, the Germans Used and Americans Need to Study", *Life*, 21 December 1942.
88   Letter: ibid., 11 January 1943.
89   Ibid.
90   Mackinder, "The Round World . . ." p. 601.

when it did, Stalin continued to believe that the West might be able to bomb Moscow but it could not win a war against the Soviet Union unless it could occupy Soviet territory, and that would take troops in number. Mackinder ended his article with the reflection that after Germany and Japan were mature as economies, India and China would emerge into prosperity. But in all a balance would be required. Reaching back into the past for the Balance of Power, he looked forward to "a balanced globe of human beings. And happy, because balanced and thus free."[91]

However sanguine the writings of Mackinder in the democratic world, the alternative vision thrown up by Geopolitics in Central Europe gives pause for thought. Perhaps even more than the notions of Reasons of State and Balance of Power, the implications of German Geopolitics underline the close (and for us uncomfortable) inter-relationship between apparently harmless, abstract and avowedly impersonal realist reasoning and the policy-directed and operational needs of Powers seeking to justify as much as clarify their behaviour in the international system. That such notions should then be used by students of international relations in years subsequent to those which originally gave rise to them and in circumstances at great remove from those that precipitated them raises awkward and important questions about the realist tradition.

It was no accident that Geopolitics achieved a revival at the very place and at the very moment when the United States was emerging as the potential Superpower; and although the term all but disappeared, the attendant ideas persisted and spread under different cover in the years that followed in various schools of International Relations from coast to coast. Spykman was in advance of his time in anticipating the role that the United States would play, and, like Mahan before him, it was not merely anticipation but ambition for his country that drove him into print. One should never assume that scholarship precludes advocacy or that advocacy entirely jeopardises scholarship, particularly in so current and controversial a field as international relations. But the development of International Relations as a subject in its own right, particularly in the United States, owed less to the absorption of Geopolitics than to other intellectual currents that flowed across the Atlantic driven by the cyclone of war that encircled the Old World.

91   Ibid., p. 602.

Chapter 5
FROM *REALPOLITIK* TO NEOREALISM

"It is curious to find that our policy makers who tend to believe that they act by sheer instinct and without any theory or philosophy, were misled by a very definite philosophy of international relations, one as a matter of fact which, until recently, has been prevalent in this country . . ."

– Arnold Wolfers[1]

The term Reasons of State had all but disappeared from works on international relations by the end of the eighteenth century. Gone but not forgotten, it none the less underpinned the twin notions of the Balance of Power and the Balance of Trade that structured the conduct of international relations in the ensuing decades. By the middle of the nineteenth century, however, it effectively re-emerged under a new label – German, this time: *Realpolitik*. It was from the heart of Central Europe that the realist tradition in international relations found its way into the United States nearly one hundred years later: imported in the mental baggage of refugees tossed uninvited and unexpectedly upon the shores of an untutored New World, as the Old World descended into a new barbarism. The United States had sought to escape from the tainted European legacy of realism. Turn-of-the-century moralist William Sumner captured this well encrusted sentiment when he noted: "The fathers of the Republic . . . meant to have no grand statecraft or 'high politics', no 'balance of power' or 'reasons of state', which had cost the human race so much."[2] To say that realism was therefore not entirely welcome in the United States is an understatement. But how and why had *Realpolitik* suddenly appeared in, and so speedily seized, Central Europe?

One might have expected that the French Revolution and its wars of conquest would be a turning-point for the conduct of international relations in Europe, that the principles of republicanism and of national self-determination would sustain unchallenged

---

1 "The Pattern of the Post-War World", Lecture to the National War College, 10 September 1947: *Wolfers Papers* 634, Series 2, Box 18, Folio 230 (Yale).
2 W. Sumner, "The Fallacy of Territorial Extension", 1896: *War and Other Essays* (New Haven 1919) pp. 291–2.

authority in the liberal camp and that the top-down preferences of the absolutist Powers would forever be discarded. The irony, instead, is that Reasons of State re-emerged under cover of the new concept of *Realpolitik*. The French Revolution had been conducted under the banner of the Enlightenment: rational, universal values as the route to freedom, liberation beyond the confines of the state. But the expansion of that revolution by the French bayonet across the old frontiers of Europe effectively aroused a backlash not only among the legitimists, who called for counter-revolution in the name of the *ancien régime*, but also, and ultimately with more lasting effect, among those who unexpectedly unmasked the universalism of the French as a cover for national self-interest and who sought to create a nation-state to defend their own, par-ticularist interests against those of expansionist France. This reaction was most evident in the German states, where support for the revolution was initially strong, but then collapsed once Napoleon invaded and sought to crush national identity. These were the fertile conditions in which the idea of Reasons of State re-emerged. Its most eminent expositor was Leopold von Ranke (1795–1886); its most famous practitioner, Otto von Bismarck (1815–98). The historian Ranke never formulated doctrine, but the ideas which von Rochau and later von Treitschke expressed could be found in Ranke's historical reflections.

Ranke reacted fiercely against the hegemonic cosmopolitanism of the Enlighten-ment, which he identified with the Napoleonic invasions that threatened the individu-ality of the state and with the spread of ideas that undermined the idea of a separate statehood. Following Napoleon's defeat, among liberals universalistic ideas of a European community emerged. As if in tandem, the reactionary *anciens régimes* of Austria and Russia also held back true statehood, in this instance by organizing the Holy Alliance to sustain the imperial status quo regardless of national identity. It was time, Ranke insisted, for each state to return to the national trajectory that had been thrown off course by the revolutionary wars.[3]

The term *Realpolitik* first appeared, as we have seen, in a tough-minded rejection of liberal idealism at the hands of von Rochau in his *Grundsätze der Realpolitik angewendet aus die staatlichen Zustände Deutschlands* in 1853. It was here that Rochau, having perhaps overlearnt the hard lessons of bitter experience in the search for German reunification, emphasised the importance of understanding "that the law of the strong [*das Gesetze der Stärke*] over political life performs a function similar to the law of gravity over the material world."[4] Only through the proper understanding and use of power could national unification be accomplished. The term was enthusiasti-cally adopted by the influential Heinrich von Treitschke (1834–96), who wrote a biog-raphy of the founder of unified Italy Count Cavour, in order to show the German

---

3   "Politisches Gespräch" (1836): Ranke, *Sämmtliche Werke: "Zur Geschichte Deutschlands und Frankreichs im neunzehnten Jahrhundert"* (Leipzig 1887) p. 329.
4   *Grundsätze der Realpolitik*, p. 1.

public "how brilliant Realpolitik is,"[5] and thereby signalled a conscious revival of Reasons of State.

It was from this mixed parentage that there emerged a figure who sought to connect the tumultuous present with the larger European realist tradition in attempting a complete vindication of the emergence of Germany as a nation-state. This was Friedrich Meinecke. Born on 30 October 1862 in Magdeburg, Prussian Saxony, Meinecke achieved academic success early, becoming editor of the prestigious *Historische Zeitschrift*, along with Treitschke, in 1895. His epochal book, *Weltbürgertum und Nationalstaat*, followed Ranke, von Rochau and von Treitschke in turning its back on the cosmopolitanism of the Enlightenment. Only by so doing, Meinecke asserted, had Germany finally attained statehood.[6] The rejection of universalist values above and beyond the state paved the way for the re-emergence of Reasons of State at the pinnacle of society's values. Thus Meinecke's forceful sequel, *Die Idee der Staatsräson in der Neueren Geschichte* (1924), provided the historical basis for the re-emergence of Reasons of State in Germany. Yet, curiously, the author was reluctant to define the very concept whose pedigree he traced so attentively through the preceding centuries.[7] Critics also seized upon a further feature, in this instance common to "a great deal of political theory, so-called. This difficulty", as Carl Friedrich of Harvard noted, echoing Kant, "is rooted in the constant confusion of political and juristic concepts, a confusion which is bred by the desire of political pamphleteers to obscure the essential logical distinction between categories of existence and categories of essence, between what is and what ought to be."[8] For all that, in 1924 Meinecke successfully reinserted Reasons of State centre stage. Meinecke's significance extended far beyond the immediate impact of his two main works. All the key realists who followed, consciously or not, built their structures on the foundations he laid: the Dutchman, Spykman, the Englishman, Carr, the German, Morgenthau, the Swiss, Wolfers, and the Americans, Tucker and Waltz. These ideas, reiterated and reformulated by Meinecke, were so deeply imbibed as almost to become a commonplace; certainly below consciousness of the need for explicit attribution.

Meinecke made his most dramatic impact on the English-speaking world, for several reasons. First, these were the men least aware of the Reasons of State tradition, which was almost entirely, certainly latterly, of continental European origin; and German political ideas ceased to carry the mark of unalloyed integrity as the Second World War approached. Second, and more importantly, the initial reaction of the Anglo-American

---

5   Letter to Salomon Hirzel, 28/11 65: ed. M. Cornicelius, *Heinrich von Treitschkes Briefe* (Leipzig 1913) pp. 437–8.
6   See F. Meinecke, *Cosmopolitanism and the National State* (Princeton 1970); originally *Weltbürgertum and Nationalstaat* (Munich 1907).
7   Noted by critic Carl Friedrich of Harvard: review in the *American Political Science Review*, November 1931, Vol. XXV, No 4, pp. 1064–9.
8   Ibid., p. 1067.

middle classes to the catastrophic human losses incurred in the First World War was to embrace liberal and utopian solutions to the problem of international conflict. The League of Nations was to become the focus of these aspirations. Arbitration, security and disarmament were the League's answers; the emphasis (with the notable and then notorious exception of France) on arbitration and disarmament. Collective security, although provided for in the Covenant, tended to be neglected by these idealists because it carried with it the threat and use of force. The universalism that reasserted itself after World War I had a strongly pacifist undercurrent. But once these ideals ran into the rocks, Meinecke's message appeared to make a good deal more sense.

The United States had opted out of League of Nations membership when in 1920 the Senate refused to ratify Wilson's commitments. None the less the utopian assumptions that riddled middle-class Britain had their counterpart in the United States, not least because they harmonised with both native Wilsonianism and historic isolationism. One natural adherent to this extension of liberal assumptions was the young Edward Hallett Carr (1892–1982). Born into Victorian but liberal Britain, Carr early on in life acquired much of the intellectual furniture of the period. Laissez-faire economics, the longstanding belief that free trade increased harmony between states, national self-determination, the dislike of military power, or at least the assumption that arms races caused war, were combined in his mind to view the transition from a devastating war to a long-sought peace as a natural reversion to the best of the old order. He like many other liberals and socialists saw in the League of Nations the natural and more humane culmination of the tradition of the Concert of Europe: a means to avert war. Carr's only doubts – like those of the economist and fellow liberal John Maynard Keynes – concerned the vengeful conditions of peace forced upon the Germans in 1919. Some of the best cynics were once great but later deeply disappointed idealists. Carr fits this picture. The ideals of a stable and humane international order based on liberal principles were shattered. First, the new small nation-states of Eastern Europe (his area of specialism) began behaving a good deal worse than even the Great Powers. Second, the onerous conditions loaded on Germany at Paris offended the liberal conscience. Third, the outbreak of the Great Depression in 1929 cut away the intellectual supports of free trade. Parallel to such reflections, Carr's absorption in the alien but enticing world of Russian culture sensitised him to the relativity of values which, when internalised into a mind long divested of the stabilising pillars of religion, left him dangerously agnostic.[9]

Carr had been conscripted into the Foreign Office in 1916 and there imbibed the 'necessities of power'. For him, therefore, Meinecke did no more than to reinforce lessons learned from experience. The process of attrition which ate away at his core liberal beliefs was never complete, however. The spirit of indignation at the harsh treat-

---

9   For further detail: J. Haslam, *The Vices of Integrity: E. H. Carr, 1892–1982* (London/New York 1999).

ment of the Germans which he shared with all liberals and socialists grew rather than reduced with time. Thus Hitler's assumption of power in 1933 appeared to Carr the logical consequence of the Versailles Treaty, and within the Central Department of the Foreign Office, which dealt with Germany, he pressed the argument for the appeasement of the Nazi regime as far as was permissible. It was only when he chose to press it further still that his remaining there became impracticable. He therefore removed himself to academia, namely a special Chair in International Relations at the University of Wales in Aberystwyth in 1936. It was with this new-found freedom and from this newly acquired ivory tower that he intended to preach the cause of appeasement.

The most important by-product of this process was the text he produced for a course on international politics, which he named "Utopia and Reality" but which eventually appeared under the anomalous title *The Twenty Years' Crisis* at the very outbreak of war in 1939. The initial motivation – to preach appeasement – thus immediately became redundant, but in the course of reasoning out his position Carr unfolded "an analysis of fundamental trends in international politics",[10] the first coherent realist theory of international relations yet in print, and he did so building largely upon personal experience, a classical education and wide reading in political thought.

The Twenty Years' Crisis, in Carr's words, was written to counteract "the glaring and dangerous defect of nearly all thinking, both academic and popular, about international politics in English-speaking countries from 1919–1939 – the almost total neglect of the factor of power."[11] He consciously saw himself as a kind of twentieth-century Machiavelli, doing for international relations what the Italian had done for politics in general. In August 1930 he had expressed approval of Machiavelli's contribution to turning the study of politics into a science by rudely brushing aside "the vague ideals of altruism and humanitarianism to which men Odid lip service and no more."[12] "Machiavelli's starting-point", he noted in 1939, "is a revolt against the utopianism of current political thought."[13] "The realists of the Renaissance made the first determined onslaught on the primacy of ethics and propounded a view of politics which made ethics an instrument of politics, the authority of the state being thus substituted for the authority of the church as the arbiter of morality".[14] He argued:

> The teleological aspect of the science of international politics has been conspicuous from the outset. It took its rise from the great and disastrous war; and the over-

10   Carr to Harold Macmillan, 31 May 1939: *Macmillan Company Archives*.
11   Preface to the second edition, 15 November 1945.
12   Review of a book on Machiavelli: *Fortnightly Review*, August 1930.
13   *The Twenty Years' Crisis 1919–1939: An Introduction to the Study of International Relations* (London 1939) p. 81.
14   Ibid., p. 31.

whelming purpose which dominated and inspired the pioneers of the new science was to obviate a recurrence of this disease of the international body politic.[15]

It was, he asserted, "hard ruthless analysis of reality which is the hallmark of science".[16]

The parallels between Carr and Machiavelli are striking, even where they diverge. Both served the state in diplomatic capacities. Both left office disappointed. Both possessed sensitive minds that reacted emotionally to changes in the international situation and to the presumed incompetence of those in power. Both were realists who none the less had within them still a strong streak of idealism: Machiavelli for the liberation of Italy; Carr for the peaceful settlement of European differences by granting Germany what was presumed to be its due. There the identification ends, however. But the similarities are undoubtedly greater than the differences. And the degree of identification that Carr felt was heightened by his reading of Meinecke's treatise on Machiavellism, which had appeared a decade before.

Carr's book revolves around the distinction between utopia and reality and here an intellectual debt was due to Reinhold Niebuhr, who had recently laid bare the unpleasant realities of domestic society in *Moral Man and Immoral Society*. Carr extends the distinction to that between theory and practice, the intellectual and the bureaucrat. On this view the intellectual tended towards the Left, "just as naturally as the bureaucrat, the man of practice, will gravitate towards the Right."[17] This was Carr speaking from direct experience. A further influence is evident in his strictures concerning the notional autonomy of intellectual thought – the influence of Karl Mannheim. Intellectuals, he wrote, "liked to think of themselves as leaders whose theories provide the motive force for so-called men of action"; in reality, however, their thought was "conditioned by forces external to themselves".[18]

Mannheim's sociology of knowledge, ultimately derived from Marx's *German Ideology*, provided Carr with the ideal instrument with which to undermine liberal idealism: "the view that the nineteenth century liberal democracy was based, not on a balance of forces peculiar to the economic development of the period and countries concerned, but on certain a priori principles which had only to be applied in other contexts to produce similar results, was essentially utopian".[19] The application of that theory to the peace settlement of 1919 resulted in the creation of political structures across Europe modelled on nineteenth-century Britain but rooted in material conditions that bore no relationship to the original. Hence Carr's conclusion that "The liberal democracies scattered throughout the world by the peace settlement of 1919 were the product of abstract theory, stuck no roots into the soil, and quickly shrivelled away."[20]

15   Ibid., p. 11.
16   Ibid., p. 13.
17   Ibid., p. 26.
18   Ibid., p. 39.
19   Ibid., p. 37.
20   Ibid., pp. 37–8.

Whereas Carr attributed considerable importance to economic factors, Machiavelli was dismissive of the power of money. The utopianism Carr described presupposed a natural harmony of interests, as we have seen from the time of Florus and Grotius. But this utopianism, Carr went on, assumed "that every nation has an identical interest in peace, and that any nation which desires to disturb the peace is therefore both irrational and immoral."[21] It is here that his assault on the self-interest of Anglo-American liberalism intersected with the case for appeasement. And it is here that Carr asserted the centrality of interests in international relations. Britain wanted peace; Germany appeared to want war. "The common interest in peace masks the fact that some nations desire to maintain the *status quo* without having to fight for it, and others to change the *status quo* without having to fight to do so".[22] The economic counterpart to this division was the tension between those advocating free trade and those promulgating protectionism. Here Carr called upon experience. As a member of the British delegation at the League of Nations in Geneva during the Slump, he heard the Yugoslav Foreign Minister attack the self-interest of the industrialised countries disguised as the demand for free trade. By the time Carr composed his book, he had no doubt also referred to List but most probably only to see more closely the reasoning out of the case that he first encountered at Geneva. "The old 'things-will-right themselves' school of economists", he wrote, "argued that if nothing were done and events were allowed to follow their natural course from an economic point of view, economic equilibrium would come about of its own accord . . . But how would that equilibrium come about? At the expense of the weakest."[23]

This onslaught on the supremacy of liberal thought shocks even today when the case for Germany appears not only anachronistic but also dangerously misleading. No one had quite so systematically analysed the conduct of international relations in such frighteningly realist terms and the epitaph Carr gave Machiavelli in this respect stands equally for his own:

> Where Machiavelli is . . . most original and most modern is in his attempt to treat politics as an ethically neutral science, not as a branch of ethics. There is an element of technical efficiency in politics which is as independent of moral considerations as are the qualities of high explosives . . . The greatness of Machiavelli is that he saw a part, though not the whole, of the truth about politics with unrivalled penetration.[24]

Carr was not alone in reacting to utopian illusions by attacking them at length and in print. On the other side of the Atlantic Spykman had led the way (see pp. 178–81). But it was the German-Jewish immigrant Hans Morgenthau (1904–80) who made the

21   Ibid., p. 67.
22   Ibid., p. 68.
23   Ibid., p. 74.
24   "Is Machiavelli a Modern?", *Spectator*, 28 June 1940.

most forceful impact. Henry Kissinger, academic and statesman, recalled that Morgenthau "made the study of contemporary international relations a major discipline. All of us who taught the subject after him, however much we differed from one another, had to start with his reflections. Not everybody agreed with him, but nobody could ignore him."[25] And here the influence of Meinecke and the tradition from which he drew is much more evident than on Carr, though Carr's impact on Morgenthau was itself not inconsiderable – indeed, it should be noted that Carr's was one of ten key books cited by Morgenthau as among those that have most shaped people's lives.[26]

Born in Coburg, Bavaria, Germany, on 17 February 1904, the son of a doctor, Morgenthau set out to study philosophy at the then fashionable centre of Marxist thought, the University of Frankfurt, but found it surprisingly out of touch with the realities of the day. Instead he moved over to law, graduating from the University of Munich and entering the Bar in 1927.[27] By then his intellect was most influenced by, as his biographer notes, "the honesty of Nietzsche, the objectivity of Weber, the empiricist postulates of Machiavelli",[28] against what Morgenthau called "the moralising reflections of the Germans".[29] He took the view strongly held by Carr (and later R. W. Tucker) that the morality of the individual had no bearing on the behaviour of the state.[30] Indeed, in the summer of 1927 he began putting together material for a work on Machiavelli. It was at this time that Morgenthau read *Die Idee der Staatsräson*, published three years earlier, only to realise that Meinecke had done the job for him.[31]

Morgenthau returned to Frankfurt to take a doctorate. He simultaneously engaged in private practice, specialising in labour law and working as a teaching assistant to Hugo Sinzheimer, the founder of progressive labour law. But he found lawyers too narrow in outlook (later on in life the term "lawyer" was to Morgenthau a term of abuse).[32] Moreover, his interest in ideas had by no means disappeared. He was determined to reintroduce politics into the law through his study of international law. And it is around this time that he came to the attention of the now prominent right-wing critic of liberalism, Carl Schmitt, who, in a landmark tract which in retrospect seems hard to appreciate, in 1928 defined politics in terms of the friend-enemy dualism.[33]

25   H. Kissinger, "A gentle analyst of power. Hans Morgenthau", *New Republic*, Vol. 183, Nos 5 and 6, 2 and 9 August 1980.

26   C. Frei, *Hans J. Morgenthau: Eine intellektuelle Biographie* (Bern 1994) p. 117.

27   For details of his student years: H. Morgenthau, "Fragment of an Intellectual Autobiography", K. Thompson and R. Myers (ed.), *A Tribute to Hans Morgenthau* (Washington DC 1977). And for his years in Germany, see J. Honig, "Totalitarianism and Realism: Hans Morgenthau's German Years", *Security Studies*, Vol. 5, No 2, Winter 1995, pp. 283–313.

28   C. Frei, *Hans J. Morgenthau*, p. 128.

29   Diary entry, 9 May 1927: ibid.

30   Letter dated 7 October 1931: ibid.; also letter of 28 October 1934: ibid.

31   Ibid.

32   He used mistakenly to dismiss Robert W. Tucker as "a lawyer".

33   See C. Schmitt, *The Concept of the Political* (New Jersey 1976). For the larger context of Schmitt's work: E. Kennedy's introduction to C. Schmitt, *The Crisis of Parliamentary Democracy* (Cambridge, Mass.

This was *Der Begriff des Politischen*. Morgenthau, clearly influenced by Schmitt, unex-pectedly received from him a flattering comment about his doctoral thesis (of which more below) and was summoned to see the professor in Berlin. But Schmitt promptly disillusioned the somewhat prickly young man by staging the meeting rather in the manner of "a public relations production".[34] If this were not disappointment enough, Schmitt then plagiarised one of Morgenthau's key ideas in the second edition of *Der Begriff*. Morgenthau, whose academic prospects could have been rapidly elevated by Schmitt's published acknowledgement of an intellectual debt, reacted with justified resentment.[35] It is worth noting, therefore, that Morgenthau's basic outlook on politics was formed before Schmitt's most important work reached the world and, in fact, also before he had laid eyes on Meinecke.

All was not lost, however. Morgenthau was determined to argue that international law was inescapably political. It therefore seemed entirely logical for Morgenthau to borrow Schmitt's famous tag and to label his thesis "The International Judicial Func-tion and the Concept of Politics" – much to the dislike of his supervisors, who insisted he cut "politics" from the title.[36] "Having learned already that international law is a par-ticularly weak kind of law, I now discovered that the main source of its weakness stems from the intrusions of international politics. From that discovery there was but one step to the conclusion that what really mattered in relations among nations was not inter-national law but international politics."[37] That step had yet to be taken, however. On completing his training Morgenthau became acting president of the labour law court in Frankfurt in 1931 but, increasingly conscious of the political dimension to the system of justice and extremely uncomfortable at the increased anti-semitism in Germany on the eve of Hitler's rise to power, he moved in 1932 to a poorly paid and, as it turned out, dead-end job at the graduate Institute of International Studies in Geneva, where the great Hans Kelsen had set up shop.

It was here that Morgenthau became an instructor in German public law but also taught international politics, international law, European government and political theory.[38] Although a disappointment, this proved a fruitful period, ending in 1935 and resulting in the publication of *La Réalité des Normes en particulier des normes du droit international*,[39] a Kelsenian work to the core. The work is no less interesting because at

---

1985); and P. Noack, *Carl Schmitt: Eine Biographie* (Berlin 1993). For an extensive discussion of Schmitt's claimed influence on the extreme left as well as the better known influence on the right, besides Kennedy's introduction, see E. Parise, *Carl Schmitt: La difficile critica del liberalismo* (Naples 1995).

34   Frei, *Hans J. Morgenthau*, p. 170.

35   Schmitt, *Der Begriff des Politischen* (Munich 1932) pp. 27 and 38: Frei, *Hans J. Morgenthau*, p. 170.

36   The title that finally emerged was *Die internationale Rechtsfluge, ihr Wesen und ihre Grenzen* (The International Law of the Air – its Essence and its Limitations), published in 1929.

37   Ibid., p. 9.

38   *Hans Morgenthau Papers* (Library of Congress), Box 66.

39   Paris, 1934.

the outset Morgenthau refused to follow the established pattern of bowing to the authorities in the field. "As far as we are concerned, we do not believe in the scholarly utility of a method which consists, to take one example, in incessantly reproducing in each new study dedicated to the connexions between international law and domestic law, all the theories that have been developed on the subject of this problem, even citing entire passages from these works known to all scholars and that everyone can get hold of. This method consisting of making of nine books a tenth, to quote Schopenhauer, is certainly proof of immense application, but it seems to us rather unoriginal."[40] Independent to the last, he was, however, prepared to acknowledge his debt to Kelsen, who thereafter became his key referee, for "the trend towards a truly scholarly knowledge of normative and, in particular, legal phenomena."[41] Indeed, Morgenthau prefaced his book with an expression of deep regret that Kelsen's pioneering work – the most profound and systematic in the study of norms – remained *ein Zwischenfall ohne Folgen* ("an incident without consequences").[42]

Kelsen had taken as his starting-point the application of Kantian thought to the field of law. Kant had drawn a clear distinction between the realms of reality and of ethics (is and ought). Kelsen used the independence of the normative sphere to draw systematic consequences for the study of law. And it is within the context of this discussion that Morgenthau first issued his opinion as to the critical distinction between the natural and the social sciences:

> The natural law of gravitation is valid . . . whether man wishes it or not. It would be the same, according to Grotius, with respect to natural law whether or not there were God to sanction its validity. Natural laws are always and necessarily effective.
>
> . . . The validity such as it is of the norms of law, of ethics or morality is on the contrary inseparably tied to the existence of human communities. It is not at all because their content is just or because it flows directly from the nature of things and from man that norms are valid, but uniquely because human will – normative will – determines [*s'incorpore*] the content of these norms to bring them into being . . . This kind of validity is thus relative; for its existence depends upon the inconstant will of men.[43]

He was not to return to this theme for some years. Like Carr, Morgenthau did not tolerate fools gladly. He was ever conscious of the "*volonté de puissance*" ("will to power"),[44] at all stages of his career, even with respect to research and writing. It would,

---

40   H. Morgenthau, *La Réalité des Normes en particulier des normes du droit international* (Paris 1934) p. vii.
41   Ibid., p. xi.
42   Ibid., p. 1.
43   Ibid., pp. 38–9.
44   Ibid., pp. viii–ix.

however, be wrong to see him as entirely inflexible. His determination to make a successful career out of the study of world politics drove him on relentlessly and forced
him into fairly humble, if not humiliating, conditions en route. After he became a professor of law, which in the Latin as well as the Germanic world encompasses politics,
in Madrid in 1935, the Spanish civil war supervened. Morgenthau, mixing with the
Republican elite, made no effort to leave – at first: according to a close friend, he "under-
estimated the depth and force of the popular revolt unleashed by Franco's coup – a
spontaneous popular movement which at that time did not fit too well in his concept
of power politics."[45] Finally, as matters went from bad to worse, in 1937 he took the best
option open to him: emigration to the United States, where he held the lowly position
of instructor in government at Brooklyn College for two years and suffered the reputation among activist Jewish Communist students of being proto-Fascist, because of
his coolly detached view of politics as *Realpolitik*.[46] Kelsen also moved to the United
States, but to the higher elevation of Berkeley, California, and to a tenured post.
He wrote well of this difficult but gifted young man, who seemed to go out of his way
not to appear a *protégé*. Morgenthau was, he wrote, a "very qualified, diligent and con-
scientious scholar". Kelsen read *La Réalité* in draft and was struck by the fact that this
was no mere reiteration of existing knowledge but a "very independent" work of
"absolutely original ideas."[47] The respect was reciprocated. Years later, after the sober-
ing experience of the Vietnam war, Morgenthau dedicated a book of essays to Kelsen,
"who has taught us through his example how to speak Truth to Power."[48] We know next
to nothing of what occurred academically at Brooklyn College, except that he taught a
great deal, including Comparative Government, International Law and Political Theory.
From there he moved to the University of Kansas in Kansas City as assistant professor,
where he also qualified for the Bar. He was brought in by the president, the ruthless and
ambitious Clarence Decker, who had just added a school of law to the campus. Decker
wanted Morgenthau to teach international relations along with law, but offered only
a one-year appointment and obliged him to repeat his course on labour law to the
evening class.[49]

He was given a damp former bathroom to work in. It must have been galling. Carr's
Twenty Years' Crisis had appeared and expressed, in part, much of Morgenthau's
pent-up hostility to liberal *naiveté* in international relations. The "extraordinary
difficulties with which I have to deal with here"[50] accumulated. In January 1940 he
sought financial support from the American Philosophical Society. His declared aim

45   G. Eckstein, "Hans Morgenthau: A Personal Memoir", *Social Research*, Winter 1981, Vol. 48, No 4,
     p. 648. Eckstein befriended him in 1931.
46   Ibid., p. 649.
47   Reference for a grant, dated 15 February 1934: *Morgenthau Papers*, Box 33.
48   H. Morgenthau, *Truth and Power* (New York 1970).
49   *Morgenthau Papers*, Box. 88.
50   Morgenthau to Conklin (American Philosophical Society), 9 June 1941: ibid., Box 4.

was to write "on the philosophical foundations of post-World War foreign politics", tentatively entitled "Liberalism and Foreign Politics." In October the money was forthcoming and he told the Society that he intended to free himself from "all routine work in connection with research as well as my functions as member of the faculty of the University of Kansas City" (including his night classes).[51] Unfortunately for him, the Society laid down that substitution for teaching was not allowed and the University was unwilling to relieve him of any duties regardless.[52] Four years later and he was still only an assistant professor; though Morgenthau was technically tenured, Decker – heartily sick of his assertiveness – gave him abrupt notification of dismissal. Legal action only delayed proceedings. He took leave in 1943 and finally resigned in November 1944.[53]

It was in these bleak conditions that the Society's grant enabled Morgenthau to go to the fundamentals and develop his own distinctive approach to international relations, a large part of which eventually made its way into print as *Scientific Man versus Power Politics*; the rest underlay the writing of *Politics among Nations*. "Foreign policy", he assumed at the outset of the study in 1940, "is an integral part of culture as a whole and reflects its theory and practice. Hence, it is only through the analysis of the general philosophy of a given time that it is possible to understand the foreign policy of this particular time." This principle applied to foreign policy in the inter-war period, the main elements of which stemmed from "the rationalistic philosophy of the seventeenth and eighteenth centuries and from the political philosophy of liberalism." He concluded that the "failure of this foreign policy is mainly due to the misunderstanding of the domestic experience with liberalism . . . The ideas of liberalism were successful in the domestic field under certain historic conditions. By generalizing those ideas and regarding them as universal truths, liberal foreign policy has applied them to the international scene where the conditions are largely absent to which liberalism owes its victories in the domestic field." This also jeopardised the "very survival of liberalism in the domestic field."[54] A year later and Morgenthau argued that "it is the modern conception of reason, its relation to the irrational forces of evil, and its functions in the social world, which is in the last analysis responsible for the general misdirection as well as for the particular failures of liberalism in foreign affairs."[55] In a memorable summing up, he attacked rationalism, the foundation of liberal thought, for drawing three conclusions: "first, that the rationally right and ethically good are identical; second, that the rationally right action is of necessity the successful one; third, that education leads man to the rationally right, hence good and successful action." These

51   Morgenthau to the American Philosophical Society, 19 October 1940: ibid.
52   American Philosophical Society to Morgenthau, 26 October 1940: ibid.
53   *Morgenthau Papers*, Box 88.
54   Report of Committee on Research: Grant No 467 (1940): *The American Philosophical Society Year Book 1941* (Philadelphia 1942).
55   Ibid., p. 212.

conclusions "failed to understand the nature of man; the nature of the world, especially the social world; and, finally, the nature of reason itself."

This led Morgenthau to fault the analogy between the natural sciences and the social sciences (so deeply imbued in the minds of those like Charles Merriam, the great political science entrepreneur at Chicago, who sought to achieve with the social sciences what had been achieved by the natural sciences, in like manner and with no conception of the differences between the objects under scrutiny).[56] This rationalism marginalised evil as "a mere negative quality. It can only be conceived as lack of reason and is incapable of positive determination based upon its own intrinsic qualities. It is nothing but an accidental disturbance of the order of the world, sure to be overcome by a gradual development towards the good." This picture bore "no semblance to reality". Morgenthau was seeking to reach back to the pre-liberal, pre-enlightenment era. "Reason", he wrote, "is like a light which by its own inner force can move nowhere.[57] It must be carried in order to move. It is carried by the irrational forces of interest and emotion to where those forces want it, regardless of what the inner logic of abstract reason would require. Its course is furthermore determined by the strength of hostile forces which, as passion, lust for power, and the like, are a permanent element of human existence." Morgenthau thus turned back to the thought of Hobbes and Spinoza, though without explicit reference to them. His conclusions were obvious. "Since the triumph of reason depends upon the relative strength of opposing irrational forces, social reform must aspire toward creating a balance of power, favorable to reason, among the irrational forces which compete for the control of human action."[58] As Kissinger has pointed out, "Being himself passionate, he [Morgenthau] did not trust passion as the regulator of conduct."[59] Morgenthau thus stood squarely within the Reasons of State tradition.

Morgenthau's immediate response to the threat of redundancy was to fire off a letter to every higher education institution in the country with a political science department. The replies were a mixture of perplexed rejection and polite shelving of his curriculum vitae for the indefinite future. He wrote, inter alia, to Quincy Wright at the University of Chicago, whose *Study of War* had made of him the best-known specialist on international relations in the country, apart, perhaps, from Spykman. Wright's reply in August 1943 was of the polite bear-you-in-mind variety, and Morgenthau would have reason to have believed that the political science department at Chicago, dominated by the scientism of Merriam and Wright's more idealistic approach to the subject, was not naturally a receptive safe haven. He was wrong, however. Before long Wright wrote

---

56   See D. Ross, *The Origins of American Social Science* (Cambridge 1991) pp. 395–7; also K. Thompson, *Schools of Thought in International Relations: Interpreters, Issues, and Morality* (London 1996) pp. 21–5.

57   He must have meant a lamp rather than "light" which, of course, does move of its own volition.

58   Report, pp. 212–13.

59   *New Republic*, 1980.

offering Morgenthau a position as visiting associate professor for the first two quarters of the 1943–4 academic year, beginning September, which would tide Morgenthau over till joining the Yale Institute for the remainder of the academic year from March 1944. It was Spykman's untimely demise that had thrown open this momentary opportunity.[60] By the time Morgenthau had left for Yale, the die was cast; they were considering him for a full-time position with tenure at Chicago, which took effect that November.

The work done under the auspices of the American Philosophical Society laid the foundations for two major publications: the first, *Scientific Man*, an attack on scientism in the study of politics, had lost none of its cogency and relevance, not least when written from its heart, at Chicago; the second, *Politics among Nations*, which synthesised lectures given at the University of Chicago from 1943, based upon "the only written record of those lectures", put together by a student in the winter of 1946.[61] Morgenthau used to lecture extemporaneously from shorthand notes which could easily pass as Chinese characters. Those lectures – "International Politics" (Political Science 261) – as transcribed are still available and it is instructive to compare them with the book that ultimately resulted. Whereas the book is discursive and at times muddled, with multiple and contradictory definitions that have inevitably been a little unkindly attacked with a certain relish by his critics (notably on concepts like the Balance of Power), the lectures are a veritable *tour de force*: an acute, vigorous, entirely consistent, wide-ranging, yet highly compressed and theoretically coherent contribution to knowledge. As in the book, the core of the thesis is the immanence of power. Lecture four, as recorded on 9 January 1946, includes the following:

> It seems to me that history shows conclusively that the struggle for power and the desire for power as the dominating motive force in the minds of statesmen and nations has been present everywhere and at all times, regardless of economic system, form of government, etc. It seems to me, therefore, from a realistic point of view the struggle for power is the very essence of international affairs.[62]

The key to the lectures and to the resulting book was both the statement above and its corollary, as given in lecture seven on 16 January:

> The desire for power among all nations leads to a basic constellation in international affairs which is intrinsically interwoven with the very structure of international politics, and that is the balance of power . . . the balance of power is the only organizing principle there is.[63]

60   *Morgenthau Papers*, Box 66.
61   H. Morgenthau, *Politics among Nations* (1st edition, New York 1948), foreword.
62   "Lectures – International Politics": *Morgenthau Papers*, Box 77.
63   Ibid.

The damage was done by Knopf, the publishers. In the summer of 1945 Morgenthau sent them an outline of *International Politics*. Unfortunately their chief adviser in this field – unnamed – thought the outline too abstract and disliked the tone, the emphasis on power: "Chapter II on the Balance of Power is based on a conception of that subject which many, perhaps most, teachers of International Relations would not share."[64] In fact, that was the very reason Morgenthau wrote the book, so he was hardly likely to give way on such a critical point. "Since I have opposed from the very beginning of my academic career the errors and weaknesses of the traditional approach to the field of international politics, I do not intend to write a textbook perpetuating these deficiencies", he brusquely retorted on 7 August 1945.[65] Knopf wanted to dilute the message, saying they wanted a "more factual and elementary book", for fear of losing sales to existing professors of international relations, whose prejudices were being attacked by Morgenthau's text.[66] They then took away his title because of objections from Frederick Schuman, whose *International Politics* had also been published by Knopf.[67] The rewriting then got out of control, much to the publisher's irritation. "When I undertook to write the book for you in a relatively short period of time," Morgenthau explained by letter in December 1946, "I thought it would be a relatively easy job consisting mainly in putting the text of lectures into printable form. When I sat down to do this job I found myself doing research on every point which I had touched on in my lectures . . ."[68] While continuously pressing for prompt completion, the publishers also kept pressing for more of a textbook. The unfortunate result was a work that was not only diffuse and extensive but rushed into its final stages. The readers' comments then further complicated matters because the editor called for further dilution and compromise.[69] Once more Morgenthau resisted: "The public must be concerned that the new situation requires a new intellectual effort, and that this book offers what is needed."[70]

The further research that added ballast to the book came courtesy of Morgenthau's graduate student, the young, enthusiastic and energetic Kenneth Thompson, who arrived in Chicago only a few months after the effort got under way.[71] Thompson, from Des Moines, Iowa, via St. Olaf's College, Minnesota, and war service from 1943 to 1946, came to study in the department because of its leading reputation in political science. Morgenthau took him rapidly on board, regarding him as "the most brilliant and most profound thinker" of all the students he had encountered.[72]

---

64   Allen Wilbur to Morgenthau, 2 August 1945: *Morgenthau Papers*, Box 121.
65   Ibid.
66   Roger Shugg to Morgenthau, 10 August 1945: ibid.
67   Shugg to Morgenthau, 19 June 1946: ibid.
68   Morgenthau to Shugg, 11 December 1946: ibid.
69   Shugg to Morgenthau, 25 May 1947: ibid.
70   Morgenthau to Shugg, 6 June 1947: ibid.
71   Morgenthau, *Politics*, foreword.
72   Morgenthau to Crane Brinton, 22 December 1949: *Morgenthau Papers*, Box 56.

Morgenthau later described *Politics among Nations*, which very soon became a best-seller, as a summary of "an intellectual experience of twenty years . . . an experience of lonely and seemingly ineffectual reflection on the nature of international politics and on the ways by which a false conception of foreign policy, put into practice by the western democracies, led inevitably to the threat and the actuality of totalitarianism and war. When this book was originally written, that false and pernicious conception of foreign policy was still in the ascendancy. This book was, indeed, and could be nothing else but, a frontal attack against that conception."[73] In his own inimitably egocentric way, Morgenthau entirely ignored Carr's prior contribution. It was also an unnecessary claim, because *Politics among Nations* made a contribution Carr could not make, because he was not an American, and would not make, because he had no sympathy for the role assumed by the United States in standing up against the Soviet Union in 1945–7. In a sense Morgenthau translated a critical part of Carr's message at a time and in a language Americans could not only understand but needed. He also added a good deal more to the message and in entirely his own terms. Arthur Schlesinger Jr. recalls those times: "wide oceans had long shielded the republic from the logic of *Realpolitik*. Americans were accustomed to viewing their actions abroad as the expressions of disinterested moral virtue."[74] The study of international relations was, he notes, at that time "in some disarray". It was "legalistic in mode and idealistic in purpose, for it was organized around the longing for a better world. Notable individuals – Nicholas J. Spykman, Walter Lippmann, Edward Mead Earle, Frederick J. Schuman – insisted on the primacy of power in the international structure, but their somber ideas had not permeated the mainstream of academic analysis."[75]

Morgenthau opened his work with an eloquent statement on the position of the United States in the world and the American perception of it, changed forever by World War II. Once self-sufficient, "Now it stands outside the enclosures of its continental citadel, taking on the whole of the political world as friend or foe. It has become dangerous and vulnerable, feared and afraid." "The multiple state system of the past . . . has been transformed into two inflexible, hostile blocs, which are morally two worlds", he went on, and concluded: "Since in this world situation the United States holds a position of predominant power and, hence, of foremost responsibility, the understanding of the forces which mold international politics and of the factors which determine its course has become for the United States more than an interesting intellectual occupation. It has become a vital necessity."[76]

Just as Carr had written *The Twenty Years' Crisis* to offset the almost complete neglect in Britain of the factor of power in international relations, so too did Morgenthau in

73   Morgenthau, *Politics among Nations* (2nd edition, New York 1954) p. vii.
74   Arthur Schlesinger Jr., "In Memoriam, Hans Joachim Morgenthau", in G. Schwab, ed., *United States Foreign Policy At the Crossroads* (Westport, Ct., 1982) p. xi.
75   Ibid., p. x.
76   Ibid., p. 8.

the American context. He therefore opened Chapter One with the blunt assertion that "power is always the immediate aim" of those conducting foreign policy. "While this fact is generally recognised in the practice of foreign affairs, it is frequently denied in the pronouncements of scholars, publicists, and even statesmen."[77] Since 1815 the exercise of power was seen by many as merely a temporary phenomenon, and here the peculiarity of the United States came into play: "the general conception which the nineteenth century had formed of the nature of foreign affairs combined with specific elements in the American experience to create the belief that involvement in power politics is not inevitable, but only a historic accident, and that nations have a choice between power politics and other kinds of foreign policy not tainted by the desire for power."[78]

Although giving formal acknowledgement to the role of ideology in both his key works, *Politics among Nations* and *In Defense of the National Interest*,[79] Morgenthau reduced the aims of all states at all times and in all circumstances to the search for power. Here he had moved substantially from the assumptions laid out to the American Philosophical Society at the beginning of the decade, and ultimately also from the methodological critique in *Scientific Man*. References to the "popular fallacy of equating the foreign policies of a statesman with his philosophic or political sympathies" completely contradicted the orientation of his original prospectus.[80] The "moving force" in the world was, he asserted, "the aspiration for power of sovereign nations".[81] This included his appreciation of the Cold War as "not a struggle between good and evil, truth and falsehood, but of power with power".[82] He wrote of "iron laws" governing international relations, as in his "iron law . . . that legal obligations must yield to the national interest . . ."[83] He condemned the "misconception . . . that men have a choice between power politics and its necessary outgrowth, the balance of power, on the one hand, and a different, better kind of international relations on the other . . . that a foreign policy based on the balance of power is one among several possible foreign policies . . ."[84] However, Morgenthau never defined the national interest or qualified this elusive search for power. The combination of ambiguous definition with a rigid determinism was then compounded with an attempt to castigate the US Government for not following iron laws and for exercising choices which in his scheme of things did not and could not exist.

Whereas Carr was ultimately indifferent to the image in which he had been cast as a hard-boiled advocate of *Machtpolitik* (Power Politics), not least because he recognised

77   Ibid., p. 13.
78   Ibid., p. 20.
79   *In Defense of the National Interest: A Critical Study of American Foreign Policy* (New York 1951).
80   *Politics* (2nd edition, 1954) p. 7.
81   Morgenthau, *Politics* (1st edition, 1948) p. 89.
82   Morgenthau, *In Defense*, p. 219.
83   Ibid., p. 144.
84   Morgenthau, *Politics* (2nd edition) p. 155.

the image to be not altogether inaccurate (as he had noted was the case with Machi-avelli), Morgenthau was extremely sensitive to being labelled a one-dimensional believer in power. Indeed, friend Arthur Schlesinger Jr. remembers him as "deeply moral".[85] And Stanley Hoffmann, who, as a fervent liberal, might be expected to detect his own, described him as "an idealist in disguise, a somewhat conservative liberal in revolt against other, imprudent liberals."[86] Morgenthau's own unyielding and ungener-ous attack on Carr for being obsessed with power, which was not fully justified given Carr's patently utopian streak – strikingly apparent in his domestic reform programme adumbrated during the war – was in reality an attempt to extricate himself from the position in which his book and the reputation had unexpectedly landed him. Indeed there was – certainly in print – less *virtù* (using Morgenthau's misleading definition) evident in Morgenthau than Carr; and quite what Morgenthau thought Machiavelli actually meant by *virtù* is a puzzle, since to Machiavelli it ultimately meant strength rather than moral virtue. Morgenthau slowly but surely shifted position over the sub-sequent two decades, with the result that he all but appeared in the opposing camp of universalism by the end of the 1960s, as his loyal but not uncritical Boswell, Kenneth Thompson, noted at the time. Morgenthau may have believed that consistency was the hobgoblin of lesser minds; but whether this was the result of personal discomfort with notoriety or a certain lassitude of mind, the published work most certainly reveals some intriguing contradictions.

It is a notable irony that one manuscript reader for Knopf had complained of *Poli-tics among Nations* that Morgenthau treated power as "something apart from the ends being sought thereby". He had no idea that only a few years hence Morgenthau would take Carr to task for the self-same failing, if that is what it was.[87] This is revealing. It shows that Morgenthau was never fully conscious of the deeper implications of the ideas he had expressed with so much emotion and energy at such length. Whereas Carr saw the immanence of power as the key to intellectual separation from prevailing ide-ologies and the only route to a more scientific understanding of politics, Morgenthau was deeply troubled by the notion, as he was by the criticism that his "realist" image attracted. He saw Carr as one-dimensional in this respect; he could not abide the thought that others thought himself likewise. Thus no sooner was *Politics among Nations* in public hands than he began telling fellow-countrymen that power was not enough.

Morgenthau's work none the less had a major impact on an entire generation of young American students of international relations. The message was reinforced by the writings of George Kennan (1904–), a scholar-diplomat and self-taught Sovietologist from the policy-making community. Like Carr, Kennan was a sensitive mind hit by the harsh realities of power. This revelation finds eloquent expression in his own

85   Schlesinger, in Schwab, *United States*, p. xii.
86   S. Hoffmann, "Notes on the Limits of 'Realism' ", *Social Research*, Winter 1981, Vol. 48, No 4, p. 657.
87   Shugg to Morgenthau, 21 February 1947: *Morgenthau Papers*, Box 121.

early work. But he never attempted to write theory. He did not need to: Morgenthau had done the job for him. Reviewing the course of US foreign policy from the turn of the century, Kennan took every opportunity to slate "the legalistic-moralistic approach to international politics" which he believed characterised White House behaviour.[88] Commenting on the US notes issued in 1899 demanding an "Open Door" to China, he wrote: "we find no greater readiness, so far, to admit the validity and legitimacy of power realities and aspirations, to accept them without feeling the obligation of moral judgement, to take them as existing and unalterable human forces, neither good nor bad, and to seek their point of maximum equilibrium rather than their reform or their repression."[89] Instead of "making ourselves slaves of the concepts of international law and morality", he wished that the United States should "confine these concepts to the unobtrusive, almost feminine, function of the gentler civilizer of national self-interest in which they find their true value . . ."[90] He welcomed Mahan's writings and deeply regretted that "Those efforts remained suspended, as it were, in the mid-air of history – an isolated spurt of intellectual activity against a background of general torpor and smugness in American thinking about foreign affairs."[91] Kennan himself completely identified with the position thus formulated by Morgenthau, not only at that time but also today.[92] "We tend to underestimate the violence of national maladjustments and discontents elsewhere in the world if we think that they would always appear to other people as less important than the presentation of the juridical tidiness of international life."[93]

The parallels between Kennan and Carr, or, indeed, between Kennan and Machiavelli are not so far-fetched. Although in later years, out of and at some distance from government while secluded at the Institute for Advanced Study in Princeton, Kennan's writing became more moralistic – indeed, far too much so for Carr's severe tastes[94] – his thoughts "On Government and Governments" have recently provided fascinating insight into the ex-official's intuitive grasp of the immanence of power, expressed in a form both Machiavelli and Carr would have immediately understood and unhesitatingly underwritten. Kennan takes a bleak, indeed an Augustinian view of politics, which echoes the higher preoccupations of late medieval Europe: "government, while worthy of respect, should not be idealized. It is simply not the channel through which men's noblest impulses are to be realized. Its task, on the contrary, is largely to see to it that the ignoble ones are kept under restraint and not permitted to go too far."[95] He

88 G. Kennan, *American Diplomacy* (Chicago 1951; revised 1984) p. 95.
89 Ibid., p. 53.
90 Ibid., pp. 53–4.
91 Ibid., p. 6.
92 In conversation with the author, September 1999.
93 Kennan, *American Diplomacy*, p. 97.
94 Haslam, *The Vices of Integrity*, p. 248.
95 Kennan, *Around the Cragged Hill: A Personal and Political Philosophy* (New York 1993) p. 54.

continues: "Efforts may be made, from time to time, by individual politicians or statesmen to use government (or to pretend to use it) for the achievement of what appears to be glorious ideals. But then the uses to which they are professing to put it are ones not inherent in its basic purposes."[96] For Kennan as for Lord Acton, power possessed a quality of its own which created temptation and therefore of itself dictated behaviour.

This was also immediately understood by practitioners, particularly the more devious. In conversation with Tito in May 1946, Stalin uttered a core truth when he spoke of the Czech Prime Minister Beneš as a "realist, when shown strength, but . . . an idealist if he felt he was in possession of strength."[97] That is to say, the mere possession of power opens the mind to possible courses of action barely conceived of before. Kennan argued more than that, however; as did Acton. Referring to the effect of power on those who enter government, he comments: "that they, once involved in it, remain wholly unaffected by the distorting discipline it exerts, I must be allowed to doubt."[98] They would form part of a ruling group and "this group will be found to be bringing to expression a wide variety of motivations, including the individual political ambitions of its various members; the interests of the group as such; the interests of the party; and finally, no doubt, such of the national interests as do not conflict too sharply with any of these more burning incentives."[99] As a result, Kennan detected two distinct voices in foreign affairs: "on the one hand, the voice of the interests of the entire country, as the regime perceives them, and to the extent it chooses to defer to them; and on the other hand, the voice of a single political faction, deeply concerned to serve its own fortunes in the face of whatever domestic-political competition confronts it and threatens it. Those two voices may at times fully coincide, but they do not usually do so; and there is no reason why they should."[100] Here the ageing and sadly wiser Kennan echoes the knowing Pufendorf.

The most comprehensive and stylish onslaught against the re-emergence of Balance of Power thinking, a key axiom in the thought of both Kennan and Morgenthau, was launched by the young German-born Ernst Haas, a social-democrat who always openly despised and castigated realism.[101] The attack took the form of a Columbia University PhD: *Belgium and the Balance of Power: A Critical Examination of some Balance of Power Theories in the Light of the Policy Motivations of the Major European States toward Belgium, 1830–1839*, submitted at the end of 1952. The initial focus of criticism was

96   Ibid.
97   From the Tito archives: *fond kabinet Marsala Juhoslavije*, reprinted in *Cold War International History Project* website, p. 9 of 17.
98   Kennan, *Around the Cragged Hill*, p. 57.
99   Ibid., p. 59.
100   Ibid., pp. 60–1.
101   Haas to the author, 28 October 1998.

the idea of "power politics": power as ends as well as means.[102] This angle was chosen not least because "The idea of power and of the use of power is essential to an approach of that highly controversial and highly lauded principle, the balance of power."[103] As Haas explained the connexion, "Given that power aspirations and power needs alone govern inter-state relations, the balance of power emerges as a device to introduce some order into an otherwise chaotic state system, a balance nevertheless based on the very motive forces of power politics itself."[104] He went on to name seven different meanings of the term balance of power, emphasising the self-evident fact, decisively demonstrated by his case study on Belgium, that its usage varied in different situations by different Powers. What he was reacting against was perfectly clear: "The balance of power, during the early years of the League of Nations, was generally thought of as an obsolete concept, useless if not pernicious. This, however, is no longer the case. Since 1940 or 1941 the term has enjoyed a sudden and spectacular revival not only in the pages of learned journals and technical discussions, but even in the daily press."[105] "There would", he continued, "be no difficulty about this development if the term were free from philological, semantic and theoretical confusion. Unfortunately, it is not."[106]

Haas was not entirely correct in his claim that the proponents of the Balance of Power were all guilty of sloppy thinking. A much more nuanced, though still obviously "realist" approach had been taken by the Cambridge historian Herbert Butterfield (1900–79), who was a contradiction in both public and private life, a deeply committed lay preacher but a disciple of Machiavelli. He made clear that when he spoke of the Balance of Power he was referring only to "the distribution of power". Like Carr, Morgenthau and Kennan, he took the view firmly that "it is better to treat power in itself as an object of science than to rely, as a matter of sentimentality, on any giant's good intentions."[107] As with Kennan, so with Butterfield, also following Acton's precept, power possessed a quality all of its own that created temptation and therefore dictated behaviour. It is here that Butterfield emphasised that defensive or aggressive behaviour on the part of states is determined less by intention than situation:

102   E. Haas, *A Critical Examination of some Balance of Power Theories in the Light of the Policy Motivations of the Major European States toward Belgium, 1830–1839* (Columbia University PhD 1953) Chapter 2.

103   Ibid., pp. 81–2.

104   Ibid., p. 82.

105   Ibid., p. 499.

106   Ibid., p. 500. The summing-up can be read in two articles published in *World Politics*: see, for example, "The Balance of Power: Prescription, Concept, or Propaganda?", *World Politics*, No 4, July 1953, pp. 442–77.

107   H. Butterfield, "The Scientific Versus the Moralist Approach in International Affairs", *International Affairs*, July 1951, p. 412.

it is not always easy to say when a given State moves from an originally defensive policy, and then from a reasonable demand for securities, to actual aggrandizement. And since Europe is honeycombed with areas that are the subject of irredentist aspirations, ethnical controversies, and nationalistic claims, the State which at a given moment becomes strong enough to assert what it regards as its rights may go a long way in aggrandizement without feeling itself to be an aggressor at all. It appears that in certain conditions States do emerge as aggressors, even if they have been well-behaved hitherto; and indeed small States often show all the tendencies that make for aggression, and are some-times more wild and irresponsible in their ambitions than the greater ones.

In anticipation of those who later claimed to substantiate a Kantian belief that a true democracy would not resort to war against democracies, Butterfield argued that "Young democracies and new nations seem to be particularly prone to irredentisms or dreams of expansion or projects of military conquest." This point was made merely to reinforce his overall message as to the accuracy of "the more traditional view that aggression is somehow related to the character of power itself, and the effect which power has upon its possessors, more or less in the sense that Acton had in mind . . ."[108]

Butterfield, like Carr and Kennan, was, for differing reasons, a voice off stage: Carr dropped international relations for the history of the Soviet Union; Kennan left government when the Republicans won power; and Butterfield remained a marginal figure in the world of political science, certainly for Americans. It was the figure of Morgenthau that predominated in the United States, long to the exclusion of all else. One figure of note, who was more of an *éminence grise* in academia and therefore of much lower profile, nevertheless had unusual links to those in power (not just in the United States but also in re-emerging Western Europe). This was Arnold Wolfers (1892–1968). The difference between Morgenthau and Wolfers bears comparison with that between Machiavelli and Guicciardini; Morgenthau always seemed the clearer, less inhibited voice and was always the lesser historian of the two. Moreover, ultimately Machiavelli uncovered his great ideal, as did Morgenthau, whereas one searches in vain for Guicciardini and Wolfers' utopia. Although never a practitioner, Wolfers had an acute empathy for the practitioner, which was bought at the price of a certain coherence of view. Kennan, for example, deep down more the absolutist scholar than the difference-splitting diplomat, always esteemed Morgenthau one of the greatest contemporary thinkers on international relations, whereas, in respect to Wolfers, he perceptively commented that the man never seemed to make up his mind.[109]

Professor at Yale from 1935, Wolfers was a *protégé* of Spykman's. Born in St. Gallen, Switzerland, on 14 June 1892 (and therefore almost to the day the same age as Carr),

108   Ibid., p. 413.
109   In conversation with the author, September 1999.

Wolfers took a law degree from Zurich in 1917 and a doctorate from Geneva in 1924.[110] After law practice upon graduation, he lectured in political science from 1924 to 1933 and then became director of the renowned Hochschule für Politik in Berlin. He went to New Haven as a visiting professor on Hitler's accession to power in 1933, and when the Nazis took over, he gladly accepted permanency at Yale.[111] Wolfers' lectures were from the outset "realist" in tone and non-theoretical in form. Their quality was high and distinguished by a sympathetic insight into the view of the international situation from the operational, diplomatic perspective, but unusually detached from the vantage-point of any one Power. A particularly striking illustration of the even-handed and empathetic quality of his mind is a piece he composed when serving as a consultant to the War Department at a crucial turning point in the conflict, the battle for Stalingrad. Stalin appeared to be making an overture to German nationalist sentiment to divide the military and the industrialists from the Nazis. Entitled "Soviet Policy Toward Germany (as evidenced in the Manifesto of the Free Germany Committee in Moscow)", Wolfers' paper argued:

The Russians are likely to be much concerned about the future orientation and sympathy of the Germans. They are very much handicapped by the fact that in most people's minds the Soviet Union is still identified with the Communist world revolution. There are few countries in Europe on whose friendship they can count. If Germany is very weak, anti-Bolshevik forces, for instance in the Catholic countries, might gain the upper hand in Europe. If Germany is hostile, she might become a partner to an all-European anti-Bolshevik front. The United States and Britain might sooner or later be found in the same camp. There is a strong temptation, therefore, for the Bolsheviks to ingratiate themselves with the Germans by offering to save them from the disgrace and dangers of unconditional surrender, occupation and unilateral disarmament.[112]

The qualities Wolfers thus exhibited were more those of the meditative and prudent practitioner or historian than of the armchair theorist working in timeless abstractions. His only theoretical work, which was largely a collection of essays (formerly lectures), did not appear until very much later, in 1962, long after he had left Yale and had taken charge of the Washington Center of Foreign Policy Research at the Johns Hopkins School of Advanced International Studies (SAIS).

The failure to produce a theoretical tract points to the core of Wolfers' approach to international relations. Although a realist by inclination, he was not, at least until well into the 1950s, fully a realist by conviction. "Power politics," he told his students in the

---

110   The thesis was entitled *Die Aufrichtung der Kapitalherrschaft in der abendlaendischen Geschichte*.
111   John Van Sickle to Ernest Jaqua, Scripps College, Claremont, California, 23 February 1937: *Rockefeller Foundation Archives*, RG1.1, Series 200, Box 416, Fldr 4943.
112   Dated 1 September 1943: *Wolfers Papers* (Yale), 164, Box 13, Folder 157.

autumn of 1944, when hopes for the postwar world still lingered, "if it is to be true to the fact, should not imply that international relations are nothing but a struggle for power or that all governments are or should be at all times engaged in an effort to acquire more power for their security. The fact is that many states are satisfied with the power they have or are negligent about their power."[113] Thus although his lectures at Yale followed a Spykman-like trajectory – "Location", "Mahan", "Geopolitical theories of power", etc. – they were delivered with a heavy dose of scepticism as to their general applicability. Wolfers was very much in favour of advancing international relations theory, but this latent dualism in his intellectual make-up quite simply made it impossible to generate a model of state behaviour based on a generalised set of assumptions. In a draft on the "Quest for Power: Methodological Introduction", he noted:

> It would facilitate the task of working out a theory of international politics if it were permissible to start with the simple and sweeping assumption that sovereign states in a multi-state system devote themselves to the single objective of enhancing their power to the utmost of their ability. But such an assumption would provide a valuable hypothesis only if it were realistic.[114]

"Nations", Wolfers believed, "are neither absolutely cooperative nor absolutely devoid of all sense of common responsibility. It can hardly be denied, however, that at the present moment [October 1947] the pessimistic view comes nearer to representing the true portrait of existing conditions. The balance of power is today a prerequisite even of effective international organization."[115] He added: "Governments, unless blissfully unaware of the intents of their countries, will almost instinctively partake in the over-all balancing process which characterises the multi-state system."[116]

What gave Morgenthau's *magnum opus* its impact and allowed the formation of a theory of international politics – however inadequate – was the singling out of power as the goal of states in their relations with one another. Wolfers, not unexpectedly, felt uncomfortable with Morgenthau's focus on power as an end in itself. In his best-known essay, "The Pole of Power and the Pole of Indifference", which contrasted the realist and idealist approaches to world politics, Wolfers argued that "power is a means to other ends and not an end in itself . . . Therefore, to treat the quest for power, positively or negatively, outside the context of ends and purposes which it is expected to serve, robs it of any intelligible meaning and, by the way, also makes it impossible to judge its appropriateness or excessiveness. It is as if an economist, in developing economic theory, were to concentrate on the accumulation and expenditure of money. He could

---

113   "Foundations of National Power", Lecture 4, "Power Politics and the Restraint of Power": *Wolfers Papers*, 634, Series 2, Box 17, No 207.
114   *Wolfers Papers* 634, Series 2, Box 16, Folio 194.
115   Ibid., Box 17, Folio 214.
116   Ibid.

not avoid painting a picture of a world of misers or spendthrifts, as the political scientist on the power level can see little but a world of insatiably power-hungry or uncon-
ditionally power-hostile political actors." A different picture emerged, he wrote, "if one
considers first the values and purposes for the sake of which policy-makers seek to
accumulate or use national power, as they may also seek alternative or supplementary
means."[117] Wolfers went on to point out that states varied in what they sought and how
they sought to attain it. States were "not single-purpose organizations like hospitals,
golf clubs, or banking establishments." In deciding between competing demands from
the domestic population, "relatively scarce means must be parceled out in order of preference and by a constant process of weighing, comparing, and computing of values.
Because policy-makers, like all men, seek to maximize value in accordance with ever-
fluctuating value patterns, one would anticipate great variations in their choice unless
something compelled them to conform."[118]

Wolfers went on to classify foreign policy goals under three headings: national self-
extension, national self-preservation and national self-abnegation. By including the
latter, and allowing for actors other than states, Wolfers marked himself off from
Morgenthau and built a bridge to the universalists. By definition those advocating
greater realism had to acknowledge the ability of their idealist counterparts to run
affairs in a contrary fashion: "Realists would not be so eager – as was Machiavelli
himself – to impress their governments with the 'necessity' of playing the game of
power politics as consistently as their opponents, were it not for fear that these governments might act otherwise."[119] His was, as before, a more nuanced approach than
that of the vulgar realist. What was lost in impact was gained in subtlety. But, by the
same token, what was lost in simplicity was also lost to theory.

For those who believed that the United States was unprepared for world power and
for those who equally believed they had something to contribute, intellectually, towards
its preparation, the lure of Washington was, and remains, hard to resist – particularly
when the influential come calling. The School for Advanced International Studies, SAIS,
had been established in 1944 by, among others, Paul Nitze, who later explained: "We
believed that the problems which concerned us sprang in part from the speed with
which the position of the United States in the world was changing and in part from the
unfortunate gap which continued to separate the academic world from the world of
practical international affairs, both of business and of government."[120] In September
1950 SAIS was incorporated into the Johns Hopkins University with, not accidentally,
training centres in countries targeted by the CIA as threatened by Communism: Burma,
Italy and Indonesia. At that time Nitze had taken over from Kennan as head of State

117   *World Politics*, No 1, October 1951, p. 48.
118   Ibid., p. 49.
119   Ibid., p. 60.
120   Nitze to Dean Rusk, President of the Rockefeller Foundation, 14 December 1953: *Rockefeller Foun-
      dation Archives*, RF, RG 1.2,SAIS 200s, Box 526, Fldr 4502.

Department Policy Planning, where he forged the hawkish National Security Memorandum NSC68, arguing for the containment of Communism by military means. In 1953 his original aim for SAIS, which was always frustrated by lack of funding and academic exclusiveness – namely, bringing together those exercising power and those studying it – seemed as far from fulfilment as ever. But his chance came with the opportunity of funding from the Rockefeller Foundation. He formally proposed setting up a centre attached to SAIS and drawing in for regular discussion four outstanding senior figures, two academic, two involved in policy, plus an equal number of research assistants. The names originally suggested were Erich Hula, Morgenthau and Wolfers, on the academic side, Charles Burton Marshall, Louis Halle and Robert Tufts on the policy side.[121] It took a while to bring to fruition. Finally in June 1957 Wolfers indicated his willingness to leave Yale, which was in some chaos through feuding over the future of international relations in the university, and move to Washington.[122]

The Washington Center of Foreign Policy Research was thus finally established at SAIS in the autumn of 1957 under Wolfers' direction. It was to be the focal point of realist thought in international relations, as Nitze originally intended. Here Wolfers carefully orchestrated a series of seminars which brought together scholars and policy-makers to focus on key issues of principle as well as of practice, general theoretical matters as well as matters of importance to US foreign policy. The first fruits of discussion, on East-West negotiations, were published in 1958. This came at the time when public opinion in the West and the emerging third world was pressing for disengagement. There was talk of creating a nuclear-free zone in Central Europe. President Eisenhower had initiated talks with the Russians on the nuclear test ban and other associated matters. The tone of Wolfers' account placed him squarely in the classical European realist tradition. He saw states as inherently expansionist and believed firmly in the Balance of Power. But, like many at the time and later, he never entirely made up his mind about Moscow: was this just Russia or was it a revolutionary state? At one moment he spoke of it as the former; at another, the latter. At the roundtable he pointed out that "The Soviet Union is at present a revolutionary power in the inter-state system. How can that revolutionary drive be countered or decreased? The desirability of negotiations will depend on whether granting the Soviet Union a place in the sun will dissipate her revolutionary tendencies or encourage her aggressiveness by whetting her appetite."[123] Elsewhere, notably in the chapter he wrote following the roundtable, he struck a rather different note: "Any government of a powerful Russia, even a non-Communist government, would be sorely tempted to take advantage of favorable opportunities for further expansion, because it would not lack grounds upon which to justify such expansion."[124] He wrote of the United States in similarly neutral terms. The

---

121   Formal proposals of 13 October 1953 to the Rockefeller Foundation: ibid.
122   Memorandum by Kenneth Thompson, 4 June 1957: ibid.
123   The minutes of the roundtable are enclosed in Part II of *East-West Negotiations* edited by Wolfers (Washington DC 1958) p. 10.
124   Ibid., p. 15.

United States, like other Great Powers in former times, was "seeking to maintain a reasonable balance of power in the world as an indispensable means of preserving the peace."[125] Wolfers maintained a distance from those who identified the conflict with the Soviet Union as an essentially ideological issue. He was overtly critical of those advocating disengagement, not least because many of those so much in favour of it – not least in the third world – were in fact beneficiaries of the US presence elsewhere. "It is not without irony that some leaders of uncommitted countries are urging the United States to pull out of Eurasia when much of the freedom of action their countries enjoy, and much of their profitable leverage against the Great powers results from the presence in their neighborhood not of one but of two rival power blocs."[126] He firmly rejected any idea that the United States and the Soviet Union stood in similar positions. The Russians had the geographical advantage. " It is one thing to obtain control of the island of North America, a very different thing to become master of all of Eurasia and its offshore islands, thereby to dominate the world!"[127] If there were to be any kind of limited engagement which, for public opinion reasons, Wolfers was disinclined to rule entirely out of court, it should be determined by the needs of the Balance of Power. "After all, the balance of power is a restraining as well as a demanding goal. Taken as a guide, it may help to discern changes in the present largely accidental military status quo that would not only be compatible with East-West equilibrium, but would serve to establish that equilibrium where it is absent today."[128] When such as Nitze challenged the notion that this was a Balance of Power system because the system was bipolar, not multipolar, and the bipolarity made for rigidity, Wolfers countered: "The bi-polar system that exists today is relatively unstable, but still, it is a balance of power system. That it is bi-polar does not mean that it is inflexible: there are certain areas of the world where power is continually fluctuating."[129] And in a remarkably perspicacious aside, he commented: "Once the balance of power is broken, once a particular nation secures a predominant position in the state system, it will be tempted to continue to expand its power vis-à-vis the other states. If the United States broke through the present bi-polar balance, its objectives (for example, of eliminating tyranny) would probably become unlimited too."[130]

Wolfers' only extended discourse on international relations, *Discord and Collaboration*, was dedicated to the fond memory of Spykman. "As late as the outbreak of World War II," he wrote, "any suggestion that the United States was – or should be – concerning itself with the world balance of power was distasteful to Americans, many of whom considered the suggestion almost cynical."[131] In the interval since Spykman's

---

125   "Limits on Disengagement", *East-West Negotiations*, p. 13.
126   Ibid., p. 17.
127   Ibid., p. 18.
128   Ibid.
129   Ibid., Part II, p. 12.
130   Ibid., p. 29.
131   A. Wolfers, *Discord and Collaboration: Essays on International Politics* (Baltimore 1962) p. 117.

death the study of international relations trailed political science generally in searching for a more scientific mode of explanation, an approach increasingly alien to Wolfers,
whose nuanced approach to the subject and kinship with policy-makers – the world of
hard compromise and his grounding in Geopolitics – made theory-building not only
uncongenial but also impracticable. It explained why he had abandoned Yale. If abstract
theory was anathema, its conjunction with re-emergent idealist universalism was
beyond the pale. Wolfers thus sharply criticised Haas – who was to become a leading
apostle of functional international integration pioneered by David Mitrany – for completely omitting the Balance of Power in further writings. Haas, Wolfers insisted, "like
some other 'modernists' in political science, has become so absorbed with the trees
(subnational groups and individual decision-makers) that the forest of power distribution and power conflict among nation-states has dropped out of sight."[132]

Although a profession divided, International Relations remained predominantly an
"American Social Science".[133] "As far as the United States were concerned," Raymond
Aron (1905–83) said of the 1950s, "they had almost a monopoly in the study of international relations."[134] After Carr's seminal contribution, and despite Butterfield's meet-
ings in Cambridge, Britain struggled to produce a thinker of any originality in the
realist tradition. Those of any stature who did emerge consciously distanced themselves
from that order. As the still fervent liberal internationalist Stanley Hoffmann noted,
"it was not in England that Carr's pioneering effort bore fruit."[135] The closest approximation was the Oxford-educated Australian Hedley Bull, Montague Burton Professor
of International Relations at Balliol College, Oxford, whose stance was self-consciously
more moralist than realist in the strict sense.[136] The decline in British thinking
was not surprising in that the period of the Cold War was an era both of unprecedented
US supremacy and of British decline. It was not that the talent did not exist. Although
intellectuals rarely respond consciously to such fundamental shifts in the power of
their own societies, the subconscious sensitivity to their working environment is
hard to ignore. The philosophy of supremacy is very different from the philosophy
of decline. Along with the decline of Britain's status in the world ran the decline in
original thought about power and international relations. Carr typically summed it up
with the tongue-in-cheek observation that once he had been interested in power but

132   Ibid., footnote, pp. 118–19.
133   S. Hoffmann, "An American Social Science: International Relations", *Daedalus*, Vol. 106, No 3,
       Summer 1977, pp. 41–60.
134   R. Aron, *Le Spectateur Engagé: Entretiens avec Jean-Louis Missika et Dominique Wolton* (Paris 1981)
       p. 236.
135   Hoffmann, "An American . . ." p. 43. For Hoffmann on Hoffmann: "A Retrospective on World Poli-
       tics", L. Miller and M. Smith (eds.), *Ideas and Ideals: Essays on Politics in Honor of Stanley Hoffmann*
       (Boulder 1993) pp. 3–18.
136   For the most sympathetic and penetrating assessment by a friend: S. Hoffmann, "Hedley Bull and
       his contribution to international relations", *International Affairs*, Vol. 62, No 2, Spring 1986, pp.
       179–95.

that now Britain was no longer a Great Power he no longer approved of the way they behaved.[137]

France, although following a far more violent and hurried decline from empire, also saw a more precipitous rise in prestige as a rehabilitated nation-state with the proud reassertion of national consciousness after De Gaulle's constitutional *coup d'état* in 1958. This should not be exaggerated, however. It was more image than reality, as De Gaulle gloomily confessed nearly a decade later: "In reality," he said, "would you believe that we are on a stage where I have been creating illusions since 1940. Now I am giving, or I am trying to give France the image of a nation that is solid, steadfast, resolute, expanding, whereas it is a nation that is out of shape [*avachie*], which thinks only of its own comfort, which wants nothing to do with history, which does not wish to fight, which does not wish to make difficulties for anyone, no less the Americans than the English. It is an everlasting illusion. I am on the theatre stage and I give every appearance of believing, I cause others to believe, I believe that it is happening, that France is a great country, that France is resolute, mobilised [*rassemblée*], whereas it is nothing. France is out of shape."[138]

Along with this phantom renaissance in international relations came the emergence of an incoherent doctrine of power in foreign policy in the person of Raymond Aron. Aron had originally moved from the prestigious École Normale Supérieure to become a journalist before the war interrupted his career. Thereafter he taught at the Sorbonne but continued to write for the press, mainly, though not exclusively, for *Le Figaro*. His earliest academic work of substance was a study of war. Thereafter, and on the basis of such work, he visited the United States at frequent intervals from the early 1950s, when Harvard is said to have offered him a post. Unusually for a Frenchman of his generation and later, he was never anti-American. The phobia with which postwar France regarded the United States (not least because of Roosevelt's maintenance of relations with the wartime Vichy regime and the postwar US opposition to French annexation of the Ruhr) created an insuperable obstacle for most, if not all, Gaullists. But Aron offered instead a tactful explanation – "A society with the reputation of being money-makers par excellence, such as the United States, is often the object of empassioned polemic"[139] – which was typical of his open-mindedness. And he absorbed a great deal from US approaches to international relations, though he never thought it proper to acknowledge this debt (nor any debt to Carr) in his own *magnum opus* on the subject, *Paix et Guerre entre les Nations*, published in English in 1966, perhaps because he was fundamentally at variance with their very spirit. In an early article, "En Quête d'une Philosophie de la Politique Étrangère", Aron displayed an olympian scepticism. "The criticism made by the realist school is useful, valuable even. It prompts us to keep a

---

137   Haslam, *The Vices of Integrity*, p. 250.
138   As told to Jacques Focart, *Tous les soirs avec de Gaulle: Journal de l'Élysée – I 1965–1967* (Paris 1977) p. 691.
139   Aron, *Le Spectateur . . .* p. 236.

cool head, to look at the world for what it is, and not to imagine what we would like it to be, to guard ourselves against abstractions. Unfortunately," he added, "moving from these generalities, reasonable but vague, the realists all too often make a mistake just as serious as that of the idealists: in confounding traditional diplomacy, that of European practice [*des cabinets européens*], with diplomacy for all time."[140] He went on to challenge both Kennan and Morgenthau in their assumption that a deal could be done with Moscow. "Is it enough to oppose to a strategy of revolution or of world conquest a diplomacy oriented on the basis of the national interest?"[141] Although the "theoreticians of the national interest" served a useful role in preventing one from being carried away by "the blind passion of ideology", Aron was more concerned lest they commit the cardinal error "of taking as the essence of international politics a practice and a theory of happier times when, within a stable civilisation, rivalry between states is limited, in the means employed and in consequences, by an unwritten code of what is legitimate and what illegitimate. When this code does not exist, we are returned to a state of nature, in the extreme sense of the term, where survival and freedom are the stakes of the conflict, where the communities engaged muster all their resources because they are wagering their possessions and their very existence. In such periods of disorder, no great Power limits its objectives to the national interest, in the sense that a Mazarin or a Bismarck would give to the term."[142] The West thus had to stand for some concept of an international order. This was not Aron's sole objection. "The primacy of foreign policy with no connexion to party rivalry at home – a theory of German historians in the nineteenth century – is no longer valid when the constitutive principle of the political units is in question."[143] In terms of immediate policy options in the Cold War, Aron could sound more hardline than any leading realist. But with respect to longer-term possibilities, he sounded like a voluntarist rather than a determinist, a feature shared with Rousseau and Kant. As he noted, "We have not yet encountered true realism, authentic realism, capable of drawing a distinction between historical practice and permanent traits in foreign policy, equally capable of not ignoring the fact that the aspiration towards values is an integral part of human reality, individual and collective."[144]

Although Aron would never have fitted in comfortably with Hoffmann's original hopes for the extinction of the state (see below, pp. 219–20), he continued to distance himself openly from the realist tradition in the United States and Britain: "the 'realist' school . . . tends to hypostatize the States [sic] and their so-called national interests, to attribute to those interests a sort of patency or permanence, and to regard events as reflecting nothing but the calculation of power and the compromise necessary to

140   *Revue Française de Science Politique*, Vol. III, No 1, January–March 1953, pp. 82–3.
141   Ibid., p. 83.
142   Ibid., p. 88.
143   Ibid., p. 87.
144   Ibid.

achieve a balance."[145] He attacked Morgenthau's rationalistic interpretation: "Is it enough to consider merely the rational elements in order to produce a sketch or paint a portrait in accord with the model's essence?"[146] Along the same lines he also argued, with a certain Cartesian delight, against the value of games theory, notably the "indeterminacy of the stakes and the limits of the game. For there to be a game in the rigorous sense of the word, for a mathematical solution defining rational conduct to be possible, there must be a beginning and an end, a finite number of moves for each of the players, a result susceptible of cardinal or ordinal evaluation for each of the players."[147]

As a result, and owing no doubt also to the opacity of his *magnum opus* – the skills of the essayist not easily translating across the extended page – Aron was perhaps even less well known to the American readership than Butterfield. One of the few realists to take an active interest in Aron's work was Robert W. Tucker: a typical response from a mind unsettled by tame conventionality, and which almost relished the challenge of a dense text, however contrary, provided it was laced with reasoning.[148] Tucker, born in southern California on 25 August 1924, graduated from the US Naval Academy at Annapolis, and went on to study international relations at the University of California, Berkeley, where, by chance, he was given the task of showing Carr around the campus on his visit in 1949. Tucker was by then a student of international law under Kelsen. Kelsen's "pure theory of law" argued that because this theory "eliminates the dualism of law and justice and the dualism of objective and subjective law, so it abolishes the dualism of law and State. By so doing it establishes a theory of the State as an intrinsic part of the theory of law . . ."[149] Tucker thus imbibed a modicum of political philosophy along with law under Kelsen. His first published work on international relations was nevertheless an article on "Professor Morgenthau's Theory of Political 'Realism' ", which appeared in 1952.[150] Here Tucker's well-honed forensic skills, building on Wolfers' critique a year earlier, made short work of Morgenthau's logical inconsistencies – much to Morgenthau's annoyance. Tucker's direct target was Morgenthau's *In Defense of the National Interest*,[151] and he attacked Morgenthau's thesis – in *Politics among Nations* – that the conduct of states is always determined by

---

145   S. Hoffmann (ed.), *Contemporary Theory in International Relations* (New Jersey 1960) p. 200.
146   Aron, *Peace and War: A Theory of International Relations* (London 1966) p. 3.
147   Ibid., pp. 772–3.
148   At SAIS Tucker adopted the technique, when working on a subject, of drawing in colleagues and students with views entirely opposed to his own, in order better to work through his line of argument. All of his work thus partakes of a dialectical form of discussion. Not everyone appreciated playing the role of devil's advocate, but, next to acting as a research assistant, it was certainly the best way of learning how to go about matters.
149   H. Kelsen, *General Theory of Law and State* (Cambridge, Mass. 1949) p. xvi.
150   *American Political Science Review*, Vol. XLVI, No 1, March 1952, pp. 214–24.
151   New York 1951.

a desire for power as "at times . . . meaningless."[152] When Morgenthau went on to confuse the issue by sometimes stating that the Cold War was an ideological struggle on a moral level and at other times calling it a purely power struggle, Tucker delighted in rigorously exposing such blatant contradictions. But it would be a mistake to assume that Tucker was not at this stage a realist. On the contrary, he was as a convinced realist all the more concerned to preserve the coherence of the realist image, if by defiant iconoclasm so much the better.

From his first post at San Francisco State College, such writing propelled Tucker into the Johns Hopkins University, ironically once Woodrow Wilson's intellectual home, on the east coast in Baltimore. Here he spent considerable time researching Reasons of State only to draw the starkest of conclusions consistent with the notion of necessity of state. As he explained, in a review of Raymond Aron's diffuse and ultimately impenetrable *Paix et Guerre*, "In threatening or in employing force – including nuclear force – the statesman merely acts as he is compelled to act. To insist, however, that his action raises moral dilemmas and forms the proper object of moral judgement is to misapprehend its nature and significance. It may of course be seen as tragic in much the same way that death is seen as tragic. Still, we do not ask whether death as such poses moral dilemmas for men, much less whether death is moral or immoral, just or unjust. It is as meaningless to pass moral judgement on death as it is to pass moral judgement on an earthquake or a flood or on any natural catastrophe. Very nearly the same has been claimed for the attempt to pass moral judgement on the catastrophes that have marked men's collective relations in the past and that may yet one day attend the failure of a strategy of mutual deterrence."[153] Some thought that the advent of the thermonuclear era spelt an end to the use of force between the Superpowers, that to speculate on the possibilities of nuclear war was to think the unthinkable. On Tucker's view the threat or use of force was unavoidable in the protection of state interests. Since 1950, he wrote, "Where change has occurred it has almost invariably been attended by the threat, if not the actual use of, force. Where force has been neither employed nor seriously threatened on behalf of interests challenged by others, such interests have been preserved, if at all, only with great difficulty. In the light of this experience it borders on the absurd to contend, though an increasing number of observers do so contend, that force has lost its utility as an instrument of statecraft."[154]

This was written as the Vietnam war got under way, a war that Tucker, along with a number of realists, opposed as against the national interest. The most substantial piece of work that appeared in these years was co-written with Robert Osgood, a former colleague of Morgenthau's, who vigorously supported the war. Their co-operation played on their strengths: Osgood, the student of strategy; Tucker, more akin to a legal philosopher, at least by training if not by vocation. What they also shared was the attraction

152   "Professor Morgenthau's . . ." p. 216.
153   Tucker, "Peace and War", *World Politics*, January 1965, XVII, No 2, p. 322.
154   Ibid., p. 324.

of being able to influence US foreign policy-making. Thus the focus of their work dealt with policy and the moral dilemmas entailed. That is what is, perhaps, so distinctive and valuable about the book: most realists run a mile when the issue of ethics or morality is raised, and dive for cover under "necessity" of state. The book, *Force, Order, and Justice*, which appeared in 1967, transcended their deep differences and dealt with the conundrums involved in the use of force and as such arguably fits more in the category of philosophy of war than of international relations *per se*. One discreet section of the work deals directly with the issue of Reasons of State, which Tucker had spent some considerable time pondering during the 1950s, reaching back to the era of Machiavelli. Here Tucker rejected the mechanistic interpretation which implied a necessity of state independent of will or moral compunction. Necessity in statecraft was, he insisted, "a choice" and "the necessity imposed upon the statesman is a 'moral necessity.' "[155] Moreover, although use of the term usually implied that what should be done was obvious and that particular circumstances were of no great consideration, Tucker underlined the essential elasticity of the notion, particularly where Great Powers were concerned, since mere survival was more rarely of immediate concern to the greater states than to smaller ones.

Ironically, Tucker's signal contribution to the theory of international relations ultimately stretched the application of necessity of state to breaking point: certainly beyond the cautionary principle of prudence. It grew directly out of issues of current policy, from which he was always excluded; it was not originally intended as a contribution to theory at all. After the devastating reduction in American morale consequent upon defeat in Vietnam, Tucker was distracted by the oil crisis of 1973–4 and two movements of thought in international relations from the utopian end of the spectrum: first, appeals for a redistribution of income between developed and underdeveloped countries (what was called by liberal universalists a New International Economic Order); and, second, the case for growing interdependence and integration of states resulting from the increased importance of non-state actors in international relations. Tucker was the foremost opponent of the first movement and a latecomer, but trenchant, critic of the second.

Tucker also sought to refute several strands of thought which created an emerging consensus on the left and within the third world in the early 1970s. They aimed to enhance the economic position of the third world in its commerce with the West in what might be seen as neo-mercantilism. They also constructed their argument alternatively in the realist terms of the Balance of Trade or in the much more emotive appeal (to the left) of what President Rafael Caldera of Venezuela used (incessantly) to call International Social Justice.

The doctrine of the Balance of Trade extended and promulgated by List had travelled a great distance since its original propagation. Witte had introduced it to

---

155   R. Osgood and R. Tucker, *Force, Order, and Justice* (Baltimore 1967) p. 266.

Tsarist Russia. But it was Lenin, with the state monopoly of foreign trade which was effected in 1918, who brought protectionism to the level of autarchy in essential goods. His purpose was less the purely economic one of facilitating infant industrial development – though this purpose came increasingly to the forefront under Stalin – than to seal off the proto-socialist state from unwelcome penetration by foreign, private capital and the evident political consequences that would flow from it. Hitler, too, cast a canopy of protection over Nazi Germany, but essentially to secure uninterrupted development of military goods free from the effects of a non-convertible currency.

It was in what the French came to call the third world that the infant industry argument drove the case for protection. The leading theorist was the Argentinian economist Raúl Prebisch. Like List, Prebisch began his career believing "firmly in neoclassical theories" of economics.[156] As in the case of List, cataclysmic events in the outer world effected a total intellectual transformation. For Prebisch it was the Great Depression from 1929 which generated deep doubt about these beliefs. The "second great crisis of capitalism" in the mid-1970s reinforced his attitude. As a young man in the Depression he served first as under-secretary of finance and later as head of the central bank. Like his counterparts in the first world he recommended orthodox deflationary policies to cut the budget deficit. But faced with a serious imbalance of payments on the foreign account, he advised "a resolute policy of industrialisation and other means oriented to this end."[157] He became a convert for protectionism, "throwing overboard" a "considerable part" of his previous beliefs.[158]

Forced out of office in 1943 when Juan Perón came to power, Prebisch finally found the time to lay the foundations of his ideas born of his experiences at the centre of policy-making. Thus by 1949, when Prebisch moved to Chile to take charge of CEPAL (Comisión Economica para America Latina), his ideas had begun to crystallise; he began writing. The most important essay appeared only in mimeographic form as "The Economic Development of Latin America and its Principal Problems" and did not find its way into print, in English, until February 1962. The argument of classical economics was that with the international division of labour there was no need for producers of primary products to industrialise, since they would automatically share in the benefits of trade and the distribution of technological progress. The idea was that the prices of manufactures would diminish as productivity increased. Prebisch argued that there was no such distribution of benefits because the increases in productivity were absorbed by the industrialised states. Arguing on the basis of data from the 1870s to the 1930s, Prebisch wrote: "while the centres kept the whole benefit of the technical development of their industries, the peripheral countries transferred to them a share

156   R. Prebisch, "Cinco etapas de mi pensamiento sobre el desarrollo", El Trimestre Economico, Vol. L (2), April–June 1983, No 198, p. 1077.
157   Ibid.
158   Ibid., p. 1080.

of the profits of their own technical progress."[159] And, as a corollary, "since prices do not keep pace with productivity, industrialization is the only means by which the Latin American countries may fully obtain the advantage of technical progress."[160]

This became known as the Prebisch-Singer Thesis, or PS for short. At the very time Prebisch produced his argument in Chile, Hans Singer published something extraordinarily similar in the United States. This was no mere coincidence, in that the UN had begun producing statistics on the relative prices of exports and imports of underdeveloped countries. Whereas these figures served to confirm Prebisch's intuitive conclusions, they acted as a catalyst to Singer's thinking. Prebisch's thesis was based entirely on the balance of trade between the United States and Latin America. Singer painted on a larger canvas. Born in 1910, Singer worked on unemployment under Keynes at Cambridge, and after a spell on local planning in the postwar Attlee Labour Government took a job in the United States, where fortuitously his involvement in local planning was mistaken for expertise in macro-economic development.[161] At the end of December 1949 Singer delivered a paper to the American Economic Association in New York. Entitled "The Distribution of Gains Between Investing and Borrowing Countries", it rehearsed most of the same lines of argument as Prebisch. The specialisation of underdeveloped countries in the production of raw materials was, he argued, unfortunate, "(a) because it removed most of the secondary and cumulative effects of investment from the country in which the investment took place to the investing country; and (b) because it diverted the underdeveloped countries into types of activity offering less scope for technical progress, internal and external economies taken by themselves, and withheld from the course of their economic history a central factor of dynamic radiation which has revolutionized society in the industrialized countries." The third reason related to terms of trade: "It is a matter of historical fact that ever since the seventies [1870s] the trend of prices has been heavily against sellers of food and raw materials and in favor of the sellers of manufactured articles."[162] On this basis, Singer argued for a radical transformation of the world economic order: "the purposes of foreign investment and foreign trade ought perhaps to be redefined as producing gradual changes in the structure of comparative advantages and of the comparative endowment of the different countries rather than to develop a world trading system based on existing comparative advantages and existing distribution of endowments."[163]

---

159   R. Prebisch, "The Economic Development of Latin America and its Principal Problems", *Economic Bulletin for Latin America*, Vol. VII, No 1, February 1962, p. 5.

160   Ibid., p. 7.

161   His own account: *A Biographical Dictionary of Dissenting Economists*, ed. P. Arestis and M. Sawyer (Hampshire/Vermont 1992) pp. 528–9.

162   H. Singer, "The Distribution of Gains Between Investing and Borrowing Countries", *The American Economic Review*, Vol. XL, May 1950, No 2 (Papers and Proceedings . . .) p. 477.

163   Ibid., p. 484.

To argue this from the intellectual remoteness of CEPAL in Santiago was one thing, to make the case within the United States in the company of neoclassical economists such as Jacob Viner and Gottfried Haberler was quite another. When Singer presented it at Harvard he came under fire from the establishment.[164] And these opinions, though sustained through the 1950s, had little impact on real politics until the number of underdeveloped states grew from a small minority of mainly Latin American countries plus India, Burma and Ceylon, to the majority in the UN General Assembly. This same process brought Prebisch to head the United Nations Commission on Trade and Development (UNCTAD) in 1963, which enabled him "to revise and develop" his thought "systematically".[165] "The developing countries", he wrote in 1964, "are still suffering from the consequences of the disintegration of the world economy which the great catastrophe of the thirties brought with it. They do not export industrial goods, except in the most meagre quantity. And since their primary [goods] exports grow so little and relative prices deteriorate, they lack the indispensable means to ensure, in sufficient measure, the imports demanded by a satisfactory rhythm of development."[166] Thereafter the argument was pressed ever more forcefully that the developed countries had a duty to rectify an imbalance which they had themselves in some sense, if not originated, then exacerbated.

Although these were arguments squarely within the realist tradition, they were pressed by the "have-not" Powers in the same manner that Carr had spoken for the equivalent economies in the 1930s. Prebisch's arguments thus found natural favour with those liberal universalists in the United States who would not normally countenance anything tainted with realism and who argued that the world was becoming more interdependent and therefore more peaceful. The idea that the international relations was merely a passing phase in world history, so noticeable in the medieval period when the state was still merely a tentative political formation, at least in the minds of those who believed in *corpus christianum* or the Holy Roman Empire as the normal structure of Europe, had its latter-day secular counterpart in the cosmopolitanism of the free-market economists. In the twentieth century belief in world government grew from the same roots and had flowered after the devastating war of 1914–18, which apparently demonstrated not only the moral culpability of the states system but also its self-destructive essence. Belief in world government, which centred on the League of Nations, emerged from the experience of the inter-war period damaged, at least for mainstream minds. In its place, however, and emerging from the same fundamentally liberal and free-market premiss, appeared the notion of functional international (or regional) integration. This idea appealed to young idealists, who particularly disliked the crudity of the Morgenthau model and who rejected the focus of foreign policy upon

164   *A Biographical . . .* p. 528.
165   "Cinco etapas . . ." p. 1077.
166   23 March 1964: Prebisch, *Nueva Política Comercial Para el Desarrollo* (Mexico-Buenos Aires 1964) p. 125.

the dominant conflict of the time – the Cold War. But many of these idealists by the 1970s sought to skirt the predominantly realist assessment of world politics and, rather than directly challenging it head on – evidently for lack of sufficient force of argument, or wracked by doubt – instead sought to undermine it from within by attrition and dilution. The more resolute searched for havens within the international system where an alternative could be sought where integration was working: rather like the building of a second Foundation, in Asimov's famous novel, while the original Foundation, now an Empire, was destined for final collapse at the other end of the universe.

One of the most determined and at the same time one of the most cautious of the functionalists of the older generation was Haas, who rejected the hitherto ineffective idealism of Mitrany, in favour of accumulating detail on elements of largely technical international co-operation. His first major post-doctoral work, on the emergence of the European Economic Community, shadowed a significant development in postwar politics, though whether it emerged quite for the reasons Haas attributed to the process is an open question. The breach with Mitrany's approach did not indicate any softening; on the contrary. In *Beyond the Nation-State: Functionalism and International Organization*, Haas declared: "It is precisely the merit of Functionalism that it broke away from the cliches of Realist political theory. Its fault lies in not having broken radically enough."[167] The objections to Realism were ideological: "The main reason for studying . . . regional integration . . . is normative: the units and actions provide a living laboratory for observing the peaceful creation of possible new types of human communities at a very high level of organization and of the processes that may lead to such conditions."[168] His belief was that *"There will be a continued drift toward supranationality . . ."*[169] Moreover, and this is an important point to note, he saw a closer relationship between international relations theory "and the rest of the social sciences"[170] as the alternative to Realism and as the best means of accomplishing his goal; hence the rapprochement with sociology and the borrowing of functionalism to explain international behaviour.

Those who shared such views congregated around the journal *International Organization*, which provided the main forum for debate and confirmation. There were differences, however. Whereas Haas had no time at all for realism *per se*, there were younger recruits who did. They emerged from the stable of Stanley Hoffmann, an Austrian by birth (1928–), and a formidably learned liberal universalist of French training, whose doctoral thesis had boldly anticipated the extinction of the state. The

---

167 E. Haas, *Beyond the Nation-State: Functionalism and International Organization* (Stanford 1964) p. 24.
168 As quoted in R. Keohane and J. Nye, "International Interdependence and Integration", *Handbook of Political Science*, Vol. 8: *International Politics*, ed. F. Greenstein and N. Polsby (Reading, Mass. 1975) p. 367.
169 Haas, *Beyond . . .* , p. 492.
170 Ibid., p. 24.

thesis in published form bore the deceptively unassuming title *Organisations Interna-tionales et Pouvoirs Politiques des États.*[171] The work is strikingly original in several respects. It has a clean Cartesian logic worthy of eighteenth-century writers like Say. It avoids the customary and obvious trap of elevating beyond reasonable credulity pre-existing or current international organisations as exemplars against which failing humankind falls disastrously short. It makes a realistic appreciation of events but then, instead of extending, as one might have anticipated, towards the logic of Reasons of State, it veers around sharply to attack "the cause of the disease: the Modern State",[172] by three distinct means: through adept verbal surgery at the expense of the formal attributes of the state; a generous view of the effect of international institutions in circumscribing the freedom of state behaviour; and, lastly, by adopting a Fabian view of the ultimate triumph of international organisation at the expense of the state itself. Sovereignty is ditched because all states have had to compromise their powers and sovereignty cannot be held in parts. This is the technical objection, which barely veils the underlying moral (liberal) objection which bursts unexpectedly to the surface: "the function of this word constitutes an incontestable danger for the development of international law or the establishment of an order in the international environment, since it at once consolidates the power of the state and the myth of the state as a person, at the expense of the individual."[173] The notion of "independence" is cut down by the same sword. Only in some kind of state of nature did true independence exist, where interaction did not take place between states. "As, and to the degree that, relations between states are established [*se nouent*], these powers [pertaining to states] become modified . . ."[174] Hoffmann even objects to "powers", except in the restricted legal form; in the end he prefers "political capabilities" (*pouvoirs politiques*) – not surprisingly the choice fell on a term that carried not the slightest sense of legitimacy. As he later con-fessed, the thesis combined "a realist analysis of state behavior . . . and a wild call for overcoming sovereignty."[175]

Since that time a certain and necessary adaptation to harsh realities could be observed that required more selective borrowing from the realist bank; but Hoffmann was not backward in asserting his values. Attacking the "narrower version" of realism which emphasised the centrality of military power to international relations, Hoffmann abhorred the fact that it "both rests on and leads to an ethical assumption: the impos-sibility of moving beyond that game, or rather of going beyond the traditional tech-niques of moderation, of which the balance of power is the most successful example. This is not only a morally objectionable postulate or conclusion, given the fate of such

---

171   Published in 1954 (Paris).
172   Hoffmann, *Organisations*, p. 417.
173   Ibid., p. 15.
174   Ibid., p. 16.
175   L. Miller and M. Smith, eds., *Ideas and Ideals: Essays on Politics in Honor of Stanley Hoffmann* (Boulder 1993) p. 9.

techniques in the past, and the formidable inequities and violations of human rights which the game has usually tolerated or even encouraged. It is", he added, "also unnecessary to accept it, since 'realism', in any version, only demonstrates that there can be no leap into Erewhon, no escape from 'the workmanlike manipulation of the perennial forces' of the political universe. It does not, and cannot, prove that one is doomed to repeat the past and that there is no middle ground, however narrow, between the limited and fragile moderation of the past and the impossible abolition of the game."[176]

As Hoffmann claimed, "I study power so as to understand the enemy, not so as better to be able to exert it."[177] This was a misleading, though a high-minded claim. It was more complex than that. In fact Hoffmann wished to use power, including military power, extensively for other purposes. Tucker used to complain that whereas Hoffmann tended to refuse to accept the use of force where state interests were threatened, he hawkishly advocated force where humanitarian causes arose (see below, p. 246). Hoffmann's young disciples were less inclined to mark out the differences separating them from the realists – as Haas preferred – and more inclined to concede certain realist premises in order to establish their ideas more securely on the agenda. They were thus willing to compromise, though the balance of their views and ideals most certainly and deliberately tilted towards Haas. The two young disciples of Hoffmann and Haas were Joseph Nye and Robert Keohane. Both had been graduate students under Hoffmann at Harvard. Nye, an Africanist, was very much of the UNCTAD school – thus very much in the Prebisch-Singer camp. African integration proved a mirage, and Nye became bored with it all. But perhaps something could be salvaged from the wreckage? Nye described his transition towards mainstream international relations thus:

> The invisible college of students of integration that had formed around Ernest Haas began to dissolve.
>
> Yet I felt that many of the insights from regional integration theory were applicable to the broader dimensions of international economic interdependence that were becoming more prominent.[178]

A milder version of functionalism and integration theory thereby emerged in the notion of Interdependence. This represented the influence of Hoffmann rather than Haas: what the somewhat jaded ex-official Charles Burton Marshall encapsulated in a sardonic aside, dismissing "the prevalent theory that when people get to know each other well, they like each other."[179]

176   Hoffmann, "Notes on the Limits of 'Realism' ", pp. 658–9.
177   Ibid.
178   Nye's testimony in ed. J. Kruzel and J. Rosenau, *Journeys through World Politics: Autobiographical Reflections of Thirty-four Academic Travellers* (Lexington, Mass. 1989) p. 203.
179   Roundtable at the Washington Center: *East-West Negotiations*, p. 35.

Keohane started out as a student of voting in the UN General Assembly, a firm if futile believer in the value of international organisations. He worked for Eugene McCarthy's campaign for the Presidency on a peace platform and then for anti-war candidates for the US Senate in 1968–70.[180] As he recalled, "Ever since my years in graduate school, I had been critical of the then-dominant school of political realism, as represented most eloquently (and confusingly) by the works of Hans J. Morgenthau."[181] He later acknowledged, somewhat to the bafflement of his subject: "a special role model for me is Ernst Haas of the University of California at Berkeley – whose student I would have been had not the Harvard mystique turned my head."[182] In 1969 Keohane wrote: "The 'plant of integration theory', as one author has written, may need pruning; but the struggling seedling of international organization theory requires watering with new concepts for rapid growth. To accomplish this we must give it greater attention and a more favored place in our garden."[183] It all sounds reminiscent of a revivalist meeting.

What Keohane and Nye came up with were the compromise notions of interdependence (already in circulation and, interestingly, a term used by Hoffmann in his thesis nearly two decades before)[184] and "Transnational Relations". Haas had sought to get away from the untrammelled nation-state by emphasising regional integration. International integration still seemed a distant prospect, even to true believers. Not until the mid-seventies did Haas come around to the position that "Integration theories are becoming obsolete because they are not designed to address the most pressing and important problems on the global agenda of policy and research."[185] The emphasis was placed instead on relations between "non-state actors". After a dinner of the board of *International Organization* in Boston in June 1968, not accidentally at the height of student discontent over the US war in Vietnam, there were expressions of dissatisfaction with current approaches to the subject and of concern to avoid "the overemphasis on intergovernmental organization."[186] Keohane and Nye, the young Turks on the board, led the way: "we tried to reconcile the insights of traditional realism with the liberal tradition that focused on economic interactions and institutions".[187] But this was disingenuous as a statement of what Nye and Keohane attempted. Hoffmann lauded them

---

180   Keohane in *Journeys*, p. 407.
181   Ibid.
182   Ibid., p. 414.
183   "Institutionalization in the UNGA", *International Organization*, Vol. XXIII, No 4, Autumn 1969, p. 896.
184   Hoffmann, *Organisations*, p. 418.
185   E. Haas, *The Obsolescence of Regional Integration Theory* (Berkeley 1975) p. 17. Readers should beware, however, of casually assuming from this title that Haas thought regional integration theory was no longer of any use.
186   R. Keohane and J. Nye, ed., *Transnational Relations and World Politics* (Cambridge, Mass. 1973) p. vii.
187   Nye, in *Journeys*, p. 204.

as the *"modernes"*, fighting the cause against a "theory of international politics which defines the states as the only actors on the world scene, makes of military power the decisive currency, and sees the hierarchy of military might *the* hierarchy in the international system."[188] Their avowed purpose was to stress "the importance of nonstate actors, of transnational and transgovernmental coalitions, of nonmilitary forms of power, and of multiple hierarchies depending on the 'issue-area' or on the international regime."[189] Their role was in fact not unlike that of Botero in his counter-offensive against Machiavelli: borrowing the form of realism but denuding it of all substance. They ignored those elements of economic relations highlighted by the Balance of Trade thinkers since the sixteenth century which made for conflict, and which were to rear their head again with the oil crisis in 1973–4, and instead blindly seized upon those elements highlighted by Florus the epitomist and later taken up by Bodin and Grotius that fixed upon those factors in trade making for peace.

The mask slipped, however, as the collapse of the US presence in Vietnam in 1975 bolstered confidence in the alternative vision. A contribution to a collection of studies on comparative modernisation gave Keohane and Nye the chance to state openly: "Faced with a growing complexity of actors and issues, a number of analysts have begun to pay more attention to transnational relations. In this article we will contend that if critiques of Realist models of world politics are taken seriously, they not only call into question state-centric conceptions of 'the international systems', but also throw doubt upon prevailing notions about international organizations. If one relaxes Realist assumptions, one can visualize more significant roles for international organizations in world politics."[190]

Their common belief that the "realist paradigm was poorly equipped to cope with these new issues"[191] was later effectively answered by Tucker – that is, if one assumed merely an attempt to understand the problem rather than also to change the world, which in the case of Nye and Keohane one could not. In their edited collection on *Transnational Relations and World Politics* these two did not dare suggest that non-state actors were more important than states as actors. But realists were unanimous in regarding non-state actors as entirely peripheral to the workings of international relations. Keohane and Nye were attempting, through purely formal deference to realist thought, to raise the status of non-state actors to the level of states within the international system. The traditional (realist) focus on relations between states had, they asserted, led to a neglect of "inter-societal interactions" and "transnational actors". The new approach "treats the reciprocal effects between transnational relations on the

---

188 Hoffmann, "Notes on the Limits of 'Realism' ", pp. 657–8. This section of the article from which the quotations are taken was a flashback to the 1970s.
189 Ibid., p. 658.
190 Keohane and Nye, "Transgovernmental Relations and International Organizations", in C. Black, ed., *Comparative Modernization: A Reader* (New York and London 1976) p. 411.
191 Nye in *Journeys*, p. 203.

interstate system as centrally important to the understanding of contemporary world politics", they claimed.[192] Yet the scholarly validity of the entire exercise was inadvertently undermined by the frank admission that this was as much an idealist enterprise as that undertaken by functionalists like Haas, whom they clearly hoped to supersede: "Students of international law and organization should . . . become involved in the study of transnational relations not merely for the sake of understanding reality but also in order to help change reality."[193] Indeed, Keohane has consistently argued that the study of international relations is "profoundly normative".[194] Those norms he defined as "humanistic, cosmopolitan and ecological values".[195]

The assumption that states were less central than they had been and that closer interaction would lead to a significant diminution in conflict was valid enough (within strict limits) in respect of Western Europe as the movement to greater integration gathered momentum, albeit falteringly. But Western Europe was a special case from which it took a leap of faith to generalise about other regions (as Nye was by no means alone in discovering) and only those with no experience of life in such regions could hold firmly to the idea that the West European experience was immediately exportable elsewhere: a Wilsonian illusion, perhaps; characteristically out of touch with reality, simultaneously both appealingly idealistic and irritatingly ethnocentric.

On top of this came US defeat in the Vietnam war, dressed up disingenuously by President Nixon and his *alter ego*, US Secretary of State Henry Kissinger, as a compromise peace, the ultimate consequence of failed military intervention opposed by some of the leading realists of the time – Morgenthau, Tucker and Waltz. "To be militarily frustrated, and eventually defeated, by so small a state is humiliating, and nothing we say can deny this", Tucker wrote.[196] Thus by the early seventies it appeared that the liberals had won the argument, on both sides of the coin, economic and political. The nature of international relations had, on their view, undergone a substantial change for the better.

It was the oil crisis precipitated by the outbreak of war in the Middle East on 6 October 1973 which heralded an entirely new era. Even before Egypt's attack on Israel, pressure was building towards an embargo on oil to the United States. Saudi Arabia was the Arab state closest aligned to Washington. On 31 August that year King Faisal warned that continuing US support for Israel made it "extremely difficult" for Saudi Arabia to maintain friendly relations with the United States and even to continue supplying the Americans with oil.[197] Moreover, all oil exporting countries were looking to raise prices to meet foreign exchange needs at a time of rapidly rising inflation following the

192 *Transnational*, pp. x–xi.
193 Ibid., p. xxix.
194 Keohane in *Journeys*, p. 403.
195 Ibid., p. 414.
196 Tucker, "Vietnam: The Final Reckoning", *Commentary*, Vol. 59, No 5, May 1975.
197 *Keesing's Contemporary Archives (KCA)*, 1973, p. 26194.

Vietnam war. Finally, after the outbreak of war the Organisation of Arab Petroleum Exporting Countries (OAPEC) agreed to cut the production of oil progressively by 5 per cent each month until the complete withdrawal of the Israelis from the territories they occupied during the war of June 1967 and the restoration of Palestinian rights. Certain Arab states went on to embargo oil sales to the United States in their entirety. By November this added up to a total of a 25-per-cent cut in production, and other members of the international OPEC cartel, such as Venezuela and Iran, agreed not to make up the difference through increased exports. As a result, within months the price of oil quadrupled. The constitutional crisis over Watergate followed in 1974. In January 1975 President Ford, delivering his State of the Union address, pointed out that "Millions of Americans are out of work. Recession and inflation are eroding the money of millions more. Prices are too high and sales are too slow."[198] The economic dislocation originating in an inflationary war in Vietnam had turned into a major crisis as a result of the oil embargo. At the outset Kissinger, Nixon's Secretary of State, had warned the Arabs that if the embargo continued "unreasonably and indefinitely", the United States would "have to consult what counter-measures it may have to take."[199] But these were idle threats. In practice the Americans had lost heart.

Whereas North Vietnam had threatened no core US interests as defined by several realists – Morgenthau, Tucker and Waltz – to Tucker the threat posed to Western oil supplies most certainly met that criterion. The standard liberal response, on the other hand, was that the embargo conclusively demonstrated the need for closer interdependence as well as the right of the less developed world to gain its share of wealth from the developed world: a curious mixture of liberal universalism at the expense of the state (i.e., the states of the developed world) and advocacy of the enhancement of state power (of the underdeveloped countries), and a contradiction never resolved. The US Government appeared impotent in the face of this unprecedented challenge. Tucker was infuriated and embarked on a series of articles in *Commentary*, a prominent and respected Jewish-American mouthpiece, not noted for empathy towards the Arab world, arguing the case for the threat or use of force to rectify the problem. "Instead of leaving the option of armed intervention open," he wrote in the first and most notorious of these pieces in January 1975, "the American government has all but foreclosed it."[200] Tucker continued: "By a kind of unspoken convention, even to ask the question apparently indicates that one is simply out of touch with the realities of today's world, that one is a latter-day Colonel Blimp or, for the more sophisticated, an imperialist *manqué*. Yet it is doubtful that the same question, raised in roughly comparable circumstances, would have had the same reception fifteen or even ten years ago." To Tucker these were "vital interests" at stake, and surely they were worth protecting through force. Those who disagreed implied "a revolutionary change in the very nature of

198   *KCA* 1975, p. 26934.
199   21 November 1973: ibid., p. 26294.
200   Tucker, "Oil: The Issue of American Intervention", *Commentary*, Vol. 59, No 1, January 1975.

international society" and moreover appeared to find the change "so indisputable as scarcely to deserve attention"[201]:

> There is little to be served by making once again the already well-worn and unavoidably abrasive observations on the legacy of Vietnam. But it is impossible not to address, however briefly, the broad conviction that armed force has lost most of its former utility and legitimacy. If this conviction is well-founded, then those who hold it should draw the appropriate conclusions for American foreign policy. The principal conclusion to be drawn – that the present structure of American interests in the world must change, and radically so – may be avoided only by assuming that in place of an obsolete policy of power and intervention we may substitute a policy of pacific interdependence rather than one that clearly points toward isolationism.

But, Tucker argued, the oil crisis was "not a manifestation of interdependence in the sense that proponents of interdependence have in mind when using the term. Nor is it, clearly, a manifestation of the 'old politics.' Instead, it is the latest manifestation – though by far the most spectacular to date – of an egalitarianism which, if permitted to run its logical course, is likely to result first in chaos and then in an international system far harsher than today's, or even yesterday's, system."[202] Two further articles in a similar vein followed over subsequent months.

The counter-blast came from Hoffmann, who wrote to *Commentary* in protest at Tucker's message. Hoffmann insisted that the new attitude rejecting the use of force had nothing whatever to do with Vietnam. It dated back to the Suez crisis of 1956, and he cited the Cuban crisis as a further example. Hoffmann was an outspoken advocate of interdependence:

> Would not the concern for a world system both less brutal and less unfair than that of the past require that we seek solutions that maximize interdependence, entangle the "newly rich" countries in the economies of the old ones, give the former an incentive to avoid – and indeed deter them from – damaging the latter, and commit the old *and* the new rich to improving the fate of the poorest nations?[203]

Tucker thought this illusory:

> it is by now apparent that the relationships between the industrialized and developing states will be characterized much more by conflict than by consensus and that

201   Ibid.
202   Ibid.
203   Letter, ibid., No 4, April 1975.

if one projects a world in which military power is increasingly at a discount this conflict may exact a heavy price from the industrialized states.

Hoffmann had asserted that influence was more important than military power. What worried Tucker was that this was another way of saying the West had become ineffective:

> it seemed to me that the competition for influence had become an increasingly expensive game that was increasingly devoid of durable consequences and this for the reason that the traditional instruments for exercising influence, particularly over the states of the developing world, had declined in effectiveness. Very few observers would care to dispute this decline and many among Western elites welcome it. Whether it is welcomed or decried, the consequences of the decline have now been vividly illustrated in the oil crisis.
>
> Does the "new internationalism", with its commitment to an ever-increasing interdependence, prevent these consequences we see in the oil crisis? To date, at least, the evidence is that it does not.

Hoffmann argued that use of force carried too high a price tag. "But", wrote Tucker, "so does the pursuit of Mr. Hoffmann's internationalism, with its 'renunciation of the use of force to redress non-military measures of coercion' and its reliance on 'solutions that maximize interdependence'." While states continued to exist in competition and conflict with one another, Tucker did not relish greater interdependence. Hoffmann appeared to take for granted current stability when in fact it rested upon an order based in the threat of force from the more powerful. Like Waltz, Tucker argued: "The prospect of a world that is ever more interdependent is scarcely a comforting one when such a world is still one of states and still one in which the bases for conflict and disorder are many and deep – if anything, more numerous and intractable than ever – while the traditional instruments for providing what modicum of order international society has enjoyed in the past are increasingly at a discount."[204]

Tucker pursued his argument into book form. Echoing Mackinder, *The Inequality of Nations* opened with the assertion that "The history of the international system is a history of inequality par excellence."[205] The form of that system was one of "international anarchy" (Norman Angell's term), characterised by self-help, which was less a right, more a matter of power. Following Carr, Tucker went on to assert that "where self-help is the principal institutional expression of order for a society whose members are vastly unequal in power, the tendency must arise to throw the mantle of right over those uses of power that, whatever their proper characterization, prove effective."[206] The

204   Ibid.
205   *The Inequality of Nations* (London 1977) p. 3.
206   Ibid., pp. 4–5.

expansion in the number of states, the steady abandonment of formal inequalities between them and the growing constraints on the use of military and economic power made it seem as though the international system was moving in the direction taken by Western societies in their formation. In the sphere of trade the successful quadrupling of the price of oil by OPEC in 1973–4 gave "an extraordinary added momentum . . . to the demands of the developing states for greater equality."[207] Those claims had surprisingly elicited support "among liberal elites" in the West, so pervasively "that the articulate few who do not share it are seen as eccentric, if not perverse."[208]

But what would the international system look like if the West gave way to these demands? Tucker expected liberals to be sorely disappointed: "there is little reason to expect that the scope accorded the exercise of the right of self-help would be significantly narrowed in the new system. At least, there is little reason to expect this unless it is assumed that, among themselves at any rate, the new states will not have the conflicts that states have had in the past, that instead they will manifest an altogether unprecedented solidarity in their mutual relations. But the record to date indicates that the new states may be expected to behave toward one another in much the same way as the older states behaved."[209] This was already apparent in areas other than disputes with the West. India was a prime example. But this was to be expected. It merely reflected "the ubiquitous operation of reason of state, the nerve root of the insistence upon preserving one's freedom of action and leaving broad scope to the exercise of the right of self-help."[210]

The point was that the new egalitarianism gave "renewed strength" to this traditional form of behaviour. It was directed not simply against disparities in wealth and power inherent in the international system, "but radical disparities in levels of development that give rise to a special kind of inequality . . . a sense of humiliation and resentment more potent than the sense of injustice bred by normal disparities of power."[211] Thus the new egalitarianism did not challenge "the essential structure of the international system but the distribution of wealth and power within this system." For it was "through the institution of the state" that this goal was being pursued. It was therefore not a revolutionary but a "traditional" challenge to the international system.[212]

Tucker was worried that acceptance of growing equality had undermined the US government's determination to defend US interests. He had only a few years before written of the prospect of using force against the Arabs if the US oil supplies were put in jeopardy. He openly regretted "the disinclination today among the developed and capitalist states to threaten or use force even when vital interests are

---

207   Ibid., p. 50.
208   Ibid., p. 51.
209   Ibid., p. 60.
210   Ibid., pp. 60–1.
211   Ibid., p. 62.
212   Ibid., pp. 63–4.

jeopardized . . ."[213] If this continued unchecked, Tucker feared a distribution in power within the existing system, "a new international hierarchy" rather than the removal of all hierarchy.[214] The growing demands for equality in the third world and the liberal advocacy of interdependence were not in fact harmonious. Tucker pointed to the "marked ambivalence toward the state" among liberal opinion. "In contrast to the outlook of the elites of most of the new states, Western liberal elites look increasingly to a global order whose basis is no longer centered exclusively, or even primarily, on the state."[215] This was, perhaps, Tucker's most effective form of attack. Few would go along with his previous call to arms, for reasons of prudence as much as of morality (and not just liberal opinion). But in calling attention to the fact that the states of the third world, like trade unionists at home, sought merely to enhance their status within the existing system rather than supplant that system, as social democrats at home and liberals abroad hoped, Tucker hit home. Indeed, his foremost and most vehement critic, Hoffmann, conceded Tucker's main charge. Hoffmann confessed to his deep disappointment barely a year later: "the anti-imperialist nations", he wrote, "show a remarkable ability at double bookkeeping. They denounce the unfair order imposed by the rich nations of the West, yet they deal profitably with several if not all of these, and they pursue their own rivalries and grievances in ways that turn the common front of the developing nations into a mass of bitter conflicts."[216] His disillusionment with the intended beneficiaries of universalist good-will was to deepen still further after the end of the Cold War removed the convenient mask of excuses for misbehaviour at home as well as abroad. Another severe critic of liberals who saw interdependence as the road to harmony was Waltz.

Postwar realists such as Tucker were not that complicated. Their politics was predictably conservative; their outlook firmly misanthropic; they sought direct influence over policy, and all the Americans among them gravitated to Washington to observe closely and seek the role of counsellor, albeit informally, at the heart of the empire; they generally preferred philosophy to theory, policy to social science. Waltz's temperament and personal political outlook have in some fundamental sense always contradicted the image of the standard realist; as complex as Carr, perhaps, though in a different manner, preferring the relative distance from power and tranquillity of Berkeley to the bustle of political networking along the north-east corridor. Moreover, Waltz is a leading theorist who believes that international relations theory has barely got anywhere – "moribund" was the term he used in 1975[217] – a view he shares with Tucker, whose most

213   Ibid., p. 116.
214   Ibid., p. 117.
215   Ibid., p. 134.
216   S. Hoffmann, *Primacy or World Order: American Foreign Policy since the Cold War* (New York 1978) p. 105.
217   K. Waltz, "Theory of International Relations", *Handbook of Political Science*, Vol. 8: International Politics, ed. F. Greenstein and N. Polsby (Reading, Mass., 1975) p. 1.

quotable comment about the theorists is: "they packed their bags but have never left the station."[218] How does Waltz put it? "I think that structural theory has at least helped focus people's minds on the theoretical problem, but I don't think there's much increase in understanding. I have often said that what Morgenthau did was translate Meinecke from German to English, and if you look at the index, you won't see Meinecke mentioned. I would translate some of Meinecke into the same words that Morgenthau used in Politics among Nations. And then Morton Kaplan translated Morgenthau from English into whatever language it was that Kaplan was writing in. I guess I think there's been very little progress. An awful lot of people became interested in I[nternational] P[olitical] E[conomy], a lot of work was churned out, but I haven't seen much progress."[219]

Waltz, the son of German-speaking working-class Americans, was born in Ann Arbor, Michigan on 8 June 1924.[220] He graduated from Oberlin College in 1948 after focusing initially on mathematics, which he found easy and enjoyed, and then shifting to economics. He moved to graduate school at Columbia intending to become an econometrician but found it unstimulating and drifted instead, under the influence of Franz Neumann (once of the Marxist Frankfurt School), into the field of political philosophy. Waltz had to seek a subsidiary field and chose international relations because, he said, he had already done international economics. The choice was once again made because it appeared an easy option until, however, the astute but relatively unpublished William Fox took charge and forced Waltz into serious study. What then happened has been recorded for posterity:

> So I started reading, reading, reading like mad; and I couldn't make head or tail of it. So many people writing in I[nternational] R[elations] were talking past each other, talking different languages really. I think I still have the faded piece of yellow paper on which I wrote down the three images: "This is why the people I am reading are not able to communicate with each other: because some of them think the major causes lie at the level of individuals or states or the international system." This was my final month as a graduate student before beginning to write the dissertation about a year and a half later.[221]

The thesis, defended at Columbia University in 1954, appeared under the title *Man, the State, and the State System in Theories of the Causes of War*. Here Waltz noted that "In international politics one is faced not only with a welter of often mutually contradictory prescriptions but also with a multiplicity of images of the world political

218   In conversation with the author.
219   "Interview with Ken Waltz", F. Halliday and J. Rosenberg, *Review of International Studies* (1998), 24, p. 386.
220   "Interview . . .", p. 371. Additional details from the author's conversations with Waltz.
221   "Interview . . .", p. 372.

problem."[222] He considered progress in the field impossible for that very reason: "The important point is that agreement on what image of international politics is valid reduces argument over prescriptions to questions of method and, more significantly, of practicability; but disagreement on what is the correct image renders discussion of prescriptions, to a large extent at least, futile."[223] This was the rationale for breaking down the literature into its core components. That literature was defined in its most extensive form: "international politics will be taken as a subject that can be subsumed under the general heading of political theory [the American term for what the British call 'political thought']. Statements relating to international politics will be considered, not as mere extensions of philosophies developed and applied to man and the state, but as logically and intrinsically related to such philosophies."[224]

The abstract with which the thesis opened thus outlined three images: the cause of war in the nature of man; the cause of war in the nature of the state; and the cause of war in the nature of the international system. Each image was represented by one political philosopher: the first by Spinoza; the second, Kant; and the third, Rousseau. "The choice of Spinoza, Kant and Rousseau", Waltz commented, "is based on a personal estimate of convenience. Any of a number of other political philosophers might have served equally well to illustrate the three images."[225]

The underlying assumption was that if one was to end the problem of war, its causes should be properly understood. An additional axiom was that "Any approach falling entirely under one image is a single-cause approach to the war problem. Such an approach", he reminded his examiners, "though in a sense it may be 'true', cannot be very useful."[226] Later still, he noted: "Some combination of our three images, rather than any one of them, may be required for an accurate understanding of international politics."[227] His reasoning ran thus: "The more sophisticated and perceptive the analyst the more surely he is led, in his attempt to understand war and peace, to a consideration of the more inclusive nexus. The third image describes the framework of world politics, but without the first and second images there are no motivating forces of action; the first and second images describe the motivating forces in world politics, but without the third image it is impossible to estimate their significance or predict their results."[228]

The thesis was published with some emendation in 1959, as *Man, the State and War: A Theoretical Analysis*. It ordered the findings of political philosophers within a

222   Waltz, *Man, the State, and the State System in Theories of the Causes of War* (New York, Columbia PhD 1954) p. 12.
223   Ibid.
224   Ibid., p. 17.
225   Ibid.
226   Ibid., p. 2.
227   Ibid., p. 24.
228   Ibid., p. 3.

behaviourist framework. In so doing Waltz sought to bridge an old and tried tradition of thought with the new (American) social sciences. He still fully expected to find employment in what the Americans call "political theory". Waltz proceeded by taking the assumptions of leading political thinkers and "asking repeatedly what differences they make".[229] As noted above, he distinguished three images of international relations. In the first image "the locus of the important causes of war is found in the nature and behavior of man."[230] In the second image "the internal organization of states is the key to understanding war and peace."[231] The third image is that "the international political environment has much to do with the ways in which states behave."[232] Although scrupulously careful to give due weight to each of the images in turn, Waltz's preference for the third image as the most decisive of the three became apparent towards the end of the work: "With many sovereign states, with no system of law enforceable among them, with each state judging its grievances and ambitions according to the dictates of its own reason or desire – conflict, sometimes leading to war, is bound to occur. To achieve a favorable outcome from such conflict a state has to rely on its own devices, the relative efficiency of which must be its constant concern."[233] On his view, "If there were but two loci of cause involved, men and states, we could be sure that the appearance of more peacefully inclined states would, at worst, not damage the cause of world peace."[234] However, "The increased propensity to peace of some participants in international politics may increase, rather than decrease, the likelihood of war."[235] Following Hobbes, Waltz accepted that governments had been formed to prevent a continuous state of open conflict within society. But in response to those who argued that international anarchy was so dangerous that world government of some form was essential, Waltz insisted that "the state of nature that continues to prevail among states often produces monstrous behavior but so far has not made itself impossible."[236] Unconvinced by the utopians, Waltz expected that the third image might "provide a realistic approach, and one that avoids the tendency of some realists to attribute the necessary amorality, or even immorality, of world politics to the inherently bad character of man."[237]

The classical philosophers he focused on were St. Augustine, Machiavelli, Spinoza, Kant and Rousseau. He identified most closely with Rousseau (partly mediated through Niebuhr) and Kant. This leads us directly into the complexities within Waltz's thought. For he not only combined an assertive realism, evident in his publications, with an

---

229   K. Waltz, *Man, the State and War: A Theoretical Analysis* (New York 1959) p. 2.
230   Ibid., p. 16.
231   Ibid., p. 81.
232   Ibid., p. 123.
233   Ibid., p. 158.
234   Ibid., p. 233.
235   Ibid.
236   Ibid., pp. 227–8.
237   Ibid., p. 238.

equally assertive liberalism, most strikingly apparent in discussion, but also a penchant for traditional political theory – evident in his early writings – with an equal taste for the scientistic approach to international relations – in later work – so characteristic of anti-realist writers like Haas. This split was marked by Waltz's tenure at Swarthmore College (1957–66) and his transfer – via Brandeis – to Berkeley (1971–94). Of course, what marks out Rousseau and Kant both is that while drawing a sharply realist image of the state of world politics into the medium term, they simultaneously held out a possibility of ultimately changing the nature of man and thereby state behaviour. Writing of Kant in 1961, Waltz remarked: "He has, as many liberals do not, an appreciation of politics as struggle, an idea of possible equilibrium [of Powers] not as simple and automatic harmony but always as something perilously achieved out of conflict."[238]

From the outset Waltz dealt severely with those who did not learn what appeared to be an obvious lesson. Two targets that presented themselves were the functionalists and those committed to the idea of interdependence.

Waltz first castigated the interdependence theorists at their inception in 1965. Departing from his customary framework of traditional political thought, Waltz had begun to stake out a more distinctive individual stance and did so initially, like Tucker, through a critique of the positions taken by others, including fellow realists. A review article in *World Politics* on "Contention and Management in International Relations" gave him an opportunity. One is struck by the cool manner in which he wrote of the fact that "In the relations of states, with competition unregulated, war will occasionally occur. Though in one of its aspects war is a means of adjustment within the international system, the occurrence of war has often mistakenly been taken to indicate that the system itself has broken down."[239] The image Waltz had formed was of states entrapped within a system which dictated the ends and means adopted by its component states. The situation was what he described as one of "self-dependence" (Tucker's "self-help"). Waltz did not see any form of centralised management of the system by the UN or any other body to be practicable. He presented the dilemma in Hobbist terms:

the self-dependence of states means that each state must develop and maintain the power upon which its security rests. Each state's quest for security must then render all states insecure. The dilemmas of international politics are cruel, and every imagined escape from them poses difficulties and dangers as great as those that now exist. States cannot entrust the management of power to a central agency unless that agency is competent to protect its client states. The more powerful the clients and

238 "Kant, Liberalism, and War": Paper prepared for an annual meeting of the American Political Science Association in St. Louis, Missouri, September 1961 – *American Political Science Review*, Vol. LVI, No 2, June 1962, p. 339.

239 "Contention and Management in International Relations", *World Politics*, Vol. XVII, No 4, July 1965, p. 729.

the more the power of each of them appears to be a threat to the others, the greater must be the power that is lodged in the hands of the manager. The establishment of a manager of power would then invite the states to use their own power in a struggle to control the central agency.[240]

To those (like Keohane) who "argued that the sharp horns of the Hobbesian dilemma are being blunted by the growing interdependence of states", Waltz had little comfort to offer:

Interdependence that locks national interests so closely together that separation is self-evidently destructive of all good things may increase the chances of peace. Short of that threshold, the new form of the old argument that war will not occur because it does not pay brings little comfort. If interdependence is growing at a pace that exceeds the development of central control, then interdependence may increase the occasions for war.[241]

In 1970 Waltz revisited the issue in "The Myth of National Interdependence." The thrust of his argument was that the "conclusion . . . often drawn that a growing closeness of interdependence would improve the chances of peace" was fallacious.[242] Moreover Waltz saw the conduct of international relations largely, if not exclusively, determined by the two Superpowers, and his refutation of the "myth" rested mainly on demonstrating that the United States and the Soviet Union were less rather than more dependent than before. "The size of the two greatest powers gives them some capacity for control and at the same time insulates them to a considerable extent from the effects of other states' behavior. The inequality of nations produces a condition of equilibrium at a low level of interdependence. In the absence of a system of international regulation, loose coupling and a certain amount of control exerted by large states help to promote the desired stability."[243]

It is worth putting a footnote to the notion of interdependence, which has largely sunk into oblivion along with other intellectual fashions in international relations theory, adopted with so much enthusiasm but destined for an unattended burial. The bankruptcy of the idea was inadvertently admitted by one of its earnest disciples in 1980. James Rosenau, unfailingly an accurate barometer of passing trends in the field, expressed puzzlement at the persistence with which governments constantly took over

240   Ibid., p. 733.
241   Ibid., p. 735.
242   K. Waltz, "The Myth of National Interdependence", *The International Corporation*, ed. C. Kindle-berger (Cambridge, Mass. 1970) p. 205. A response to Waltz's attacks appears in R. Rosecrance and A. Stein, "Interdependence: Myth or Reality", in C. Black, ed., *Comparative Modernization*, pp. 368–91.
243   Ibid., pp. 222–3.

issues raised by non-state actors. "Why is it," he wrote, "I keep wondering, that national governments always succeed in intruding themselves into the authority structures that form around the new issues and thereby transform such issues into *their* problems?"[244] An unkind response might be that the problem would not arise for a realist. The tendency of the liberal universalists to allow fundamental analysis to be swayed by elevated hopes has not infrequently undermined their credibility.

Kenneth Thompson recalls Waltz remarking in the early 1960s that he "was not satisfied with the theoretical rigor of *Man, the State and War* and planned to devote several years exclusively to the study of the history and philosophy of science."[245] Later, when Waltz was attacked for positing axioms at the base of his theory which did not match reality, his reading of scientific method stood him in good stead. The approach he took was identical to that outlined by the economist Milton Friedman, who, anxious to elevate the study of economics to the level attained by the natural sciences, cited examples in natural science in his own defence of a method which is at first sight counterintuitive. He wrote: "Truly important and significant hypotheses will be found to have 'assumptions' that are wildly inaccurate descriptive representations of reality, and, in general, the more significant the theory, the more unrealistic the assumptions (in this sense)."[246] Friedman continued:

> The reason is simple. A hypothesis is important if it "explains" much by little, that is, if it abstracts the common and crucial elements from the mass of complex and detailed circumstances surrounding the phenomena to be explained and permits valid predictions on the basis of them alone. To be important, therefore, a hypothesis must be descriptively false in its assumptions; it takes account of, and accounts for, none of the many other attendant circumstances, since its very success shows them to be irrelevant for the phenomena to be explained.
>
> To put this point less paradoxically, the relevant question to ask about the "assumptions" of a theory is not whether they are descriptively "realistic", for they never are, but whether they are sufficiently good approximations for the purpose in hand. And this question can be answered only by seeing whether the theory works, which means whether it yields sufficiently accurate predictions.[247]

Friedman went on to attack the "confusion between descriptive accuracy and analytical relevance".[248] This was, indeed, Waltz's method. Tactically its strength against

---

244 J. Rosenau, *The Study of Global Interdependence: Essays on the Transnationalization of World Affairs* (New York 1980) p. 33.

245 K. Thompson, *Schools of Thought in International Relations: Interpreters, Issues, and Morality* (Baton Rouge/London 1996) p. 139.

246 M. Friedman, *Essays in Positive Economics* (Chicago and London 1953) p. 14.

247 Ibid., pp. 14–15.

248 Ibid., p. 32.

criticism for any failure to match his premisses against historical reality was logically sound. Problems arose, however, in pivoting so much of its value on the capacity for prediction.

In a letter to Hoffmann, Carr argued that "no science of international relations exists. The study of international relations in English speaking countries is simply a study of the best way to run the world from positions of strength."[249] This is precisely how Waltz's most acclaimed work, *Theory of International Politics*, was received by certain sceptical critics. From the princely elevations of Oxford, and with the privileged vantage-point of a Power long in secular decline, Bull, with characteristic immodesty, bluntly expressed the forthright opinion that "Waltz's own, truly 'systemic' explanation proves to be an elaborate defence of the dominance of world politics by the superpowers."[250] One might retort that Bull's work, in his rejection of the notion of Great Power dominance, equally reflected Britain's relative weakness.

The *Theory of International Politics* is an elegant treatise of unusual force and rigour that has preoccupied those in the field for the better part of two decades. Written with accustomed clarity and energised by Waltz's usual fixity of purpose and emotionally charged sense of conviction, it can claim to a much greater level of originality than most recent books, realist or otherwise. Waltz brought to it a close identification with classical political thinkers (above all Kant and Niebuhr), sustained critical attention to strategic studies, and years of absorption of method from the philosophy of the natural sciences. Yet its core image is at least five hundred years old: that of the Balance of Power. The theory Waltz evolves is a Balance of Power theory, which, as he explains, "is a theory about the results produced by the uncoordinated actions of states."[251] It is this, he argues, that will "give general and useful answers" as to "why a certain similarity of behavior is expected from similarly situated states."[252] It is a deeply conservative thesis, but written by a committed liberal. As with Machiavelli and Kant, with Carr and Morgenthau, so with Waltz, we are here treating of a realist driven to his position out of frustration with the accuracy and workability of the universalist vision, but retaining a passionate commitment to a liberal vision of the domestic order. The *Theory* rationalises Superpower dominance of the international system by arguing, as Waltz had done elsewhere and earlier, that the bipolar system was the most stable and that it had created the possibility of peace in a world otherwise tempted to war. It also exculpates both Powers from blame for the situation, not least the Russians, who were otherwise held responsible for the Cold War by Waltz's fellow countrymen. The antiseptic neutrality with which Waltz viewed the behaviour of the Superpowers and his expressed aversion to the arms race led by the United States were at least as much anathema to the American establishment as to the diehard left. The preference is also an unusual

249   See Haslam, *The Vices of Integrity*, p. 252.
250   H. Bull, "International Relations", *Times Literary Supplement*, 4 January 1980.
251   K. Waltz, *Theory of International Politics* (New York 1979), p. 122.
252   Ibid.

one for a realist in that most realists developed or sought to develop a world-view from the balcony of statesmen; inevitably this meant a unit-level of analysis in international relations and a natural identification with someone's idea of the national interest. To study international relations from the vantage-point of the system is by definition to count oneself out as a future national security adviser.

Waltz, a hard taskmaster like Morgenthau, made few nods in favour of his contemporaries. He disposed of rivals with clinical precision: "Among the depressing features of international-political studies is the small gain in explanatory power that has come from the large amount of work done in recent decades."[253] Waltz attacked Hoffmann protégé Richard Rosecrance's *Action and Reaction in World Politics* on the grounds that the "Systems as he describes them have no effect on the actions and the interactions of states."[254] Similarly, he reproached Hoffmann's own various attempts, albeit in an amicable tone, for the fact that "system-level causes become entangled with unit-level causes and the latter tend to become dominant."[255] Towards the founder of systems theory in international relations, Morton Kaplan, he was more demanding and therefore more severe: "The propositions he offers are about decision-making units and the rules they follow rather than being about the effect of different international systems on such units."[256] Having thus scythed what he saw as wasteland down to the last stalk, Waltz then began laying his own landscape.

There is no grand unifying theory in physics, and biologists continue to disagree over evolution. It is therefore hardly to be expected that an all-encompassing theory of international relations should have yet to see the light of day. And Waltz did not create one. Instead he aimed to put in place a theory that would explain certain key elements and only those elements pertaining to the workings of the international system, not its units. "I wrote a theory of international politics and not a theory of foreign policy", he insisted.[257] It was for others to create theories that account for unit-driven behaviour. As Waltz himself acknowledged, "to explain state behavior in international politics requires a theory of foreign policy as well as a theory of international politics."[258] Disagreement with Waltz might then arise as to the relative significance of unit-driven as against system-driven behaviour.

Waltz targeted all explanations of state behaviour that lie within the boundaries of the state. These he appeared to identify with factors making for change. "One who believes that he can account for changes in international relations must also ask how its continuities can be explained."[259] His answer was that the "enduring anarchic

253   Waltz, *Theory of International Politics*, p. 18.
254   Ibid., p. 42.
255   Ibid., p. 45.
256   Ibid., p. 56.
257   Waltz, "Letter to the editor", *International Organization*, Vol. 36, No 3, Summer 1982, p. 680.
258   Ibid., p. 681.
259   Waltz, "Theory of International Relations", p. 68.

character of international politics accounts for the striking sameness in the quality of international life through the millennia . . ."[260] The fundamental explanation for behaviour was thus analogous to that of the geopoliticians, situational: not "what states are like and how they interact, but . . . how they stand in relation to each other."[261] His entire focus was thus on "causes" that "operate among the actors collectively that are not found in their individual characters and motives."[262] Here the influence of his earlier vocation for economics is most in evidence. Waltz construed the workings of the international system as the operation of the market in which the individual character and decisions of the firm prove less important than the determination of price and survival by the sum total of firms in the market: Adam Smith's "invisible hand". It is also on the same level of thought as that of the social psychologists' view of the behaviour of man as a psychological being socialised by the collective behaviour of other individuals.

Latter-day Waltz stood squarely within the traditions of the social sciences but also, and equally, squarely within the much older Balance of Power tradition. As we have seen, this stream of thought diverged into two distinct and alternative lines: the one presupposing the balancing as a choice open to statesmen when faced with overwhelming hostile power; the other predicating the Balance as a force of nature. The former was by far the most popular, from fifteenth-century Italy through to the twentieth century, its most elegant expositors, Fénélon and Bolingbroke, holding sway at the turn of the eighteenth century. This conception highlighted the crucial role of the statesman, and subjective factors such as good judgement, astute timing and prudential perspicacity. In direct contrast, its *alter ego*, first identified by Botero in his *Relatione della Republica Venetiana*, saw the system of states operating as a mechanism ultimately ordained by the Almighty. It is this – perhaps with the omission of the Almighty – that Waltz adopted as his own. Here the statesman is effectively reduced to the status of mere mechanic, who fine-tunes a motor whose outer orientation is determined by objective forces much larger than his own.

The existence of states and their dominance were as central to Waltz's thinking as to that of any realist. Thus the *Theory* lambasted interdependence and transnationalism with as much vigour as before. They were processes that took place within an overarching structure. That structure was composed by states. While that structure persisted, those processes occurring above or below the level of the state would not predominate.[263] But, as Waltz also pointed out, we have no need to enquire into the nature of each state to explain the continuities in state behaviour, which were remarkably well sustained over time. It is the nature of the structure that indicates the persistence of

260   Ibid.
261   Ibid., p. 69.
262   Ibid., p. 70.
263   *Theory*, p. 95.

certain forms of behaviour. And here, once again, the similarities with the ideas of Geopolitics reappear. Whereas in Geopolitics the geographical location of the state both constrains and encourages forms of action, for Waltz the structure of the international system "acts as a constraining and disposing force on the interacting units within it."[264] The only factor that disposes one to discriminate between the nature of states is the difference in their capabilities. Thus a general theory of international politics "is necessarily based on the great powers."[265]

Where the theoretical structure begins to wobble is as a result of certain contradictions within the text, where the fluency of Waltz's pen has presented matters at one point as a matter of more or less – evidently to win over doubters – and at another point – where doubters have now been shed or converted – in terms of absolutes. For instance, as in his presentation of the three images in *Man, the State and War*, he informs us that "Causes at the level of units and of systems interact, and because they do so explanation at the level of units alone is bound to mislead."[266] It logically follows that to do so at the level of the system alone – which is what Waltz's theory does – is similarly bound to mislead. In other words, although apparently even-handedly dealing with the advantages and disadvantages of unit-level and systemic-level explanations, Waltz in fact applies the most severe standards only to unit-level explanation; and where, later in the text, he deals with systemic-level explanation those standards are silently allowed to slip. He later defended himself against the accusation of ignoring unit-level behaviour by saying that "Political scientists, if they are not well versed in what theories are like and how they are constructed, may slip into thinking that what an author fails to concentrate his attention upon, he takes to be inconsequential."[267] But if one focuses exclusively on one side of the equation, the reader has to assume that the writer has chosen what he believes to be the most important; and when the writer goes on to attack all those who do focus on the other side of the equation, the reader is bound to assume that the writer thinks them mistaken. All of the emphasis in Waltz is placed upon "the similarity and repetition of international outcomes".[268] And it is never entirely clear whether this is because the international system has always been the same or because the postwar, bipolar system is critical. In other words, if this is an explanation by system, which kind of system is crucial, or is it merely a matter of all systems in general and at all times?

This leads us into a crucial flaw, which may be inherent in this kind of theory-building, and, if so, raises the question whether this kind of theory-building is of any lasting value: the omission of the factors of time and change, notably within the units

264   Ibid., p. 72.
265   Ibid., p. 73.
266   Ibid., p. 68.
267   Waltz, "Letter to the editor", p. 680.
268   *Theory*, p. 67.

and not merely in respect of capability. "What continues and repeats is surely not less important than what changes", Waltz insists.[269] But he neglects to ask whether what changes is thereby not as important as or even almost as important as what continues and repeats. He acknowledges that a theory of international politics, as against a theory of foreign policy, can "explain only certain aspects" of what states do.[270] But his theory throughout implies that the aspects it explains are the critical ones. In addition Waltz tells us that a theory has "explanatory and predictive power".[271] Elsewhere, when defending the failure of prediction, he denies he is trying to predict, merely to explain.

Like most other realists, with the noted exception of Morgenthau, Waltz has never assumed rationality in foreign policy decision-making, given "the vagaries of men and the unpredictability of the individual's reaction to events . . ."[272] "Since making foreign policy is such a complicated business," he writes, "one cannot expect of political leaders the nicely calculated decisions that the word 'rationality' suggests."[273] Thus, although Waltz considered a world divided between the two Superpowers more stable than one divided between a multiple of Powers of more equal weight, not least because "In a multipolar-conventional world, difficulties multiply because a state has to compare its strength with a number of others and also has to estimate the strength of actual and potential conditions"[274], it is the effect of the balance of power that ensures stability; not the intentionality or presumed conscious rationality of the various leaders. In other words, the system itself imposes a certain degree of rationality on behaviour not much differently from the conditioning of Pavlov's dogs to salivate on the sound of a bell associated with food. What lies beyond that limited sphere is to be left to theories of foreign policy. Waltz presented his theory as covering only a limited domain.

What has been presented as a variation of the Waltzian model, though in fact a self-standing entity, is the work of Stephen Walt. Once Waltz's student at Berkeley, Walt both impressed and exasperated him by the stubborn independence that bolstered his intellect (a mirror-image of the master, perhaps). Where Walt struck out on his own was in the chance realisation "that states ally to balance against threats rather than against power alone." He therefore proposed a "balance of threat theory as a better alternative than balance of power theory."[275] In his aversion to the role of disembodied power, Walt leads the reader back to the territory of more traditional realism, where the nature of the state matters; otherwise why would he emphasise the importance of "perceptions"

269   Ibid., p. 70.
270   Ibid., p. 72.
271   Ibid., p. 69.
272   Waltz, "Stability of a Bipolar World", *Daedalus*, Vol. 93, No 3, 1964, p. 906.
273   Waltz, "A Response to my Critics", R. Keohane, ed., *Neorealism and its Critics* (New York 1986) p. 330.
274   Waltz, "The Emerging Structure of International Politics", *International Security*, Vol. 18, No 2, Fall 1993, p. 73.
275   S. Walt, *The Origins of Alliances* (Ithaca and London, 1987) p. 5.

and "ideology" along with power?[276] Walt's world in contrast to that of Waltz is a Humean or Kantian rather than a Hobbist universe, a subjectivist as well as an objectivist realm. He also reaches to factors such as space, a critical presumption of Geopolitics. But the key variable is the eye of the beholder. And he believes this approach to be vindicated by the absence of the appearance of any serious counter-balance to the United States to as the unique superpower after the collapse of the Soviet Union in 1991. "The anomaly of states failing to balance U.S. power largely vanishes if we focus not on power but on *threat*."[277] He therefore recommends the United States to walk softly if it intends carrying a big stick. The contrast with Waltz could not be greater, since for Waltz it is the mere possession of power that will assure counter-balancing. Waltz still awaits a countervailing coalition to offset US power. None has yet appeared. But does Walt's assumption that power in and of itself carries no life of its own really withstand scrutiny? If the Kennanite view that power will inevitably corrupt its possessor – a view that Wolfers shared, particularly with respect to a United States bereft of the Cold War adversary – holds true then the neorealist vision may still be realised.

The untidy and unexpected breach in the apparently impregnable front of neorealism blasted open by the abrupt collapse of the Soviet Union not only lent all the more credibility to Walt within the realist camp, it also presented an unprecedented opportunity for a revival in liberal universalism. Longstanding adversaries of Waltz now argued the contribution of neglected international institutions to the world's problems. It had, for instance, always been argued that the only reason for the failure of the United Nations as a security organization was the Soviet veto; so it was not beyond the bounds of possibility that, with the sudden and as yet unaccountable disappearance of the USSR, constructive solutions on a global plane could now be found. Advocates of this position ranged from the historian Paul Kennedy at Yale to theorist John Ruggie at Columbia. Both in their different ways hastened to invest a good deal of time and energy to making multilateralism a reality. In an outburst of futile enthusiasm Kennedy completely reoriented the direction of his research and Ruggie ended up joining the UN as assistant secretary. Collectively this group had, since the unattended burial of interdependence and the birth of "regime theory", become known as "neoliberal institutionalists". They fast became the target of that energumen, John Mearsheimer at Chicago, whose thinking on realism was "closer to Waltz than to Morgenthau."[278] Mearsheimer had opened himself to attack by over-hastily predicting conflict between the Powers in Europe unless a new balance of power were created.[279] It was not and no conflict

---

276   Ibid., p. 10.
277   Walt, "Keeping the World 'Off-Balance': Self-Restraint and U.S. Foreign Policy", *KSG Research Working Paper Series* (Harvard), October 2000, p. 18.
278   "The False Promise of International Institutions", *International Security*, Vol. 19, No 3, Winter 1994/95, p. 9, footnote 20.
279   "Back to the Future: Instability in Europe After the Cold War", ibid., Vol. 15, No 1, Summer 1990, pp. 5–56.

occurred. Instead attention shifted to the destabilisation and then the crumbling of Yugoslavia as a unitary state.

What this experience underlined was that neorealism was, indeed, no reliable predictor of state behaviour. Not for the first time, the true effectiveness of realism in terms of theory was not evident until a demolition job was called for, in this case once the faith in liberal institutionalism was once again shown to be fallacious after experimentation by government. Mearsheimer's assault launched in 1995 thus carried the kind of credibility that his musings half a dozen years earlier could not deliver. Despite the fact that his version of realism was closer to Waltz than to Morgenthau, Mearsheimer merited Robert Jervis' definition as an "offensive" realist: i.e., more Hobbist than Kantian.[280] His vision is, indeed, more zero-sum than that of Waltz:

> Realism paints a rather grim picture of world politics. The international system is portrayed as a brutal arena where states look for opportunities to take advantage of each other, and therefore have little reason to trust each other. Daily life is essentially a struggle for power, where each state strives not only to be the most powerful actor in the system, but also to ensure that no other state achieves that lofty position.[281]

Where Mearsheimer comes into his own, however, is in emphasising that liberal institutionalists have provided plausible explanations for state behaviour only on the margins of the main issues in international relations – trade and the environment rather than security and war – and in his caustic dissection of the arguments of the constructivists who claim it is all a matter of ideas but then call in evidence of the world of practice to back up their arguments. But here, too, Mearsheimer tends to overplay his hand in assuming that relations between developed democracies such as Britain and France are in some fundamental sense on the same level of potential conflict as, say, between Israel and Iraq. Once again, neorealism's assumption that the entire international system works on Hobbist principles, all states in equal measure, leads analysts up a blind alley. The case made by liberal universalist Michael Doyle of Princeton – another Hoffmann *protégé* – that democracies do not war with one another, even if they war with other regimes, surely contains a core truth, however untidy it makes our attempts to generalise about state behaviour regardless of constitution, culture and ideology.[282]

It should occasion no surprise that in the 1990s no less than at every other epoch,

---

280   R. Jervis, "Realism, Neoliberalism, and Cooperation: Understanding the Debate", ibid., Vol. 24, No 1, Summer 1999, pp. 48–50.

281   "The False Promise . . .", p. 9. For more: *The Tragedy of Great Power Politics* (New York 2001).

282   For the original argument, derived from Kant: "Kant, Liberal Legacies, and Foreign Affairs", *Philosophy and Public Affairs*, Vol. 12, Nos 3–4, Summer and Fall 1983, pp. 205–54 and 323–53, respectively. For a milder restatement: *Ways of War and Peace: Realism, Liberalism, and Socialism* (New York/London 1997) pp. 258–77. It is here that the constructivists have something of a case to make.

the debates at the level of theory mirrored what was happening at the level of policy-making. The liquidation of the Soviet Union represented not only the extinction of a major threat to US security but also the extinction of the core challenge to US supremacy, just as Wolfers feared. If the United States faced no security problem of any significance, it could logically choose between two main paths: a return to isolationism or the imposition of its values and interests on the rest of the states system. The former fitted ill with the global spread of US trading interests, even if it matched a groundswell of national sentiment far removed from the East coast. The alternative of forcing US values onto the rest of the international system exactly matched Stalin's comment in 1946 that Beneš was currently a realist because he lacked power, but with strength he would become an idealist (see above, p. 202). The exertion of US hegemony would require an act of will since it would inevitably entail sacrifice, not only material but also in blood. In the strange new world of choices, US liberals began arguing in favour of interventionism across the globe; and at their head, academically, sat Stanley Hoffmann, the very man who argued against intervention in the Gulf to safeguard US oil supplies in the 1970s, but who now argued for intervention on moral grounds almost anywhere, regardless of security or material interests.

Having become disillusioned by the events of the 1970s, in particular by discovering just how self-interested governments of the third world could be, and witnessing "the gap" between the "good intentions and contradictory policies"[283] of the Carter administration, which he had supported, Hoffmann then became even more disillusioned on learning how "murderous" the second and third worlds could be. The problem for Hoffmann and fervent liberal universalists was how to equate their vision of what was supposed to be happening – "the empirical revolution of interdependence and globalisation that both deprives states of much of their 'operational', that is, effective, sovereignty and transfers many of their previous functions to a largely private world capitalist economy that is beyond national control and under very meagre inter-state control"[284] – with the obvious fact that "Anomie and chaos may well be with us for a long time."[285] Whereas Tucker was contemptuous of, and worried at, what Hoffmann disparaged as "America's new doctrine of (American) combatant immunity" for the defence of material national interests (such as control over overseas sources of oil), Hoffmann was concerned for other, more elevated, universalist reasons.

As far as Hoffmann was concerned, Clinton was on probation and likely to fail parole. National Security Adviser Anthony Lake claimed that "we are helping to create a world where tolerance, freedom and democracy prevail."[286] Hoffmann, however, felt bitterly

283   Hoffmann, "In Defense of Mother Teresa: Morality in Foreign Policy", *Foreign Affairs*, Vol. 75, No 2, March/April 1996, p. 172.
284   Hoffmann, "The Politics and Ethics of Military Intervention", *Survival*, Vol. 37, No 4, Winter 1995–6, p. 31.
285   Ibid., p. 49.
286   Quoted in J. DeParle, "The Man Inside Bill Clinton's Foreign Policy", *New York Times Magazine*, 20 August 1995.

betrayed at the failure of Clinton, like Carter, to take liberal universalism to what he saw as its logical conclusion. Lake described himself as a "pragmatic neo-Wilsonian".[287] Hoffmann's first broadside, delivered in the spring of 1995, measured the administration's actions against its much heralded, pious convictions. "After two years," Hoffmann snapped, ". . . pragmatism is more visible than Wilsonianism."[288] What worried him in particular were Lake's statements that Washington would press the liberal internationalist agenda only where US interests were clearly defined; that, in Hoffmann's words, "the spread of liberalism was not *ipso facto* an American interest", which Hoffmann saw as "an inadvertent but remarkable concession to traditional realism."[289] Once again, realism was gaining the upper hand, even where liberal universalism seemed to have every opportunity of dominating policy. Whereas Carter had the excuse that the Cold War tied his hands, Clinton held every apparent advantage. No wonder Hoffmann was disturbed, and, thrown back on the questionability of the programme that had so far failed, he was even given to speculate that "an examination of the plight of liberal internationalism must shift to the flaws and limitations of liberalism itself."[290] There were, after all, evident contradictions between the demands of "human rights versus the expansion of free trade".[291]

However, doubts about liberal universalism's own internal contradictions were soon suppressed as Hoffmann sought to take on the more urgent task of forcing the administration back to the observance of fundamentals. The resulting manifesto appeared at the end of 1995 as "The Politics and Ethics of Military Intervention". This argued for military intervention "when domestic turmoil threatens regional or international security and when massive violations of human rights occur."[292] Anticipating the objections of realists, Hoffmann began by arguing that the concept of the " 'national interest' . . . should be widened to incorporate ethical concerns": somewhat like the political counterpart to suggesting that a road should "merely" be modified to become a runway for aircraft. Such interventions would not necessarily have to be legitimised by the UN Security Council, nor would they require the assent of the government of the country concerned. Instead of being reassured that greater international integration would produce greater harmony, Hoffmann was now shocked at "the multitude of totally or partially failed, troubled and murderous states whose claims to sovereignty are either unsustainable or unacceptable."[293] His original objections to the "disease of the Westphalian system", to sovereignty, namely that the Great Powers misbehaved in the states system and that they should collapse their independence for the sake of an integrated

287   Ibid.
288   Hoffmann, "The Crisis of Liberal Internationalism", *Foreign Policy*, No 98, Spring 1995, p. 159.
289   Ibid.
290   Ibid., p. 160.
291   Ibid., p. 159.
292   Hoffmann, "The Politics . . .", p. 29.
293   Ibid., p. 31.

world order that effectively disposed of the state, now instead became an objection to the exercise of sovereignty by certain states only. In Hoffmann's words, "the moral good of sovereignty must yield to superior imperatives".[294] Presumably that did not mean that other countries could intervene in the United States to defend the human rights of those blacks subjected to the death penalty in such number. Since the United Nations could not be counted upon to act, the United States should act unilaterally and do so with "a new, broader and more far-sighted definition of the national interest".[295] The criteria for intervention "would be massive violations of human rights, which would encompass genocide, ethnic cleansing, brutal and large-scale repression to force a population into submission, including deliberate policies of barbarism, as well as the kinds of famines, massive breakdowns of law and order, epidemics and flights of refugees that occur when a 'failed state' collapses."[296] On this basis it is difficult to imagine which states of Africa or Asia would survive as independent entities. This doctrine is precisely what Wolfers feared if ever the United States were to emerge unchallenged as the leading world Power. By default, since Hoffmann was sufficiently a realist to recognise that "collective enterprises simply will not succeed unless there is a clear political will behind them, which must be provided either by a major state . . . or by a coalition",[297] he ends up arguing for a right of unilateral intervention by the United States: the final triumph of Gladstonian liberal universalism.

In the realist camp, with Tucker effectively in retirement from current comment, a one-time *protégé* now ensconced at SAIS and former member of Hoffmann's department, Michael Mandelbaum, was more concerned at the degree to which the administration had bought into the liberal universalist programme. This – and no doubt Hoffmann's restatement of basic principles – prompted a caustic attack on the Clinton record, bitterly entitled "Foreign Policy as Social Work". Mandelbaum denounced the three "failed military interventions" (Bosnia, Somalia and Haiti) that "set the tone and established much of the agenda" of US foreign policy from 1993 to the time of writing at the end of 1995.[298] Although on somewhat uncertain ground in arguing that "Historically the foreign policy of the United States has centered on American interests, defined as developments that could affect the lives of American citizens",[299] which implied that the use of military intervention in the past had not been directed by Wilsonian idealism, Mandelbaum was on firmer ground in his characterisation of National Security Adviser Anthony Lake's idealism and its consequences under "a president less interested in international affairs than at any time in the previous six decades".[300] Lake subscribed to a Manichean ideology that fitted oddly with his

294   Ibid., p. 35.
295   Ibid., p. 36.
296   Ibid., p. 38.
297   Ibid., p. 48.
298   *Foreign Affairs*, Vol. 75, No 1, January/February 1996, p. 16.
299   Ibid., p. 17.
300   Ibid., p. 19.

reputation among colleagues as an "apparatchik", though, one should remember, he resigned from Kissinger's staff in 1970 for ethical reasons over the catastrophic decision to bomb Cambodia. "Now," Mandelbaum announced, "I think, our society has come back to where we were in World War II, that there are evil forces out there . . ."[301] He went on to astonish cooler heads in expressing the generous but wildly inaccurate view that "Mother Teresa and Ronald Reagan were both trying to do the same thing", with "one helping the helpless, one fighting the Evil Empire."[302] Having established the obvious – namely that they were trying to do entirely different things – Mandelbaum then extended the image to devastating effect:

> While Mother Teresa is an admirable person and social work a noble profession, conducting American foreign policy by her example is an expensive proposition. The world is a big place filled with distressed people, all of whom, by these lights, have a claim to American attention. Putting an end to the suffering in Bosnia, Somalia, and Haiti would have involved addressing its causes, which would have meant deep, protracted, and costly engagement in the tangled political life of each country.[303]

In short, Mandelbaum found this project dangerously impracticable, given the far-reaching aims and the inability to carry US public opinion even part of the way towards their fulfilment.

Not one to cave in under pressure, Hoffmann then wrote "In Defense of Mother Teresa". Here he further emphasised his view that "the opposition between interests and values is a sham" (a point with which Tucker would have agreed, though from the opposing vantage-point with respect to which values).[304] But Hoffmann's appeal for selective intervention on the grounds of "moral duty"[305] marks himself from all realists. The issue is: how do you ensure that this is unravelled from material US interests? The problem is one that the liberal philosophy makes difficult to acknowledge: the manner in which power is itself not merely a tool for higher uses, but has its own determining quality. Arguably, what lay between the good intentions and the contradictory policies of both the Carter and Clinton administrations that Hoffmann supported was the reality of power rather than the collective failure of the men trying to wield it.

301   Ibid.
302   Ibid.
303   Ibid., p. 18.
304   Hoffmann, "In Defense of Mother Teresa . . .", p. 173.
305   Ibid., p. 174.

Conclusion
THE RELEVANCE OF REALISM

"Well, it may be all right in practice, but it will never work in theory"[1]

– Warren Buffett[2]

The pedigree of thought in international relations merits concentrated attention not least because ignorance encourages fallacious assumptions about the degree of novelty in theories of our own age. It also exposes assumptions lying within the grain of thought peculiar to the times in which they arose; which circumstances now lie in the distant past but still exert the pull of attraction without our being fully aware of the source. What the historical record shows is that the fluctuations and reversals in fortune between realism on one pole and universalism on the other have been a recurrent feature since early modern Europe. One should therefore be wary of assuming that either the one or the other has finally triumphed.

Some have boldly declared realism dead.[3] One of those same pens has drawn the conclusion that the emergence of the European Union represents the victory of universalist aspirations through the operations of the "commercial interest".[4] In justification of this revival in liberal economism, the argument is made that the "primary motivation of those who chose to integrate was not to prevent another Franco-German war, bolster global prestige and power, or balance against the superpowers."[5] Moreover, we are equally confidently informed that "German willingness to move toward EMU and set a date for the IGC at Strasbourg in December 1989 is generally attributed to the sudden opposition to unification following the fall of the Berlin Wall. The German

---

1   Readers will recognize this as the inverse of Kant's *Das mag in der Theorie richtig sein taugt aber nicht für die Praxis.*

2   Letter to shareholders 1985: *The 1984 Annual Report of Berkshire Hathaway Inc.*

3   See J. Legro and A. Moravcsik, "Is Anybody Still a Realist", *International Security*, Vol. 24, No 2, Fall 1999, pp. 5–55.

4   A. Moravcsik, *The Choice for Europe: Social Purpose and State Power from Messina to Maastricht* (Ithaca 1998) p. 3. Also (pp. 15–16) "the pursuit of economic interest is the fundamental force underlying the integration."

5   Ibid., p. 4.

government was forced to offer a quid pro quo to remove French opposition to unification; some allege that other governments suddenly had a greater incentive to lock Germany into Europe. Yet such claims", we are also assured, "are based on no more than Mitterrand and Kohl's public rhetoric and apparent coincidence in timing."[6]

The verbatim record of their secret discussions is, however, now a matter of public record. And it is striking how the traditional realist vocabulary reappears to confirm precisely what we originally supposed had happened. The fall of the Wall prompted near panic in Paris. "A Germany reunified would represent a double danger for Europe", President Mitterrand argued in private. "Through its power. And because it would drive into alliance Great Britain, France and the Soviet Union. This would ensure a war in the 21st Century. Europe has to be constructed at great speed to defuse German reunification."[7] After Chancellor Kohl announced, without any advance warning to Mitterrand, that the Federal Republic would seek reunification, Mitterrand bluntly warned Foreign Minister Genscher that if German reunification was not delayed until the achievement of European union, Bonn would find itself confronted with a triple alliance (France, Britain and Russia) "and that would end in war." But "if German union is effected after that of Europe, we will help you."[8]

At a summit shortly thereafter with President Gorbachev focused entirely on the German problem, Mitterrand emphasised the urgent need to "make progress in the construction of the European Community" in strongly realist terms: before reunification became a *fait accompli*, Russia and France, he stressed, were together "responsible for the balance of power."[9] And when the twelve heads of state and government of the EEC met at the Élysée to consider matters, the language chosen by Kohl to be reassuring was also staunchly realist: "For the majority of my citizens, reason of state demands that the FRG remains in the [European] Community."[10] Presumably the term was used to add weight to Kohl's reassurances. Coming from a German, it might as easily have aroused untimely and bitter memories in its emphasis on statism as the ultimate rationale for decision. The threats proved futile. Reunification was not held back to await European union, but there was no way Germany could avert isolation without following up as speedily as possible with European union.

The rapid and renewed acceleration of European integration was thus an extension of Balance of Power thinking rather than its abandonment for the universalist ideal of a Europe without frontiers. The strength of the revival of realism in the first half of the twentieth century and its efflorescence in the United States can be attributed to the power of argument of various pens, and those we have considered should certainly be accorded their due. But here, as in Europe, it was ultimately force of circumstance

6   Ibid., p. 437.
7   Entry, 5 November 1989: J. Attali, *Verbatim* (Paris 1993), p. 333.
8   30 November 1989: ibid., p. 354.
9   Ibid., p. 363.
10   Entry dated 18 November 1989: ibid., p. 343.

that triumphed, and in itself explains why those such as Carr and Morgenthau took up the cudgels against utopian illusions about international relations. Hirohito and Hitler's armies crashed through the rickety fence erected by the League of Nations and thereby shattered the Panglossian aspirations that pervaded pre-war Britain and the United States. Stalin and his successors in Moscow subsequently did the rest. For such reasons even so devoted a moralist as Stanley Hoffmann has felt obliged to acknowledge, in startling moments of candour, the contribution of realist thought in combating "unrealism".

In the past, realist thought mirrored as well as controlled and rationalised the conduct of international relations. As such it may have provided "no more than a penetrating central insight" into the dynamics of the states system. It never strayed far from the world of practice, at least when practice remained faithful to its traditions. And, as a former participant pointed out, "practical statecraft will always be about four-fifths a matter of instant reactions to immediate pressures and opportunities".[11] While statesmen of our own time continue to think and decide within the categories espoused by realists – even if in public they use the sophist language indicative of a more ideal world – realism will continue to find a place in the study of international relations.

In debate, however, it has become customary to refer to something called "realist theory"; and, consciously or not, this imposes upon a loose and fragmented assemblage of thought a degree of coherence which is arguably unjustified and unnecessary. To make the realist tradition a subject of study is therefore a conscious attempt to emphasise both its breadth of thought and the length of time realism has persisted. It represents an attempt to escape from overly simplistic, ethnocentric and ahistorical notions associated with a particular school in international relations. The realist tradition is to be seen as a spectrum of ideas of varying hues from light to dark rather than as a fixed point of focus with sharp definition that distinguishes itself exclusively and at every point of the compass from its idealist counterparts.

It is for this reason that one can find idealists such as Rousseau and Kant possessed of a fundamentally realist analysis of what was then current in international relations. It is for this reason that convinced liberals such as Morgenthau or Waltz can simultaneously be realists in international relations. To the disgruntled critic – notably the idealist in the methodological as well as the political sense – this fuzziness is unsatisfactory; rather than a strength, it is seen as a source of weakness. But then we are not dealing here with the natural sciences; and even at the outer limits of the natural sciences – notably on the tiniest scale of quantum mechanics and the universal scale of cosmology – the degree of precision lessens to a disturbing degree. Within political science the very subject matter is ultimately ourselves. Inevitably a price is therefore paid in matters of precision. As Keynes wrote in another, though not entirely inapposite, context, better imprecisely correct than precisely wrong.

---

11   G. Liska, "The Vital Triad: International-Relations Theory, History, and Social Philosophy", *Social Research*, Winter 1981, Vol. 48, No 4, pp. 704 and 703.

However, this does not mean a clear distinction cannot be drawn between realism and idealism (or "unrealism"). Realist thought depends upon a premiss which universalists refuse to accept: namely, the primacy of the state. At the core of the realist tradition also lies the insistence that considerations of morality which would normally apply to the individual within society should not apply to society acting in relation to other societies. Rules of prudence take precedence over rules of morality, since the dominant community – the state or society – has transcendent needs and commands prior loyalty. It is this that most clearly marks the realist from the universalist. Beyond this, distinct differences emerge in the approach taken by various carriers of realist thought. To some the differences that exist are not so much marked by the difference of time – the twentieth century in contrast to other centuries – because, many realists would normally maintain, the conduct of international relations has in its essence not altered that much; the differences, rather, arise from particular alignments of thought which are based upon independent assumptions routed in parallel but through separate channels across time, whether or not their progenitors are aware of this process.

We have, for instance, Robert Tucker, whose main alignment reaches back to Machiavelli and the Reasons of State tradition. Kenneth Waltz, on the other hand, stands furthest along a continuum dating from Botero. Whereas Tucker and Machiavelli take a dim view of man's nature as a point of departure, Waltz and Botero focus on the operations of a states system determined by laws of nature independent of the nature of man. What both groups of realists have in common is in seeing conflict as normal rather than exceptional, in seeing the solution to conflict within international relations as extremely limited, and in regarding issues of morality as of no direct relevance to these affairs. Where they differ is in sourcing the precise causes of these problems.

The refusal to accept that individual morality should be the touchstone for international relations has always alarmed universalists on the grounds that amorality opens the floodgates to the worst forms of human behaviour and that, moreover, the realists have formulated concepts such as Reasons of State and the Balance of Power to justify them. The historical record reveals that these concepts, though undoubtedly in practice all too frequently licensing the worst forms of behaviour, were actually instituted precisely in order to contain them – assuming, of course, that their complete eradication was beyond our limited means.

The signal achievement of Reasons of State was to lay down clear lines of priority to ensure the survival of the nascent state in the emerging system. It arose in response to weakness, division and subjugation by other Powers. It set the weight of opinion against universal ideals, personal ambition or sectional interest as the determinants of foreign policy. It highlighted the need to offset the adverse impact of the emotions in the conduct of state affairs to ensure that the interests of the state as a whole took priority. It was intended to ensure that policy was rationally devised to secure ends that served the welfare of the state as a whole. Far from assuming rationality in statecraft, those who called for the enforcement of Reasons of State saw it as their role to create rationality out of violent chaos, to forestall the ruler from indulging emotion and to ensure that passion was subjected to reason. This is, perhaps, the least understood foundation of realist thought. It also became an analytical device for making sense of state behaviour. The danger was that, as an analytical tool, it assumed something that was at the same time a norm directing human behaviour. A further weakness both as guide and advertised practice lay in the fact that, like other political concepts, its very flexibility could be stretched to mask the very practices it was intended to end.

Reasons of State led logically to the Balance of Power. The Balance of Power, too, had its strengths as an explanation of state behaviour and as a guide to policy. Most notably it emphasised the degree to which a state's actions were determined by the overall system of which it was but a constituent part. It was originally devised to forestall the worst: the danger of universal monarchy, which not only hard-bitten ex-professionals such as Guicciardini but also armchair liberals such as Kant believed was a danger greater than war itself. Matters left to themselves would, they feared, otherwise result in the domination of Europe by one Power. Only through the conscious attempt to keep the capabilities of the various Powers in balance could the security of all be preserved. The concept of the Balance of Power thus built upon the assumptions of Reasons of State: unchecked passions would result in disaster. An additional feature, which has also been utterly forgotten in the urge to dump the concept, is the belief that the Balance of Power constituted not just a system of disciplined behaviour for the welfare of the state but also a shared community of interests between states: the sense, ever since the fragile Italian city-states system collapsed under the immense weight of the French invasion, that collective action was a virtue in and of itself as a safeguard against the collapse of the entire system.

The main weakness of the Balance, however, lay in its mechanistic form. The analogy with mechanics could go only so far in explaining any kind of human behaviour, and since states are the outer shell of societies, and those societies are subject to dynamics determined in large part by consciousness and intentionality, the Balance of Power left these other dimensions untouched. Yet their actions may prove critical in any given situation. Because conscious or intentional factors exist does not, of course, necessarily mean they will make themselves effective. The degree to which they are determinant varies through time and across circumstances. Over the decades, indeed the centuries, the extent to which the Great Powers are purely reactive within the system and the extent to which they are pro-active in altering the dynamics of the system shift with the years. Any attempt to predict behaviour, short or long term, which ignores this element is bound to fail for this very reason: the x factor comes from within society, whose dynamics do not lie within the realm of the international system but whose dynamics affect that system.

As with Reasons of State, so with the Balance of Power: idealist critics such as Ernst Haas have very effectively seized upon the various uses and abuses of terminology across history to argue for dispensing with the concept entirely. In defence one might plausibly argue that no concept in politics has ever gone unscathed by misuse and downright misrepresentation. The fact that Louis XIV used the Balance of Power to justify a bid for universal monarchy in Europe no more undermines the validity of the concept than did Hitler's justification of universal empire in Europe by the needs of national self-determination. And in our time politicians daily abuse terms such as democracy and liberty. It is, and always was, the very authority of such concepts that attracts and attracted their misuse. The questions that should, instead, be addressed are, first of all, whether the concept, as originally formulated and intended, explains how policy was directed, and, second, whether it can serve to identify and explain policy thereafter, allowing for its exploitation as a source of legitimacy for misbehaviour. It most certainly explains the policies of some – such as Churchill or Nixon – but not others – such as Neville Chamberlain or Carter. It would therefore be unwise to assume that a universe of explanation can be pivoted on its workings. That would leave us – like Waltz – baffled by, and impatient at, the absence of a coalition emerging to counter-balance US hegemony today.

Those who wrote so forcefully and persuasively about Reasons of State and realist thought in general not infrequently did so in emotional revolt against the harshness of the times and against the illusions that seemed so costly an indulgence. This most certainly applies to Machiavelli, to Bodin and to Hobbes in early modern Europe; it almost certainly equally applies to Carr and Morgenthau in the twentieth century. Bear in mind that these were, on the whole, reluctant realists: sensitive and penetrating, in some cases utopian, minds that over-reacted to dramatic, unheralded and therefore unexpected outbursts of violence and their consequences. Realist thought in that sense emerged and re-emerged at moments of crisis when its lessons had been long forgotten in happier times. That is to say, it was in part the acceptance of alternative and more optimistic modes of thought that contributed to the crises that resulted in their eventual substitution by realism. But it is equally clear that there never was a final victory of the one over the other; it seems to reflect a dialectic that mirrors the dichotomy of human nature and the human condition.

The key question for us today in respect of whether or how much we have to learn from their writings is how far those times were typical and to what degree, if any, they bear relevance to our own. To abstract the full force of the conclusions of Machiavelli and Hobbes in application to, for instance, relations between Russia and the West today or, to put it at its most ludicrous, relations between the United States and its NATO allies would, of course, be absurd. The times were very different and it was that context which prompted the arguments *in extremis*. The counterpart to this is all too easy to slip into: the opposite assumption – comfortable for some, less comfortable for others – that current, relatively benign circumstances will continue indefinitely, or current trends will develop further in their existing direction.

The only lesson from history is that change rather than progress is inevitable. Theories of international relations that focus on equilibria and provide no real explanation for abrupt shifts in patterns of change are therefore bound to prove unsatisfactory. We should therefore be wary of assuming that the present improvements in relations within the first world and between the first and second worlds are, under all conditions, irreversible. We must also bear in mind that conduct within the third world – and those areas bordering upon it – not infrequently bears more relation to sixteenth- and seventeenth-century Europe than the Europe of today – and, even then, who can forget Bosnia?

The argument can plausibly be made that it is a mistake now to see the entire states system as a homogeneous whole, when its components, although subjected to a similar process of socialisation, have entirely different ages and entirely different political cultures and varying levels of economic development. This, of course, suggests that the nature and maturity of the units matter and that there may, indeed, be a teleology at work such as in the Kantian tradition equating more pacific behaviour with a linear advance towards political democracy. It is striking, however, that the foremost advocates of the Kantian peace act as though only the behaviour of the Great Powers is of consequence – a curious and oblique reflection of, and a backhanded compliment to, realist thought.

It is, in short, too tall an order to expect that a theory explaining the behaviour of some can successfully explain the behaviour of all. It is obvious that today Britain and France behave differently towards each another than from the fourteenth to the nineteenth centuries and that Pakistan and India behave more in the manner of Britain and France in past centuries. Nothing was ever more stark, for instance, than the contrast between the self-righteous moralism of Nehru in international relations and his actual policies. In other words it might be helpful to see the system as stratified and as a differentiated whole, with segments scattered along a continuum of time and therefore circumstance and varying degrees of necessity.

The caveat, of course, is that if some behave worse than others and behave that way towards others, then there is a tendency for all behaviour to sink to the most common denominator in reacting to worst practice. One should not therefore expect behaviour between first and third world countries to partake of the same qualities as relations within the first world. Moreover, as the quotations from both Kohl and Mitterrand indicate, the realist tradition still predominates even within the first world at times of crisis in international relations. The point may be that where once arms were used to decide differences within the Western half of Europe, money now determines the balance; that the old struggles have been elevated to a higher and less fatal level for resolution. That this would mark learning in international relations, a core improvement, should not be denied. But neither should it be overlooked that these are still rival Powers in contention over interests that divide them because they answer to different communities; and that it is only the ultimate, in this case shared, prospect of mutual annihilation that has tamed the beast.

The distinction between the first and the second or third worlds is equally evident in respect of the Balance of Trade. In the second world, newly liberated from state socialism, the tussle between Smithian notions of the free market and the protectionist model that reached its zenith under Stalin is as yet unresolved. We may be justified in positing that East-Central Europe at least will take the path favoured by the Western democracies. The case of Russia is more problematic. The case of the third world, with the exceptions of Hong Kong (as part of China), Taiwan and Singapore, supports acceptance of the Balance of Trade as a model of behaviour, an answer to the natural imbalance of power in commerce between states at very different levels of industrialisation. Malaysia is a classic reincarnation of Colbert's protectionist model. Others are more or less at the same stage. And as for Geopolitics, the foreign and defence policies of Israel, India, Pakistan and China bear convincing testimony to the importance of geographical determinants in making for strategies focused on security through territorial expansion to natural frontiers.

The question that naturally arises is why the realists make so much headway despite loud protestation and moral condemnation from their opponents? One answer, which not everyone could be expected to accept, is that their outlook has matched the reality they have claimed to describe. Certainly, it is striking how even those with utopian projections, whether More, Rousseau or Kant, had to allow for far more resistance from the nature of man, of society or of the nascent European states system than one might have presupposed from their core beliefs. But, sharing this view or no, other factors play a role. First, these were years of great upheaval and instability, most particularly the sixteenth and the first half of the seventeenth century, so that many – however radical in other ways – clung to the nascent nation-state as to a life-raft in stormy seas; it was not so much that the raft was enticing as that no other practical means of survival lay to hand. Second, the immediate alternatives, in the form of universal empire and the universal church, had crumbled – the empire from the centrifugal forces of economic change and its political consequences, the church as a result of the revolution from within launched by Martin Luther, which in itself produced a revived Catholicism that cemented the new divide – while a distant alternative, the secular universalism of free trade and peace, awaited the awe-inspiring rise of industrialisation and would thus far have to be accepted on trust without any track record, let alone one of success. Third, those advocating idealist alternatives were all too often tainted with special interest, whether it be Campanella, Postel, Grotius, Vitoria, or, indeed, Adam Smith. Perhaps what is most striking is the stark divergence between the high-minded professions of universalist ideals and their cynical realisation in practice as they pass through the prism of the state. Power looks less like a neutral instrument for higher ends, more like a determinant in its own right, a particular irony for those – like Hoffmann – who seek to foster larger ends in pursuit of the destruction of power. For all the progress made, and we should not now deny what has recently been achieved after much bloodshed, we are still far from much hoped-for utopias envisaged by Kant and Rousseau, let alone that of Karl Marx, in the compass of the globe.

Index